COMRADES BETRAYED

A volume in the series

Battlegrounds: Cornell Studies in Military History
Edited by David J. Silbey

Editorial Board: Petra Goedde, Wayne E. Lee, Brian McAllister Linn, and Lien-Hang T. Nguyen

A list of titles in this series is available at cornellpress.cornell.edu.

COMRADES BETRAYED

JEWISH WORLD WAR I
VETERANS UNDER HITLER

BY MICHAEL GEHERAN

CORNELL UNIVERSITY PRESS

Ithaca and London

First published 2020 by Cornell University Press
Printed in the United States of America

Library of Congress Cataloging-in-Publication Data

Names: Geheran, Michael, 1971– author.
Title: Comrades betrayed : Jewish World War I veterans under Hitler / by Michael Geheran.
Description: Ithaca [New York] : Cornell University Press, 2020. | Series: Battlegrounds : Cornell studies in military history | Includes bibliographical references and index.
Identifiers: LCCN 2020013010 (print) | LCCN 2020013011 (ebook) | ISBN 9781501751011 (cloth) | ISBN 9781501751028 (epub) | ISBN 9781501751035 (pdf)
Subjects: LCSH: World War, 1914–1918—Veterans—Germany. | Jewish veterans—Germany—Social conditions—20th century. | Antisemitism—Germany—History—20th century. | World War, 1939–1945—Jews—Germany. | Jews, German—History—20th century. | Masculinity—Religious aspects—Judaism.
Classification: LCC D639.V48 G34 2020 (print) | LCC D639.V48 (ebook) | DDC 305.892/404308697—dc23
LC record available at https://lccn.loc.gov/2020013010
LC ebook record available at https://lccn.loc.gov/2020013011

To my parents, John and Christa, in love and gratitude,
and my wife, Anna, for being my partner in every adventure

Contents

Acknowledgments

A few sentences could never fully express my gratitude to everyone who helped bring this project to fruition. Without the assistance from my mentors, colleagues, friends, and family, and the support of key institutions, I simply could not have done this work.

First and foremost, I wish to express my deepest gratitude to Thomas Kühne. His meticulous and at times highly critical feedback made my work immeasurably better, and over the years he introduced me to a community of scholars with similar interests, which has expanded my academic universe immensely. I would also like to thank Geoffrey Megargee and Omer Bartov, who offered invaluable counsel, criticism, and encouragement over many years, and who suffered through all of the project's various iterations. I have been blessed to receive assistance from many individuals who have given their time to read and comment on sections of the manuscript at varying stages. For this, I am indebted to Dirk Bönker, Jason Crouthamel, and Dennis Showalter, as well as Benjamin Ziemann, Andrew Donson, and Erika Kuhlman, who reviewed the draft manuscript for Cornell University Press. I count myself lucky to have learned from their scholarship, example, and wisdom; any shortcomings and errors are mine alone.

Over the years, I have profited enormously from professional interactions and personal conversations with numerous brilliant individuals, who have inspired me in ways they may not be fully aware of. In particular, I would like to say thank you to Taner Akçam, Betsy Anthony, Frank Bajohr, Sarah Cushman, Werner Dirks, Małgorzata Domagalsk, Debórah Dwork, Stefanie Fischer, Roland Flade, Jürgen Förster, Tim Grady, Anna Hájková, Ainslie Hepburn, Peter Lande, Natalya Lazar, Andrea Löw, Jürgen Matthäus, Eliot Nidam, Michael Nolte, Darren O'Byrne, Devlin Scofield, Matthew Shields, Joanna Sliwa, Jaan Valsiner, Michael Wildt, and Kim Wünschmann. I am also appreciative of Richard Card for his editorial and stylistic advice.

The Strassler Center for Holocaust and Genocide Studies at Clark University brought me into contact with a warm, talented, intellectually curious group of colleagues. I could think of no more nurturing home for a long academic journey. A gracious thanks to my fellow graduate students at the Strassler Center. With great compassion and humor, we have shared our work and worries with one another, offering constructive critique and repairing one another's egos when necessary.

David Frey, Colonel Gail Yoshitani, and Lieutenant Colonel Nadine Ross, along with other members of the Department of History at the United States Military Academy, provided an invigorating environment in which to pursue history, all while we endeavored to teach the skills of our discipline to new generations of future officers. I cannot think of a more exciting place to be a history professor.

I am also enormously grateful to Emily Andrew and the editorial team at Cornell University Press, for the enthusiasm with which they have seen this book through from conception to publication. A special thanks to Alexis Siemon, who offered meticulous yet kind assistance throughout production. In the end, I could not have hoped for a smoother production and review process.

I am also indebted to the many Holocaust survivors and their family members who gave so much of themselves when they agreed to be interviewed for this project. Their contributions are truly inestimable. Many thanks to Johanna Neumann, Kaethe Wells (Schohl), Gerald Weiss, Roger Trefousse, Marion Blumenthal Lazan, Ernest Haas, Lorenz Beckhardt, and Yvonne Klemperer. Many collections of letters and documents remain in private hands, usually in the possession of family members. I am particularly indebted to Ulrich Lewin, who shared his father's surviving military records, photographs, and private letters with me.

I want to thank the numerous institutions that have generously supported my work. This book was made possible (in part) by funds granted to me through an L. Dennis and Susan R. Shapiro Fellowship at the Jack, Joseph and Morton Mandel Center for Advanced Holocaust Studies of the United States Holocaust Memorial Museum. The statements made and views expressed in it, however, are solely my responsibility. I am also grateful to the Emerging Scholars Program at the Mandel Center for its support in the preparation of the manuscript and of the book proposal. Much gratitude is owed to Jo-Ellyn Decker, Suzanne Brown-Fleming, Steven Feldman, Robert Ehrenreich, Megan Lewis, and the wonderful staff at the USHMM, who provided efficient and valuable assistance as well as kindness and hospitality. In addition to introducing me to numerous scholars with shared interests, my involvement with the German Historical Institute has deepened my knowledge of modern German history and the Nazi period. A grant from the Fulbright

Commission made it possible for me to spend over a year in Germany conducting preliminary research for this project. I am also grateful to have received funding from the Leo Baeck Institute, the Society for Military History, the Central European History Society, the German Academic Exchange Service (DAAD), the International Institute for Holocaust Research at Yad Vashem, and the Conference on Jewish Material Claims against Germany.

Most importantly, however, this endeavor would never have been possible without the lifelong, unconditional love and support of my parents, John and Christa Geheran, who instilled in me a passion for learning and a strong work ethic at a young age. Their unwavering encouragement, interest, and enthusiasm sustained me throughout my studies and early career. My late grandparents, Anna and Emil Bellinger, gave me a love of history that has endured. Perhaps my greatest supporter has been my wife, Anna. She has shouldered enormous burdens taking care of our beautiful daughter, Karoline, while I completed the manuscript, and listened to more discussions about World War I and Nazi Germany than any nonhistorian should ever have to endure. Her patience and support cannot be measured, and she has once again proven that I am the lucky one in our marriage. I cannot thank them enough; I dedicate this manuscript to each of them in love and gratitude.

Abbreviations

BA-MA	Bundesarchiv-Militärarchiv, Freiburg
BArch	Bundesarchiv, Berlin
BayHStA/II	Bayerisches Haupstaatsarchiv, Munich
BHStA/IV	Bayerische Hauptstaatsarchiv, Abt. IV, Kriegsarchiv, Munich
CV	Central Association of German Citizens of Jewish Faith (Centralverein deutscher Staatsbürger jüdischen Glaubens)
DTA	Deutsches Tagebucharchiv, Emmendingen
HHL	Harvard Houghton Library
HStADD	Haupstaatsarchiv Dresden
HStADü	Haupstaatsarchiv Düsseldorf
HStAS	Hauptstaatsarchiv Stuttgart
IfZ	Institut für Zeitgeschichte, Munich
JMB	Jüdisches Museum Berlin
LBINY	Leo Baeck Institute, New York
NCO	noncommissioned officer
NIOD	NIOD Instituut voor Oorlogs-, Holocaust- en Genocidestudies, Amsterdam
NSDAP	National Socialist German Workers' Party (Nationalsozialistische deutsche Arbeiterpartei)
OKH	Army High Command (Oberkommando des Heeres)
OKW	Wehrmacht High Command (Oberkommando der Wehrmacht)
RGBl	Reichsgesetzblatt (Reich Law Gazette)
RjF	Reich Association of Jewish Frontline Soldiers (Reichsbund jüdischer Frontsoldaten)
RSHA	Reich Main Security Office (Reichssicherheitshauptamt)
RV	Reich Association of Jews in Germany (Reichsvereinigung der Juden in Deutschland)

SA   Sturmabteilung
SPD   Social Democratic Party of Germany
               (Sozialdemokratische Partei Deutschlands)
SS   Schutzstaffel
StAH   Staatsarchiv Hamburg
StArFr   Stadtarchiv Freiburg
StArN   Stadtarchiv Nürnberg
StArW   Stadtarchiv Würzburg
StAW   Staatsarchiv Würzburg
USHMMA   United States Holocaust Memorial Museum Archives,
               Washington, DC
YVA   Yad Vashem Archives, Jerusalem

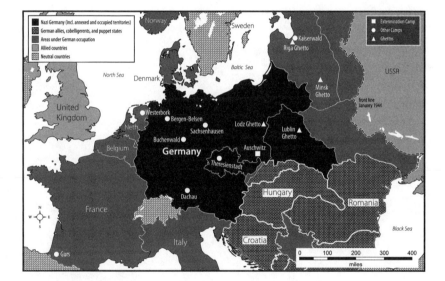

Major camps and ghettos in Nazi Germany and German-occupied Europe.

COMRADES BETRAYED

Introduction

        In November 1938, Julius Katzmann, a Jewish forty-seven-year-old World War I veteran and a lifelong resident of Würzburg, appeared to have defied the Nazis' attempts to marginalize him from German society. Katzmann was co-owner of a successful textile business, H. A. Fränkel, which, despite relentless Nazi agitation, had continued to prosper after Hitler's rise to power in 1933. Katzmann had a number of non-Jewish friends and business contacts, including officers of the local military garrison, and, as the Gestapo itself grudgingly admitted, he was widely respected in the local community. Katzmann contradicted the Nazi propaganda image of Jews as effeminate, self-serving, and inherently un-German. He identified himself first and foremost as a German national, and when war had broken out in 1914, he had rushed to the colors and taken part in some of the bitterest fighting on the Western Front. After the war he returned to Würzburg and fought against Communist revolutionaries who had briefly taken control of the city, and throughout the 1920s and 1930s became an active supporter of conservative political causes. After 1933, when other Jews were forced out of their professions, saw their businesses "aryanized," and were pushed to the margins of mainstream German life, Katzmann's service record ensured that he was exempted from Nazi racial laws. Despite increasing Nazi provocation, he gave the outward impression of leading a secure middle-class existence.

This all came crashing to an end on 9 November 1938, Kristallnacht. That night, the Nazis unleashed a storm of violence across Germany, vandalizing thousands of Jewish-owned businesses and homes and hauling tens of thousands of Jewish men to jails and concentration camps. Katzmann was taken into custody by Nazi authorities—one of some thirty thousand Jewish men rounded up in the wake of the pogrom—and was sent to Buchenwald the following day.

Katzmann's arrest, however, provoked a backlash: several employees at H. A. Fränkel drafted a petition to the Reich Chancellery in Berlin, imploring Hitler to release their boss. The petition writers didn't object to the violent antisemitic campaign that had devastated Germany's Jewish community. "We stand behind our *Volksgenossen* [racial comrades] . . . [and] do not challenge National Socialist principles," they wrote. Yet Katzmann, they argued, was "an exception" and had nothing in common with the "Polish and unclean Jews" who were apparently deserving of Nazi retaliatory measures. His service as a German officer in World War I, where he was twice wounded and awarded the Iron Cross, in addition to his record battling Communists, had "proven his Germanness."[1] The petition was signed by twenty-five of Katzmann's employees, several of whom were members of the Nazi Party. "The tragedy of this case is acknowledged by the enclosed signatures of each of the firm's SA and SS men," it stated. "With Katzmann, one can genuinely speak of a *German* Jew, one who had always declared that he will remain a German until it kills him."[2]

Katzmann was discharged from Buchenwald on 17 November.[3] The petition appears to have been instrumental in securing his early release, and, not coincidentally, less than two weeks later, an order from Hermann Göring called for all Jewish war veterans incarcerated after Kristallnacht to be paroled, suggesting that other, if less dramatic, interventions on behalf of Jewish veterans had occurred. Thus as Jewish men across Germany were shipped off to concentration camps, awaiting uncertain fates, Jewish veterans of the Great War were summarily freed from Nazi custody and given a respite, until the Second World War, when all exit routes to Jews were closed off.

The incident says something remarkable about Jewish veterans and how their wartime experience shaped their responses to National Socialism. When Katzmann's employees argued that he had "proven his Germanness" because he had fought for Germany during the Great War, they were linking military sacrifice with status, recognition, and a claim to national belonging. Such a rationale undergirded the belief that wartime sacrifices would—or should—be compensated with social entitlement, that the discriminatory measures targeting other Jews shouldn't apply to Katzmann because he'd "fulfilled his duty to the Fatherland."[4]

Until his arrest, Katzmann had no intention of leaving Germany. He remained German in the face of evidence that the Germany he'd known no longer considered him one of its own. Current scholarship on the Holocaust contends that most Jews had become "neighborless" or suffered a "social death" by 1935.[5] But stories like Katzmann's contradict that notion, and show how Katzmann, and others like him, confronted persecution, deportation, and antisemitism, and used their status as heroes of the Great War to discredit the claims of Nazi propaganda. The primary aim of this book is to write Jewish war veterans into the history of Nazi Germany and the Holocaust. It examines how Jewish veterans responded to Hitler's seizure of power in 1933, which coping and survival strategies they developed, and why so many remained convinced that Germany would not betray them, even as the Holocaust unfolded around them.

In retrospect, it is difficult to understand the motives of these Jewish victims. How did they cope under the circumstances? What choices did they make that allowed them to believe they would be safe from increasingly virulent antisemitism? What drove Jewish veterans to endure such overwhelming degradations and dangers to their lives? Why did they continue to hold out, even when the situation was clearly hopeless? And what do their behaviors and reactions tell us about soldiering, war, masculinity, and identity?

Not surprisingly, in their writings Jewish veterans emphasized abstract concepts such as honor, manhood, and courage. The ability to "prove" oneself, whether on the battlefields of Flanders in 1914 or against Nazi thugs on the streets of Berlin in 1933, mattered immensely to this generation of Jewish men. Through the discursive link between military service, citizenship, and national belonging, it was not just in Germany that the military occupied a central place where images of masculine behavior were shaped, a development the historian George Mosse refers to as the "militarization of masculinity."[6] In part, this explains why despite having suffered a humiliating defeat at the hands of the Allies, the soldiers of the German Army were welcomed back as heroes in 1918, and seen as having passed a collective test of manhood. After four bloody years of fighting in the trenches, they saw themselves as a kind of masculine elite, having demonstrated their manhood through participation in war. The term *Frontkämpfer* (frontline veteran) communicated aggressiveness, resolve, and active participation in battle, differentiating the "real" soldiers who had faced the enemy in combat from the alleged cowards and shirkers in the rear.[7] This specific conception of manhood embodied the masculine image of the rational actor, the stoic warrior, who retained control of his mental faculties even in times of fear-inducing, life-or-death situations.[8] The power of this image was rooted in public discourses in Germany, which elevated sacrifice and performance of duty (*Pflichterfüllung*) as the highest expression of manhood.[9] These narratives enabled Jewish former soldiers to imbue their identities with a moral legitimacy alongside other German veterans of the Great War and become potentially equal members of this privileged class of men. Especially after World War I, when antisemitic activists charged that Jews had been complicit in Imperial Germany's downfall, this status gained precedence over other markers of status (class, wealth, education, etc.) as Jews consciously engaged in projecting a physically strong, assertive Jewish male image to counter antisemitic propaganda.[10]

This book argues that Jewish veterans oriented themselves toward this normative masculine identity, and cultivated a distinctive manner of thinking and behaving, where courage, self-assertion, and endurance became the measure against which ideal manhood was evaluated. To be sure, masculinity was not a homogeneous concept available to or practiced by a majority of men. Rather than conforming to a dominant ideal, Jewish veterans incorporated elements of their own backgrounds and personalities as part of their male self-image. The crucial point, however, is that by orienting themselves toward these hegemonic qualities, Jewish veterans could tap into prevailing discourses on military heroism, affording all a means to assert themselves, regardless of whether all men could or did act.

Another leitmotif in Jewish veterans' writings was comradeship, the feeling of solidarity that develops when individuals of different backgrounds collectively confront extreme hardships or life-threatening situations. Comradeship was the central experience of the Jewish cohorts who experienced World War I in the trenches, where they often developed powerful bonds with their gentile fellow soldiers. This solidarity was situational, ad hoc, extemporaneous. Yet it gave force and expression to a shared, sacred experience that provided collective meaning.[11] After the fighting had ended, comradeship articulated itself as a more abstract expression of group consciousness, awakening expectations of a common identity and a basic level of mutual recognition among soldiers. Crucially, it provided a mechanism of inclusion for Jewish veterans, for it allowed them to make the case before a nationalist audience that they too had fought in the trenches, where they had sacrificed and died alongside their Christian fellow fighters.

During the Nazi years, Jewish veterans were arguably the single group that antisemites were most reluctant to persecute. War-decorated Jews, including thousands of former officers and war invalids, contradicted Nazi antisemitic stereotypes in the starkest of terms. Many conservative Germans, including certain "moderate" members of the Nazi Party—the same groups who not only supported Hitler's antisemitic policies but in some cases initiated them—were unwilling to apply these policies to Jewish veterans who had "proven their Germanness." From 1933 well into the start of the Final Solution in 1941 and beyond, even those Germans responsible for committing horrific crimes against humanity during the war never fully accepted the unlimited racial antisemitism of Hitler and his closest followers. There were limits to antisemitism in Nazi Germany, and perhaps nothing shows them more clearly than the case of the Jewish Frontkämpfer.

In Germany, Jewish identity was hardly monolithic. The "Jews" were a heterogeneous group with little or no sense of collective identity; only from an outsider's perspective did they appear to constitute a coherent collective. In 1933, approximately five hundred thousand Germans identified themselves as Jews, a figure that represented about 0.77 percent of the country's overall population.[12] The majority of these individuals were self-described "assimilationists" who, like Julius Katzmann, were members of the liberal Reform movement. They belonged to the middle class, spoke German, considered themselves first and foremost natives of Germany rather than Jews, had adopted German names, customs, and manners of diet and dress, and would not necessarily have been recognizable as Jewish.[13] Then there were the Zionists, who professed a distinct Jewish national, cultural, and racial identity. Although many Zionists came from acculturated, middle-class families, they saw themselves not as "German" Jews, but as Jewish citizens of Germany, and expressed a transnational solidarity with their coreligionists throughout Europe. There were also about one hundred thousand Orthodox Jews living in Germany, although very few had lived in Germany when World War I broke out. Most were not German citizens, having belonged to families that had immigrated to Germany from Eastern Europe after 1918. In general, these immigrant populations lived a life steeped in Jewish tradition, isolated from mainstream German life.

The question of Jewish identity becomes even more complicated when considering the more than one hundred thousand Germans who did not identify as Jews, but were categorized as such according to Nazi "racial" definitions.[14] They included individuals who had actively renounced their religious affiliation by converting to the Christian faith or had parents or grandparents who had been born Jewish but were baptized as Christians. Others were entirely secular and did not think of themselves as being Jewish. Such cases in particular reveal how the imposition of Nazi racial categories led to the forcible disrupting of older notions of status and identity.

There were roughly eighty thousand Jewish First World War veterans living in Germany when Hitler came to power. Among them there were liberals and conservatives, members of the political Far Left, civil servants, entrepreneurs, the unemployed, German nationalists, atheists, and socialists. There were Jews who understood themselves to be Catholic or Protestant and did not identify with other Jews. Still others were devout Reform Jews, observant Orthodox Jews, or Zionists. Yet despite the diversity of backgrounds and experiences, they often came to a common understanding of their experience. First and foremost, wartime experience, the so-called *Kriegserlebnis*, provided the context for their identity; as ex-soldiers, they shared memories of military service, comradeship, and violence, as well as a generational consciousness.[15] To be sure, war experiences were diverse—the conflict was long, its campaigns scattered, and the forms of military service varied considerably—yet the experience of combat provided a connecting thread and offers insights into how war and identity were intimately connected.

Julius Meyer, a veteran of the Western Front, had been one of thousands of Jews incarcerated at Buchenwald in the wake of Kristallnacht. He became something of a father figure to the younger prisoners there, who looked up to Meyer for his self-discipline, resolve, and determination to overcome the hardships of the camp, qualities he chalked up to the lessons he had learned twenty years earlier as a soldier. One of the younger prisoners asked Meyer why members of the front generation, "after such a long time, twenty years onward, still bring up experiences from the war and draw comparisons to them on nearly every occasion. Surely," the young man reasoned, "you've had plenty of time before and after the war to live under much different circumstances and form other impressionable experiences." Meyer admitted that he did not have a good answer. He found it difficult to put his feelings into words and limited his response to banal descriptions of war as a "momentous event" that took place when he was at an "impressionable, young age." "But," he acknowledged, "as is the case with many others of my age . . . it was impossible to prevent memories of the war experience from arising so frequently, and here in the camp more so than ever."[16] The exchange says something important about how Meyer's attitude and his behavior during the Nazi years were tied to his military past and the high status of the Frontkämpfer. Veterans constructed an identity around it. They embodied a German Jewish identity that conformed to a specific type of masculine ideal, one that exerted a substantial influence on the generation of German Jews who had fought in World War I. Jews had gone to war in 1914 determined to prove their mettle as tough men and good soldiers; their bravery and endurance in the trenches earned them the respect of their comrades, even Germans with an abiding resentment of Jews. As soldiers, they had been under immense pressure to demonstrate their worthiness to other Germans; after the war, they vowed to remain German amid rising antisemitism, defying stereotypes of Jewish cowardice by exemplifying courage, loyalty, and a willingness to stand up to those who would question their honor. Their writings reveal that enduring the rigors of combat, earning the respect of gentiles, and becoming part of a larger community was the central experience of their lives. It strengthened their sense of belonging to the nation, created and reinforced bonds with other Germans, and led to the development of distinctive expectations and behaviors that were quite different from those who did not experience the war firsthand.

The first comprehensive scholarship on German Jewry during World War I, from the 1960s and 1970s, portrayed Jews as a marginalized, self-confined group, distinct from mainstream society in Germany, whose decades-long strive for equal rights and social acceptance ended disastrously in 1914.[17] The patriotic enthusiasm at the beginning of the Great War, this narrative held, ended abruptly with the "Jew Count" in 1916, when German officers, suspicious that Jews were avoiding frontline combat, ordered a census of Jewish soldiers serving in the army. These histories fed the perception that for Jews, antisemitism was the enduring memory of the war and that the Jew Count had been the decisive moment when German-Jewish relations unraveled. The war is portrayed as an endpoint, the "crisis of the German-Jewish symbiosis," in a long trajectory of failed integration.[18] With their hopes of social acceptance shattered, Germany's Jews turned to Zionism or disabused themselves of the hope that German society would accept them. One of these historians, George L. Mosse, in *The Jews and the German War Experience, 1914–1918*, points out that the war failed to assimilate Jewish soldiers into the German ranks; the enduring memory of the war, he claims, was antisemitism.[19]

But the attitudes and mores of civilians and fighting troops were decidedly different. Antisemitism drew considerable attention in the Jewish press on the home front, and it unleashed fierce debates among Jewish intellectuals as well as religious and community leaders in Germany. But recent analyses of letters and diaries from the field have revealed that the reactions of Jewish soldiers were far less dramatic, providing little evidence that German-Jewish relations at the front were in "crisis."[20]

In the early 2000s, some historians embraced a more nuanced view of the experience of Jewish soldiers in the Great War, and several have challenged the Jew Count and narratives of Jewish disillusionment, claiming that antisemitism was not the driving force between Jews and other Germans at the front.[21] Tim Grady's *The German-Jewish Soldiers of the First World War in History and Memory*, in particular, argues that relations between Jews and other Germans did not end abruptly after 1918.[22] Grady's book throws new light on how Jews and other Germans created a shared memory of the First World War, which persisted throughout the Weimar era, even into the early years of the Third Reich. Derek Penslar and Sarah Panter, in their comparative, transnational approaches, also maintain that antisemitism wasn't the driving force behind German-Jewish relations at the front; rather, the horrors of trench warfare far more shaped the war experience of both Jews and non-Jews involved in the fighting.[23] These works do not downplay the persistence of antisemitism in the German military—for many Jewish soldiers it was a feature of everyday life—but there is little evidence that it irrevocably damaged Jewish morale or lessened Jewish soldiers' faith in the German cause. The publication of Tim Grady's *A Deadly Legacy: German Jews and the Great War*, in particular, has moved the field in new directions, and many historians, including the present author, recognize the need to examine soldiers as a distinct segment of the overall Jewish population.[24]

Despite recent trends in the field of First World War studies, much of the scholarship on the Holocaust upholds narratives of Jewish disillusionment, tending to view Jewish ex-servicemen through the same lens as Jewish civilians or intellectuals, relegating soldiers' experience to the periphery of German persecution.[25] These studies have yielded a rich understanding of an array of topics related to the Nazi persecution of Jews in Germany, yet give only scant attention to the military background, training, and wartime experiences of veterans.[26] This is a significant omission, for many Jewish men who fought in the First World War had been shaped by their service in the Kaiser's military. We see this most clearly through Jews' high rate of participation in the postwar veterans' movement, their attendance at regimental reunions, and their repeated invocations of the war in private letters, diaries, and memoirs. Persecution meant something different for veterans and nonmilitary Jews, and so did coping and survival strategies during the Holocaust. Other studies detail what National Socialists understood by "Jews," and assume that veterans were categorized no differently from nonveterans, but in the Weimar years, and after 1933, veterans did experience persecution differently from nonmilitary Jews.

In the Nazi *Volksgemeinschaft* (people's community), race was the dominant criterion for determining community membership; in the end, it alone decided between life and death. Over the past decade, however, scholars have considerably expanded the understanding of the nuances and local dynamics of the Nazis' anti-Jewish campaign by examining additional categories of discrimination, including gender, age, political milieu, location, education, and profession,[27] and the picture of Jews' situation in Nazi Germany becomes richer in detail, more complete, and arguably more complex. Status, specifically the social prestige conferred by wartime military service, is not irrelevant in this field, yet work in this area is sparse.

This book emphasizes the complexity of Jewish war experiences as well as the multifaceted memories of the war, antisemitism, and Jewish reactions to it. Moving beyond an institutional approach solely focused on veterans' organizations and militaries, it seeks to offer a broader account of how fighting in the war affected individual German Jews as they confronted discrimination, state-sponsored terror, and organized mass murder under the Nazis. It examines the generation of Jewish men who fought in World War I as a distinct subset of the Jewish population, and considers how gender, background, and their wartime experiences affected their thinking and behavior under Hitler.

Though there is great value in grappling with the Great War's effect on Jewish war veterans' multifaceted identities, the focus of this book is deliberately narrow. First, as the combatants of the First World War were exclusively male, it focuses predominantly on men. Although thousands of Jewish women were directly impacted by World War I—including those who became widows because of the war, or lost fathers, brothers, sons, and other loved ones—because of the specific political, legal, and social circumstances, these women require a comprehensive study of their own. Second, most veterans in this book came from the predominantly urban, educated middle classes, as members of this group were more likely to document their experience in diaries and memoirs, and had the financial means to escape Nazi Germany after 1933. This does not reflect the composition of the Jewish front generation, however. In 1914, rural Jews made up nearly a third of the Jewish population, and as recent studies have shown, their reactions and motivations were often different from those of their "bourgeois" counterparts.[28] Despite these limits and exclusions, focusing on the Jewish Frontkämpfer enables us to broaden our understanding of the Jewish men who fought in the Great War and how they coped under Nazi oppression. It also tells us a great deal about the ways in which a soldier's identity rested on his memories of the front and expectations of status, which, as we shall see, did not abruptly end in 1918 or 1933.

Jewish experiences during World War I cannot be reduced to a single *Kriegserlebnis*, but as chapter 1 shows, Jews were united in the hope, as they joined thousands of other German men rushing to the colors in 1914, that the spirit of national unity would obliterate antisemitic stereotypes. Their participation in the immense violence of an industrialized war led to the formation of powerful bonds with gentile Germans, fueling Jewish hopes that the war would be the culmination of the long struggle for social acceptance.

Germany's devastating defeat in November 1918 left the German nation tattered and fragmented. When the war ended, Jewish veterans, like so many other Germans, looked forward to a return to normalcy. Instead, the returning soldiers found themselves embroiled in civil war, insurrections from the Right and Left, economic upheaval, and an unprecedented outpouring of antisemitism. Historians have traditionally portrayed the fourteen turbulent years of the Weimar Republic as a period of Jewish disillusionment, but as chapter 2 argues, Jewish veterans used their record of fighting in the trenches to discredit the claims of antisemitic activists and generate ambivalence among a German public that saw former soldiers as persons to be respected, regardless of background.

Chapter 3 extends this argument into the early years of the Third Reich, demonstrating that Hitler's seizure of power in 1933 did not bring "social death" for the Jewish Frontkämpfer. The reign of terror the Nazis unleashed on Jews, Communists, and other groups stood in marked contrast to their failed attempts to marginalize Jewish ex-servicemen, whose record of service in the front lines in World War I enabled them to claim and negotiate a special status in the new Germany. Jewish veterans did not break with their identity as Germans, and continued to demand recognition of their sacrifices from the German public as well as the Nazi Party.

Moving from Hitler's consolidation of power following Hindenburg's death in 1934 to the eve of Kristallnacht, chapter 4 examines the changes to Jewish war veterans' legal status after the Nuremberg Laws in 1935 and the ways in which many of these men tried to retain their sense of Germanness in the face of intensifying state-sponsored terror and persecution. Although the Nazis succeeded in banning Jews from the civil service and most veterans' organizations, this did not mean that Jewish veterans were abruptly cast to the margins of German public life. Not all Germans shared Himmler's radical vision of a racially purified *Volksgemeinschaft*. This inconsistency in experience—persecution on the one hand, and limited solidarity with the German public on the other—obscured the gravity of the Nazi threat, leading many Jewish veterans to contemplate accommodation with the Third Reich.

Chapter 5 analyzes the massive deterioration of the situation of Jewish veterans after 1938 and the intense debates between the higher echelons of the Wehrmacht, SS, and Nazi Party officials over the remnants of the special status that they, at this stage, still enjoyed. It also examines Jewish veterans' ongoing attempts to preserve their honor as prisoners in the Nazi concentration camps following the mass incarcerations after Kristallnacht. As they were rounded up, physically and verbally assaulted, and deported to Dachau, Buchenwald, and Sachsenhausen, Jewish veterans not only relied on their military training and memories of the war to overcome the ordeal; they also remained committed to preserving their honor and their dignity. This also held true for those Jewish veterans deported to the ghettos of Lodz, Minsk, and Riga in late 1941.

The Wannsee Conference in January 1942 established Theresienstadt as the destination for highly decorated and war-wounded Jewish veterans. The German public's negative reaction to the deportations of Jews that began the previous year, together with interventions by senior officers, pressured the SS to create a special camp for "privileged" types of German Jews. Theresienstadt was merely a ruse, a way station on the road to Auschwitz. But as chapter 6 shows, despite the brutal conditions they faced there and at other Nazi camps, Jewish veterans' connection to their former status and their identity did not abruptly end.

The book closes with a short glimpse into the history of Jewish veterans after 1945, as the survivors of the camps returned to Germany, outlining ruptures and continuities in comparison with the pre-Nazi period. Jewish veterans imposed different narratives on their experiences under National Socialism. As the past receded into the distance, it became a concern for the survivors to engage with the past, which they variously looked back on with nostalgia, disillusionment, or bitter anger.

A final note: the Nazis lumped together an extremely diverse group of people who often had little in common except that they were categorized as Jewish. In this regard, to a certain extent this book must mimic vocabulary used by the Nazi perpetrators. Individuals not referred to as "Jewish" in other contexts are subjects of this book only because they were identified, persecuted, and murdered as Jews by the Nazi regime, while in certain contexts the term "Aryan" is used to describe Germans whom the Nazis classified as non-Jewish.

CHAPTER 1

Reappraising Jewish War Experiences, 1914–18

The long-standing historiography of German Jewry during World War I has typically followed a linear trajectory that begins with Jewish enthusiasm in 1914, as Jews celebrated the war in the belief that it would obliterate antisemitic stereotypes and level any remaining barriers to social equality. Despite volunteering to fight at the front lines in large numbers, however, Jews' hopes ended disastrously amid increasing antisemitism, culminating in the so-called Jew Count (*Judenzählung*) in November 1916.[1] Only since the early 2000s have studies shown that military and political developments were often perceived differently in the field than on the civilian home front. Military discipline, comradeship, almost daily exposure to hardships and life-threatening dangers, and the experience of combat created a distinctive habitus among the Jewish combatants, one that set them apart from their civilian counterparts back home in Germany. A study of the Jewish combatants raises a series of overarching questions: Did Jewish soldiers experience the war differently than other Germans? To what degree was Jewishness a factor at the front? How did Jews react to antisemitism in the field? Could the comradeship of the front lines overcome antisemitism? Were Jewish soldiers able to successfully discredit antisemitic stereotypes?

Jewish Service in the German Military

Relations between Jews and other Germans in Imperial Germany were marked by acceptance despite the existence of antisemitism. After Jews were granted legal equality and all the rights of German citizens following Germany's unification in 1871, they gained access to the major functional spheres of society as well as in everyday life, and became firmly established in the German middle class. Numerous studies have shown that German Jews were highly integrated in their local communities, participating in all spheres of social, cultural, and associational life.[2] Although discourses complaining about alleged "Jewish influence" in the media, finance, or the arts were common, antisemitic parties were confined to the political fringe prior to 1918. A small faction of radical nationalists demanded stripping Jews of their rights, on the grounds that they belonged to a foreign ethnic group, but if political power is any indicator of the success of these ideologies, then their resounding defeat in the 1913 parliamentary elections seems to provide little evidence that this rhetoric actually resonated with the general public.[3]

Antisemitism had, however, made serious inroads in two important spheres in German society: the youth movement, especially in university student fraternities, and perhaps the most important institution in Imperial Germany—the army. The Prussian officers' corps traditionally saw Jews as poor patriots, physically weak, effeminate, and inherently unsuited for soldiering.[4] Along with socialists and members of the working class, many German officers regarded Jews as politically "unreliable," believing that their perceived lack of strong moral character and leftist political leanings threatened to open the army to liberalization.[5] Although there were no legal restrictions prohibiting Jews from obtaining a commission, in practice they were all but barred from entering the officers' ranks. To become an officer in the Prussian Army, a soldier had to not only pass the required physical and practical examinations, but also obtain the endorsement of his regimental commander. His candidacy then had to be unanimously approved by all of the officers in the regiment by way of a secret ballot. A single negative vote was sufficient to disqualify a candidate, regardless of his qualifications. Between 1885 and the outbreak of World War I, not a single Jew was on the roll of active or reserve officers in the Prussian Army.[6] Only in Bavaria did Jews stand a chance of entering the officers' ranks. In 1913, 129 Jewish soldiers in Bavaria held reserve commissions.[7]

Discrimination in the military had serious implications for Jewish men. The army was an institution of immense stature in Imperial Germany, and widely regarded as the "school of the nation" among the German middle class. As all German men were obligated to serve a three-year stint in the armed forces, there can be little doubt that conscription legitimized these negative stereotypes before a significant swath of German society.[8] Anti-Jewish prejudice was based primarily on religion, not race, as conversion to Christianity offered some Jews a path to obtaining an officer's commission. Yet there can be no doubt that it intensified the sense of dishonor and estrangement of German Jews, who had practically no chance to pursue military careers.

Despite Jews' being barred from the officers' corps, military service remained a key issue in Jewish discourses on emancipation and held a particular attraction for young Jewish men struggling to unburden themselves from stereotypes of frailty.[9] In a society where young men were expected to fulfill masculine ideals that were inseparable from the image of the soldier, the army was seen not merely as the "school of the nation," but also as the "school of manhood," where adolescents underwent a masculine rite of passage that made them into "real men." Soldiers demonstrated selflessness, bravery, and the readiness to sacrifice self for a higher cause, placing the nation and their communities over personal safety. This was the ultimate expression of manhood. The tough, powerful physique of the soldier ran counter to the image of the Jewish man as feeble, effete, and weak, and donning the Kaiser's uniform promised young Jewish men social prestige, status, and a chance to earn the respect of other men. This is precisely what attracted Victor Klemperer to the army. As a young boy growing up in Berlin, he was fascinated by the military, and one of his favorite pastimes was to watch the soldiers of the nearby grenadier regiment drill and march in formation. Both of his brothers had been declared "unfit" for active military service, and he too was convinced that someone as "scrawny" and "hunchbacked" as he was would never be accepted by the army. When he reported for his physical exam in 1903, he was elated when the medical examiner told him, "Although you have no muscles, you are completely healthy and the military will toughen you up."[10] The fact that he "was not physically inferior and hunchbacked, like it was often said," filled Klemperer with "great joy"; he rejoiced at the prospect of being considered "useful."[11] It came as a particularly severe blow when, several weeks later, he was reexamined by another doctor after reporting for duty in Halle and deemed too frail. Klemperer was sent home, "completely dismayed." "My physical competence," he wrote, "of which I had been so proud, had come to nothing."[12]

Becoming a soldier was the most visible expression of one's allegiance and willingness to self-sacrifice for the nation. In Germany, military service was grounded in a long-standing tradition in European political thought that emphasized the inherent connection between national citizenship and soldiering. In theory if not in practice, it gave the soldier a claim to individual rights and freedoms grounded in the belief that someone who is willing to die for the fatherland has a claim on full recognition as a citizen.[13] The language of heroism in public discourses reinforced and perpetuated these ideals throughout German society, equating military service with social and political belonging.[14] For Jews, however, soldiering held a greater significance. As the highest form of civic virtue, it was a pathway to social acceptance and a means to demonstrate Jewish worthiness for equal rights.

The Spirit of 1914

Recent studies have laid to rest the notion that an all-embracing war euphoria swept Germany in 1914. While enthusiasm visibly manifested itself in cities and larger towns, this sentiment was largely restricted to the liberal and middle classes. There was little jubilation among the working class or in rural communities, where news of the impending conflict was mostly greeted with uncertainty and resignation.[15] On the surface, however, the "Spirit of 1914" seemed to rally the nation together. In big cities and university towns, large crowds in favor of the war marched through the streets, pubs and cafés were overflowing with people singing patriotic songs, and throngs of volunteers rushed to enlistment depots to join the army. Out of common crisis emerged a newfound solidarity. Businessmen, intellectuals, university students, and the majority of the urban middle classes saw the war as a means to end decades of bitter domestic strife, and to unite a society fractured by social conflict and class difference. Labor unions, interest groups, religious organizations, and political parties of all stripes seized the moment, believing that an enthusiastic endorsement of the German war effort would further their political agendas, be it voting reform in Prussia, social solidarity, or the repudiation of antisemitism. Even the Social Democratic Party (Sozialdemokratische Partei Deutschlands, or SPD), the erstwhile opponent of the monarchy's authoritarian nation-state, pledged its support to Kaiser Wilhelm. Thus, the *Burgfrieden*—the fortress truce—was established.

To acculturated German Jews, the war was a catalyst for social change; it represented the long-awaited moment for them to publicly demonstrate their loyalty to the fatherland and surmount the last hurdles toward complete integration in German society. Kaiser Wilhelm's famous speech before a delegation of Reichstag deputies, in which he vowed to no longer recognize political parties or religious confessions but "only Germans," emboldened

Germany's Jewish population. Jewish newspapers, synagogues, and interest groups across Germany immediately responded with public exhortations in support of the government. Germany's largest Jewish organization, the Central Association of German Citizens of Jewish Faith (Centralverein deutscher Staatsbürger jüdischen Glaubens, or CV), published a proclamation just two days after the Kaiser's speech: "Call to Arms! To German Jews! In this fateful hour, the Fatherland calls its sons to the colors. That every German Jew is prepared to sacrifice blood and property for this cause, as required by duty, is obvious. Fellow Jews! We call on you to *rise above your simple duty* and devote your strength and energy to the Fatherland!"[16]

Zionist organizations such as the Zionist Federation of Germany (Zionistische Vereinigung für Deutschland) responded with similar declarations of support, urging all Jewish men to take up arms and local communities to back the German cause.[17] A powerful impetus for Zionists was that the war was being fought against Russia, widely regarded as Jews' greatest oppressor. Standing shoulder to shoulder with their Jewish brethren in Russia, they saw a victorious German campaign against the Tsar—"the archenemy of all Jews"—as an opportunity to free millions of East European Jews from oppressive, autocratic rule.[18]

The feeling that Germany had been provoked into a defensive war by the Entente reinforced Jews' sense of solidarity with other Germans. "We feel that we are being attacked," Herbert Sulzbach noted in his diary as he enlisted with the Sixty-Third Field Artillery Regiment in Frankfurt am Main. "And that feeling, of having to defend ourselves, gives us unbelievable strength."[19] In universities throughout Germany, Jewish student fraternities, such as the Salia in Würzburg, urged their members to enlist before the moment passed, "to spill their hearts' blood on the grim battlefield for the honor and glory of our beloved Fatherland."[20] Ernst Marcus was one of thousands of Jews who volunteered for the army. For him, the wave of euphoria in his home city of Breslau was an overwhelming, if imagined, moment: "The mood in those days was unforgettable; only then did I ever feel a real enthusiasm, a genuine solidarity that transcended class, status, and political persuasion. There was an overriding consensus: Germany was being attacked, the English, this nation of shopkeepers, were denying Germany its place in the sun, and therefore this battle for our honor and our existence was justified."[21] In Munich, Victor Klemperer was also gripped by the patriotic hysteria sweeping through German cities. As he watched columns of troops file past, marching through the streets to the accompaniment of music and throngs of cheering spectators, Klemperer found himself "moved to tears every time."[22]

Jewish responses from August 1914 did not differ dramatically from those of other Germans of the same class and background. Jewish autobiographical sources articulated narratives common among young, middle-class German men, such as love of fatherland, performance of duty (*Pflichterfüllung*), and a desire to prove their male self-worth. Many volunteers, like Karl Löwith, were drawn to the sense of adventure the war promised: "The passion for 'living dangerously,' which Nietzsche instilled in us, the desire to throw ourselves into adventure and to test ourselves . . . these and similar motives led me to welcome the war as an opportunity to live and die more intensely."[23] Fritz Goldberg also saw the war as an exhilarating, empowering moment. Invoking the romantic imagery of heroism and combat as a masculine rite of passage, he eagerly followed his classmates to join a local regiment. The war, he wrote, "was not a break with our past; on the contrary, it was a confirmation of everything we had been taught to believe. We were raised in the spirit of heroism—now its hour had come. Love of Fatherland was our beacon—now all that mattered was to prove it. The Kaiser and his army were the highest authority—now we yearned to heed their call."[24]

Like many German men in 1914, Goldberg embraced romantic notions of combat, manhood, and performing acts of bravery on the battlefield that would make him a hero. Aspirations of heroism encouraged thousands of Jews to volunteer, with Kaiser Wilhelm's words still echoing in their ears. It was the moment for these young men to prove themselves and to be celebrated by their communities back home. Their induction into the army was an entry ticket into a privileged, exclusive male fraternity. "I had gotten to know the men of our society from up close," wrote Ernst Marcus. "Now I was one of them."[25] Even Carl Zuckmayer, who later penned the famous antiwar play *The Captain of Kopernick*, looked back on the moment he joined a local regiment in 1914 as a validation of his masculine worth. "It seems absurd," he wrote, "but with one stroke, one became a man."[26] Failure to pass the military physical examination, on the other hand, was a mark of shame for Jewish men; it represented their failures as men and went to the essence of their male honor. "It was seen as a disgrace to be unqualified for the army," David Kollander recalled, as his older brother endured untold verbal abuse by his schoolmates after failing to pass the initial muster.[27] Max Kronenburg also received the dreaded classification "unfit," due to a heart condition. Undeterred, he traveled to a neighboring town and petitioned several local units until taken up by a field artillery regiment.[28]

The majority of Jewish soldiers did not volunteer, however, but fought because they were drafted.[29] In Nuremberg 1,543 Jews served during the war, of whom roughly 11 percent had volunteered.[30] The percentage was slightly higher in Würzburg, a university town, where 52 out of the 398 Jewish men who entered the army had joined voluntarily.[31] By contrast, a study of the Bavarian Rhön, a rural, agricultural region in northern Franconia, indicates that only 2 of the total 280 Jewish soldiers had volunteered.[32] Thus, while war euphoria was prevalent among the educated middle classes, in rural communities there was little enthusiasm to motivate Jewish farmers and cattle traders to volunteer for the army; for them a prolonged military campaign meant chronic labor shortages, especially during critical planting and harvesting seasons.[33] When war broke out, Louis Liebmann, the son of a cattle dealer in Hesse-Nassau, tried his best to avoid the draft as long as possible. In his memoir, he rails against the widespread war cheering and "Hurrah-Patriotism" and unabashedly recounts his ongoing efforts to avoid serving in combat.[34] Liebmann's behavior was atypical of most rural Germans, Jewish or Christian. Yet his case reminds us that not every German Jew was willing to subordinate himself to the rigors of military life and risk an early death on the battlefield.

There were discernible differences in the attitudes, motivations, and expectations of the Jewish men who went to war in 1914. What they shared, however, were two overarching hopes: to discredit the antisemitic stereotype of the unmanly, unpatriotic Jew, and that German society would recognize their sacrifices. The last part was crucial. Whether as a war volunteer or conscript, the soldier expected that his sacrifices would be recognized later on; he wanted to be welcomed back to Germany as a hero and as a "real" man. This expectation provided the impetus for individuals to go headlong into the trenches, to risk death, wounds, and disfigurement for the fatherland.

Jewish Front Experiences

Individual wartime experiences were contingent on a range of social and situational factors, central to which were a soldier's expectations in August 1914 and the extent to which they were being fulfilled. This gap between expectations and reality undergirded Jewish expressions of enthusiasm, hope, ambivalence, and disappointment. In addition to Jewish soldiers' age, education, profession, and temperament, their cultural and religious identity—and sense of integration into German society—largely determined how they perceived and reacted to wartime events, and how these events were later transfigured into memory.[35]

A second decisive factor in shaping soldiers' experiences was the capacity in which they served—that is, whether they fought as part of a combat unit at the front or performed a support function behind the lines. For soldiers engaged in the actual fighting, the encounter with extreme violence formed a central element of their war experiences. They underwent face-to-face encounters with the enemy and were thrust into situations that others would find difficult to imagine. Combat created unparalleled levels of fear and duress, putting soldiers in sometimes daily confrontations with life-or-death situations. Prolonged shelling by artillery, the deafening noise of grenades and small arms fire, and days, even weeks, living in the mud and rain without opportunities to bathe or change one's clothes, amid rats and the corpses of soldiers ripped apart by shellfire, were realities that distinguished the experiences of the fighting troops from the soldiers stationed in the rear.[36]

Despite the horrific realities of protracted, industrial-style warfare, there was a "constructive" side to military violence. Combat was an exercise in community building; it established social bonds. Mortal danger created a powerful sense of community among the soldiers who endured it. Confrontations with death, mourning fallen comrades, fear of wounds and dismemberment, and killing were experiences that transgressed the norms of civilian society. Confronting them together fed the experience of community.[37] Amid the constant dread of being killed or crippled by hostile fire, Edwin Halle, an artilleryman on the Western Front, felt a sense of reassurance being in the forward trenches, among his comrades: "Between us chaps here up front, the inner comradeship is more pronounced than ever. The proximity to the enemy welds people even closer together. Here in the earth, where one can glimpse only a sliver of sky, in the mud through which one wades, one realizes that we are little more than the worms that root around underneath us. Life can be extinguished in an instant: that was made clear to us by Schlitte's sudden death. Yet here, we felt especially safe."[38]

What Halle described was a solidarity born of survival; this central, overriding emotion engendered cooperation and mutual dependence between members of a military primary group.[39] This dynamic enabled soldiers to survive; they fought together under extreme conditions, and continued to do so even after their initial enthusiasm had faded.[40] Combat forged a powerful microlevel solidarity between the men who endured it, bonds that withstood social and ideological rifts, including antisemitism. An oft-repeated claim in letters written home was how proximity to danger erased distinctions of class, religion, and social background in the field, as inner tensions, prejudices, and personal rivalries were displaced by solidarity in what George Simmel called the "extreme environment" of war.[41] "That I am at the front smooths over a lot of things that would normally provide fodder for constant conflict, as everyone is afraid and is committed to each other," wrote Alfred Koch, a war volunteer from Offenbach am Main who served with

Field Artillery Regiment No. 21 in Flanders. "Hopefully things will stay that way."[42] Another artilleryman, Herbert Sulzbach, also preferred the forward-most trenches to the quiet areas behind the lines, "because the comradeship and selflessness become more pronounced the greater the danger."[43] Joachim Beutler, who served with an infantry regiment in Flanders, was even more explicit in a letter to his parents: "We receive several attacks daily from Frenchmen and Negroes, accompanied by volleys of hand grenades, the crackling of machine-gun bullets overhead, to the point where one believes hell on earth has finally come. One consolation for us in these dark hours is our comradeship. . . . I never experienced anything in the way of antisemitism here, times are too serious for that."[44]

Such "extreme experiences" certainly did not characterize everyday life in the front lines. The great material battles on the Western Front, such as Verdun and the Somme, continue to shape popular perceptions of World War I, but there were prolonged lulls in the fighting, and combat deployments were punctuated by extended periods of rest and refitting behind the trenches.[45] Yet these moments of crisis, where soldiers depended on comrades to survive, however fleeting they were, would be remembered by the combatants long after the fighting ended.

Studies have shown that comradeship encompassed far more than "hard" masculinity of the type that inspired acts of bravery and resilience among soldiers engaged in combat. It incorporated elements of a "softer" altruistic side, bringing relief and psychological sustenance to soldiers confronted by daily violence.[46] The primary group assumed the role of a surrogate family, providing reassurance to men confronted by loneliness, deprivation, and the omnipresence of death. After enduring the shock of coming under hostile fire for the first time, Julius Fürst found salvation among his fellow soldiers. "Once those first horrible days have passed," he wrote to a friend, "you stop thinking, you are pushed inexorably towards the others, to your comrades: they have experienced the same thing, in their souls the same chaos reigns, they must surely know the way."[47]

Comradeship also offered a space for Jewish soldiers to cope under the brutality of antisemitic superiors. In his diary, Edwin Halle praises his fellow soldiers for sustaining him through the rigors of basic training, especially after it was revealed that his battery commander, Lieutenant Schröder, was an unapologetic Jew hater. The man "had a grudge against us Jews from the very beginning: Adler, Telheimer, Rosenthal and me," Halle wrote. "He makes no secret about being an antisemite."[48] A few days later, the lieutenant falsely accused Halle of committing a minor infraction. He was punished and arbitrarily sentenced to a short period of confinement to the barracks, an incident that left him bitter and deeply disillusioned about his prospects in the army:

> I am without question a patriot in body in soul and have done everything within my power to serve the Fatherland. I learned—I wanted to excel! But with such treatment one loses it, the commitment to becoming a soldier. If one's honor is besmirched in this way, it is like suffering a moral death. And here I lodge my complaint: if from now on I am no longer able to do what is required of me, that man who now leads our battery and despises me for no reason—because I am a Jew—is responsible! God forgive me! There are limits, at which even the best man loses his bearing![49]

Halle felt shame for allegedly discrediting the reputation of the battery and leaving his comrades "in the lurch." As he returned to his outfit to await the judgment of his fellow soldiers, he was "afraid to look at anyone" and "unable to overcome the feeling of having been dishonored." To Halle's surprise, he was enthusiastically welcomed back. "When I reported back to the battery this afternoon, the sense of elation was enormous," he wrote. "It felt good, to experience this heartfelt joy shown to me by not only my comrades, but also my superiors, from privates all the way up to the staff sergeant."[50] Such incidents suggest that amid the helplessness of soldiers subjected to a system of hierarchy and obedience, comradeship provided comfort, reassurance, and a sense of empowerment. Although Halle was outraged over the injustice, it was quickly forgotten. His dignity was restored by the devotion of his comrades, and the confrontation did not fundamentally change Halle's commitment to the German cause.

Like Halle, Otto Meyer also became the target of antisemitic slurs during basic training. The twenty-nine-year-old small business owner from Rheda, Westphalia, was drafted into a Prussian foot artillery regiment in 1915 and immediately singled out by a racist sergeant. "As a Jew, I was particularly berated," he wrote his wife in April 1915. "Yet I don't complain about this, my sweetheart. You cannot imagine the inner peace I have achieved. My patriotism is not affected by these things either, for what can the Fatherland do about it?"[51] Meyer related few details to his wife about what happened, yet his reaction says something significant about how acculturated Jewish soldiers responded to antisemitism. Despite the setback, he continued to view his military experience as generally positive. The behavior of the antisemitic noncommissioned officer (NCO) did not undermine his self-understanding as a German of Jewish faith. Meyer encountered prejudice in different forms throughout the war. His diary is punctuated with expressions of resignation, bitterness, and disbelief. Yet amid such disappointments, the dominant thread in his writings is not antisemitism, but the sense of community among his fellow soldiers. "Comradeship," Meyer wrote on 28 April 1915, "makes it possible for me to remember the spiritual amid the overwhelming physical experiences and exertions."[52] He formed deep attachments to the other men in his unit, and when he was promoted to sergeant, his feelings were conflicted as it meant transferring to a different unit and leaving behind his comrades. "I have waited for this day with longing," he wrote. "My military adolescence is now completed, the time of manhood now begins; I realize that I have to take leave of other things as well, the carefree camaraderie and the wonderful cohabitation with the others, the commoners and really shabby ones alike. Whether I shall be able to live together with my old comrades as before, the one-yearers who will also become noncoms, is not yet certain."[53]

It would be a mistake to imagine that comradeship hinged on the presence of enduring personal relationships or friendships. As Thomas Kühne and Benjamin Ziemann have shown, the bonds forged between soldiers, thrust into roles from which they could not escape, were characterized foremost by contingency.[54] In his diary, Fritz Frank described good relations with his comrades throughout the entire conflict, insisting time and again that "common crisis and work weld us together," yet not once did he ever mention anything resembling a deep personal connection or friendship.[55] Alfred Koch maintained a regular correspondence with his mother and brother, Richard, that lasted through almost four years of war. In general, the army was no place for expressions of misery, self-doubt, or vulnerability, and as the war dragged on, Koch's letters began to assume the quality of a private confessional. Stitched together and preserved by his mother after he was killed at Soissons in April 1918, the letters reveal the frustration of a young man from a privileged upper-middle-class background forced to live in close quarters with rural peasants and "shit farmers" who, in Koch's eyes, behaved like animals: "If you knew what that means: when one lives 14 hours a day, side-by-side with people you would otherwise not even spit in the face. These people are built to completely different specifications than we are. 90% animal. . . . I regard my fate, which has brought me into ongoing association with these people, foremost as my contribution to the great sacrifice."[56]

Confronted with lower-class male behavior for the first time, Koch struggled to accept being forced to live with people to whom, under normal circumstances, he would never have gotten close enough to spit on. "One has to take the position," he complained to his parents in October 1914, "that the majority of people stand on a much, much lower cultural level than even the most degenerate Jewish beggar. . . . One can only regard them as a different species of people who cannot be compared to us."[57] Koch's inability to "fit in" was a recurring preoccupation throughout his wartime writings, as his letters conveyed a persistent sense of aloneness: "How rarely one meets another person with whom one can talk about something else besides the usual battery gossip. Since I've been here in the regiment, I haven't found anyone."[58] But despite his personal feelings of distance, Koch acknowledged the bravery and competence of his fellow soldiers under fire. "Despite everything, I am quite lucky to stand among my comrades," he wrote on 17 March 1917. "They are primitive chaps, but also skillful and full of love."[59]

It is striking that Halle, Meyer, and Koch described comradeship in fundamentally different ways. While they experienced (and acknowledged) the mutual cooperation of soldiers under fire, for Koch this solidarity was functional, extemporaneous, and impersonal. His letters conveyed nothing of the sort of emotional attachment or group identification described by acculturated Jews like Halle or Meyer. These findings reveal that comradeship encompassed far more than human behavior in extremis. Very often it articulated itself as something intangible, as an organizing discourse, an abstract means of self-identification and expression of group consciousness.[60] Jewish writings from the field suggest that the soldiers saw comradeship as a mechanism of self-definition, a sign of inclusion, and a category through which they interpreted their sense of belonging with other Germans. It determined not only how and with which spiritual attitude they experienced the war and endured its hardships, but also how they would remember it when the fighting ended.

"At least in war everyone is equal," Walther Heymann wrote to his wife, alluding to his realization that at the front, enemy fire did not distinguish officers from conscripts, or individuals of different class and social backgrounds.[61] He was seemingly elated by the fact that he, as a Jew, felt a deep sense of togetherness with his comrades, something he had never experienced before the war in civilian life. This revelation led Heymann to contemplate heroic, redemptive death on the battlefield, for "it is not a mere phrase, that who dies, sacrifices himself for all, even the survivors. To pay with one's life is undoubtedly difficult. But in death as in life, in the service of a cause, one must be prepared to die, even as cannon fodder."[62]

Like many of his fellow "assimilationists," Albrecht Mugdan described the outbreak of war in 1914 as an exhilarating, empowering experience. The son of upper-middle-class parents in Breslau, Mugdan saw it as a kind of adventure, a rite of passage, and a means to escape the predictable routines of civilian life. His handwritten, hastily scrawled postcards and letters from the field exhibited an immense pride at serving in the front lines and obtaining an officer's commission in an elite alpine regiment. An "unforgettable" moment occurred just two months before Mugdan was killed at Verdun, when Kaiser Wilhelm paid an unexpected visit to his regiment and personally pinned the Iron Cross on his chest.[63] But the decidedly nationalistic tone of Mugdan's writings was not solely the result of actual wartime experiences. The style and tenor of his writings did not change from the beginning of the war until he was killed. This finding suggests that Mugdan's attitude was not shaped exclusively by the positive experiences he described in his letters, but also by the values and expectations of his social milieu. It should be remembered that the CV saw the conflict as an opportunity to "forge a brotherhood that is everlasting," and in general, this is how Mugdan portrayed his war experience.[64] Life at the front was invariably described as "good" and "very nice," even during those times his unit was engaged in combat and suffering casualties. He repeatedly praised the solidarity in his platoon; relations with his fellow soldiers were "unconstrained and cozy," and "better than I could wish for."[65] Mugdan felt at home among comrades, emphasized the sense of oneness between officers and men, and saw himself as part of a community of fate bound by a common mission and purpose, where race and background were seemingly irrelevant. Exposure to danger invigorated this sense of belonging. After an engagement with enemy soldiers, he wrote, "The comradeship among us members of the first platoon becomes ever stronger. We all understand each other very well and are inseparable. It is truly wonderful, and I believe this solidarity is a reflection of everything we experience together."[66]

To Mugdan, this fraternal bond became a self-affirming war experience, an expression of self-identity and group identity driven by a desire for community with other Germans. As Robert Nelson writes, comradeship was more than a mere psychological reaction, but also "pre-war socialization followed by the wartime search for self-justification."[67] For soldiers like Mugdan, who did not identify themselves as Jewish in a cultural sense, the military primary group was their own, and the acceptance of Jews as "comrades" by the gentile frontline community strengthened their identities as German Jews. "It never occurred to me during this war that I am a Jew," wrote Nathan Wolf. "I feel one with my comrades, and they with me, so that it never enters our consciousness; we all feel German and especially *Badisch*."[68] The authors' Jewish faith often remained in the background, seemingly eclipsed by the exigencies of the war. At no point in his letters did Albrecht Mugdan mention being a Jew.[69] While such cases were the exception, most contemporary diarists made only veiled or situational references to Jewish identity. Rather, they tended to elevate the "we" of the primary group—that is, the sameness and commonality with other Germans.

If acculturated Jewry saw the solidarity of the trenches as the fulfill-
ment of their hopes that the war would meld Jews and other Germans into
a greater national community, some Jewish servicemen regarded it with
ambivalence and disappointment. The orientation to comradeship and the
"fatherland" were central political-moral values for Wolf and Mugdan, and
held far greater importance than they did for the devout Jewish philosopher
Franz Rosenzweig. Rosenzweig self-identified neither as Orthodox nor as a
Zionist, but nevertheless embraced a distinct Jewish national and cultural
identity. His wartime letters described the "front experience" with a sense of
disappointment, claiming that the experience of living and fighting alongside other Germans merely intensified the sense of separateness between
Germans and Jews. The feeling of otherness, he wrote, "is never switched
off except when one happens to meet someone else who is also 'different,'"
meaning Jewish. Comradeship, in Rosenzweig's eyes, did not bridge differences or bring Germans closer together; it was merely "enforced togetherness in spite of otherness."[70] His letters contrast the deepening sense of
alienation between Jewish and Christian soldiers in the field to the comfort
and sense of community derived from meeting other Jews at field religious
services or when they were fortunate enough to be assigned to the same unit.
The idea that Jews should sacrifice self for the "we" of the German *Volk* was
anathema to Rosenzweig. To a far greater extent, he saw "solidarity" as an
expression of Jewish distinctiveness, a means to assert the honor of Jews who
fought not as Germans, but as Jewish citizens of the German nation.

Despite months of enduring hardships and dangers together in battle,
Alfred Koch's comrades—the members of his artillery battery—whom he invariably described as "dependable," "trustworthy," "efficient," and "skilled,"
remain obscure and more or less anonymous. At no point are they mentioned
by name, nor do we ever learn much about their backgrounds, values, or
personalities. The only other soldiers Koch described in detail were *Glaubensgenossen* (comrades in faith), a more affective term that frequently appears in
the writings of Jewish nationalists or religious Jews, and gave expression to
a sense of shared identity.[71] This solidarity did not hinge on the actual presence of Jewish comrades or face-to-face relationships; far more it revealed
itself as identification with a more abstract Jewish consciousness. As the only
Jewish soldier in his battery, Koch's detachment from his "comrades" was assuaged by the joy he derived from reading letters or the division newspaper
and learning about other Jews who had been promoted or received the Iron
Cross, occasions that brought him such happiness, "as if it were my own."[72]
At the heart of his writings was a moral imperative, a devotion not to his gentile comrades or the fatherland, but to his *Glaubensgenossen*. "What is always

closest to my heart," Koch confided to his brother just two weeks before he was killed, "is to do my share to strengthen and honor the Jewish name."[73]

Perhaps the most frequently cited Jewish autobiographical source from the First World War is the diary of Julius Marx.[74] Marx's writings are frequently used to support claims that antisemitism was the defining Jewish wartime experience, and therefore they require closer attention. The author portrays himself as an acculturated German Jew whose run-ins with antisemitism eventually led him to embrace a newfound sense of Jewish identity. Yet historians must take into account that the diary underwent several revisions before it was published in Switzerland in 1939, as a protest against Kristallnacht and the policies of the Nazi government, and reconsider its value as a contemporary source.[75] From what is known about Marx, he came from a devout Orthodox family and was himself deeply religious.[76] This may explain why, in terms of language and semantic tone, his writings bear a striking resemblance to postwar Zionist narratives. It is quite clear, for example, that at the war's outbreak Marx was already skeptical about Jewish prospects for emancipation. In October 1914, an NCO, under the pretense of humor, mocked him as a "cowardly Jew," an incident that caused Marx to request a transfer to a different unit and declare that the solidarity of August 1914 was a farce, one that merely papered over deep-seated divisions that had existed before the war. "At war's outbreak every prejudice seemed to have vanished, there were only Germans then," he wrote. "Now one hears that old, slanderous talk *again.*"[77] The proposition that fighting alongside other Germans would be rewarded with social acceptance was at best illusory, if not naive. His writings convey an increasing disenchantment about the prospects of Jewish assimilation, as he painstakingly chronicled how anti-Jewish hostility intensified as the likelihood of a German victory diminished.

A notable feature in the writings of Zionists and religious Jews is the mention of prewar antisemitic incidents. The authors tended to portray anti-Jewish hostility as a feature of everyday life in Germany before 1914, and Marx too suggested that the deteriorating relations between Jews and gentiles he witnessed at the front had a precedent. After the incident involving the antisemitic joke, he wrote, "*Once again*, we are Christians and Jews, rightists and leftists, officers and conscripts, and no longer just soldiers."[78] Repeated confrontations with antisemitic superiors, together with taunting from fellow soldiers, led him to see the much-exalted comradeship as a facade. Only when "shells come crashing down," he wrote, did these tensions subside. "All of a sudden there aren't Christians and Jews anymore—only people, strained to the utmost to overcome their fear of death so they can perform their damn duty and do their part—and then you have it: community—a stream of altruism—comradeship—humanity."[79] Marx went on to describe a growing sense of estrangement from other Germans, as the front experience merely reinforced an insurmountable feeling of otherness, of "being alone among comrades."[80]

The fact that such events are as well detailed as they are shows their clear significance to those involved. Such reactions can be understood only within the context of a Jewish minority in Germany that rejected the premise of assimilation and advocated Jewish separateness. Crucially, however, soldiers' perceptions of comradeship and their reactions to discrimination were rarely indicative of a wartime reevaluation of preexisting beliefs and values. Rosenzweig, Koch, and arguably Marx did not undergo a profound spiritual or political transformation between 1914 and 1918. Rather, these experiences were used to legitimize existing attitudes that individuals had brought with them into the war.

Confronting Antisemitism

When Joachim Beutler wrote that amid "volleys of hand grenades, the cracking of machine-gun bullets overhead," times were "too serious" for antisemitism, he lauded the one thing that the inhumanity of war could never taint: comradeship.[81] In doing so, he gave voice to the hopes and expectations of acculturated German Jews, who were convinced that the exigencies of combat would leave no room for old prejudices, that the solidarity forged under fire would bridge differences of class, religion, and background.

Beutler was not alone in foregrounding the positive elements of his war experience in his letters home. What is remarkable about this account, however, is that the topic of antisemitism was broached, even when it was not present. It suggests that Jews remained ever vigilant in the front lines, continually interrogating their surroundings, and that the writers had probably encountered some form of prejudice previously, whether before or sometime during the war. Beutler's letters tell us little about why or in which context antisemitism was brought up, whether in response to a question, a statement to allay the concerns of family, or an affirmation of the writer's ideological conviction. Yet they suggest that antisemitism, even in absentia, exerted a significant influence on Jewish thinking and behavior during the war.

What frequently arises in Jewish writings from the field, for example, is the image of the shirker (*Drückeberger*). Even in the absence of direct confrontations with these stereotypes, many Jewish soldiers expressed concern about being associated with the "cowardly Jew," the weak, second-rate soldier, who purportedly dodged his obligation to serve in combat. Ever conscious of such stereotypes, many Jews reacted like Ernst Löwenberg, who turned down an offer by his platoon leader to work behind the lines as the company clerk. "I have spoken as my inner conscience demands," he wrote to his parents. "As a Jew, I have no right to sit behind a desk."[82] Löwenberg had been an enthusiastic soldier throughout the war. He described close relations with his comrades and "never felt antisemitism," except from certain officers. He made no mention of personal encounters with anti-Jewish prejudice, yet the prospect of being regarded as a shirker by his fellow soldiers was deeply troubling to him, and undoubtedly had a precedent.

The need to counter antisemitic stereotypes through acts of bravery is a recurring theme in the letters of Alfred Koch. When he volunteered for the army in August 1914, Koch was dismayed to discover that he had been assigned to a baggage train, not to the fighting troops as he had wanted. He found serving in a supply unit boring, tedious, and humiliating—an "infamy" (*Infamie*), as he put it.[83] So when the opportunity arose to volunteer for an artillery unit, Koch took it, describing the decision as his "duty" (*Pflicht*). "If I hadn't taken the first opportunity to get away from here, the accusation that I was suited only for the [baggage] train would have been completely justified," he wrote. "For it would have meant that I chose to stay despite having the chance to leave."[84] Koch did not mention from whom such an "accusation" might have come. Yet such utterances reveal that it mattered immensely to him to be regarded as a brave soldier, especially in the eyes of gentile society. In a letter to his brother written just before his death, he again justified his decision to leave the safety of the supply depot in order to serve in combat:

> It was an unbearable thought to stand there as the archetype of the Jewish rear-area soldier, a luxury which has commanded a price, one that I am now prepared to pay in full awareness of the consequences. I would have deserved more pity had I declined and remained a sutler. Furthermore, I had the gratification of winning the respect of my superiors and soldiers. In the battery, I have the reputation as being one of the "coldest" ones, and for me this has always been a most worthwhile goal, not for my personal vanity, but as seen from a higher perspective.[85]

Koch's behavior was calculated; he felt compelled to prove his competence and courage under fire to his non-Jewish comrades, and by doing so, obviate any suspicions that he might be a coward. The Jewish rear-area soldier was tainted with the stain of unmanliness, and Koch deemed it essential to demonstrate that he was not afraid to risk his life in battle. His letters make no mention of actual, face-to-face encounters with this stereotype. But the image of the unmanly Jew haunted him; it was a foil through which he evaluated his behavior, compelling him time and again to disassociate from stereotypical "Jewish" traits.

This kind of implicit antisemitism exerted a powerful influence on Jewish behavior in the front lines: it governed the way Jewish soldiers interpreted and reacted to certain situations, and it determined how they carried themselves in the presence of their gentile comrades. The majority of "German" Jewish men who fought in World War I entered the conflict believing that rigorous demonstrations of bravery and conformity could succeed in changing German perceptions of Jewry.[86] In their letters, Jews expressed immense satisfaction at having seemingly disabused other Germans of their antisemitism. "At my post at the front I had never felt any kind of class differences," wrote Hermann Lehrer. "First of all, there really were no antisemites, and the only antisemitic lieutenant had only been one previously at home; he is now a great friend of the Jews with whom I use the informal 'du.' "[87] Letters like these were enthusiastically collected and published by Jewish newspapers, and held up as proof that long-established stereotypes and antisemitic tropes could be subverted by Jewish valor.[88]

Antisemitism manifested itself in more tangible ways, however, from jokes, teasing, and gossip to outright hostility and exclusion. It did not distinguish between Zionist, Orthodox, and acculturated Jews, yet Jewish soldiers interpreted and reacted to it in often dramatically different ways. In general, the letters and diaries of acculturated Jews rarely mention incidents involving taunting or anti-Jewish jokes by comrades, and when they did, most responded like Fritz Goldberg, who brushed them off as "very general and never directed against the individual," attributing them to the same kind of teasing that went on between the Protestants and Catholics he grew up with.[89] Others attributed racism to the officers' corps or the war ministry, but only rarely to comrades. Yet one wonders how many soldiers consciously avoided potential confrontations by concealing their Jewishness, like Hermann Berel Barsqueaux, who wondered whether the "good camaraderie" in his unit could be attributed to the fact that "the others don't know which religion I belong to."[90]

A persistent setback encountered by the majority of the Jewish soldiers examined in this book was exclusion from the officers' corps. Not untypical is the experience of Bernhard Bing, a middle-aged factory owner from Nuremberg who served in an artillery resupply train of the Sixth Bavarian Reserve Division on the Western Front. The forty-one-year-old Bing was repeatedly commended by his superiors for his performance. He had already been promoted to sergeant when, at the urging of his company commander, he submitted his application for an officer's commission, easily passing both the written and oral examinations.[91] But his nomination was rejected after it was put to the obligatory vote before the board of regimental officers, because the commander of the regiment allegedly "did not want to promote any Jews to the officer ranks."[92] This is the first and only time in his diary where Bing mentioned anti-Jewish discrimination. It is also the only point where he referred to himself as a Jew. The setback did not deter him, however; he was eventually promoted to lieutenant after transferring to another unit.[93] Bing's diary leaves little doubt that the injustice left him bitter and outraged. But it did not shake his strong identification with Germany or visibly weaken his faith in the prospects of Jewish assimilation. His resolve did not diminish; Bing remained a loyal soldier and a good comrade. At least, this is how he presented himself in his diary.[94]

Bing's response to discrimination can be extended beyond the individual case, for it says something important about how many acculturated Jews acted in the face of adversity. He attributed the setback to a single antisemitic actor; at no point did he conflate the injustice with the presence of a broader, endemic Jew hatred in the military. Moreover, he drew a clear distinction in his diary between his comrades and the racist officer who derailed his promotion. Bing's conviction that fulfilling his duty as a soldier, and fighting side by side with other Germans, would be rewarded with social recognition after the war remained unshaken. This was a recurring message in his diary: despite reversals and disappointments, he never questioned his identity as a "German of Jewish faith," and remained convinced that the example he set would help change the status of Jews in Germany. These beliefs did not abruptly end as a result of discrimination. Jews' silence regarding antisemitism, therefore, should not be understood as proof that it was absent; rather, their self-understanding as Germans and Jews was not severely challenged because of it.

The letters of Alfred Koch reveal that he too was no stranger to antisemitism in the German military, yet from the outset he interpreted such incidents in a very different way. Exclusion from the officers' corps left Koch resentful and disheartened, and also strengthened his belief that Jews would never be accepted as equals by German society. Writing before the war, as Koch fulfilled his one-year voluntary military service, he lamented that, as a Jew, the opportunities for advancement were all but closed to him. "Despite all my acceptance," he wrote, "it offends me that the prospects for promotion are so bad. It makes one lose all enthusiasm for this whole business. I can do everything at least as well, and many things even better than the

Gojims [gentiles]. As a result, my somewhat slumbering Zionism has been reawakened."[95] It was at this time that Koch mentioned Bernhard Bing, who had served in the same unit before the war: "A noncommissioned officer told me: 'We know, our Captain simply does not promote Jews like everyone else.' The year before there was a Nuremberg Jew here, Bing, who had supposedly been very competent, from a good family, and he never even made it to officer candidate. A very nice chap, he is now away participating in a field exercise."[96]

The sources do not reveal whether Koch and Bernhard Bing ever encountered each other before the war, or if Koch was merely relaying what he had heard from others. It is striking, however, that the incident negatively impacted Koch, while Bing himself never mentioned it. In fact, even though neither ever described actual face-to-face encounters with antisemitism during their time in the army, on 30 September 1916 Koch confided to his brother that he had been keeping his Jewish identity a secret, because he was certain that "everyone from the General to the stable boy was a *Judenfresser* [Jew hater]."[97] This kind of implicit antisemitism was a recurring theme in his war letters. If antisemitism was ignored or suppressed by many acculturated Jews, the picture that emerges in Zionist writings is of a pervasive divide separating Jews from their Christian fellow soldiers: a deep-seated prejudice that reinforced an innate Jewish distinctiveness, something that public avowals of solidarity or shared suffering could not erase.

A far more difficult question to answer is how gentile Germans viewed their Jewish comrades. Studies of letter collections from World War I have unearthed little evidence of a consistent, verifiable Jew hatred among German soldiers.[98] The wartime diaries of Ernst Jünger and Franz Schauwecker, who later rose to prominence in the national right-wing political milieu, make no mention of a "Jewish problem" at the front, nor does the first edition of Erich Ludendorff's memoir, published in 1919, contain any derogatory revelations about Jewry.[99] Recent studies have also disproven postwar claims of discrimination in the proportion of medals awarded or the number of promotions given to Jewish soldiers, which were actually equivalent to those of non-Jews.[100] The surviving officer personnel records of the Bavarian Army, which include performance evaluations, after-action reports, and medal commendations, provide little evidence that Jewishness was a factor at the front: Jewish officers were recommended for promotion, commended for their bravery by superiors, and enjoyed comfortable relations with their men and immediate chain of command.[101]

It would be wrong to imagine, however, that anti-Jewish prejudice receded during the war. One has to look no further than the diary of Victor

Klemperer, who had converted to the Protestant faith in 1912. While on leave in Munich, he observed a Jewish ceremony attended by several soldiers wearing the Iron Cross, leading him to wonder, "What are they really fighting for? Really and quite simply for the Fatherland? Or for the attainment of a Fatherland? Or so that they can later get ahead in their careers?"[102] At the front, however, deeply held racist beliefs did not prevent antisemites from forming powerful bonds with their Jewish fellow fighters. During the war, Julius Fürst befriended a fellow officer in his regiment, Ludwig Zeise, a self-described "nationalist and radical anti-Semite." Yet the fact that Fürst was Jewish did not undermine the emotional bonds between them. The two men engaged in frequent and often heated discussions over the "Jewish Question," and when Zeise was transferred to a different sector of the front, they continued these debates in their letters. In a remarkable exchange from late in the war, the two officers engaged in a contentious argument over whether Jews could ever be fully assimilated into German society. For his part, Zeise charged that "Jewry" constituted a foreign ethnic group living on German soil, pointing out Jews' alleged lack of enthusiasm for the war as evidence of their incompatibility with the German *Volk*: "The Jew has been spared in this war, in great disproportion to the rest of the population, one only has to count the Jews who are at the front; those who did not stay at home got 'hung up' in the rear echelon (medics, radio operators, truck drivers—I know for a fact that these units often comprise up to 30% Jews)."[103]

It is unclear whether Fürst responded to these allegations, for he was killed in April 1918. After his burial, his widow received condolences from Zeise. "I have lost a friend for life," Zeise wrote. "Friendship in the field, it binds us stronger than any formed in peaceful times. . . . We understood each other inwardly, perhaps because outwardly our temperaments were so different and we often had conflicting opinions."[104]

Friedrich Solon, in his memoirs, described his regimental commander in the war as "an anti-Semite of the highest order. He never directly articulated this, but it was clear enough how he felt about me." Solon endured the officer's antisemitism throughout the war. In the same passage, however, Solon mentions two other Jews in his regiment, besides himself, who earned the Iron Cross First Class, and that he was promoted to lieutenant in 1918, which would have been impossible without the recommendation of the commanding officer.[105] These examples are a testament to the prevalence of antisemitic thinking in the officers' corps. At the same time, however, they reveal that Jewish soldiers were accorded friendship and respect in their military primary group, even by those gentiles who normally shunned any association with Jews.

Holding the Line

Much has been made of the Jew Count, the infamous census of Jewish soldiers implemented by the Prussian War Ministry on 11 October 1916.[106] It
was carried out on the premise of unfounded accusations that Jews were
shirking frontline military service, and its purpose was to ascertain the
number of Jewish soldiers in combat units in proportion to those serving in
support roles behind the lines. Many historians portrayed the measure as a
watershed in German-Jewish relations, and despite recent studies that make
a strong case for the contrary, it is a view accepted by many scholars to this
day. The implications of the Jew Count would be far more egregious after
1918, however. As the census results were never revealed to the public, the
mere fact that it had been carried out legitimized and reinforced antisemitic
stereotypes propagated by political groups on the nationalist Right after
the war.[107] The census shook Jewish morale on the home front. It provoked
intense debates among Jewish intellectuals, activists, and community leaders, and drew considerable attention in the Jewish press.[108] Yet it was rarely
mentioned in Jewish writings from the field. The census did not come up in
any of the more than eight hundred letters written by Jewish soldiers to the
director of their former Jewish community orphanage in Berlin.[109] Neither
Herbert Sulzbach, Nathan Wolf, or Bernhard Bing mentioned it in their diaries, nor did the census arise anywhere in the letters of Alfred Koch or Franz
Rosenzweig, which is all the more surprising as both were astute commentators on politics and Jewish affairs throughout the war.[110] The silence is confounding. It suggests that many Jews were not even aware of the census as
it was being carried out, or that it was simply dismissed as another example
of harassment "from above"—that is, by the officers' corps.[111] Those Jewish
soldiers who wrote about the Jew Count in their diaries and letters expressed
outrage, shock, and disbelief. Yet with very few exceptions, anger over the
incident subsided rather quickly, and there is little evidence to suggest that it
fundamentally changed German-Jewish relations at the front.[112]

In general, confrontations with antisemitism did not result, as Derek Penslar puts it, in "a Nietzschean reevaluation of values."[113] While, of course, examples exist of acculturated Jews turning their backs on integration, this, the
sources suggest, was a relatively rare occurrence. Far more common were
men who, although disappointed, continued to embrace assimilation and,
in doing so, sustained a key element of their identities as "German" Jews.
The tone and discursive style of Jewish soldiers' writings remained the same
before, during, and after the census was carried out. They had experienced
discrimination long before October 1916. They encountered it before the

war, at school and universities, in the workplace, even amid the euphoria of July and August 1914, and they continued to do so after the Prussian War Ministry's infamous order. Antisemitism did not intensify or diminish over time but was ever present. It was the *Normalzustand* at the front.

During the final months of the war, Jewish soldiers placed a far greater emphasis on the worsening military situation and the collapse of the political order, suggesting that German defeat and the revolutionary upheavals at home preoccupied Jewish thinking far more than antisemitism. To Herbert Sulzbach, the thought of Germany laying down its arms was "horrifying" and "incomprehensible."[114] He said that as he donned his officer's uniform for the last time to bid his troops a final farewell, "It felt like I was going to my own funeral."[115] Fritz Beckhardt, a pilot with Jagdgeschwader 3, refused to surrender his plane to the French. Beckhardt volunteered for the Flying Corps in 1916, where he racked up an impressive tally of seventeen kills by war's end. Under the terms of the November 1918 armistice, the Germans had fourteen days to evacuate the Western Front and turn over their aircraft. But Beckhardt defied the Allied demands and flew his Siemens-Schuckert D.III fighter to Switzerland instead, where he was promptly apprehended by Swiss authorities and sent back to Germany.[116] And Wilhelm Lustig, who had predicted a German victory a few weeks earlier, ended his diary on 11 November 1918, with "a bleeding heart, in deep sorrow for the Fatherland. May God grant me the strength to help in its rebuilding. I still have faith: Germany will not perish."[117]

These responses were not, on the whole, a radical break with traditional values and attitudes. A minority, overwhelmingly Zionist and nonassimilated Jews, saw the war experience as a vindication of their belief that Jews formed a unique and distinctive culture, an inherent "otherness" that assimilation could never bridge. For most German Jews, who were committed to integration, discrimination did not lead them to lose faith in the German cause; they continued to fight and die for Germany and for their ideals as before. Although confrontations with Jew hatred were taken seriously, examples of "bad" comradeship were the exception at the front, as Jewish writings juxtaposed these incidents with memories of inclusion, togetherness, and belonging. Such memories, as Julius Fürst wrote before he died, "could be forgotten only with greatest difficulty."[118]

CHAPTER 2

The Politics of Comradeship

Weimar Germany, 1918–33

Much of the literature on German Jewry during the Weimar Republic continues to embrace the notion that Jewish soldiers returned to Germany in 1918 embittered and deeply disillusioned by the endemic antisemitism they encountered in the trenches, and by the realization that their struggle for social acceptance had failed.[1] In the years that followed, amid rising antisemitic tensions, Jews allegedly withdrew from mainstream German life to find solace in their Judaism. Intellectuals and Zionist activists held that the front experience persuaded many Jews to turn their backs on assimilation and embrace a newfound Jewish separateness.[2]

One searches in vain, however, in the writings of Jewish soldiers for evidence that wartime antisemitism led to an abandonment of prewar attitudes and beliefs. Letters and diary entries written during the final weeks of the war showed no signs that Jewish soldiers had abandoned their ideals or that their desire to see Germany emerge victorious diminished; the celebratory language of the writings of socialist and leftist soldiers, who enthusiastically greeted the revolution and the downfall of the monarchy, was largely absent.[3] To be sure, German-Jewish relations underwent a significant change after 1918, prompting Jewish veterans to form their own organization. Some Jewish soldiers had indeed returned from the war shaken by antisemitism, an experience that pushed some to the extremes of Zionism, others to accelerated assimilation. But there is little evidence that such reactions extended beyond a radicalized minority.

Heroes of the Great War

Twenty years after the First World War, Friedrich Solon reflected on the meaning of his wartime experiences as he composed his memoirs. Discharged from the army in 1918 as a highly decorated officer, he recalled how his experience fighting in the war had not only solidified his faith in the possibilities of assimilation, but deepened his spiritual bond with Germany "more than ever before": "The Jewish blood that had flowed, the ever-present comradeship which I, like everyone else, could rely on through hardships and danger, left me with no doubts that I could begin my old life again, emblazoned with my dignity and achievements, but with even greater esteem and success than before. . . . With uncertain expectations I had marched off to war, with great hopes I returned. Despite the many disappointments that followed . . . by and large I feel enriched by the war experience."[4]

Solon wrote these passages in London in 1940, as a refugee from the Nazis, having fled Germany the year before in the wake of increasing persecution and fear for his family's safety. Despite the trauma and hardships of four years of war and his experiences under National Socialism, Solon believed then, as he had in November 1918, that Jewish sacrifices for the fatherland had not been in vain. As a war volunteer and frontline soldier, he earned a field commission in a Prussian artillery regiment, received both classes of the Iron Cross, and felt assured that his sacrifices would be rewarded with recognition by German society.

The ways in which Jewish former combatants like Solon not only experienced the war but remembered it afterward is crucial to determining how they constructed their identity as veterans.[5] Like all soldiers who returned to Germany after the fighting ended on 11 November 1918, Jews began to think about their frontline experiences in a fundamentally different way. Against the backdrop of defeat, revolution, and economic uncertainty, former soldiers engaged in a process of reflection and self-justification, as they struggled to make sense of the war and their participation in it. The way they talked about and communicated these memories to others was central to who they were; these experiences formed a central part of their identities. In the months and years that followed, wartime events acquired new meaning, as former soldiers, now distanced from the traumatizing realities of the trenches, retrospectively transfigured their wartime experiences into memory.[6]

It would be a mistake to imagine that Solon's attitude and memories of the war represented a universal Jewish experience. Yet certain elements of his experience—such as the expectation that German society would acknowledge his sacrifices—have significance beyond the individual case, for despite repeated brushes with antisemitism, Jewish soldiers' abiding faith in military sacrifice did not abruptly end with the armistice in November 1918. To be a war veteran meant belonging to a desired status group in postwar German society, someone to whom both the nation and the community owed a debt of honor. When they had gone to war in 1914, they believed—and were repeatedly told—that their suffering in the defense of the fatherland would make them heroes in their communities and pillars of German society. Now they demanded recognition for their sacrifices.

Of course, the high status accorded to the Frontkämpfer of World War I was largely symbolic, manifesting itself in the form of social prestige that acknowledged the suffering of four bloody years of fighting for the nation. But it was legitimized and reinforced to the general populace through public rituals, such as the consecration of war memorials, national holidays, and a variety of wartime commemorations. The power of this discourse was rooted in its abstraction. It was free of political and racial connotations and enabled Jews to invest their identities with moral legitimacy alongside other German veterans, rather than follow a particularist Jewish path. For in theory if not in practice, the "thanks of the fatherland" was symbolically bestowed on all former combatants, irrespective of class, religion, political affiliation, or former military rank.[7] For Jews, Frontkämpfer became a status that held greater significance beyond public expressions of heroism or expectations of state beneficence. It became a demonstration of Jewish valor and allegiance to the fatherland, a sign of belonging, and a means to combat antisemitic stereotypes perpetuated by the radical nationalist Right.

In the Shadow of the *Judenzählung*

Germany's defeat in November 1918 and the subsequent revolutionary upheavals gave new life to prejudices that had been dormant, if not suppressed, for most of the conflict. Jews suffered an outpouring of anti-Jewish sentiment throughout the Weimar years, which was unprecedented in both its scale and its form. In the war's immediate aftermath, however, the extremist organizations perpetrating these attacks were still too weak and disorganized to make serious inroads into mainstream German society or to influence the wider remembrance of the war. Jewish veterans continued to respond positively to nationalist politics after November 1918, with many joining the postwar paramilitary fighters in the Freikorps, who assisted the army in battling Communist uprisings in Berlin, Munich, and the Ruhr, and fought Polish separatists in the eastern provinces of Posen and Silesia.[8] The Freikorps drew a great deal of former officers, such as Alwin Lippmann, who organized and led the "Freiwilliges Volkswehr-Bataillon Oberschlesien" during the Silesian Uprisings from January through October 1919.[9] It also attracted a number of Jewish university students, intellectuals, and middle-class idealists, such as Ernst Kantorowicz and Gerhard Masur,[10] to name but a few. At least eighteen Jews served in the Freikorps Würzburg, a brigade-sized unit that participated in the campaign to unseat the Munich Räterepublik (Soviet Republic) in 1919. The unit's personnel roster included three Jewish officers—including Benno Schwabacher, one of the battalion adjutants, and Eugen Stahl, who commanded an infantry company—indicating that Jews were active at all levels of command.[11]

Some Jewish veterans undoubtedly saw joining the Freikorps as a further means to change negative German perceptions of Jewry in the postwar years, believing that fighting Communism would be perceived as tangible proof of loyalty to the fatherland. Yet the age, experience, and background of the volunteers suggest that most had been motivated by the same reasons as other Germans of the same class and background.[12] A high proportion of the Jewish volunteers were former officers, who possibly aspired to a career in the new army, the Reichswehr, or hoped their participation would positively effect a new postwar order. In regions where there was an actual threat of a Communist takeover, as was the case in Würzburg, the number of volunteers was much higher. Others were motivated by anti-Communist convictions or by the fear of the chaos that a full-blown revolution would unleash. One such volunteer was the SPD activist Kurt Sabatzky, who returned to Berlin in November 1918, "gun in hand," and promptly joined the pro-republican Regiment Reichstag to defend the government quarter against Spartacists.[13] In general, Jewish participation in the Freikorps reflected an established pattern of military service, which suggests that nationally minded Jews were tolerated, if not always welcomed, in traditionally antisemitic organizations of the nationalist Right.

At the same time, however, contemporary sources leave little doubt about the ideological penetration of race-based antisemitism into many Freikorps units. The most notorious example, perhaps, is the Marine-Brigade-Ehrhardt, whose brutality against Jewish civilians has been well documented.[14] There were also times when Jewish Freikorps soldiers themselves became the target of antisemitic attacks. Joseph Kurt, a former NCO in the German Air Force (Luftstreitkräfte), enlisted with the Freikorps Brussow after being threatened by a group of Communists in Berlin. He was selected to lead a detachment of one hundred men during the fighting in the capital in January 1919, before redeploying to Silesia later that year to fight Polish separatists. It was there that a group of soldiers from a neighboring outfit approached his unit and demanded that they "hand over the Jew," declaring that the Freikorps "was no place for Jews." Kurt was saved by the intervention of his comrades, who threatened the aggressors with armed force if he were harmed. Fearing for his safety, however, Kurt discharged himself several days later.[15]

Kurt's testimony requires closer attention. The fact that his comrades' intervention saved his life throws light on the microlevel solidarity that developed between Jews and other Germans in the field, one that could withstand racial and ideological prejudices. Yet despite Kurt's military background and record fighting Communists, in the minds of certain radical antisemites, as a Jew he was an "enemy," one that had to be combated at all costs. The incident is emblematic of a broader shift in antisemitic thinking that occurred in Germany after World War I. The breakdown of traditional authority in 1918, and the revolutionary turmoil that followed, precipitated a radicalization of the nationalist Right that fundamentally changed antisemitism and discourses on the Jewish Question. This "new antisemitism," to use Anthony Kauders's term, infused existing anti-Jewish prejudice with racist ideology.[16] Whereas classic antisemitic thinking equated Jews with liberalism, greed, and an unwillingness to self-sacrifice for the fatherland, by the mid-1920s, race had established itself as the predominant form of discourse on the Jewish Question. These debates were no longer restricted to the radical fringe of the nationalist Right as they had been before the war, but would eventually reach into all strata of German society, including groups and individuals that had previously shunned any association with racism.[17]

The Jew Count was one of the driving forces behind Weimar antisemitism. What was important was not the census itself, however, but the way in which it was interpreted after the war. Because its findings were never publicized, the census fueled speculation and wild rumors about the Jewish war record. It became a rhetorical weapon for the Far Right, which, in a calculated effort to undermine Jewish claims for equality and recognition for having risked their lives for Germany, accused Jews of shirking frontline combat. These accusations were not solely the work of openly antisemitic and extremist organizations such as the Alldeutscher Verband (Pan-German League) or Reichshammerbund (Reich Hammer League); they also came from former high-ranking officers of the Imperial Army.[18] Eager to deflect blame for their own military failures, former generals such as Erich Ludendorff and Colonel Max Bauer, a radical antisemite and former adviser to Hindenburg, charged that a conspiracy of socialists, pacifists, and Jews had undermined the fighting power of the German Army during the final spring offensives of 1918, which would have otherwise culminated in a German victory.[19] These allegations formed the core element of the *Dolchstoßlegende* (stab-in-the-back myth), and they threatened to tarnish Jewish honor ineradicably.[20]

Accusations of shirking—that Jews had collectively sought refuge in comfortable, rear-area postings while "real" Germans had died facing the enemy—humiliated Jewish veterans, the impact of which is difficult to overstate. Shirkers were men without honor, cowardly soldiers who were unable to endure the rigors and deprivations of war; they survived by hiding behind the forward ranks, and stood by as others did the fighting. By attacking Jews' loyalty and performance under fire, the extreme Right sought to obliterate Jewish claims for recognition based on their wartime sacrifices. The slur on Jewish masculinity also fed into antisemites' efforts to feminize Jewish men by making it impossible for them to assert their masculinity through performance of military duty or achieve social respect for having risked life and limb for the fatherland. The Jew Count gave these accusations a veneer of credibility. It generated ambivalence, uncertainty: a reasonable doubt. To Jewish ex-servicemen, these allegations came as a shock. Writing in 1920, Samuel Jacobs, an observant Jew from a village outside Hannover, claimed he had never encountered antisemitic prejudice during the war. Jacobs had been an enthusiastic soldier, referred to himself as a "loyal German warrior" in his memoirs, revealing that his time in the army had left a deep impression. But now, in the wake of Germany's defeat, the fact that his bravery was being questioned left him angry and disillusioned. "A bitter feeling comes over me now, when I see today how we Jews are marked as second-class citizens," he wrote. "One tries to deprive us of our most sacred possession: our honor."[21] This sentiment was echoed by Leo Löwenstein, chairman of the Reichsbund jüdischer Frontsoldaten (RjF), who wrote in 1927 that even though attacks against Jewish lives and property were of grave concern, "even harder to bear were those against our honor."[22]

Jewish organizations, led by the Centralverein (CV), countered this antisemitic campaign with statistics on Jewish war service, painstakingly compiled by activists and local communities across Germany. Efforts had already been underway during the war to document the number of Jewish soldiers who had served in combat, how many had been decorated, and how many had been killed. Local memorial books dedicated to the Jewish war dead were published not only to commemorate the fallen, but also to promote the extent of Jewish sacrifices and fend off accusations of Jews' lack of patriotism.[23] The results of these efforts were published in Jacob Segall's extensive report, which concluded that approximately one hundred thousand Jews had served in the German military between 1914 and 1918. Eighty thousand Jewish soldiers served in the front lines, thirty-five thousand were decorated, and twenty-three thousand were promoted, two thousand of whom were commissioned as officers.[24] Segall further calculated that twelve thousand of the Jewish combatants had been killed in action, which represented a fatality rate of 12 percent. This figure was slightly below the 13.49 percent death rate estimated for the German military as a whole, a discrepancy Segall attributed to the low Jewish birthrate in the late nineteenth century, which had resulted in a proportionate shortage of military-age men, and the higher level of education among Jewish conscripts, who had a greater likelihood of being placed in desk jobs than their comrades.[25]

A Sobering Reality

These statistics did little to temper the controversy ignited by the Jew Count. Weimar antisemitism was not the logical or inevitable consequence of the First World War. It gained momentum gradually, moving in phases of increasing and receding intensity, culminating in two unprecedented waves of antisemitic violence: the first between 1923 and 1924, and again from 1930 to 1932. These upheavals were not precipitated solely by Germany's defeat, but were fueled by a series of interrelated developments that prepared the ideological ground for a radicalization of the political Right. First, the prominence of Jews in the Spartacus League, in the Communist insurrections in Munich, Berlin, and the Ruhr, and in the Council of the People's Deputies (Rat der Volksbeauftragten), the provisional government that negotiated the terms of the armistice with the Allies, led many Germans to associate Jewry with the revolutionary movements that brought about the demise of Imperial Germany.[26] As these events played themselves out, a parallel development was taking place within the political Far Right, where traditional antisemitic and anti-Communist stereotypes merged into the equation "Jewish-Bolshevism."[27] This was not an empty formula: Bolsheviks were seen as an insidious and subversive "enemy," hiding in plain sight, bent on undermining Germany's unity from within. Portraying Communism as a global conspiracy led by Jews enabled the nationalist Right to legitimize its antisemitic stance, claiming that fighting Communism also meant fighting Jewry.[28]

A second factor was the immigration of approximately seventy thousand Jewish refugees from Russia and Poland between 1914 and 1919. These overwhelmingly Orthodox Eastern European Jews were disliked by all the major political parties and were commonly portrayed as a predatory minority that deprived ordinary Germans of badly needed resources, and sapped Germany's economic well-being through their unscrupulous business practices. The presence of the Eastern European Jews provoked lively and highly publicized discussions about definitions of citizenship and German national identity in the Reichstag, with many politicians—including Jewish organizations—calling for stricter immigration laws to protect the Reich from a further influx of this foreign, un-German minority.[29] It also inflamed anti-Jewish sentiment throughout Germany, providing the nationalist Right with a potent image that legitimized its antisemitic stance.[30]

The third and most important factor, however, were the economic crises that rocked the Weimar Republic throughout the 1920s, upheavals that coincided with massive outbreaks of anti-Jewish violence. The hyperinflation of 1923, sparked after French troops marched into the Ruhr in retaliation for the German government's intentional default on reparations payments, sent the German economy into a death spiral, wiping out the savings of almost the entire middle class. The German public responded to this catastrophe with an outpouring of jingoistic, nationalist sentiment, breathing new life into extremist political movements, as accusations that Jews were fomenting revolution while simultaneously benefiting from the financial unrest sweeping Germany fell on increasingly fertile ground. Election results from 1924 point to a resurgence of the conservative Right, while newer groups on the radical fringe, such as the National Socialist German Workers' Party (Nationalsozialistische deutsche Arbeiterpartei, or NSDAP), attracted growing numbers of disaffected Germans of all stripes.[31]

The fears articulated in the press, that political radicalism had caused the economy and the general order to collapse, combined with the tangible and very real consequences of the economic crises, were catalysts for an unprecedented wave of antisemitic violence that began in 1923. Stephan Kunreuther, who had spent four years at the front as a soldier, described that period as "at times even worse than the war."[32] Anti-Jewish sentiment manifested itself in the singing of antisemitic songs, graffiti, cemetery desecrations, smashed windows, and vandalized storefronts. It was also responsible for physical attacks against Jews, ranging from personal altercations and street brawls to pogrom-like violence in Berlin in November 1923, which left one person dead and more than two hundred shops damaged or ransacked.[33] That antisemitic mobs did not make distinctions between World War I veterans and other Jews is revealed by a report filed by the Nuremberg police on 11 November 1923, which described how a war-wounded Jewish man was harassed and threatened in broad daylight, and subsequently chased down by "a horde" of youths on one of the city's busiest streets. The attackers eventually caught up with the man and beat him until he lost consciousness; doctors later confirmed that he had suffered two knife wounds to the head.[34]

A far more difficult question to answer is whether the "front experience" actually succeeded in changing German perceptions of Jewry, as the Jewish volunteers in 1914 had hoped. Did the solidarity forged between Jews and other German frontline soldiers extend beyond the war? Although comradeship stood at the center of intense public and literary debates after 1918, as both the Left and Right promoted what they saw as the "authentic" war experience, the bonds between former soldiers fundamentally changed after the fighting ended. The dynamic that forged a powerful solidarity between individuals of different class, religious, and political backgrounds on the battlefield transgressed the norms of civilian society. It was situational, ad hoc, immediate—a response to a crisis of physical survival. These bonds undoubtedly instilled a powerful sense of togetherness and belonging among members of a military primary group engaged in combat, but ties with comrades often ended when discharged soldiers reentered civilian life and left their military past behind.[35]

Certain sociological studies have claimed that prolonged periods of cooperation and positive interactions with "out-group" members can lessen or negate prejudicial attitudes toward that group, seemingly validating the Jewish hopes articulated in 1914, that the battlefields of World War I could indeed, as the CV had put it, "forge a brotherhood that is everlasting."[36] It was a desire that was universally expressed by Jewish soldiers during the war. Julius Fürst, who was killed during the final German offensives in 1918, had been certain that "the stereotype 'Jew'" would be discredited when Germans confronted "the humanity of the individual Jew . . . who was a friend and a comrade."[37] Nathan Wolf had expressed a similar hope in his war diary, when he noted on 1 April 1917 that "out here, we are all brothers and want to remain so after the war."[38] Yet there is little evidence that positive encounters with Jews during the war tempered old prejudices in the minds of antisemites. After all, antisemitism was an image of "Jewry" that had little to do with actual circumstances.[39] Ernst Frank, a former soldier who became a Zionist after the war, encountered this mentality again and again, as he was told by former comrades, "You know, if all Jews were like you, one wouldn't find it necessary to rail against the Jews."[40]

This was an issue that simultaneously fascinated yet perplexed Richard Wolf. As a former officer and convert to Christianity, Wolf strongly self-identified as a German national, not a Jew, and frequently engaged in vibrant debates with his colleagues on the Jewish Question. These discussions afforded him unique insights into the ambivalences and seemingly contradictory attitudes that characterized postwar conservative political thought, which he described at length in his memoirs. As far as Wolf was concerned, the majority of German nationalists "were personally not antisemites." But the fact that each "retained a personal Jewish scapegoat; for example, the universally despised Tucholsky," suggested that the abstract image of the "Jewish parasite" never ceased to "haunt their minds." "In all seriousness," Wolf wrote, "they believed that Jews had the power to stop antisemitism through 'good behavior' and by rooting out the distasteful elements among them."[41]

This same attitude was described by Leopold Rosenak, a former rabbi in the German Army who served under Hindenburg and General Ludendorff during the war. He had formed a warm and collegial relationship with both officers, which is why in 1921 he asked the former commander in chief to use his influence to rein in "antisemitic rowdies."[42] Hindenburg's reply was revealing. He thanked Rosenak for the Jews' "cooperation during the Great War," which the old field marshal "remembered most vividly." Yet he made clear, "I do not involve myself in political matters, on principle. The adverse actions of bad Jewish elements are doubly hard to bear, as they primarily occur in the economic and political sphere and are often supported by wealthy capital. See to it that your decent co-religionists renounce this evil and dedicate themselves to their own betterment. Then one will cease holding the entire race accountable for the wrongdoings of the unfortunately not so few."[43]

Hindenburg articulated a set of beliefs that were common among the mainstream political Right.[44] It became an article of faith among the conservative middle classes that Jews had not sacrificed in equal numbers as other Germans, that they had been overrepresented in the revolutionary movements that had brought about the monarchy's demise, and that "Jewry" exercised a disproportionate influence on German culture, economy, and society. These views were no longer confined to the radical wing of the nationalist Right, but reached into nearly every stratum of German society after World War I. Like Hindenburg, many conservative organizations justified their antisemitic stance as a defensive measure, a necessary means to guard against the unfettered power of Jewry. To be sure, most conservatives made distinctions between "Jewry" and their Jewish comrades.[45] They saw "their" Jews as standing apart from mainstream Jewry, as having proven their Germanness by being brave soldiers and good comrades. Put differently, by acting German and having demonstrated their allegiance to Germany, the Jewish Frontkämpfer had shed the qualities of the "Jew." Thus while doors were opened for Jewish comrades, there was a parallel view that Jews had the means to end discrimination by behaving "decently"—that is, by discarding their Jewish sensibilities.

Less certain is how far these convictions penetrated socialist and working-class milieus, and the degree to which this ideology resonated with the average German. One needs to look no further than Erich Maria Remarque's antiwar novel *The Road Back* for evidence that by the 1930s, antisemitic stereotypes had also penetrated left-wing discourses on the war.[46] Of course, this does not mean that all or even a majority of Germans approved of antisemitism, much less tolerated violence against Jews. Even among the organizations and political parties of the Right, there were dissenting voices and ambivalent positions over the Jewish Question, and it remains a matter of contention among historians whether antisemitism represented a coherent trend, let alone a "mass phenomenon," in Weimar Germany.[47]

Germans, Jews, and Antisemites

If patriotic Jews like Friedrich Solon tended to impose a positive narrative onto their frontline experiences, to some Jewish veterans, it all looked quite different. Increasing vandalism and harassment, in tandem with the virulent antisemitic propaganda of the Far Right, persuaded some Jewish ex-servicemen like Willy Cohn to rediscover their spiritual bond to Judaism.[48] A schoolteacher by profession, Cohn experienced warm relations with his comrades during the war, received the Iron Cross Second Class, and had joined the citizens' militia (Einwohnerwehr) when his home city of Breslau was threatened by Communists. Yet for him, Jewish sacrifices had "all been for nothing."[49] He returned from the war embittered by his experiences in the army, not because his Jewishness had alienated him from his fellow soldiers, but because his dream of earning an officer's commission had been thwarted by an antisemitic superior. Even more distressing than this personal setback was Cohn's perception that everyday Germans did not appreciate Jewish sacrifices during the war. These disappointments precipitated a spiritual crisis, not overnight, but one that manifested itself through a series of "very long and serious inner struggles," which inevitably propelled him toward Zionism.[50]

Scholars should be careful not to overstate the scope and extent of these reactions, however. It is simply not true, as one historian claimed, that "the Jewish generation that had come back from the trenches did not find a welcome" in postwar Germany.[51] If membership in Zionist organizations is any indicator of the success or popularity of this movement, then its modest appeal seems to provide little evidence that this ideology resonated with mainstream German Jewry. The number of Jews belonging to the Zionist Federation of Germany (Zionistische Vereinigung für Deutschland) had actually doubled after World War I, but it had stood at less than ten thousand prior to 1914.[52] The growing fascination with Zionism during the 1920s can be mainly attributed to members of the Jewish "war youth generation," who had been too young to be called up for military service and had observed Imperial Germany's downfall and the rise of the Far Right as adolescents.[53] But for the majority of the Jewish combatants, those who had experienced the war firsthand, if there was a spiritual crisis resulting from the disappointment of a positive expectation, then these views were confined to a small minority.

This did not mean that Jewish veterans were oblivious to the intensifying antisemitic discourses in Germany after 1918. They were outraged and resentful over slander in the press and rising incidents of public violence. Yet in Samuel Jacobs's case, antisemitism did not radicalize him to the extremes of Zionism, nor did it diminish his faith in Germany. Like many Jewish veterans, his writings mention confrontations with Jew hatred, but these incidents were attributed to extremist organizations or lone actors, not to an endemic prejudice against Jews. Jacobs refused to believe that his gentile comrades would be duped by baseless allegations of Jewish shirking invented by the extreme fringe of the nationalist Right:

> Before I end my journal, I want to especially pay tribute to a fact, so as to clear up any future preconceptions: none of my many superiors ever disadvantaged me in any way due to my religion. All accorded me the same respect and recognition as my comrades of a different faith. And when today my heart bleeds over all the postwar events, I, as a loyal German fighter, aside from the suffering that I carry with me every day as a result of my shattered nerves, am filled with agony and sorrow over the downfall of our German Fatherland.[54]

Whereas the writings of Zionist and conservative-religious Jews tended to contemplate the larger meaning of the Jew Count and the pervasiveness of anti-Jewish sentiment in German society, patriotic "German" Jews like Jacobs imposed their own narratives onto their war experiences. They tended to gloss over memories of hardship and disillusionment after the war and framed their recollections in more positive terms, emphasizing their ability to cope with and endure the increasing belligerence of the extreme Right. The main feature of these highly ritualized postwar narratives was comradeship. The memory of togetherness, solidarity, and belonging with other Germans in the trenches became a powerful beacon of collective memory. It manifested itself as a postwar search for self-justification, one that gave acculturated German Jews a means to impose meaning on the past, to craft a compelling narrative of national sacrifice and a positive vision for the future. Highly representative of this discourse was Hermann Klugmann's memoir, which elevated comradeship as the defining memory of the First World War. "At the front," he wrote, "the experience of comradeship came into the foreground: all religious, social, and other distinctions vanished, everyone shared each other's burdens. Common destiny proved to be a bond that would endure over the years."[55] For Klugmann, as for many Jewish veterans, such memories provided a means to overcome antisemitism and transform wartime suffering into renewed faith in assimilation.

Despite the prevalence of antisemitic discourse, the Weimar years also witnessed extended periods of prosperity, optimism, and promise. There were periods of calm, as well as long stretches when nothing happened, when extremist movements seemed discredited and a return to normalcy seemed possible. Jewish veterans' writings give little indication that antisemitism caused major disruptions in their daily lives during the postwar years, or that it profoundly undermined their sense of security and belonging in the middle class. To be sure, quiet periods were punctuated by renewed tensions and setbacks. Jews remained ever vigilant against antisemitic agitation, and in regions with a strong Far Right presence, many lived in a perpetual state of what one writer called "heightened anxiety."[56] Yet most autobiographical sources suggest that Jewish ex-soldiers adapted to the turbulent political climate, indicating that day-to-day relations between Jews and Christian Germans were marked by continuity rather than radical change. Veterans fell back on traditional sources of stability after the war, such as family, religion, business, and community life. For many, like Wilhelm Lustig, Jew hatred played a largely irrelevant role in their day-to-day interactions. Lustig lived in the highly volatile border region of Upper Silesia and reported that his first encounter with antisemitism did not occur until 1922, during the German-Polish border referendum, when he was accosted by members of the extremist Deutschvölkische Freiheitspartei (German Völkisch Freedom Party). Yet this "movement," according to Lustig, remained a small yet vocal minority before 1933, and failed to disrupt his personal or professional life in any meaningful way.[57]

In other cases, Jewish invocations of military sacrifice apparently succeeded in countering antisemitism. In November 1918, Edwin Landau returned to his home in Deutsch-Krone, West Prussia, a bastion of the burgeoning radical nationalist movement (and later the NSDAP). Despite the strong presence of the extreme Right, Landau's carpentry business thrived during the Weimar years, partly as a result of social networks established by virtue of his military background. "I brought back with me from the field a firm resolve, energy, and drive," he wrote. "And so I pursued the expansion of my business with renewed vigor, at which I gradually succeeded. I earned the trust of the public authorities, and because I was a Frontkämpfer, I was supplied with contracts, so much so that I had to hire an additional craftsman."[58]

Such cases suggest that inclusion and tolerance in the face of antisemitism was common for Jewish former combatants, even those living in regions with a long history of antisemitism such as eastern Prussia. There were certainly limits to local integration. Where relations between Jews and Germans had been historically strained, such as at universities and in the German youth movement, these tensions were often radicalized after the war.[59] But in the minds of many German nationalists, the record of fighting in the trenches transcended antisemitic stereotypes, for oftentimes the same elements of German society that normally did not tolerate "Jews" opened their doors to Jewish comrades.

While Jewish writings attest to a high degree of integration and acceptance in the Jews' local communities, they also reveal that veterans' behavior continued to be shaped by the specter of the Jewish shirker. This hypervigilance manifested itself most visibly as a desire to disassociate oneself from the image of the cowardly Jew. Many Jewish veterans also expressed contempt for those military-age Jewish men who did not serve in the war, alleging that they in particular were responsible for reinforcing the same negative stereotypes perpetuated by the Far Right.[60] Joseph Levy, upon returning to his home in Frankfurt am Main in 1918, looked on "in despair" as some Jews joined the revolutionary soldiers' and workers' councils that wrested control of the city from government authorities. He condemned this behavior as "unforgivable," for it "played into the hands of our opponents, giving them a weapon with which to attack us and blame us for fomenting revolution."[61] In the eyes of Edwin Landau, not all Jews had been "blameless" when it came to explaining the spread of antisemitism after the war, especially "those who hadn't been soldiers, but stayed home and managed a thriving business."[62] Even Willy Cohn, despite his growing disillusionment with Germany, railed against those Jewish men who had "stayed at home" during the war. "I can imagine (they) left a bad impression on the public, especially when so many . . . were visible throughout the capital," he wrote.[63]

Nevertheless, the overall picture gained from the writings of the Jewish former combatants is that most Germans saw the Frontkämpfer as someone who had risked his life and well-being for the nation, and someone to be ultimately respected, a belief that transcended class, geographic location, and political allegiances. Although antisemitism was a significant factor in the discursive world of newspapers and political propaganda, face-to-face interactions with Jews who had visibly performed their duty, and often courageously, seem to have thwarted most attempts to demonize Jewish veterans as cowards and unpatriotic shirkers. It would be wrong to understand these findings as a refutation of the depth and extent of Weimar antisemitism; rather, they suggest that the prestige of having earned the "thanks of the fatherland" made possible networks of relations that were not open to Jewish civilians. In the complex and intricate pattern of local, day-to-day interactions, relations between Jews and Christians typically remained strong, as ordinary Germans reacted positively to Jewish invocations of military sacrifice, despite the persistence of antisemitism.

The Politics of Comradeship

Fighting in World War I led to particular expectations of recognition, not only vis-à-vis the German public, but also from other comrades and the greater community of former soldiers. A central issue, therefore, is to what degree antisemitism permeated German-Jewish relations in the postwar military and veterans' community. Put differently, did Jewish sacrifices and evidence of bravery at the front discredit antisemitic stereotypes among the former combatants? While some veterans fell back on military networks and maintained connections with members of their old unit, most studies suggest they were the exception rather than the rule.[64] Ex-soldiers' organizations universally claimed to sustain the spirit and ideals of wartime comradeship, yet according to the historian Antoine Prost, "The veterans' association was not the direct heir to the group that consisted of soldiers under fire."[65] In his landmark work on the organized veterans' movement in postwar France, Prost argued, "No doubt they might talk of the same places and the same battles, but they did not take part in them at the same moment or in the same trench. They did not fight cheek by jowl with one another. Within the framework of a veterans' club they could thus meet war companions of the same generation and the same area, but it was not with these particular individuals that they had shared the most significant and most intense moments of life at the front."[66]

If we believe Prost, very few members of veterans' organizations had actually fought together during the war. Germany's case is more complex, however, due to the local recruitment practices of the Imperial German Army.[67] German regiments recruited from a specific city or geographic region, so it was not unusual for ex-soldiers from the same unit to encounter each other after the war in the streets of their hometowns or at a local

veterans' gathering. Yet Prost is right in asserting that peacetime comradeship had little in common with the military primary group at war, where soldiers depended on each other in order to survive. The environment that produced this dynamic had no existence beyond the trenches. For many Great
War veterans, comradeship articulated itself as something far more abstract:
an expression of group identity, a category through which former soldiers
retrospectively interpreted the war and their participation in it.[68]

In the antagonistic political atmosphere of the 1920s, debates on the war
and the reasons for Germany's defeat engendered bitter divisions within
the veterans' community.[69] The moderate Left, represented by the pro-
republican Reichsbanner Schwarz-Rot-Gold (Reichsbanner Black-Red-Gold),
set out to defend the fledgling Weimar Republic, arguing that Germany's
ruin was the result of incompetent military leadership and the egoism of
the Prussian officers' corps.[70] On the opposite end of the ideological spec-
trum stood an array of organizations from the nationalist Right, the largest
and most important of which were the Kyffhäuserbund (Kyffhäuser League),
Stahlhelm—Bund der Frontsoldaten (Steel Helmet—League of Frontline
Soldiers), and, to a lesser extent, the Jungdeutscher Orden (Young German
Order).[71] These groups cultivated a heroic interpretation of the war, universally rejected the republic, and promoted a militarist, nationalist revival in
Germany, a position that became increasingly uncompromising throughout
the 1920s. The ideology of the "stab in the back" stood at the center of conservative war remembrances. In what became a nationalistically charged political myth, the Right argued that the German Army had not been beaten in
the field, but had fallen victim to a conspiracy of socialists, Communists, and
Jews who had sown discontent and weakened Germany's fighting spirit.[72] As
warring political factions debated and contested the causes of Germany's
defeat—and competing visions for its future—it was no longer an individual's
war record that determined membership in veterans' associations, but ideology, party credentials, and in some cases race.

In January 1919, the accusations that Jews had been cowards, traitors, and
"bad" comrades led to the creation of the RjF, an organization dedicated to
fighting antisemitic attacks and preserving Jews' "honor as German front soldiers."[73] By adopting the semantic title "Frontsoldaten" (frontline soldiers),
the RjF defined itself as an exclusive organization of former frontline combatants, and simultaneously promoted the extent of Jewish war service to
the broader public.[74] Its chairman, Leo Löwenstein, was a highly decorated
former officer who had joined the Fatherland Party in 1917 and became a
member of the moderate-conservative German People's Party (Deutsche
Volks Partei) after the war.[75] A respected chemist, Löwenstein worked on

several military projects for the Reichswehr throughout the 1920s, a position that enabled him to forge important connections in the German Army and Defense Ministry.[76] The RjF was a marginal force in the veterans' movement during the early years of the republic, with a membership that never surpassed fifteen thousand. However, the outpouring of antisemitism precipitated by the economic crisis in 1923 brought thousands of new members into its ranks.[77] In that year alone, the RjF established forty-five new local chapters, and by 1924 its member rolls grew to over thirty-six thousand—more than double what they had been three years before.[78] By the mid-1920s, the RjF incorporated nearly half of all Jewish veterans in Germany, making it one of the few veterans' organizations to represent a near majority of its constituent population.

In terms of image and self-representation, the RjF did not fundamentally differ from veterans' associations of the nationalist Right in the way that it narrated and remembered the war experience. It cultivated a heroic style of commemoration that embraced nationalist discourses on the *Frontgemeinschaft*, the overarching frontline community that had allegedly transcended class, ideology, and religious denomination.[79] Löwenstein was convinced that evidence of Jewish valor could succeed in changing German perceptions of Jewry, that public demonstrations of patriotism, conformity, and a pronounced "soldierly spirit" would refute any charges of Jews' not being German.[80] The RjF consciously avoided a Jewish victimization narrative that portrayed Jews as the innocent victims of a racist officers' corps, and railed against left-wing organizations for what it believed were unfounded attacks on the Prussian military.[81] It portrayed its war memories as "German" memories, reflecting on the meaning and legacy of the conflict from a nationalist perspective. Its membership journal, *Der Schild*, in tandem with its memorial volumes and published letter collections, stressed the commitment and selfless devotion to the fatherland that melded all Germans into a tight-knit fraternity at the front. Harking back to those moments during the war "when there were no Catholics, no Protestants, no Jews, no Center Party supporters and no Social Democrats, no Poles and no Danes, or men from Lorraine; but Germans" allowed the RjF to portray itself as an organization of comrades and loyal German Frontkämpfer.[82]

After the war, the RjF vigorously challenged accusations of Jewish shirking, exhorting its members to confront right-wing agitators. Its bombastic tone and assertive public image must be viewed against the backdrop of a community that portrayed itself as unequivocally German, yet simultaneously struggled to unburden itself of persisting suspicions of cowardice. Its rhetoric was part of a concerted effort to engage war veterans from the nationalist camp, to disabuse ambivalent Germans of their antisemitism, and to earn the grudging respect of the conservative Right. Although it maintained close relations with the Reichsbanner, the RjF simultaneously drew sharp distinctions between itself and the leftist organizations that conservatives accused of being defeatists and traitors, resulting in a sometimes tenuous relationship vis-à-vis pro-republican veterans' groups.[83] But distancing itself from left-wing narratives served the RjF's larger goal of winning over its detractors on the right and cultivating ties with more moderate associations such as the Kyffhäuser League, as well as local regimental associations.[84] It interpreted the presence of prominent nationalist guests at its annual gathering, such as the writers Walter Bloem and Rudolf Binding or former officers such as General Paul von Schoenaich, as an affirmation of German identity and proof that its efforts were paying off.[85]

Existing studies have largely overlooked the RjF's extensive cooperation with the German military, the Reichswehr. This is a significant oversight, for until 1933 German military officers were a regular sight at RjF official events and public dedications of Jewish war memorials.[86] What makes this collaboration remarkable is that the Reichswehr eschewed public appearances with nonnationalist, leftist organizations. It refused to appear in public with the Reichsbanner, and even shunned the Reichsbund der Kriegsbeschädigten und Kriegsteilnehmer (National Union of War Wounded and War Veterans) for its perceived pacifist, antimilitarist stance.[87] Yet at the RjF's annual "front soldiers' day," where the opening ceremonies typically included flag consecrations and the playing of the national anthem, the Reichswehr routinely sent an honor guard to march alongside the long processions of uniformed RjF members.[88] There is little doubt that such gestures of mutual solidarity were symbolic. However, as the Reichswehr was the official curator of the legacy of the Kaiser's army, its willingness to share the public stage with Jewish veterans should not be overlooked. These ritualistic displays of comradeship served an important function, for the RjF choreographed them in a way that communicated solidarity and singleness of purpose, promoting the vision of a united soldierly community to the broader public. The symbolic elements of these rituals, which often included the black-white-red flags of the Imperial regime, were a public expression of loyalty and deference to the "old" army. They communicated a kind of mutual respect between soldiers, a sign of recognition that attested to the heroism and national "reliability" of the RjF.[89]

The Reichswehr lent the Jewish veterans' organization valuable legitimacy. Its endorsement of the RjF served to weaken a crucial element of right-wing discourse: that Jews had shirked their duty at the front, and had flocked to the radical Left after the war. Löwenstein regarded the Reichswehr as a key ally against the Far Right and later described the army's relationship with his organization as "favorable and supportive."[90] Other higher-ups in the RjF, such as Kurt Sabatzky, a district leader in East Prussia, attributed their ability to counter antisemitic propaganda from the NSDAP to none other than Generals Blomberg and Reichenau, who would later become some of the staunchest supporters of Adolf Hitler.[91] What made this kind of collaboration possible? And how did the German military reconcile antisemitism and the ideology of the "stab in the back" with its support of the RjF?

The German military was a traditional bastion of antisemitism in Imperial Germany, and there can be no doubt that such attitudes were energized by the defeat in 1918 and fears of an all-out revolution and its consequences.[92] For many officers, the specter of the Russian Revolution, of "Bolshevik conditions," the loss of control over millions of men, violence against officers, and the possibility that ruling elites would be held responsible for Germany's collapse, prepared the ideological ground for an uncompromising stance against "Jewish Bolshevism" in the postwar German Army. In 1920, General Walther Reinhardt, in his capacity as Prussian war minister, thought it necessary to remind his staff that the army was obliged to abide by its tradition of remaining above politics: "As in all political questions, the Reichswehr should strictly desist from any involvement in the Jewish Question. The personal opinion of the individual for or against Jews is his own prerogative."[93] Reinhardt addressed the issue of antisemitism again the following year, in a speech to Reichswehr troops during Easter celebrations in 1921:

> I also want to define openly my position regarding the Jewish question, in the interest of internal peace. Whoever among them does damage to the German fatherland, or is merely indifferent to it, must be fought in the sharpest manner; but whoever as a German Jew sympathizes and fights with us must be welcomed and respected. The spirit of mammon and greed is contemptible; we must refute it in Jews and in Christians; but above all we must not, through love of pleasure or carelessness, become the slaves of money and thus the slaves of Jews. This defensive kind of antisemitism is praiseworthy; it operates not in malicious actions against Jews, but through self-restraint.[94]

Reinhardt was perhaps the only senior officer to take a public stand against antisemitism after the war. Yet his views were driven by pragmatism, not compassion or liberal sympathies. Like other Germans of his caste and profession, he saw antisemitism as a legitimate defensive measure that was necessary to keep "Jewish influence" in check, yet he also recognized it as a divisive ideology that had the potential to weaken the morale and discipline of the army.[95] Most importantly, Reinhardt's drawing of a distinction between "Jewry" and "German Jews who fight with us" warrants closer attention. Like other officers, he did not conflate Jewish comrades with the mass of "un-German," revolutionary, or socialist Jews. To the contrary, Jews who had proven their German credentials during the war were accorded "welcome and respect." He did not see a conflict of interest in condoning "defensive" antisemitism while simultaneously maintaining close ties with the RjF. The following year, Reinhardt attended a wreath-laying ceremony to commemorate the Jewish war dead in the Stuttgart synagogue as the RjF's official "guest of honor."[96] General Werner von Fritsch adopted a similar attitude; he declared in 1924 that "in the last resort, Ebert, pacifists, Jews, democrats, black, red and gold, and the French are all the same thing, namely the people who want to destroy Germany. There may be small differences, but in the end it all amounts to the same."[97] Fritsch's hostility toward Jews, however, did not dissuade him from maintaining close ties with a Jewish officer from his wartime regiment, whom he assured that he "would never forget the close comradeship of the war that had bound them together."[98] In certain contexts, then, a basic level of mutual recognition between former soldiers trumped social and ideological rifts, including antisemitism, and vague notions of comradeship between veterans persisted, even during the politically divisive years of the Weimar Republic.

Nowhere, perhaps, were such ambivalences and conflicting views as apparent as in the Stahlhelm. As the largest ex-soldiers' organization of the political Right, with a peak membership approaching half a million by the early 1930s, the Stahlhelm combined a militant brand of nationalism with an antidemocratic, anti-Communist, and increasingly antisemitic worldview.[99] It was not originally an openly antisemitic organization, however. Its militarism and embrace of the *Dolchstoß* had always been pronounced, but when it was founded in 1919, antisemitism was neither a foreseeable nor a foregone conclusion within it. Established as an ex–front soldiers' organization and self-defense league, it claimed to represent "a coalition of comrades who learned the value of true comradeship in the hardest days of fighting at the front, and who continue to embrace this comradeship in peacetime, without regard to rank and class, religion and party affiliation."[100] Until 1924, the sole requirement for membership was six months of frontline military service. Precise figures on Jewish membership are unknown, yet it is believed that several hundred Jews joined the Stahlhelm between 1919 and 1924, mainly former officers such as Stephan Prager, who was one of the founding members of the Düsseldorf chapter.[101]

At its annual meeting in 1924, the Stahlhelm adopted the "Aryan Paragraph," which officially banned Jews from belonging to the organization. That decision, however, was preceded by two failed attempts to prohibit Jewish membership, as Franz Seldte, the group's chairman, subscribed to a more traditional conservative worldview that recognized neither "Jews nor non-Jews, but [only] Stahlhelm men."[102] By 1924, however, the political winds in Germany had shifted. The outburst of nationalistic, antiforeign sentiment during the hyperinflationary period reinvigorated extremist groups such as the Pan-German League, whose influence inside the organization increased substantially. Tensions between the conservative wing and a growing extremist faction resulted in the election of a cochairman, Theodor Duesterberg, a radical antisemite and Pan-German member, who successfully led the *völkisch* block in its campaign to rid Jews from the Stahlhelm.[103]

Despite the adoption of the Aryan Paragraph, connections between Jewish war veterans and certain elements of the Stahlhelm did not suddenly end.[104] The Stahlhelm was a highly decentralized organization, with final decisions on membership and personnel policies resting with local district branches. Decisions on whether or not to expel Jewish members or admit Germans of partial Jewish descent were typically made by the *Ortsgruppenführer* (district leader). Several local chapters refused outright to discharge their Jewish members, and in some cases the measure was simply ignored. Jewish writings further reveal that in some regions a basic level of sociability between the Stahlhelm and the RjF remained intact. Adolf Asch, an RjF member in Berlin, reported a "friendly" working relationship with the nearby Stahlhelm office; at times the two associations even coordinated mutual outings and events, as well as joint appearances on national holidays such as Memorial Day (Volkstrauertag). And although its members were supposed to avoid appearing at RjF-specific events in any official capacity, in Fulda in May 1926, a Stahlhelm delegation attended the unveiling of a memorial plaque to the Jewish war dead in the city's synagogue.[105] On a local level, at least, mutual recognition between old soldiers apparently outweighed ideological rifts, considerations to which newer, extremist groups such as the NSDAP were not bound.

In its newspapers and speeches, the Stahlhelm frequently railed against "Jewry," yet at the same time, it was hesitant to openly denigrate Jewish ex-servicemen. In 1925, it published a joke in its newsletter, insinuating that Jewish soldiers had avoided combat by feigning wounds or illness. At a Jewish field hospital, the joke went, the medical staff had been sitting around for weeks with nothing to do, waiting for a casualty to arrive. They were finally called into action after a Jewish soldier dropped a typewriter on his foot. The RjF responded by demanding a public apology—and the Stahl-helm obliged.[106] It retracted the joke and publicly apologized for having dis-respected Jewish comrades "who had fought together with us at the front."[107] The following year, when an article in its monthly newspaper pledged to maintain its fight against "international Jewry," the Stahlhelm felt compelled to clarify its stance to the RjF, assuring Löwenstein that its statement did not apply to Jewish former combatants of the Great War.[108]

Two conclusions can be drawn from these cases. First, it is difficult to speak of an ideological consensus when it came to the Jewish Question. Not all Reichswehr officers or supporters of the nationalist Right were in denial about the true causes of Germany's defeat, much less actively promoted a mythical conspiracy of Jews and socialists.[109] Although antisemitism formed one of the core tenets of conservative-nationalist political discourse after 1918, these convictions coincided with fundamental disagreements, ambiva-lences, and opposing viewpoints. Certain factions of the conservative Right undoubtedly shared the near-universal antisemitism of the NSDAP, but there were often bitter and long-standing discussions about Jews that reflected di-verse and frequently shifting opinions on the Jewish Question. Second—and more important—antisemitism coexisted alongside older, more traditional discourses on military sacrifice and national belonging. These rationales did not simply vanish because of antisemitism. They were neither mutu-ally exclusive nor incompatible with each other, but acted in tandem. Many Germans, including some unapologetic antisemites, distinguished their Jew-ish comrades from the mass of ordinary Jews. On a personal level and in face-to-face relations, Jewish war veterans were accorded respect, and experi-enced inclusion and warm relations in the military and veterans' community and other traditionally antisemitic circles. The mutual coexistence of these discourses permitted German officers or members of organizations such as the Stahlhelm to not see a contradiction in maintaining ties with Jewish "comrades" while simultaneously striving to keep their ranks free of Jewish influence.

Regimental Associations

In June 1929, Max Senator, a former officer and convert to Christianity, peti-tioned the Stahlhelm district office in Kolberg, demanding to know why the organization considered him, a highly decorated former officer, "unworthy" to become a member.[110] Senator had served as a medical officer in a Prussian infantry regiment during World War I, earned both classes of the Iron Cross, and was promoted to the position of company commander (*Oberststabsarzt*).

Despite this impressive résumé, Senator's appeal was rejected on the grounds that he was a Jew.[111] Remarkably, though, the Stahlhelm district leader, Wedigo von Wedel, admitted in a handwritten internal memo that Senator was a "respectable man," whom he and several other members of the Kolberg chapter knew personally. The reason for this personal affiliation was that Senator, Wedel, and several other Stahlhelmers belonged to the same regimental association in Kolberg.[112] This revelation points to patterns of relations in smaller, local veterans' associations that were markedly different from those in the nationally based leagues (so-called *Wehrverbände*). The Kolberg regimental association was not exceptional in this regard: Jewish veterans often coexisted alongside comrades holding concurrent memberships in Far Right leagues such as the Stahlhelm and Jungdo, as well as leftist groups like the Reichsbanner. What made this coexistence possible? In which contexts did the "front experience" cultivate social networks that transcended ideological and political allegiances?

During the Weimar Republic, regimental associations fulfilled a largely symbolic role, which was to preserve the traditions and the wartime legacy of the Imperial German regiments.[113] Thousands of local associations were in existence throughout Germany after World War I, rivaling the nationally based leagues in terms of both scope and the number of active members.[114] A Berlin address book from 1921, for example, lists 161 veterans' leagues, of which more than 120 were unit-based associations.[115] The sheer number and diversity of these associations make it difficult, if not impossible, to make general statements about their prevalent character and institutional culture. Yet unlike the national leagues, whose self-image and patterns of sociability were increasingly intertwined with the major political movements, regimental associations dedicated themselves to planning and building local war memorials, preserving soldiers' cemeteries, commemorating holidays and the anniversaries of important battles, and honoring the war dead. They were inherently middle-class organizations that publicly promoted a conservative interpretation of the war. Their get-togethers and public commemoration events often became popular local attractions, replete with music, flag waving, drinking, and dancing, and were designed to communicate the heroism and sacrifices of the German soldier.

Despite their pronounced nationalist self-image, the members of these associations were not homogeneous in their backgrounds and political convictions. A look at the membership lists from different associations reveals that a considerable number of them were craftsmen, skilled workers, and artisans, as well as merchants and landowners, indicating that some associations managed to attract a significant working-class following, reflecting a social and professional diversity that would have been unimaginable prior to 1914.[116] To be sure, regimental associations probably attracted more middle-class idealists than committed socialists, but the diverse demographic base was not lost on the members. "Despite the fact that a significant part of the working-class population is red," an article from an association's newsletter declared, "those who belong to ex-soldiers' associations do not hesitate to demonstrate their belonging through active participation at our events." The author of the essay, himself a Stahlhelm member, went on to laud the mutual cooperation between left- and right-wing veterans in all aspects of associational life: "Even though I know that the various parties are represented in my Guards' Association [*Garde Verein*], that, for example, nearly the entire executive board, as opposed to me, thinks and votes democratically, it surprises me time and again how they are all attached to their old regiments, and how they attend the commemorations in Berlin, Potsdam and Spandau just to be with old comrades again."[117]

Jewish veterans were also strongly represented in regimental associations.[118] In Göppingen, the former field rabbi Arnold Tänzer served on the executive board of his local association and authored the memorial book commemorating its fifty-year anniversary.[119] Max Schohl, a former infantry officer, avoided joining the RjF, opting instead to become a member of the Kyffhäuser League and the association of his old regiment in Florsheim. He reasoned that active and visible participation in the non-Jewish veterans' community was key to discrediting antisemitism.[120] The RjF, for its part, encouraged its members to join non-Jewish associations, and sources reveal that a high percentage of Jewish veterans held concurrent memberships in the RjF and local, unit-based organizations.

Regional differences were the most important factor that shaped the organizational culture, practices, and ideological outlook of local associations. In large cities such as Berlin and Hamburg, in the Rhineland, and throughout the southern and predominantly Catholic regions of Germany, there was no discrimination between religious denominations at reunions and remembrance events. In Würzburg, the Association of the Ninth Royal Bavarian Infantry Regiment kicked off its yearly three-day festivities with concurrent religious services in the city's Catholic and Protestant churches and its synagogue.[121] However, in other regions where relations between Jews and Germans were traditionally strained, these tensions also revealed themselves in local association culture. In Nuremberg, the association of the Eighth Royal Bavarian Field Artillery Regiment passed a resolution forbidding the flying of the regimental colors during Jewish burial services, a move that prompted many Jews to quit the organization.[122] And in Konstanz in 1925, the rabbi was denied opening remarks at the commencement ceremonies during the annual gathering of the Sixth Badisches Infantry Regiment "Kaiser Friedrich III."[123] Yet despite these setbacks, one has to look no further than the newspapers of the extreme Right for evidence that Jews continued to play a major role in association life, even in Nazi strongholds such as Nuremberg. The Nazi Party's weekly tabloid, *Der Stürmer*, repeatedly attacked local veterans' associations for what it called "Jew friendliness."[124] It was particularly incensed by the behavior of Bavarian Crown Prince Rupprecht, who was seen dining with several Jewish former officers during a regimental get-together on "Garrison Day" in the nearby city of Fürth in 1925.[125]

This basic level of mutual respect was grounded in a collective identity built around memories and shared experiences within the exclusive context of the regiment. This nostalgic invocation of comradeship, of fighting together, "shoulder to shoulder," in the same battles, was the framework for collective memory. It instilled a sense of community among its members, providing the experience around which the associations' patterns of sociability coalesced. The annual reunions and parades, followed by beer drinking and get-togethers at the local *Stammtisch* (regulars' table), did more than just satisfy the sentimental and nostalgic attachments to one's old unit; they provided a public identity and a platform from which veterans could renew and sustain bonds of comradeship begun in wartime. Jewish writings attest that many former soldiers rekindled connections with members of their old regiments after the war. Adolf Asch, a member of the association of the Reserve-Field Artillery Regiment No. 43, wrote about meeting former wartime comrades at his yearly reunions, including the same medic who had bandaged his wounds at Verdun.[126] The funerals of deceased veterans similarly brought together old comrades. After Walther Gottheil's father died in the early 1920s, he was buried with full military honors by his regimental association. A number of his father's comrades attended the funeral, some of whom were also members of the Stahlhelm.[127]

Connections with former comrades were arguably small scale and limited, but the cultivation of these relations, which in some cases went back to the war, was a major factor in explaining Jewish integration in the postwar veterans' movement. The sense of community was built more around mutual experiences, or memories of those experiences, and less by political loyalties. In an advertisement for its 1922 annual reunion in Würzburg, for example, the association of the Ninth Infantry Regiment demanded that participants "leave politics at home" and "celebrate the memory of old, loyal friendships."[128] The tradition of remaining "above politics" manifested itself most visibly in the dedication of war memorials. A distinguishing feature of the thousands of monuments constructed across Germany during the 1920s and early 1930s is that they paid tribute to each member of the regiment or local community killed in the war, irrespective of background, religion, or political affiliation.[129] The names of the regiment's war dead were typically inscribed in chronological order of death, with no differentiation between Jews, Protestants, or Catholics. The dedication ceremonies, which usually reflected a heroic interpretation of the war, stressed the bravery and selfless sacrifice of each of its fallen soldiers.[130] Those men who had made the ulti-mate sacrifice for their comrades, the regiment, and Germany were honored together, as equals.

These developments should not distract from the gradual radicalization of the conservative Right during the Weimar Republic. If before 1914 nation-alists had been willing to tolerate Jews being perceived as fully assimilated into German culture, by the late 1920s many demanded the exclusion and separation of the Jewish community from the rest of society. Yet Jew hatred was by no means a universal or stable phenomenon in Weimar Germany; tolerance and social acceptance coexisted alongside antisemitism. In the discursive world of newspapers and political speeches, the nationalist Right universally condemned "Jewry." However, on a local level, where group and individual relations ran deeper, acceptance was the norm, not the exception.

In general, despite a deep-seated polarization between various social and political milieus after the war, there was not an unbridgeable gulf between the experiences and memories of Jewish and gentile German veterans. As members of the educated middle class, Jewish ex-servicemen saw the war as a psychologically transformative experience and a cornerstone of identity and social status. The majority continued to identify strongly with the Ger-man nation and its soldierly traditions. They maintained their patriotism in the face of efforts by the radical nationalist Right to cast Jews as enemies of the national and social body, and as threats to the sacred memory of the "front experience." Despite heightened tensions, Jewish veterans did not abandon hope that their service would be recognized by German society, nor did Weimar antisemitism precipitate a radical "break" with their Ger-man identity.

CHAPTER 3

"These Scoundrels Are Not the German People"

The Nazi Seizure of Power, 1933–35

The Nazi "seizure of power" on 30 January 1933 ushered in an unparalleled wave of antisemitic violence and discrimination throughout Germany. What made Hitler's twelve-year Reich "unprecedented" was that racism constituted the core tenet of the Nazis' vision for Germany's renewal.[1]

From the beginning, the impetus behind National Socialist policies was the removal of "non-Aryans" from all spheres of German public life and the creation of an ideologically and racially homogeneous *Volksgemeinschaft* (people's community). Jewish war veterans responded to the Nazi takeover with rigorous assertions of identity, in a desperate, ambiguous struggle to challenge their status as members of the out-group and secure some form of agency against the regime. The success of these interventions in the early months of 1933 convinced many veterans that they retained the backing of the German public and conservative forces in the government, and that the Nazi antisemitic campaign could be thwarted by evidence of Jewish valor. This tension—between Nazi antisemitism and older discourses on military sacrifice and national belonging—brings into relief the Third Reich's struggle to exert its racial policies on preexisting social and political milieus.

Jewish Reactions to the Nazi "Seizure" of Power

The Nationalist Socialists' vision of a purified, racially uniform "people's community" obliterated older notions of status, achievement, and recognition—the underpinnings of Jewish veterans' claims for inclusion in the German national body.[2] In the Nazi imagination, Jews constituted a people without roots in the fatherland, a racial minority that was biologically incompatible with the German nation and could never be assimilated. This last point was crucial. The claim that Jews were genetically predisposed to certain "un-German" characteristics, which decades of integration could never erase, found expression in the earliest Nazi political pamphlets and press articles, and it was a position stressed and repeated in official propaganda throughout Hitler's twelve-year Reich. An op-ed letter by a NSDAP district leader in Saxony published in a local newspaper in 1932 exemplifies this ideology:

> Lock up a dog of an inferior race or a mixed breed for five years with ten German shepherd dogs and try to teach the beast the noble bearing of a shepherd dog (loyalty, obedience, watchfulness, etc.), and the attempt will fail completely; the cur will always keep its inferior attitude, which is in the blood (unreliability, insidiousness, viciousness, disobedience, etc.), and the same is true for the human race. . . . A foreigner can adopt the language, customs, and rituals of his host nation, but he cannot escape from his skin, no matter how often he would like to do this.[3]

The fact that German Jews professed a strong spiritual bond to Germany and strove to assimilate into German culture was not only irrelevant to the Nazis but also dangerous. They saw the "German" Jew as a particularly insidious enemy because he operated unrecognizably, disguising himself behind the facade of Germanness. "Assimilation" was a ruse, a means for Jews to pursue their selfish agenda under the guise of bourgeois respectability. Antisemitic activists saw Jews' invocation of German nationalism, conversion to Christianity, and military service as further evidence that Jews had become adept at "mimicking" the mannerisms, language, and culture of their host nation in an attempt to conceal themselves amid an unsuspecting German public.[4]

The categories "conservative" and "Nazi" do not adequately describe the ideological differences on the Jewish Question, yet German reactions to the persecution of Jewish Frontkämpfer oftentimes assumed the character of a dichotomy. If the mainstream conservative Right conceded that some Jews had indeed fought bravely in the trenches, and that someone who was willing to die for the fatherland was ultimately to be respected, to the Nazis the issue of race rendered this distinction insignificant. This "biologically" grounded principle did not make exceptions for the Jewish veterans of World War I. Even though Nazi propaganda reiterated the claim that Jews had avoided combat, to the Nazi mind, race rendered discussions over the number of Jews who had served at the front irrelevant.[5] "How do the Jews . . . arrive at the claim that they are entitled to our gratitude for their achievements in the field?" an antisemitic newspaper article from 1934 asked its readers. "From Jewish circles in Germany one lately hears the oft-repeated claim that they had performed their national duty during the war . . . yet not a single example is known to us, where Jews had been genuinely motivated by 'national' principles to sacrifice on behalf of their hosts. When they did so, their actions were guided by other motives; to acquire power, wealth, high office, or prestige."[6] The NSDAP county leader (*Kreisleiter*) of Cochem was even more blunt, reminding his fellow party members in July 1934 that "there is no such thing as a decent Jew": "All this talk about Jewish frontline soldiers is the biggest nonsense. Why was there a considerable surplus of women in the German population after the war, while among Jews there was a surplus of men? The Jew knew how to evade the front. One would find them behind desks in the rear areas during the war. Only in isolated cases, when the Jew failed to secure a cushy job for himself, did he end up at the front, not because of his love for the Fatherland."[7]

Thus even Jews who had ostensibly fought bravely during the war, the Nazis argued, had not done so out of loyalty to Germany. Even in the uniform of the German Army, they had been nothing more than "perpetual swindlers." Behind the mask of the Frontkämpfer stood the Jewish enemy, who appropriated this image in order to acquire power and deceive the German people.

National Socialism thus upended the long-standing link between military service and national citizenship, which had been firmly embedded in European political discourses since at least the French Revolution.[8] It rejected older notions of inclusion based on status, performance of duty, service to the community, or shared experiences as a basis for national belonging; under Hitler, race became the official marker of German identity. Preventing Jews from turning their military sacrifices into claims for membership in the Volksgemeinschaft swept away the underpinnings of Jewish assimilation, for to the Nazis, evidence of bravery in the field did not change the fact that Jewish blood flowed in their veins, a fact that predisposed them to subversive attitudes toward National Socialism. Thus the centrality of military service—"the most sacred citizens' duty"—as credible proof of Germanness was relegated to insignificance.[9]

Despite the fact that the Nazis had been quite open not only about proclaiming their beliefs but also in stating what they intended to do once they were in power, for many Jews the reality of Nazi persecution became obvious only in hindsight. Contemporary reactions to 30 January make clear that Jews had not taken everything the Nazis had said literally, nor did they comprehend what a Nazi dictatorship would actually mean, with all its consequences. Jewish organizations and individuals expressed uncertainty or, at best, a sense of cautious skepticism. On the surface, the reactions of war veterans did not differ dramatically from those of other Jews of the same religious and political milieu.[10] Whereas Zionists overwhelmingly saw National Socialism as a vindication of their long-held belief that Jews would never be fully accepted in German society, acculturated German Jewry expressed hope that Hitler's government would be brief, or at the very least that conservative statesmen and institutions would put a brake on Nazi radicalism.[11]

A deeper analysis, however, reveals overarching similarities in the ways that Jewish Great War veterans reacted to these events, as well as commonalities in thought, perception, and behavior. First, they shared the belief that their status as ex-soldiers would protect them from Nazi discrimination, that they retained the backing of the army and the German public. Like other ex-soldiers, Jews returned from the war with the expectation that the suffering and privations in the trenches would be acknowledged, at least on a symbolic level. Irrespective of ideological or religious background, they were virtually united in their belief that they had fulfilled their obligations as German citizens and had earned the right to be accepted as legitimate members of the German nation. These beliefs did not come to an end on 30 January. The gap between these expectations and the realities of Nazi rule undergirded Jewish expressions of optimism, disappointment, or uncertainty in the first years of National Socialism.

Second, Jewish veterans vehemently challenged Nazi authorities determined to undermine their war record. During the Weimar period, Jewish veterans embraced an assertive means of defending their rights and status as Frontkämpfer. Their appeal to nationalist values had been a successful card with which they could trump antisemitic activists, as invocations of military sacrifice often earned them grudging respect in political circles that did not normally tolerate Jews. Doors that remained closed to Jews were sometimes opened for those who were "comrades." The success of this strategy, adopting conservative narratives on the *Frontgemeinschaft* to obliterate antisemitic stereotypes, lived on in the memories of the Jewish front generation and was integral to their thinking and behavior during the Nazi years. To be sure, not all veterans shared these attitudes, and not all Jews who expressed these convictions were veterans. Rather, there was a disproportionate occurrence of these attitudes among Jews who were also veterans.

The April Boycott

The first concerted, nationwide measure undertaken by the Nazis against the Jewish community was the so-called April Boycott on 1 April 1933. Its goal was to stir up anti-Jewish sentiment and incite popular outrage over foreign boycotts and "atrocity propaganda," which an international consortium of Jews had allegedly orchestrated against Nazi Germany.[12] Judged from this standpoint alone, the boycott was a failure, a fact the Nazi leadership largely conceded. Despite the strong presence of the Sturmabteilung (stormtroopers, or SA), many Germans either reacted with indifference to the Nazi propaganda campaign or defied the measure altogether. Of greater importance for this book, however, is how Jewish veterans perceived the boycott, and with which means they responded to it.

In Wesel, a small city in Westfalia, the Nazi district leader, apparently on his own initiative, had already organized a local boycott of Jewish businesses several days before. It was there that Erich Leyens printed large quantities of fliers decrying the Nazis' treatment of former soldiers:[13] "Our Reich Chancellor Mr. Hitler, the Reich Ministers Frick and Göring have repeatedly made the following proclamations: '*In the Third Reich, whoever insults a frontline veteran will be punished with incarceration!*'" The pamphlet asked its readers, "Is this the reward of the Fatherland: placards on the front of the door demanding that no one do business at our establishment?"[14] The following morning, when the SA arrived to take up positions in front of his department store, Leyens was waiting. Wearing the uniform of his old wartime regiment with the Iron Cross First Class he had earned as an officer on the Western Front during the First World War, Leyens positioned himself next to the stormtroopers and distributed the leaflets to passersby. This brazen defiance of Nazi authority caused a sensation in the town, as pedestrians stopped to take in the spectacle, many reacting "with open dismay" at the sight of the brownshirted SA men harassing a former soldier of the Great War.[15] According to Leyens, "Voices were raised, loud and clear, in support of the statement on the leaflet. Men gave vent to their indignation. Women, crying, came up and embraced me."[16] A crowd gathered, and before long throngs of "protest customers" pushed their way past the sentries into Leyens's store; by early afternoon, the NSDAP district office ordered the SA troops to pull back. Local newspapers lauded Leyens's "courage" and "self-determination" in challenging his accusers and "proving" his "Germanness,"[17] while the Centralverein

Main Office Berlin reminded its constituents that "such firm interventions can be successful, even today."[18]

Wesel was not an isolated case. Multiple sources reported similar incidents in cities and towns across Germany on 1 April, where Jewish shop owners, donning medals and uniforms from World War I, drew support from the local public and "discomfited the SA men who stood around with their placards."[19] One has to look no further than the case of Max Haller, a former U-boat officer and a Zionist, for evidence that these responses extended beyond the acculturated Jewish community.[20] As he stood before his business with his medals on display, the crowd of onlookers eventually grew so large that it brought traffic in that section of Berlin to a standstill. Eventually the local police chief had to intervene, "politely" imploring Haller to desist. Haller reported the incident to the main Zionist newspaper in Germany, *Jüdische Rundschau*, describing how he, "a small businessman, won the respect and approval of his fellow citizens," and that he had done so "in a neighborhood with a particularly strong nationalist following."[21] Thus even among the conservative Right, the same segment of the population that enthusiastically welcomed the fall of the republic and supported Hitler's rise to power, the sight of former soldiers being subjected to the same treatment as "ordinary" Jews by Nazi authorities elicited sympathy for the victims, as most Germans responded positively to ideological rationales emphasizing war, the military, and conservative values.

Jewish veterans used the boycott to effectively subvert a crucial element of Nationalist Socialist discourse: the claim that Jews had been cowards and unpatriotic shirkers during the war. Nazi propaganda tirelessly repeated the well-worn antisemitic tropes stressing the physical and moral inferiority of Jews, the alleged cowardice of the Jewish soldier during the First World War, and his unwillingness to sacrifice for the fatherland. Racist caricatures depicted Jewish men more or less identically: short, stocky, with crooked feet, bent postures, protruding bellies, and bearded, unshaven faces—the antithesis of the German soldierly male. These portrayals were calculated: they exemplified traits meant to convey physical and moral depravity, weakness, and, by extension, an inherent incompatibility with soldiering. They were intended to remind Germans that Jews were unworthy of emancipation and social acceptance, that they could never be assimilated into the new "people's community." Yet on 1 April, Jewish war veterans turned these claims on their head. Focusing on an already well-established connotation—the prestige of frontline military service—they were able to appropriate and exploit the positive image of the Frontkämpfer for maximum effect. In these carefully

choreographed demonstrations, their aim was to display a pronounced soldierly image, to present themselves to the public as comrades and as loyal
German fighters. Medals, uniforms, war wounds, and prosthetic limbs were
displayed as a means to occupy public space and discredit the claims of Nazi
propaganda in a highly visible manner. Speaking from the privileged position of the Frontkämpfer, Jews offered their rebuttal of Nazi propaganda
as something they could legitimately speak out about, giving voice to the
perspectives of former front soldiers who had been "there."

To be sure, not all Jewish veterans stolidly accepted their duty to "endure"
the hardships meted out by the Nazis.[22] For some, the sight of "Jewish shopkeepers hanging their Iron Crosses in their store windows" was not a sign of
Jewish resilience, but "a reminder of [Germans'] disgraceful conduct."[23] In
the Nazi stronghold of Deutsch-Krone, West Prussia, stormtroopers spared
Edwin Landau from the indignities inflicted on other Jewish business owners
on 1 April. Numerous "protest customers" visited his store that day, including local policemen, members of his veterans' association, and an official
from the mayor's office. Yet these gestures of solidarity failed to compensate
for the behavior of most of Deutsch-Krone's citizens, who "wore smiles on
their faces and could scarcely conceal their satisfaction" as Hitler's antisemitic campaign unfolded. The fact that other Jews were deprived of police
protection and became targets of arbitrary violence was too much for Landau to bear. "And for this people [*Volk*] we young Jews had once stood in the
trenches, in the cold and rain, and spilled our blood to defend the nation,"
Landau wrote. "Were there no comrades left from that time who were disgusted by this behavior?"[24] For Landau, 1 April was a turning point. It signified "my inner separation from my former fatherland," as he put it. "From
that day forward, I would be a German no more."[25]

Landau's case shows that Jewish attitudes after 1933 were informed not
only by how German society acknowledged their sacrifices during World
War I, but also by the degree to which ordinary Germans were seen as ac-
celerating, condoning, or restraining the regime's antisemitic excesses. In
general, however, the failure of the April Boycott precipitated a sense of
hope and short-lived optimism in the Jewish veterans' community, reinforcing their belief that they had the backing of the German people and could
outlast the regime. If Germans' reactions on 1 April are any indication of
how older, more conservative notions of national belonging resonated with
the German public, then the support for Jewish veterans seems to provide
some evidence that most Germans did not equate former combatants of the
war with the abstract Jewish enemy touted by Nazi propagandists.

The Frontline Veterans' Exemption

Interventions against Nazi discrimination were not restricted to defiant shopkeepers on 1 April, but also took the form of written appeals to newspapers and public officials, as Jewish veterans deployed their status as a means to influence local developments. In the first weeks after the Nazi seizure of power, veterans could still find a willing ally in the uncoordinated mainstream press. In a letter published by the *Deutsche Allgemeine Zeitung* in March, Paul Rosenthal railed against the "bitter injustice of accusing Jews in general of being un-German," appealing directly to the comradeship of Germany's community of former soldiers: "I therefore call on all my comrades from the war: do not forget us in these days, do not forget us, shield us from demeaning generalizations, and stand up for us so that old front-soldiers may take part in the rebuilding of the 'national' Germany, even if they were born as Jews."[26]

Rosenthal lauded the one thing that racial and ideological differences could never taint: comradeship. Framing his case in the rhetoric of the *Frontgemein-schaft*, he reminded readers of Jews' readiness to sacrifice themselves for Germany and for their comrades, invoking the nationalist myth that all soldiers had been equals under hostile fire. The authors of these petitions hoped such appeals would ultimately force Hitler to integrate former soldiers into the new political order, and Rosenthal's is one of several letters published by the non-Nazi press in early 1933 calling attention to the "tragic fate" befalling the Jewish front generation.[27] The fact that the *Deutsche Allgemeine Zeitung* was a prominent newspaper of the political Right, one that simultaneously endorsed Hitler's anti-Jewish campaign, openly published such letters is a testament to the inclusionary power of the military sacrifice narrative, and to its resonance with a segment of the population that overwhelmingly approved of the Third Reich.

To give potency to their claims, the Jewish veterans avoided references to Judaism or lifestyle, emphasizing traits such as comradeship, performance of duty, and their inherently German sensibilities. Often they pointed to their family history, documenting a distinguished record of service to the fatherland and their commitment to the "national" cause, in particular noting voluntary enlistment, wounds, promotions, and medals for bravery. Willi Gans's appeal to the district president of Kassel after his dismissal from the local locksmiths' commission, inquiring why, despite "willingly spilling his blood before the enemy" during the war, he was "no longer counted as a full-fledged German," was not exceptional in this regard; it was a sentiment that was stressed, repeated, and rephrased in petitions to institutions, clubs, politicians, and local officials across Germany.[28] The focus of veterans' efforts, however, was Reich president Paul von Hindenburg, a figure of immense stature in Jewish circles. In one of many letters received by the former field marshal, Hanns Silberschmidt, who had suffered severe wounds to his head, chest, and shoulder during the final German offensive in 1918, implored Hindenburg to ensure that "German Jews who, like every other comrade, fought and bled for the German people and Fatherland, be spared from the abominable disgrace of expulsion from the Volksgemeinschaft. . . . I am German not just through citizenship, according to the law, but also by my attitude and behavior. But I am also German by fate, for I have spilled my blood for Germany as a German soldier."[29]

This discursive strategy was not new. It consisted of situating Jewish participation in the war within a broader narrative of sacrifice for Germany, of reminding Germans of the time when, as the RjF had put it, "enemy bullets did not distinguish between Jews and Christians."[30] Portraying themselves as comrades, and as Frontkämpfer, was designed to establish a sense of continuity from the trenches to the present day, despite all the violence and upheaval. These claims were juxtaposed with the Nazis' treatment of former frontline soldiers, which violated the most basic principles of comradeship and soldierly honor.

Hindenburg and most conservative audiences reacted positively to invocations of military sacrifice, which was evidenced during Nazi efforts to pass the so-called Law for the Restoration of the Professional Civil Service in April 1933. This legislation was the opening phase in the *Gleichschaltung* (loosely translated as coordination or synchronization) of the government, which was intended to expel "unreliable" elements—Communists, social democrats, and Jews—from state and federal positions and replace them with members of the Nazi Party.[31] Yet days before the scheduled passage of the bill, Hitler received a letter from Hindenburg admonishing the NSDAP for its brutality against First World War veterans, declaring it "intolerable" that "Jewish civil servants who had been disabled in the war should suffer such treatment." He wrote, "As far as my own feelings are concerned, officials, judges, teachers, and lawyers who are war invalids, fought at the front, are sons of the war dead, or themselves lost sons in the war should remain in their positions unless an individual case gives reason for different treatment. If they were worthy of fighting and bleeding for Germany, then they must also be considered worthy of continuing to serve the Fatherland in their professions."[32]

This was the only time Hindenburg intervened in the regime's anti-Jewish policies. He did not seem bothered by the Nazis' brutality against Jewish

Germans overall, and his earlier correspondence with Leopold Rosenak just after World War I leaves little doubt about the depth of his antisemitic convictions.[33] Like other members of his caste and political milieu, however, he simultaneously expressed deep reservations about holding former soldiers and their families to the same standards as "Jews."[34]

Hitler knew that without the old field marshal's support, he could never win the army's backing, which at this stage he needed to stay in power.[35] Grudgingly, he assured Hindenburg that the civil service law would include exceptions for those "members of the Jewish people who were once compelled, by the requirements of the law, to perform service in the war."[36] Hitler was left with no other alternative. The amendment to the law—the so-called *Frontkämpferklausel* (frontline veterans' clause)—exempted any individual who "as part of a combat unit, participated in a battle, an engagement, in trench fighting, or in a siege."[37] It also protected war-wounded and disabled veterans, former members of the Freikorps, and any individual whose father or son had been killed in action during World War I.[38] The wording of the veterans' clause, which stated that "a civil servant who fought at the front for the German Reich or its allies during the world war has, in any case, proven his national reliability through his deeds back then," marks this as a classic conservative text.[39] In the first year after the Nazi takeover, it was still the conservative-nationalist sections of the educated middle classes that populated key agencies in the government, the judiciary, and the officers' corps, and largely shaped public discourses about the war and the ways in which military service and national belonging were articulated and talked about in public.[40] Jewish veterans still retained their mouthpiece, the forces that emulated and praised traditional patriotic virtues in German society.

The RjF took credit for the inclusion of the veterans' exemptions in the April 1933 civil service law, but there is actually little evidence to substantiate this claim.[41] It is true that the organization petitioned conservative members of the government and the military after 30 January, even meeting face to face with members of the Reichs Chancellery and key cabinet ministers, including Hermann Göring.[42] Owing to his connections in the German military, Leo Löwenstein also secured the backing of distinguished military figures such as retired field marshal August von Mackensen, as well as senior active-duty officers like General Werner von Blomberg.[43] Yet the RjF's high-level lobbying efforts tend to obscure the broad consensus of support that undergirded the veterans' claim for inclusion, forcing Hitler to maneuver between the demands of NSDAP hardliners, who urged more aggressive action on the Jewish Question, and those of his conservative coalition partners. The pattern was the same everywhere in Germany: even among

Germans with strong nationalist sympathies, including some "moderate" National Socialists, the same groups who lauded Hitler's anti-Jewish policies both publicly and privately, there was a parallel view that Jews who had risked health and life for the fatherland had, to some extent at least, "proven their Germanness."[44]

Such attitudes were not confined to a specific class or party affiliation. If activists in the Nazi Party argued that Jewish soldiers had fought not out of conviction but because military service was "forced upon them" by the draft, there is little evidence that these views resonated with the general public.[45] The civil service law, with its antisemitic elements yet simultaneous privileging of military service, largely corresponded to the demands of the conservative German middle classes, who greeted the measure with approval. Herbert Sulzbach received several letters from members of his old regiment in 1933, several whom had since joined the NSDAP, expressing relief that "as a frontline fighter, the Aryan regulations have caused you no hardship."[46] The same sentiment reveals itself in Victor Klemperer's diary, in which he described frequent encounters with openly antisemitic Germans whose attitudes changed after discovering he had served at the front during the war.[47] In Karl Löwith's case, after 1933 the Marburg University professor found himself lecturing to classrooms full of students in SA and SS uniforms, who "respected me as a lecturer, but even more so as an ex-serviceman." These same students, he wrote, saw "the elimination of all those Jews who happened not to be protected by war service—because they were either too young or unfit for army service—as a matter which need not be discussed."[48] The proposition that "my wartime military service confirmed my Germanness" was a rationale Löwith encountered again and again throughout the Nazi years, and his memoir is one of many autobiographical sources that point to the strength of older discourses that the Nazis found difficult to crack.[49]

The veterans' clause constituted a major symbolic victory for Jewish war veterans. At the same time, however, the practical implications of the law should not be overstated. In 1933 the number of Jews in the civil service did not surpass five thousand, about half of whom retained their posts due to the frontline service provision.[50] The law had no impact on the majority of the Jewish community, who were predominately small business owners, private sector employees, and livestock dealers. Moreover, paragraph 4 of the law provided for the dismissal of any civil servant due to "political unreliability," a provision that targeted current and former members of pro-republican organizations such as the SPD or the Reichsbanner.[51] This was the fate of Inge Deutschkron's father, who, as an SPD member, was spared from the provision banning Jews from the civil service by dint of his military service, yet was dismissed anyway because of his political affiliation.[52] So while Jewish veterans and their families with solid nationalist credentials initially kept their jobs, former leftists and those who had belonged to groups such as the Reichsbanner not only faced financial ruin, but also became the first targets of Nazi terror.

The Enabling Act, which effectively ended parliamentary rule and gave Hitler virtually unlimited power in Germany, unleashed a reign of terror against the political Left that was, until then, unsurpassed in scale.[53] "Prior membership in the Social Democratic Party or the Reichsbanner was deadly," wrote Alfred Oppler, as the Nazis subjected former members of these organizations to arbitrary arrest, interrogation, and physical abuse, irrespective of their military background.[54] Many prominent SPD activists shared the fate of Max Hirschberg, a highly decorated officer who was arrested on 9 March 1933 as a potential "enemy of the state" and spent five months in *Schutzhaft* (protective custody).[55] The phrase "politically unreliable" was so vague that it potentially encompassed anyone who had previously belonged to a pro-republican or leftist political group, including pacifist organizations or Freemasons' lodges. The lawyer Karl Rosenthal had been a frontline officer in the Fourth Bavarian Infantry Regiment during the war, was repeatedly decorated, and had joined a local citizens' militia to help crush the Communist insurrection in Würzburg in 1919.[56] Yet in 1935, the Gestapo accused him of having engaged in "subversive activities" because he had joined a Freemason "field lodge" during the war.[57] This was apparently evidence enough for Nazi authorities to accuse him of having helped "thrust the dagger into our backs."[58]

The conflation of the political Left with national "unreliability" and disloyalty to the fatherland was nothing new; it followed a tradition prevalent among the nationalist Right. The Left was widely seen as inciting the revolution in 1918 and installing the republic, sweeping away the monarchy and, with it, the legitimacy of conservative rule in Germany. In the minds of the old elites, who still exerted considerable influence over the government and its institutions in 1933, socialists, pacifists, and Communists had forfeited the "thanks of the Fatherland" by adopting "revolutionary" worldviews that undermined Germany's renewal. As Karl Rosenthal and others in his situation soon learned, fighting in the trenches did not compensate for "political unreliability" in Hitler's Reich.

The real significance of the veterans' clause, however, is that it established Jewish Frontkämpfer as a status group in Nazi Germany.[59] To be sure, this status was relative. It did not bestow official power or influence on veterans; at best it offered limited and largely symbolic protections to a community that lived through most of the Third Reich in a state of perpetual crisis. It allowed many Jews to remain employed for a brief time; others, such as the war wounded and disabled, gained access to material resources that would prove critical in later years—public transportation, medical care, and food rations not available to other Jewish Germans. Crucially, it defined veterans as a category distinct from "ordinary" Jews. Veterans were a group nominally entitled to special rights, privileges, and exceptions—a dichotomy that entered public discourse in Nazi Germany. Research has shown that the German public increasingly classified people according to National Socialist racial criteria after 1933 ("Non-Aryans," Jews, half-Jews, *Mischlinge*, etc.).[60] Frontkämpfer became a status that increasingly informed public discussions about the Jewish Question during the Nazi years, and it gave veterans a means to defy the category "Jew" and be considered members of a subordinate yet privileged minority.

At this early stage, political considerations required Hitler to exercise tactical restraint in his campaign against the Jews. There is no question that Hitler fundamentally opposed the exclusion of Jewish veterans from the regime's anti-Jewish campaign, and it was an issue that the Nazi leadership was not willing to compromise on.[61] In order to achieve that goal, "to show the German people the way," the Nazis would have to unmake the boundaries that separated war veterans from "Jews," to transform public discourses on race and national belonging and make all Jews the same in the minds of everyday Germans.[62] This shift in values could occur only against the backdrop of a massive social reordering: the existing power relations in the government and its institutions, the press, and the veterans' movement, which largely determined public discourses about military service and national identity, would have to be swept aside. The first step in this process was to sever Jews' ties to their most prominent bases of support: the military and veterans' community.

"Where Are My Comrades Now?"

In March 1933, the *Berliner Tageblatt* reported on a veterans' gathering organized by the RjF in Berlin; it was attended by representatives from the major ex-soldiers' associations, including the Stahlhelm and the Kyffhäuser League as well as several regimental and war-wounded organizations.[63] The RjF intended to use the occasion to publicly affirm its commitment to the new Germany and appeal to the veterans' community for solidarity, as Jews feared an ever-greater onslaught of violence and discrimination by the Nazis.[64] When the RjF speaker took the podium to open the meeting, his remarks were cut short by jeers and heckling from a group of SA men who had made their way into the assembly hall. Scuffles and commotion broke out in the audience as the stormtroopers proceeded to shout down the speaker, briefly leading to the meeting's suspension. "Many shameful things took place," wrote Gerhard Lissa, one of the RjF members in attendance. "Jewish ex-soldiers, crippled or blinded in the war, were insulted and abused by young scoundrels who had never even heard the whistle of a bullet."[65] Yet it was members of the Stahlhelm who silenced the SA men and restored order to the hall until the arrival of the police. The proceedings resumed, and before the evening was over, numerous members of the non-Jewish veterans' leagues proclaimed their solidarity with the RjF. One of them was the chairman of a local regimental association, who introduced himself to the audience as a "convinced Jew hater." Despite the man's professed support for Hitler's regime and its antisemitic ideology, he urged his fellow veterans not to abandon their Jewish "comrades from the war."[66]

This spontaneous act of unity, perhaps the only public demonstration of solidarity with Jews from the organizations of the nationalist Right, draws attention to the persistence of a basic, mutual recognition between former soldiers, one that often took precedence over deep ideological rifts, including antisemitism. The RjF saw the Berlin meeting as "proof" that "the bonds of comradeship had not been torn to pieces by the events of the day,"[67] noting that all participants in the ensuing discussion, even "a few National Socialists," were unanimous in their belief that "the Jewish Frontkämpfer must not be shut out of the Volksgemeinschaft."[68] In light of later developments, this optimism may seem naive or at best misguided. Yet in early 1933, these hopes were not irrational. In comparison to other Jews, war veterans retained close connections with non-Jewish associations during the first year of the Nazi regime. It was not unusual for Jews to be included in local war commemorations in 1933 and 1934, as was the case at the unveiling of the Eighty-First Infantry Regiment's memorial to its war dead in Frankfurt am Main, which included simultaneous religious services in the Christian churches and the city's West End Synagogue.[69] And despite the army's overall enthusiasm for Hitler, the Reichswehr invited representatives from both the RjF and the Stahlhelm to attend the swearing-in of new recruits in Ludwigsburg on 9 April 1933. According to the *Ludwigsburger Zeitung*, the garrison commander's opening remarks declared that "the army does not recognize any differences of class, status, religion, or origin. We belong to and serve the entire German Volk without distinctions."[70]

From the standpoint of the regime, these developments were both embarrassing and frustrating; they also represented significant hurdles to the complete removal of Jews from all spheres of public life.[71] The April Boycott had made all too clear that evidence of Jewish bravery could reduce the credibility of Nazi racist doctrine *ad absurdum*. The Nazis had to respond to this. The removal of Jews from associations affiliated with the German military was a vital step in the Nazis' anti-Jewish strategy, one that would not only deprive Jewish veterans of a public stage but also help erase the memory of Jewish war service from public consciousness.

Efforts had already been underway to bring the veterans' movement under government control. The Reichsbanner was the first victim of Nazi terror; after the seizure of power, its leaders had been arrested or thrown into concentration camps, and the organization was officially outlawed in March 1933.[72] Although the Stahlhelm had been an alliance partner of the National Socialists, Hitler also regarded it as a potential source of opposition, and by July 1933 the Nazis absorbed the majority of its chapters into the SA Reserve. Its first chairman, Franz Seldte, became part of Hitler's first cabinet and eventually joined the NSDAP, while Theodor Duesterberg, who had spearheaded the Stahlhelm's efforts to ban Jews in 1924, was driven out of the organization after a Nazi newspaper revealed he had a Jewish grandfather.[73] Germany's largest veterans' organization was the Kyffhäuser League, which counted 2.8 million members and served as the umbrella organization for most of the twenty-nine thousand local *Kriegervereine* (ex-soldiers' leagues) scattered throughout Germany.[74] Although it had always cultivated and promoted a pro-monarchist, national-conservative ideology, the Kyffhäuser distanced itself from the divisive debates on the Jewish Question that had embroiled the Stahlhelm from the mid-1920s on. After 30 January, however, the league wasted little time discarding its "apolitical" stance.[75] At the annual gathering in May 1933, its president, General Rudolf von Horn, declared that the league "fully supported the National Socialist Revolution," and stood "united and ready to fulfill its duties at the disposal of the Reichs Chancellor Adolf Hitler."[76] Horn may have been motivated by a desire to preserve the Kyffhäuser's autonomy and save it from the fate that befell the Stahlhelm, but there is little doubt he was also motivated by a genuine enthusiasm for the new order.[77] Six months later, without any pressure from Nazi authorities, Horn announced on 1 October 1933 that "non-Aryans" were prohibited from joining the Kyffhäuser League. All Jews and Christians of Jewish descent who belonged to the organization would have thirty days to voluntarily resign or else face expulsion.[78]

The impact of this decision is difficult to exaggerate: it meant that with one stroke, all veterans' organizations holding corporative membership in the Kyffhäuser League—roughly 90 percent (excluded for the time being were most officers' associations as well as regimental and specialist associations)—would be required to expel their Jewish members. The news came as a shock to Jewish veterans.[79] The veterans' community was a site of male status and interaction, and expulsion not only left veterans alienated and humiliated but deprived them of a means to assert their status in the community. The non-Jewish veterans' association in particular had become a keystone of their socially defined identity, a significance reinforced by their perceived integration into an exclusive, conservative—and traditionally antisemitic—sphere of German society. In an impassioned letter to Horn, Max Schohl explained how the expulsion left his "sense of German comradeship deeply shaken": "When in the murderous Battle of the Somme artillery fire rained down on my company, none of the men under me, neither enlisted personnel nor officers, asked me if I were Aryan or non-Aryan: all looked in comradely trust to their company commander. . . . And today, should it be as if all this had simply not happened? Should this comradeship, proven in blood and suffering, simply evaporate into nothing? I cannot and will not believe this, for to do so would rob my life of all meaning."[80]

Horn never responded to Schohl's appeal. Yet despite the veterans' community's embrace of National Socialism after 1933, there is little evidence that Kyffhäuser League members greeted the expulsion of their Jewish comrades with a similar consensus of support. Local records suggest that the implementation of the measure was a solemn affair: the announcements in newsletters and membership journals were brief, tersely worded, conveying nothing of the celebratory language that had accompanied Hitler's ascent to power or the government's crackdown on leftists and Communists earlier that year.[81] Several associations openly defied the directive. The Düsseldorf *Garde Verein* submitted a written protest to Horn, declaring that "we will not leave our Jewish comrades in this time of crisis, those who have stood by our Fatherland, to our association, and to the black, white, and red flag for decades, in both good times and bad times. For us, it is not a matter of background, but the decades-long record of loyalty that is decisive."[82] And in Stuttgart, the officers' association of the Twenty-Ninth Field Artillery Regiment declared in its newsletter that "the expulsion of any members is out of the question. As Frontkämpfer, non-Aryan members of the officers' association will remain members, just like before."[83]

The Kameradschaftlicher Verein Deutscher Soldaten (Comradely Association of German Soldiers), an association of over four hundred former soldiers based in Berlin, went even further: its members voted to leave the Kyffhäuser League.[84] The internal meeting report from the group's "emergency" gathering on 14 October 1933 states that Horn's order presented the association with an unresolvable moral dilemma.[85] According to its chairman, Alfred Salomon, it was now forced to reconcile two of the German military's most sacred virtues—obedience and comradeship—for the Aryan Paragraph was "an order, and we as soldiers are expected to carry this order out. Even with heavy hearts we commit ourselves to it if it's in the interest of our Fatherland." At the same time, however, the order contradicted an inviolable principle of soldierly honor, leaving the association with only one "honorable" course of action: "Wherever our old comrades stay, there we will stay too. There is nothing that can separate us from our old comrades. We shall rise and fall with them. We do not know what the future will bring, but we will do our best to secure the continued existence of the association. Whether or not we are successful in achieving our goals, is out of our hands."[86]

Salomon argued that the association had an obligation to withdraw from the Kyffhäuser League. The proposal was greeted by applause and shouts of approval from the audience. Several members stood up and gave speeches offering encouragement to their Jewish colleagues, and proclaimed "a vow of true comradeship, in the name of the Aryan comrades." According to the meeting minutes, the vote to leave the Kyffhäuser was unanimous. After the meeting adjourned, the "comrades sat comfortably together into the late-night hours over glasses of beer."[87] From that point on, the Verein continued to operate as an "independent association" until at least July 1935.[88]

Such reactions complicate the long-standing debate over the German military community's embrace of Nazi ideology after 1933.[89] Opposition to antisemitic measures in the veterans' movement was serious enough to draw the attention of the highest levels of the Nazi government. In December 1934, Heinrich Himmler, at the time acting chief of the German police, sought Hitler's advice on how to proceed against the Verband der Bayerischen Offiziers-Regiments Vereine (Association of the Bavarian Officers' Regimental Leagues), after the group rejected the order to expel all Jews. Himmler suggested coercion or disbanding the association outright, complaining that "the further presence of Jewish members in the Bavarian Officers' Regimental Leagues is unacceptable in the present day and is merely intended to devalue the movement and its program in the eyes of the public."[90] Hitler's response is revealing. He instructed his police chief to do nothing, reassuring him that "the question of Jewish membership will, over time, resolve itself."[91]

Hitler was right. Individual protests should not detract from the larger pattern that was developing after 30 January: the individual stages of the *Gleichschaltung* were initiated and implemented not by Nazi authorities, but rather by key individuals such as Horn, or by the associations themselves.

The newsletters of local veterans' organizations across Germany expressed a near-unanimous approval for Hitler and the direction of the new government, oftentimes through pledges of loyalty to the new regime. Others, like the Württembergischer Frontkämperbund in Stuttgart, went even further. Its chairman, General Ernst Kabisch, required each member to complete a questionnaire attesting that they belonged to a National Socialist organization. Those who did not "spiritually follow the path" were expelled and "wished the best of luck" in finding their "own special way."[92] Most associations complied with the Aryan Paragraph and did not hesitate to cast out their Jewish members, offering at best symbolic professions of solidarity and sympathy to their former comrades.[93] These measures were not orchestrated from the Reich Chancellery in Berlin, but rather point to the widespread enthusiasm for the regime from "below," which encouraged and empowered various local actors to press ahead with their antisemitic agendas.[94]

The German Military and the Jews

That the German military not only enthusiastically greeted Hitler's rise to power but later played a substantial role in the murder of the European Jews between 1939 and 1945 has become abundantly clear to scholars since the end of the 1970s,[95] and to the general public since at least 1995, thanks in part to the so-called Wehrmachtausstellung (Wehrmacht Exhibition) organized by the Institute for Social Research in Hamburg.[96] Perhaps more than any other institution in Germany at the time, the German military had the most to benefit from the Third Reich: the repeal of the Versailles Treaty, the creation of a militarized people's community, and the long-hoped-for military expansion were all but certain under Hitler. Nevertheless, the Reichswehr (later Wehrmacht) not only was ideologically heterogeneous but also displayed considerable variation in how it reacted to National Socialism. It may seem remarkable, for example, that the Kyffhäuser's initiative to expel "non-Aryans" drew sharp criticism from a number of high-ranking military officers, including General Werner von Blomberg, the German war minister. Less than a week after the decision was announced, Blomberg informed Horn that "these measures go way beyond what the Reich government requires of German civil servants." He wrote, "The current wording of your decree from 1 October 33 abruptly casts many accomplished Frontkämpfer out of the community to which he belongs on the basis of his entire life's work. . . . Let me therefore propose that your directive from 1 October be amended, so that as in the Civil Service law, those frontline veterans who can prove that they fought honorably at the front during the World War, are spared from these stipulations."[97]

Blomberg did not press the issue, however, and his protest had no bearing on the implementation of the policy. In any case, by early 1934 new developments were emerging that would profoundly change the German military's relationship to the Nazi regime. Amid the intensifying power struggle between the army and the SA, Blomberg was increasingly forced to fend off accusations of "Jew friendliness" or "insufficient commitment to National Socialist ideals" that were routinely leveled against the military by the Nazi press. He initially responded to these attacks with public pronouncements of loyalty to the new regime.[98] But in a move undoubtedly calculated to strengthen the army's position vis-à-vis the SA, Blomberg announced in March 1934 that he would apply the racial criteria set forth in the civil service law of April 1933 to "all officers, deck officers, non-commissioned officers, and enlisted personnel of the Wehrmacht," a decision that forced all "non-Aryans" serving in the armed forces into early retirement, with the exception of frontline veterans of World War I.[99] In what followed, the Reichswehr discharged roughly 70 officers, officer candidates, and enlisted men of "non-Aryan" background.[100] Blomberg's sudden about-face was undoubtedly a tactical maneuver, a "conscious attempt" to gain Hitler's support to act against Röhm and the SA, who were perceived as a threat to the German military's status as the nation's sole bearer of arms.[101] It was no coincidence that on the same day that Blomberg announced the Aryan Paragraph, he also notified senior commanders about his intention to introduce the Nazi eagle onto Reichswehr uniforms, a decision he justified on the grounds that it would demonstrate the army's unwavering allegiance to the new Germany.[102]

The sole voice of dissent to these antisemitic policies came from Colonel Erich von Manstein, who lodged a protest to his superiors after learning that one of his former company commanders faced expulsion.[103] Manstein framed his criticism of the Aryan Paragraph around the concept of caste honor, warning that the adoption of Nazi policies presented a grave threat to the exclusivity and autonomy of the German officers' corps. His letter to General Ludwig Beck on 21 April 1934 struck a defiant tone, declaring that it was "incompatible" with the army's honor "to renounce one's loyalty to comrades in order to sidestep political difficulties."[104] Manstein praised the Nazis' ongoing efforts to remove Jews "from the professions of judges, lawyers, and doctors," as there was "no doubt that a rigorous cleansing was in order." He found it troubling, though, that civilian authorities were imposing laws on soldiers, for the army should "have the right to judge soldiers differently than civil servants," and "not bend to the will of outsiders."

He declared, "The honor of these young men is all our honor," invoking a widely shared conviction in military circles that only soldiers could legitimately criticize or judge their own.[105]

This was the same Manstein who, seven and a half years later as commander of the Eleventh Army in the Soviet Union, issued an order asking his troops to understand "the necessity of the harsh atonement of Jewry, the spiritual carrier of the Bolshevik terror," and presided over the murder of thirty-three thousand Jews in the Crimea in 1942.[106] Yet in 1934, despite his "rigorous support of National Socialism and racial awareness," he was "deeply moved" when he learned that a former subordinate faced dismissal for having a Jewish grandmother, and saw it as his "duty to do whatever necessary to help him."[107] Of central importance are Manstein's ideological justifications for exempting Jewish soldiers from Nazi racial laws. In a ten-page memorandum to Beck, titled "Thoughts on the Retroactive Implementation of the Aryan Paragraph in the Wehrmacht," he argued that soldiers were worthy of exclusive rights on the basis that they were "willing at every hour to sacrifice their lives for the Fatherland," and that "this willingness makes it impossible not to consider them full-fledged Germans."[108] "In the past," he asserted, "if the Reich was prepared to demand a soldier sacrifice his life at any given hour, it cannot legally say to him suddenly, 'you are no longer a real German.' Whoever voluntarily became a soldier, who had been ready at every hour to give his life for the German people, he has become German on the basis of this willingness. He has proven his *Aryan disposition*, whether his grandmother is Aryan or not."[109]

Manstein's rationale, that performance of duty and a readiness to sacrifice for the fatherland constituted crucial markers of German national identity, holds a significance beyond the individual case. The conflation of "Jewry" with liberalism, pacifism, socialism, and Communism, all the while making limited exceptions for Jews who had proved their "Aryan convictions" through wartime service in the German military, was a view that resonated with many conservative Germans and, if we believe Manstein, "the majority of the officers' corps."[110]

The writings of "non-Aryans" serving in the Reichswehr appear to corroborate this claim. Hans Lebram, one of a handful of German naval officers of Jewish descent, remained confident, until the weeks leading up to his dismissal, that as a soldier he would be spared from Nazi racist legislation. "I have not detected the slightest trace of apathy or distrust," he assured his father in early May 1933. "Quite the contrary, everyone is particularly friendly toward me. I also don't believe that this will change in any way."[111] Otto Lewin, a baptized Jew who had been retained by the Reichswehr after

1934 by virtue of his frontline military service, expressed similar sentiments. Lewin had volunteered for the army in 1913, and when the First World War broke out the following year, he served as a field medic in a Prussian infantry regiment. In September 1916, his unit was engaged in the bitter fighting around Verdun, where Lewin earned the Iron Cross and a promotion to sergeant for carrying wounded soldiers back to German lines under enemy fire. After the armistice, he settled in the West Prussian city of Schneidemühl and began a successful career as an orchestral musician. Yet Lewin had been an enthusiastic soldier and enjoyed his time in the army. Despite the horrors of Verdun, he looked back on his days of soldiering with nostalgia. "My great passion for the soldiery profession," he later wrote, "drove me time and again to find a way to wear the gray uniform once again." He found his opportunity in 1923, when he reenlisted as an NCO in the army music corps (*Heeresmusikkorps*), assigned to the Sixth (Prussian) Pioneer Battalion in Minden. Over the next eighteen years, Lewin never perceived any overt prejudice or discrimination in the German military; even the events of 1933 failed to diminish his faith in Germany or his "great affection for the soldierly profession."[112] As the Reichswehr expelled other "non-Aryans" from its ranks, Lewin continued to aspire to a career as a soldier. He received encouraging signs in October 1934, when he was promoted to *Feldwebel* (staff sergeant) and selected to train a new detachment of troops at the garrison in Höxter.[113]

In general, the expulsion of Jews did not generate much attention in the German military. Although there were ongoing and often passionate debates in the armed forces about the continuing validity of national sacrifice, privileges of status, and the importance of recognizing wartime merits, the efforts of some officers to symbolically preserve the honor of expelled Jewish soldiers must be viewed against the backdrop of the Reichswehr's unbridled enthusiasm for the new order.[114] For most officers, comradeship with Jewish soldiers was an abstraction; it did not arouse any controversy outside of those units where Jews had been present. To be sure, officers like Walther von Reichenau, who embraced National Socialism and its racist worldview without reservation, openly and privately endorsing its antisemitic policies, were the exception. But there was a discernible tendency in the officer corps to understand the expulsion of Jews as unfortunate yet justifiable on the basis of the army's future prospects in Hitler's Reich. Blomberg and Manstein were representative of their caste and profession. Despite initial reservations about the fate of their comrades, they were not opposed in principle to the broad outlines of Nazi antisemitic policy and quickly aligned themselves with the regime. They ultimately accepted the Aryan Paragraph and its consequences. The "affront to the army's honor" did little to dampen their enthusiasm for the new government in the long term, as time and circumstances would later prove them quite willing to overlook the less pleasant aspects of Hitler's program.

The murders of two army officers by the SS on 30 June 1934 provide a useful corollary to the eviction of Jews from the military and veterans' community.[115] The shooting of former chancellor Kurt von Schleicher and retired general Ferdinand von Bredow forced the officers' corps to confront a serious moral dilemma. But when Blomberg invoked the bonds of comradeship as a means to rally the army, he did not mean solidarity with the murdered officers. To the contrary, he urged the army to turn inward, to find solace from within. "Comradeship" allowed the officers' corps to assuage the moral burden of complicity and turn a blind eye to the crimes committed by the regime. Group solidarity was absolute. It did not concern itself with individual fates or moral dilemmas on which the basic principles of "soldierly honor" rested.[116] The symbolic gestures of support and pledges to rehabilitate the honor of the murdered officers merely concealed the indifference toward anything that did not benefit the greater community. Outrage over the crime quickly abated, because in the end the army knew it would be the ultimate beneficiary of the new regime.[117] Like Schleicher and Bredow, Jewish comrades were a compromise, a moral concession that the Reichswehr had willingly made in return for its place as the "second pillar" of the new Reich.

Mixed Messages: Life in the Third Reich, 1933–35

Until the passage of the Nuremberg Laws in late 1935, the majority of Jewish war veterans escaped the same economic strangulation and social isolation as other Jews, who were thrown out of their professions and subsequently faced with impoverishment. Even as the overall situation grew progressively worse with constant defamations, local boycotts, and the threat of looming "aryanization," most Jewish veterans adjusted to their changed circumstances, falling back on traditional sources of stability such as family, religion, business, and community life.[118] The veterans' clause provided many Jewish ex-servicemen with a seemingly "tolerable situation," preserving a degree of financial sustenance and secure employment prospects, which led many to postpone their plans to leave Germany.[119] Their decision to remain in Germany was contingent on the belief that the lifespan of the Nazi regime would be brief, or that Hitler would eventually be forced to scale back his antisemitic agenda. While Zionists were quick to recognize the futility of assimilation and began organizing mass emigration, most Jewish veterans in the assimilated camp continued to contemplate the possibility of reconciling themselves with the new regime.

That the veterans' exemptions were a ruse, a tactical maneuver by Hitler, is obvious only in hindsight. What was important at the time was that these laws were backed by stronger forces, not only Hindenburg but also senior ranking officials in the armed forces, the judiciary, and the government. "The repeated assurances from the highest leadership that Jewish ex-servicemen would retain their offices 'with full honors' was widely believed," Karl Löwith wrote. His situation, and that of the other "protected" faculty at the University of Marburg, "seemed legally secure at the time, and [we] continued our lectures without experiencing students causing trouble as they had elsewhere."[120]

A far more pressing issue, though, is how Jewish war veterans perceived and experienced persecution in everyday life after 1933. Despite violence in the streets and the growing virulence of antisemitic propaganda, diaries and memoirs suggest that relations between Jewish veterans and Aryan Germans were not marked by radical change.[121] In Krefeld, despite living next door to an *Obersturmbannführer* of the SS, Ilse Strauss reported that the man displayed a grudging respect for her father's status as a World War I veteran. "My father had taken to wearing his war ribbons in his buttonhole and Heggers took good note of it, keeping well away from Papa," she wrote. "We lived in peace there."[122] And while Alfred Schwerin described the tangible impact of antisemitic persecution on his family and personal relationships, veterans' status ensured that crucial social networks remained intact for the time being. His leather retail business prospered, and until 1937, Schwerin "never once contemplated the problem" of having to leave Germany. He retained his old business contacts and maintained good relations with local officials, who respected him as a former soldier and saw him "as an innocent victim of arbitrary justice."[123] Schwerin also kept a sizeable circle of Aryan acquaintances, including some "National Socialists who were in no way antisemitic . . . and never hesitated to greet and speak with me in public."[124]

Jewish veterans initially saw encouraging signs in continued economic existence and Germans' pronouncements of sympathy. Many salaried employees initially retained their jobs, as veterans could still turn to the courts to compel their employers to comply with statutes protecting ex-servicemen. In the traditional Nazi stronghold of Cottbus, for example, a Jewish man identified in court documents only as Krebs sued the owner of a shoe store after being "unjustly" fired. The judges ordered the store owner to reinstate Krebs, declaring that "as a veteran, the defendant has proven himself in such a way that customers in this city, who normally would not have anything to do with Jews, never fail to show their personal respect." Krebs's presence, the court ruled, "would not bother anybody."[125] Some Jewish shop owners even saw their businesses thrive in the first years after the seizure of power. For Stephan Kunreuther, antisemitic violence had a marginal impact on his day-to-day interactions. Kunreuther lived in Fürth, a town bordering Nuremberg, and witnessed firsthand how one of his business partners, a Jew and an SPD member, was placed into "protective custody" after 30 January, subsequently losing all his Aryan friends and clientele as a result. But, Kunreauther wrote, after the 1 April boycott, "we were not bothered any further, and continued to run our store with good success, despite the bad times."[126] Things were "going well" into 1938, for "to this day, the Nazis hadn't bothered me or my business." Kunreuther remained on edge, however. "A change will come," he wrote. "But when?"[127]

It would be a mistake to imagine that the privileged Frontkämpfer were oblivious to the Nazi threat, or immune from the violence and intimidation that descended on Germany after 30 January. As time went on, Jewish expressions of determination and resilience were increasingly accompanied by a heightened sense of anxiety. Contemporary writings leave little doubt that the threat of state-sanctioned terror, denunciation, arbitrary violence, and impending financial ruin threatened Jews' sense of security and belonging in Germany. Victor Klemperer, who presented himself publicly as a resolute German patriot, confided uncertainty in his diary. He retained his professorship as a result of his service record, yet sensed the exemption provided but a temporary reprieve from what was to come. "That awful feeling of thank God I'm alive," he wrote on 10 April. "The new Civil Service 'law' leaves me, as a frontline veteran, in my post—at least for the time being. But all around rabble-rousing, misery, fear, and trembling."[128]

The privileging of military service also failed to conceal the incessant antisemitic incitement that radically transformed public space after the Nazis came to power. Vandalism against Jewish shops and houses of worship, and columns of Hitler Youth marching through the streets chanting antisemitic slogans, became a regular feature of public life under Hitler, one that no Jew could evade. Antisemitism confronted Jews at work, at home, while walking down the street or shopping, in restaurants and cafés, even on weekend getaways. "It seemed that as a Frontkämpfer, I was protected according to the letter of the law," wrote Alfred Oppler. "But there were other dangers that still threatened. . . . It was no longer possible to forget which demon and which criminal attitude threatened to destroy our Fatherland, this land of poets and thinkers."[129] Hardly a diary or memoir fails to mention the indignation caused by groups of SA men or Hitler Youth singing, "When Jewish

blood spurts from the knife, then things are going well again" (Wenn's Juden-
blut vom Messer spritzt, dann gehts nochmal so gut).[130] If the psychological
toll these provocations inflicted was downplayed in veterans' writings, it was
described vividly by the family members of ex-servicemen, such as Annemarie Wolfram: "This song was incessantly sung at gatherings and marching
formations. Even the school children were infected by it. One cannot begin
to imagine what effect this song had on those who, despite being Jews, had
the honor of losing an arm or a leg or even their sight for the Fatherland.
I remember many such shameful occasions, when severely wounded Jewish Frontkämpfer, war cripples, were forced to endure this song as a great
mockery."[131]

Perhaps the most disturbing aspect of the Nazi takeover was the almost
complete inaction of the police in the face of growing violence from party
thugs. The Decree for the Protection of Volk and State of 28 February 1933
permitted the SA and SS to arrest Jews on the basis of Schutzhaft (protective custody), even for the most trivial of offenses. In many small towns and
rural communities, especially in traditional bastions of the Nazi Party such
as Franconia and West Prussia, even veterans were left reeling by the experience of suddenly finding themselves without protection.[132] Writing from
his hospital bed following a severe altercation with the Nazi stormtroopers,
Julius Meyer, was shaken by the "terrifying" revelation that "one could no
longer expect to receive help." Meyer, who had endured three years in the
trenches of Flanders, realized that fighting back was pointless. Any form of
self-defense," he wrote, "however futile, would allow them to accuse me of
being the attacker."[133] Erich Leyens, who had courageously stood up to the
SA during the April Boycott, equated the mounting Nazi threat with the
sense of powerlessness he had experienced at the front lines, under enemy
fire: the "feeling of paralysis, to be delivered helplessly before random and
all-powerful acts of violence. It was just like back then: [shells] were impact-
ing everywhere."[134] Despite Jewish veterans' protections from antisemitic
legislation, their writings make clear that a crisis mentality permeated their
day-to-day lives after 1933, as they found themselves under constant threat of
physical violence and denunciation, and increasingly cut off from their pos-
sessions and personal freedoms. It was an atmosphere saturated with anxiety,
where, Fritz Goldberg wrote, "We became startled by every loud step, by
every ring of the doorbell."[135]

Even as Jewish ex-servicemen suffered boycotts, threats, and indignation,
they did not conflate these actions with the existence of a pervasive antisemitism in Germany. Anti-Jewish violence was overwhelmingly attributed to
"party thugs," not everyday Germans, and Ernst Marcus voiced a sentiment

common in Jewish veterans' writings when he asserted, "These scoundrels [the Nazis] are not the German people."[136] Many former soldiers were apparently unwilling to believe that expulsion from the German military or the Kyffhäuser League signified the public's endorsement of the regime's policies, consoling themselves that these measures came in response to Nazi coercion. They expressed this conviction repeatedly in letters and diaries, and Victor Klemperer was not alone in doubting the Nazis' ability to mobilize German public opinion on the basis of Jew hatred. "I cannot understand why the Nazis have made this point of their program [the Jewish Question] so central," he wrote in April 1933. "It will sink them."[137]

In hindsight, Klemperer's comments may seem irrational. It should be remembered, however, that the NSDAP itself had raised doubts about Germans' commitment to Hitler's antisemitic agenda. The public's overall lack of interest in and enthusiasm for antisemitic propaganda and other forms of incitement against Jews was a constant source of frustration for Nazi authorities, and if the secret morale reports collected by the Gestapo are to be believed, at no point between 1933 and 1945 did German public opinion reflect the goals and tactics of the regime.[138] But this tendency should in no way distract from the growing popularity of Hitler's government. Over time most Germans tolerated, if not accepted, the exclusion of the Jews.[139] Nor should it obscure the fact that at a minimum, a low level of antisemitism was an essential precondition for the regime's anti-Jewish campaign, for it allowed many Germans to overlook some of the more unsavory aspects of Nazism, while others—despite sympathy for individual Jews—took comfort in the knowledge that Hitler was combatting excessive "Jewish influence."

Nevertheless, if Germans applauded the regime's campaign against "international Jewry," then public attitudes were different toward Jews who had fought for Germany in the Great War. In the weeks and months after 1933, wartime comradeship proved to be a stronger bond than party loyalty, as many Germans did not see a contradiction in standing up for Jewish former comrades while simultaneously professing support for Hitler. After Max Strauss was dismissed from his job in June 1933, a comrade from the war reached out to console him. "Throughout our 25 years of friendship, I have known you to be a German man, one who performed his duty and did his part as a frontline solder," he wrote. "At the end of the day, the elimination of the Jews from German life is first and foremost intended to render these foreign parasites from the East and the folks at the Kurfürstendamm harmless. Chin up! For I am fully convinced that objective-minded people respect in you the frontline soldier . . . and therefore acknowledge your rights."[140] In Berlin, when local authorities accused a Jewish lawyer of being a Communist sympathizer, one of his former comrades, a Nazi Party member, intervened. "I would be a scoundrel if I were to leave him in the lurch now," he asserted in an official statement. "Despite our racial differences, I consider him a decent, irreproachable chap, one who should not be held responsible for the transgressions of his evil-minded contemporaries. For my old war comrade, I must take up the cudgels."[141]

Such acts of solidarity did not escape the attention of the Gestapo. In June 1935, its Potsdam office disapprovingly noted, "It is outright alarming and deeply deplorable that Jews are receiving recommendation letters from high-ranking members of the Wehrmacht," leading the official to conclude that there was an "insufficient understanding of the Jewish Question in Wehrmacht circles."[142] Another report from Hildesheim complained that "despite repeated public condemnations, a certain retired Lieutenant Colonel Niemann explicitly continues to maintain his connections to Jews," an attitude the Gestapo official deemed "typical" of some conservative segments of the population.[143] So if most Germans accepted the Nazis' argument that Jews were a foreign body inherently hostile to the National Socialist order, public opinion reflected the opposite trend in the case of Jewish Frontkämpfer: they were generally seen as having demonstrated their national reliability or, as Karl Löwith put it, "confirmed their Germanness."[144] This inconsistency in experience, or "mixed signals," to use Marion Kaplan's term, led veterans to constantly reevaluate their future prospects in Nazi Germany.[145] It fed Jewish hopes that they could outlast the Nazi regime, or that Hitler's antisemitism could be kept at bay by German public opinion and conservative forces in the government. Although Ernst Bloch, a highly decorated former lieutenant, admitted to a comrade that "the future for us looks darker than ever," he was not intimidated by what lay ahead: "My position toward Germany in these past months is clearer, purer, more determined, and more dedicated than ever. If I cannot let go of the dishonor that has been inflicted on us, I think of the time when we carried the German flag through Romania on horseback. Those years of struggle for Germany have given my life the direction I've always followed. And so, I hope my heart will be strong enough to stay the course and overcome the struggle, hardship, and humiliation."[146]

Perhaps at no other time during the Third Reich were these inconsistencies as evident as in July 1934, when Hindenburg announced the issuing of the so-called Ehrenkreuz des Weltkrieges (Honor Cross of the World War), to mark the twentieth anniversary of World War I. The decoration would be presented to "every German" who had served honorably during the war; in addition, a special class of the award, the Ehrenkreuz für Frontkämpfer, was established exclusively for combat veterans.[147] Eligibility was determined solely by frontline service; no distinctions were made on the basis of religion, race, class, or former military rank.[148] No doubt anticipating objections from Nazi authorities, in March 1935 the War Ministry declared that "a general exclusion of Jews from being awarded the Ehrenkreuz is out of the question."[149] The distribution of the awards commenced in 1934, although in some areas the government was still issuing medals in late 1935.

Not surprisingly, the RjF and CV greeted this news with outpourings of enthusiasm, reminding their constituents that "it is the duty of each and every Jew who served at the front" to apply for and wear the medal publicly and "proudly."[150] Jewish private correspondence, too, reveals that this "important medal" awakened old feelings of pride and esprit de corps, fueling hopes that conservative forces would put a brake on Nazi radicalism. One has to look no further than the diaries of the Zionist Willy Cohn for evidence that this enthusiasm extended beyond the ranks of assimilated Jewry:

> Then went to the police to receive the Honor Cross for Frontkämpfer; one had to sign that you had gotten your passport back. Then the chief of police gave a short speech, in which he pointed out that we should wear the medal with honor; he was conferring it in the name of the Führer and on behalf of the police president. The whole war period came rushing back as well as everything that we had experienced since then. The police chief then handed each one of us the certificate and shook our hands. When names were called one responded with "here!"—just like one used to do it in the military—and then clicked your heels together![151]

Jewish veterans saw the awarding of the medal as an opportunity to remind their Nazi oppressors, as well as everyday Germans, just how significant their sacrifices during World War I had been. The Gestapo office in Kassel reported with undisguised contempt that "through the awarding of the Ehrenkreuz to Jewish frontline veterans, the assimilationists once again felt themselves equal to Aryan citizens."[152] Another report from Potsdam complained that "the Jews are becoming increasingly confident of victory," sarcastically noting that the medal was given to "Jews who allegedly served in battle (apparently it suffices when a Jew is cut off at a supply depot and under siege for a few hours in order to be classified as a 'Frontkämpfer')."[153]

The enthusiasm in Jewish circles was not universal. The irony of being recognized for wartime service amid an overall climate of terror and expropriation was not lost on the Würzburg physician Albert Dreyfuss: "Is it not a mockery to receive an Honor Cross? How can the accompanying certificate begin with 'In the name of the Führer and Reichs Chancellor,' in a time where one berates Jews as shirkers, as cowards, as nationless underlings, and whatever other nice expressions there are?"[154] The contradictions were particularly striking in a letter from the CV's regional office in Pomerania to the police chief in Stettin on 20 March 1935, requesting help in preventing the spread of graffiti on Jewish storefronts. Days earlier, the letter noted, "the slogan 'traitor to the people' was smeared on the Hoffmann furniture store, 31 Breite Street, whose owner had received the medal for frontline veterans [Ehrenkreuz] that very morning."[155] For most Jews, however, the Ehrenkreuz held a greater significance. Amid an atmosphere of growing uncertainty, it was an important marker of acceptance, signaling membership in the larger community of Great War veterans, and a means to discredit Nazi propaganda in the eyes of the German public. It enabled veterans to distance themselves from the Nazi stereotype "Jew," and claim special privileges based on past performance of duty for the fatherland, even as the regime systematically stripped away their rights.

In their private writings, Jewish veterans portray Reich President Hindenburg's death on 2 August 1934 as a watershed in the chronology of persecution. Despite his overall indifference towards the Nazis' campaign of terror against Germany's Jews, Hindenburg remained a larger-than-life figure and a source of confidence among Jewish veterans of World War I. After all, the old field marshal had intervened on their behalf and sorted things out with Hitler, keeping the Nazis' radicalism in check. His presence seemed to provide an abstract psychological reassurance, as Jewish ex-servicemen expressed an almost unshakeable sense of trust in his personal integrity and his power to save them from something far worse.[156] Even retrospective accounts by Jewish refugees written after 1938 seldom question this infallibility. With few exceptions, they depict Hindenburg as a person of "absolute integrity" who in the end became a fellow victim of the regime, a senile old man who had been exploited by Hitler.[157] The depth of these convictions can been seen in the Jewish community's massive public outpouring of grief on 3 August, accompanied by speeches and tributes by Jewish organizations and community leaders. Even the Zionist *Jüdische Rundschau*, which was usually sparing in its praise for high-ranking officers or the nationalist Right in general, described the deceased president as an "honorable figure," declaring that all "Jews of the war generation felt themselves to be citizens and soldiers of Hindenburg."[158] These reactions were not lost on Nazi officials either. Gestapo offices in virtually every region in Germany noted disapprovingly that many Jews displayed the old black, red, and white imperial colors as a sign of tribute.[159]

Hindenburg's death was a "coup d'état," Klemperer wrote, for it meant that the Nazis would be able to seize total power "in silence, drowned out by hymns to the dead Hindenburg."[160] Even though the protections Hindenburg put in place were largely symbolic, to the minds of many Jewish veterans, his passing led to "a perceptible worsening of our situation," the moment when "all inhibitions were now cast aside."[161] It even left Zionists such as Willy Cohn depressed and fearful of what lay ahead, dashing any prospects for further reprieves from Nazi terror. "With him, an era has died," he remarked. "Germany's future will now become even darker."[162]

Tolerance and limited solidarity amid a general atmosphere of repression defined Jewish veterans' *Alltag* (routines of everyday life) between 1933 and 1934. Legal exemptions gave veterans a means to evade becoming targets of anti-Jewish policies and gain a reprieve from persecution, if only a partial or temporary one, as recognition for past service to the fatherland stood in marked contrast to Hitler's racist ambitions. Gestures of solidarity by everyday Germans solidified their belief that Germany would not betray them, even as they struggled under Nazi oppression. It deceived many Jewish veterans into believing they could evade the designation "Jew" and be treated as members of the in-group, or at least as a tolerated, protected minority. Nowhere are these disparities as obvious as in the German military and the veterans' community, where, despite Jewish veterans' expulsion from the Kyffhäuser League, a basic level of mutual recognition among former soldiers remained intact. Yet these bonds would be severely tested as Hitler consolidated his power, and the restraints on unfettered Nazi rule were swept aside.

CHAPTER 4

Jewish Frontkämpfer and the Nazi Volksgemeinschaft

Reich President Hindenburg's death on 2 August 1934 shifted the regime's internal balance of power, effectively ending conservative influence in Hitler's government and removing the last obstacles to totalitarian rule.[1] These developments also brought about an immediate intensification of antisemitic persecution that targeted those Jews who had thus far eluded the regime's exclusionary policies, as the forces that had backed exemptions for Jewish frontline veterans either were swept aside or became fully vested in the Nazi project. Yet accepting persecution was anathema for the Jewish men who had been raised and socialized in the culture of the German military. Amid intensifying repression, Jewish veterans continued to assert themselves publicly, falling back on legal exemptions and vital networks of affiliation in order to evade or lessen the impact of Nazi racial laws. Relations between Jewish ex-servicemen and the German public, which often adhered to older notions of comradeship and status, remained surprisingly stable, albeit with limitations. These findings contradict much of the scholarship on German Jewry under Hitler, which contends that Jews experienced a "social death" by the time of the Nuremberg Laws of 1935 at the latest, and that any illusion of coexistence evaporated under the full weight of the regime's racial policies.[2]

Jewish Frontkämpfer and the Masculine Habitus

Before examining Jewish life in the Germany of the Nuremberg Laws, it is first necessary to look at which coping strategies Jewish veterans developed after 1933, and what persecution and loss of status reveal about their self-image, their behaviors, their habitus. The members of the Jewish front generation were more than just former wartime combatants; this was merely one role and one identity among many that defined them. As previous studies have pointed out, ex-servicemen held a variety of coinciding social identities.[3] Jewish veterans also defined themselves by their regional, social, and religious background, by their professions and education. They were husbands, fathers, sons, and Jewish victims of Nazi oppression. Thus, reducing the Jewish Frontkämpfer to a struggle of honor and status can obscure the range of personal and collective identities they developed and maintained. At the same time, however, their writings during the Nazi period are a testament to the centrality of the First World War in shaping their lives. As they described their struggles under the Nazis, they conveyed the very qualities associated with the ideal soldierly male: resilience, determination, vigilance, self-control, and strong nerves in the face of danger. These were the qualities that had kept them alive in 1914–18, and they are key to understanding how Jewish veterans coped under Hitler's twelve-year Reich.[4] Preserving this distinctive identity both within and outside the Jewish community was central to who they were. Especially after 1933, it took precedence over class, politics, place, and other determinants in their lives, for on a basic level it undergirded veterans' belief in their own agency, without which their attitudes and responses to Nazi persecution cannot be understood.

In the first years after Hitler's seizure of power, many Jewish veterans closely oriented themselves toward this identity. This was especially true for Jewish men who did not conform to the antisemitic image of the Jew—that is, those men whose appearance and mannerisms were deemed more "Aryan" than Jewish, and who could more easily exploit mainstream public narratives on masculinity. Self-assertion gave them a means to challenge the stigma of belonging to the out-group by generating ambivalence among a non-Nazi public that saw the Frontkämpfer, irrespective of race or background, as somebody who was ultimately to be respected.[5] "As a frontline soldier, I am a modern-day Schutzjude [protected Jew]," declared Walter Tausk in July 1933 after observing a group of SA men harass Jewish pedestrians in Breslau. "If these scoundrels come after me, I'll show them my teeth."[6] For Tausk as for other Jewish veterans of World War I, the elevated status of the Frontkämpfer demanded specific concepts of manliness and the promotion of military ideals; it meant a refusal to admit defeat and it meant remaining "full of determination and taking up the hard fight with fate," as Kurt Rosenberg put it. "I know that it will be a hard fight," he wrote, "but, with teeth clenched, I also know that I have a strong will and a healthy spirit on my side."[7] Threatened by loss of status, many felt the need to stand up to Nazi thugs publicly in order to prove their male honor; this was one of the central concerns in their writings during the early Nazi years. In Hamburg, Siegbert Gerechter openly challenged another patron in a café after he brazenly made antisemitic jokes, an incident that nearly ended in a physical altercation. The man eventually backed down, however, after Gerechter identified himself as a combat veteran and made clear that he would not stand for such insults.[8] There were times when physical violence did break out, as was the case in Beuthen in July 1934. A report filed by the police states that Curt Kochmann confronted two local youngsters after they shouted, "Get out of the street, you damn Jews" at several passersby. Kochmann challenged the young men and berated them for their behavior, declaring that he, as "a loyal citizen who had served the country in war and peace," had the right to go about unmolested. As Kochmann turned to leave, one of the youths punched him in the back of the neck, calling out, "As a front soldier, you can still kiss my ass." The police detained the two assailants, yet the outcome of the investigation is unclear.[9] And in Allenstein, East Prussia, an SA adjutant in civilian attire overheard Max Levy make derogatory remarks about Nazi stormtroopers during a local parade. The adjutant confronted Levy and threatened to "put him in his place," whereupon Levy struck the man, knocking him to the ground, and injuring him badly enough to send him to the hospital.[10] It took several SA men to apprehend Levy in his apartment later that day, where he put up a "considerable fight" before being handed over to police.[11]

Self-assertion was first and foremost a protest against the Third Reich's antisemitic policies, yet it was also meant to show the Nazis as well as the German public that, as one Jewish veteran put it, "one could not call us cowards."[12] Their accounts of the early Nazi years suggest that war veterans were not merely concerned about protecting their families and surviving physically, but also strove to preserve their honor, their male self-worth. They say something important about Jewish veterans' embrace of hegemonic, masculine ideals, for by presenting themselves as active and courageous fighters, the writers invoked the exact opposite of the negative traits ascribed to Jews by the Nazis. To be sure, this was a tactic driven by necessity: as the NSDAP accused Jews of being "cowards," "shirkers," and "traitors to the *Volk*," it was necessary to show the German people that these accusations were simply not true. Germans' reaction to the boycott of Jewish stores on 1 April 1933 had made it all too clear just how effective this kind of self-exhibitionism could be, exposing the victims of Nazi terror as former soldiers, men who had risked their lives fighting for Germany. In general, these responses reflected a specific type of masculinity: manliness was demonstrated not by sheer strength, physique, or fighting back physically, but by boldness, risk-taking, and the ability to stand up for oneself.[13] These were attempts to salvage something of lost status and manhood, to protect an identity that was under threat. The significance of acting despite the inherent danger to self underscores the correlation between action and a strong masculine identity.[14] Masculinity was linked to action, initiative, and decisiveness, while femininity was associated with passivity, a division that differentiated the Frontkämpfer from the rest of the supposedly passive Jewish population. At least this is what the Jewish veterans' writings suggest. By calling attention to their courage and willingness to act, Jewish veterans left no doubt that they had a grasp on the situation and remained in control of their destinies. These behaviors were a function of their values and the internalization of status. They were the consequence of the veterans' past encounters with antisemitism and the responses and feedback from German society.

One of the means by which Jewish veterans coped under the degradations inflicted by the Nazis was to denigrate the manliness of the SA and SS. The fact that members of Hitler's "elite" had been too young to ever "hear the whistle of a bullet,"[15] that they "were still wearing their diapers" while the Jewish Frontkämpfer had been in the trenches,[16] was used to destroy their credibility as soldiers and men. These "brutes" and "bullies,"[17] these "heroes in SS uniform,"[18] may have appropriated the outer vestiges of the German military, but their behavior and indecency exposed them as frauds, weaker men who resorted to arrogance and brutality in order to compensate for their lack of masculine gravitas. Although Robert Connell argues that masculinities were foremost a means to guarantee "the dominant position of men and the subordination of women," these examples remind us that homosocial relationships were crucial in the practice of male gender identities.[19] Presenting the Nazis as a male underclass allowed Jewish veterans to reestablish a sense of superiority over their oppressors and preserve a positive image of themselves under increasingly adverse conditions.

Jewish veterans' early successes combating antisemitism reinforced the idea that military sacrifice remained an important ingroup-outgroup criterion in German society. There was an almost universal tendency among Jewish former soldiers to wear their battlefield decorations in public after 1933, a practice strongly encouraged by the CV and RjF.[20] Jewish private writings, too, attest to the practice of "peddling one's wartime accomplishments,"[21] calling it a "widespread phenomenon" among victims of the Nazi regime, both Jewish and Christian.[22] War medals on a Jewish man had a particular poignancy: they were proof of bravery, an assertion of equal status and manly self-respect. "The brazen promotion of wartime military service was the only thing that proved successful in many cases," wrote Alfred Schwerin, "because it still generated a certain degree of respect among the ordinary German, and because most of the time the simple, less-indoctrinated party member did not know how to respond to this."[23] It was an attempt to project a specific identity, a kind of self-exhibitionism that often saved Jews from arbitrary arrests, detention, or protective custody, when sympathetic policemen and local officials "recognized (us) as comrades."[24]

What these examples suggest is that veterans were able to exploit public space as a shield, for until Kristallnacht the open abuse of individuals decorated for "bravery before the enemy" was a boundary the Nazis were reluctant to cross. The persecution of former soldiers in public evoked deep anxieties about the meaning and worth of "the fatherland's thanks" and soldiers' sacrificial losses. This was to be expected in a society where military values were cultivated and promoted, and where the armed forces and former combatants of the Great War were accorded a high level of social prestige. The Frontkämpfer was an object of veneration during the Third Reich. His "national reliability" was taken for granted, attested to by Nazi discourses about military heroism and the generation of frontline soldiers who had sacrificed life and limb for the fatherland.[25] Jews were able to tap into the militaristic rhetoric of the regime by creating ambivalence among a non-Nazi public that saw the frontline veteran as somebody who had "proven his Germanness."

The Holocaust makes such symbolic assertions of identity seem naive and misguided, and some would argue that the conditions faced by Jews in Nazi Germany became so dire that considerations of manliness or honor were relegated to insignificance. Like other Jewish victims, veterans' fundamental concern was to survive physically, to protect their families, property, and professions. But they also fought to preserve an identity—and to this belongs their masculine self-worth, which was increasingly put to the test by Nazi persecution. After all, this is precisely what the RjF had been encouraging its members to do since 1933: "to fight as upright men for our right to live in the Fatherland . . . [to demonstrate] heroism, not only on the battlefield, but everywhere."[26] Ironically, Jewish veterans' embrace of the dominant martial values at the time had no impact on the dominant antisemitic stereotype; to the contrary, the veterans even reinforced it. As they fought their disempowerment and humiliation by reminding themselves and their oppressors of their status as war heroes, they disassociated themselves from "unmanly," nonmilitary Jews. In doing so, they confirmed, unconsciously and most likely inadvertently, Nazi stereotypes about Jewish men's alleged effeminacy and disloyalty to the fatherland. When a resident of Euskirchen complained to the NSDAP district office in January 1935 that local party activists had pasted an antisemitic placard to the shopwindow of a Jewish former soldier, something "out of line for a man who gave three years of his life for the German Fatherland," the district leader (*Kreisleiter*) responded by publishing the complainant's letter in the local newspaper as a warning to "those circles who maintain the view that there are still decent Jews."[27] In the accompanying op-ed letter, the district leader conceded that some Jews had indeed fought bravely during the war, and that "the National Socialist state granted Jewish front soldiers special privileges, which do justice to their services at the front." Yet it was precisely this—the high status accorded to the allegedly few Jewish frontline soldiers—that only confirmed Jews' selfishness, greed, and indifference to Germany. "On reflection," he continued, "it can be said that [the term] 'even decent Jews' is grounded in the unspoken assumption that the majority of the Jews are indecent Jews. If a Jew was indeed a brave front soldier, then this is particularly worthy of recognition because most of his racial comrades [*Rassegenossen*] saw the bloodshed of the World War as a particularly favorable business opportunity and pursued it with the most unscrupulous skill."[28] These contradictions, that the supposedly small number of Jews who'd fought in the trenches in World War I exposed the indecency of the vast majority, were stressed, repeated, and rephrased by Nazi Party activists throughout the Third Reich.[29] Thus by drawing attention to their status and masculinity, and benefiting from its privileges, Jewish veterans played a mutually constitutive role in promoting and reinforcing the masculine norms valued by German society under Hitler. Unintentionally and probably unwittingly, their behaviors had the effect of denigrating the masculinity of nonveteran Jews, thereby reinforcing their subordinate position and condemning them to effeminacy, at least rhetorically.

Although for some Jews the logical means to respond to Nazi oppression was by embodying the hegemonic masculine ideal, not all former soldiers conformed to this image, or they were unable to translate it into action. Victor Klemperer, a convert to Christianity who was persecuted as a Jew by the Nazis, had served in an artillery unit during the war. He had shunned the "hurrah patriotism" of the veterans' associations during the Weimar years, and expressed little interest in attending annual regimental reunions, but he remained proud of his military service, declaring in 1938 that "my rebelliousness and free spirit always combined with a healthy Prussian militarism. My love for the army . . . stayed with me until 1933, even longer actually, as

I had long hoped that salvation would come from the army."[30] He retained his job as a university professor in Dresden until December 1935, thanks to his service during the First World War. Even after his expulsion, Klemperer continued to receive sympathetic treatment from Aryan Germans once they learned they were dealing with a veteran of the war, from the "friendly, obliging senior official" at the pensions office[31] to the "paternal" foreman at the cardboard box factory where he was required to perform forced labor in 1944.[32] Recognition by gentiles was a central element of Klemperer's masculine identity. Even though he did not embrace all aspects of the hegemonic ideal, he clearly reaped some of the dividends this status offered.

The diary of Walter Tausk, a salesman in Breslau, is particularly revealing in this regard. His writings describe an atmosphere of intensifying fear and uncertainty after the Nazi takeover, as the Jewish population was subjected to an outpouring of harassment, humiliation, and physical abuse by members of the Hitler Youth and SA. Yet Tausk related these events as a detached onlooker; the torment and injustices he described were inflicted on others. As Jews in Breslau faced daily harassment in the streets and were forced out of their professions, Tausk noted with a certain degree of pride that he'd been awarded the Ehrenkreuz in recognition of his service in the First World War. He further took comfort in knowing that his Aryan clientele had remained loyal; his customers continued to address him with the informal "du," while fellow war veterans still called him "Kamerad."[33] During the first year of the Third Reich, Tausk seemed confident that he would not share the fate of the other Jews, claiming he would show Nazi thugs his teeth if they were to "come after" him.[34] In doing so, he invoked the quintessential traits of the soldierly male: determination, vigilance, self-control, and calm nerves in the face of fear-inducing, dangerous situations. He presented himself as an active, rational actor, someone in control of his mental faculties, whose status and temperament gave him the means to avoid the fate of other Jews, who were victimized by the Nazis with seeming impunity. Yet despite his professed willingness to fight back against his tormentors, Tausk never followed through on these claims. He rationalized his inaction in his diary, seemingly consoling himself that "one has to keep his mouth shut—otherwise one will end up in the concentration camp Breslau-Dürrgoy."[35] His sole act of defiance during the Nazi years was to hang an old Prussian flag from his apartment window in order to show the Nazis that "I was a Prussian, had been a wartime participant at the front and don't let others dictate my beliefs."[36] Thus we see a fundamental incongruence between the masculine qualities the writer articulated and his unwillingness—or inability—to put this rhetoric into action.

In theory if not in practice, veterans' status provided some space for Tausk to benefit from his record of frontline military service during World War I. Yet multiple tensions and contradictions surface in Tausk's writings, as he struggled to reconcile his self-image as a former soldier with the fact that he had been rendered powerless by Nazi persecution. By 1936, after his customers had abandoned him and his financial situation unraveled, he recorded periods of prolonged inactivity that resulted in serious bouts of depression. He was deprived of his ability to work—a core element of masculinity—and the Nazis gradually stripped him of his status and success in the community. Increasingly confined to his apartment, Tausk felt himself sliding into a state of nervous exhaustion. His diary became a kind of private confessional as he described a downhill struggle with anxiety and extended periods of inactivity, a situation that left his nerves and self-confidence "totally shot."[37] Time and again, he emerged shocked and demoralized as he was pushed to the margins of mainstream German life and increasingly exposed to the effects of Nazi persecution. The torment inflicted by the Nazis was temporarily assuaged by his reassuring himself that he had been through "far worse during the war," or by occasional interactions with Aryan "comrades," but by 1938, even they had abandoned him. By then, his diary suggests, he had been diminished by passivity, his nerves "fraying,"[38] "at the end,"[39] "broken,"[40] and so forth, a situation made worse by Tausk's awareness that he had failed to live up to the standards of militarized masculinity he had so cherished.

Taken together, the writings of Klemperer and Tausk reveal that the gradual, incremental persecution of Jews in the early Third Reich forced Jewish men into inaction, conflicting with their previous identities as active, respected members of German society. They further show that the concept of a hegemonic identity is complicated by an individual's private writings, which brought numerous tensions such as fear, self-doubt, and uncertainty to the surface, qualities that are in conflict with the masculinized soldierly identity these men gravitated toward. Crucially, however, even though such men fell short of this ideal, they did not reject it, and they thereby benefited from its hegemony.

The Meaning of Military Service in the Context of the Nazis' Exclusionary Policy

The privileging of Jewish military service posed a serious problem for the Nazis, for it threatened to undermine the most basic principles of Nazi antisemitic propaganda. The prestige accorded to the Frontkämpfer of the Great War enabled Jewish war veterans to maintain contacts with Aryan Germans and preserve networks of affiliation that had been closed to other Jews. This loophole had to be eliminated. In order to complete the total isolation of Jews from German society, the Nazis had to change popular perceptions of "decent" Jews and make all Jews the same in the eyes of the German public.

Two key pieces of legislation enacted in 1935 fundamentally changed the status of the Jews in Nazi Germany: the Military Service Law of May 1935 (Wehrgesetz) and the so-called Nuremberg Laws (September 1935). On a fundamental level, these laws were designed to strip Jews of their basic rights as German citizens, to define them as a separate and foreign body distinct from the Nazi Volksgemeinschaft, and to pressure them to leave Germany. Yet these measures should not detract from one of the Nazis' far more ambitious goals: to subvert traditional discourses on military service and citizenship, and establish race as the central category of German national identity. The Nazis recognized the discursive power of military wartime sacrifice and were all too aware that most Germans regarded active participation in war as a legitimate claim for belonging to the nation. In order to change these perceptions—and change how Germans talked about race and belonging— the Nazis had to erase the distinctions between veterans and "ordinary" Jews. The goal was to reduce the Jewish Frontkämpfer to the status of nonentities, to make them "invisible" to the rest of the German population.[41]

Although the Nuremberg Laws are generally seen as the decisive turning point in the legal status of the Jews in Nazi Germany, it was the Military Service Law of May 1935 that marked the first comprehensive step in depriving them of one of their most basic rights as German citizens: military service. This landmark legislation not only reinstated universal conscription in Germany but officially established "Aryan descent" as a prerequisite for becoming a soldier in the German armed forces.[42] The law thereby invalidated the link between military service and belonging to the nation, and with it the pathway for Jews to claim the rights of citizenship and inclusion in the national community. Amid calls for all "German men" to dedicate themselves to the national revival, exclusion from the military left the younger generation of Jews visibly and permanently ostracized.

The ruling was also an affront to the Jewish men who had served in World War I. The RjF and CV had tirelessly petitioned military and senior government officials for the inclusion of "non-Aryans" in the draft.[43] Exclusion from the military had a symbolic and psychological impact on the Jewish veterans' community, especially among former officers, some of whom had aspirations to serve in the new Wehrmacht.[44] Many letters and diaries equated exclusion from the draft with loss of status and "inalienable rights," and regarded it as a sign that further accommodation in Hitler's Germany would be impossible.[45] "The battle to strip away the veterans' protections goes on," Kurt Rosenberg recorded on 30 April 1935. "One debates exactly what the loss of citizenship rights means for Jews—merely loss of active and inactive voting rights, of becoming a soldier—or are more legal deprivations on the way?"[46] The Gestapo recorded similar concerns in its internal morale reports, such as the one filed in Munich on 21 June 1935, which described "frantic activity" among "German-Jewish assimilated organizations" owing to the new conscription law, which Jews hoped would have allowed them to "reconnect with their German identity."[47] Another report noted that many Jews had hoped inclusion in the military would have provided a "partial solution to the Jewish Problem,"[48] believing it could have strengthened claims for "special privileges . . . citizenship rights in the future . . . and freedom from the unfolding Ghetto."[49]

Historians have often portrayed the passage of the Nuremberg Laws as a watershed, an endpoint that signified the expiration of the veterans' clause.[50] But the privileging of Jewish military service did not suddenly end in November 1935. The laws, specifically the Reich Citizenship Law (Reichsbürgergesetz), fundamentally redefined civil law in Germany, for they granted only "citizens with German blood" full political rights, while Jews were officially classified as "subjects of the state." They also rescinded most of the legal protections for Jewish frontline veterans that had been codified in the Civil Service Law of 7 April 1933. Yet the first supplementary decree to the Reich Citizenship Law stipulated that "frontline veterans will continue to receive their current salary as a pension until they reach retirement age."[51] In theory, this meant that all Jews previously exempted under the veterans' provision of the Civil Service Law would receive full pay until they retired, at which point they would be eligible for their regular pensions. To be sure, the actual dispensation of pension payments was not in accordance with the letter of the law, and the payments were systematically reduced over the course of the Third Reich.[52] Nevertheless, the amendment ensured that the forcibly "retired" Jewish civil servants were not faced with immediate financial destitution. Second, the legal and medical professions were not affected by the new Reich Citizenship Law. Jewish physicians and attorneys in private practice had already lost much of their Aryan clientele since 1933, but it was not until fall 1938 that their law licenses were officially revoked.[53] Thus for many Jewish veterans such as Hermann Pineas, a neurologist living in Berlin, the "only immediate repercussion" of the Nuremberg Laws was having to dismiss his Aryan maid.[54]

The third and perhaps most important exception to the Nuremberg Laws was the protections for Jewish war invalids (*Schwerkriegsbeschädigte*). These men, technically classified as former soldiers with over 50 percent disability, were entitled to the same welfare benefits as Aryan "war victims," a status that persisted, if in name only, for the duration of the Third Reich.[55] Legislation passed during the Weimar Republic had established hiring quotas for larger businesses and government institutions, and made it illegal for veterans to be fired without the welfare office's consent.[56] The laws remained in effect after 1933, and were supplemented by additional legal protections in July 1934, as Hitler made good on his promise to elevate the disabled "heroes" of World War I to the status of "Honorary Citizens of the Nation."[57] The government overhauled the state's welfare assistance program for veterans, war widows, and their families by increasing monthly disability payments and introducing a new "frontline soldiers' supplement" (Frontzulage), which entitled all war-wounded veterans to an additional sixty-reichsmark annual disability payment.[58] Thus as Jews in Nazi Germany were categorically stripped of welfare benefits, Jewish war invalids still had access to state medical care,[59] public transportation,[60] and tobacco ration cards,[61] and were exempt from legislation requiring Jews to surrender their drivers' licenses.[62] As late as 1942, when food rations for Jews were drastically reduced, Jewish war invalids were exempted from this measure and entitled to the same allotments as the Aryan population.[63]

In some cases Jewish war invalids were dismissed from their jobs for being Jews, only to have their dismissal overturned on the account that they were protected under the War Victim's Law.[64] Oftentimes, the Nazis pressured private firms to fire their remaining Jewish employees, only for the case to be taken up by the local veterans' welfare office (Hauptfürsorgestelle für Kriegsbeschädigte), which was mandated by law to ensure that every war-disabled veteran had access to work in Hitler's Germany. As late as 1941, the head of the Stuttgart War Victims' Welfare Office tried to negotiate an agreement with a local business owner in order to prevent the dismissal of Siegfried Horn, a war-crippled Jewish veteran.[65] In the end, "local conditions" prevented Horn from keeping his job in Stuttgart, but the welfare office succeeded in relocating him to Berlin, where he was placed with a new firm.[66]

With Hitler in full control of the government and its institutions, why were restraints still being placed on Nazi Germany's anti-Jewish program? What prevented the government from effecting the complete isolation of Jewish veterans from German society? From the perspective of antisemitic hardliners, "the Jews" were to be defined as a homogeneous group that became the object of higher-level Nazi decision-making, yet many officials still hesitated when applying these criteria to former soldiers of the First World War. Jewish veterans were aided by senior government ministers who sympathized with their appeals for special concessions, as well as by mid-level bureaucrats, public servants, and local law enforcement, who agreed to listen to complaints and grievances, and by the general public, who continued to express solidarity with veterans in day-to-day encounters. Leo Löwenstein, the RjF chairman, credited the continuance of pensions for the Jewish war wounded to the "sympathetic attitude" of senior military officers,[67] while a number of CV officials similarly praised the "extraordinary efforts" of state and local welfare offices.[68]

Official government documents shed light on the tortuous and convoluted bureaucratic path that such interventions often took. A supplementary decree to the Reich Citizenship Law, passed on 21 December 1935, mandated that all remaining state-employed Jewish teachers, physicians, lawyers, and notaries be "retired," a move that threatened six hundred Jewish notaries, almost exclusively frontline veterans. Unlike civil servants, notaries' income depended on private clientele, and so they were not eligible for fixed government pensions as were former salaried civil servants. Faced with financial ruin, a group of Jewish attorneys led by Julius Fliess and Fritz Arnold, both former officers who had suffered debilitating wounds during World War I, appealed to the War Ministry and the Justice Ministry for help.[69] In a letter to the war minister, Field Marshal Werner von Blomberg, Fliess and Arnold argued that their forced retirement contradicted the will of deceased Reich president Hindenburg, who years earlier had declared that "any professional disadvantages for Frontkämpfer must be avoided,"[70] and that "the army could not simply leave these comrades in the lurch."[71] But if the War Ministry had once been willing to voice its opposition to Nazi racial policy in defense of "soldierly honor," by late 1934 this support had become increasingly passive. Blomberg, who had opposed the expulsion of Jews from the Kyffhäuser League a year earlier, had "no objections" when asked by the Interior Ministry about his position on the rescinding of the veterans' clause in November 1935.[72] Around the same time, he issued an order requiring all members of the armed forces to prove their Aryan ancestry.[73] Blomberg did concede that Jews with severe wounds ought to be spared from antisemitic regulations for the sake of "honor," but such pronouncements of solidarity were increasingly made in passing.[74] Even more surprising, perhaps, is that when the Labor Ministry, in response to Fliess and Arnold's petition, proposed a compromise that would have kept the six hundred war-wounded Jews in their positions as notaries,[75] it was Blomberg who vetoed the suggestion, remarking that retaining any Jewish public servants was "not desired."[76] Blomberg's unwillingness to support the Jewish former officers was most likely an effort to avoid further accusations of

"Jew friendliness," and a sign that the political winds in Germany had shifted by late 1935.

If the War Ministry was no longer willing to intercede on behalf of its Jewish comrades, Fliess and Arnold found an ally in the ninety-year-old World War I hero and retired field marshal August von Mackensen, who brought the matter up with Hitler on 3 December 1935. Mackensen was undoubtedly sincere when he praised Hitler for his success in combating the "sordid influence of Jewry on the daily life of the nation," yet he urged the Führer to adopt a more lenient approach when it came to comrades, who had suffered severe wounds in battle. If they were going to be forced from their jobs, he insisted, at the very least they deserved "adequate monetary compensation."[77] Fliess and Arnold also had the backing of the Reich Labor Ministry (Reichsarbeitsministerium), the agency responsible for implementing and enforcing Nazi Germany's labor laws as well as caring for the war wounded. Upon receiving Fliess's petition, a Labor Ministry official reminded Blomberg that "Jewish Frontkämpfer are worthy of special considerations." As "the *severely war-disabled* Jewish notaries would be the *first ones* who would become unemployed and destitute," he argued, "such a development would receive little understanding, especially as the law of 13 December 1935 underscores the place of honor accorded to war-wounded frontline veterans."[78] Pressured by Mackensen and the Labor Ministry, the government reinstated the protections for the war-wounded Jewish notaries.

The Reich Labor Ministry, whose intervention was decisive in this case, was headed by Franz Seldte, the former senior chairman of the Stahlhelm. It was Seldte who had attempted to block the Stahlhelm's adoption of the Aryan Paragraph over a decade earlier. In January 1933, he was one of three nonmembers of the Nazi Party to join Hitler's cabinet, becoming minister of labor, a post he held until 1945. Seldte's commitment to the Nazi regime and its racist ideology, as well as his active participation in the persecution and exploitation of the Jews, is beyond dispute. Under his leadership, the Labor Ministry spearheaded the regime's efforts to expropriate Jewish income, savings, and property.[79] It was also instrumental in formulating and implementing the Reich's compulsory labor policy after 1938 and systematically stripped German Jews of their welfare benefits and public relief.[80] Seldte's interventions, however, prevented war-disabled Jews from being forced into impoverishment. As early as September 1933, the Labor Ministry argued that all wounded veterans interned in concentration camps should be entitled to receive emergency allowances.[81] The following month, it urged "sympathetic consideration" for any disabled veteran adversely affected by the Civil Service Law.[82] And when the fifth supplementary decree to the Reich

Citizenship Law revoked all Jewish law licenses on 30 November 1938, the Labor Ministry, backed by Mackensen, secured a provision that allowed a small number of attorneys to apply for reinstatement as "consultants,"[83] a group exclusively comprising "Frontkämpfer, those who had suffered serious wounds."[84]

It was not just officers or conservative nationalists who harbored reservations when it came to persecuting disabled veterans. Party hard-liners such as Rudolf Hess, one of the authors and proponents of the Nuremberg Laws, personally intervened on more than one occasion to demand that the Jewish war wounded remain protected under the War Victims Law.[85] Thus, despite attempts by the Nazi leadership to put their concept of total racial segregation into practice, the exigencies of the situation ran counter to their intentions. Such cases help us understand how the Nazi system of persecution operated: tensions between center and periphery played a crucial role in radicalizing Nazi anti-Jewish policy, but also in preserving certain "privileged" groups, and even establishing new ones. While the Nuremberg Laws provided a catalyst for an escalation of antisemitic persecution, "moderate" forces in the government and the military demanded concessions in the name of soldierly honor, against which the Nazis still lacked a credible rebuttal.

Life in Germany under the Nuremberg Laws

Did Jewish veterans emerge from the period after the Nuremberg Laws with their sense of Germanness intact? At which point did life in the Third Reich become unbearable? Were veterans' coping strategies sufficient to mitigate the effects of Nazi persecution in the long term? To be sure, there were discernible differences in how Jewish veterans reacted to Nazi persecution; experiences varied considerably across different regions, cities, occupations, and age groups, between urban and rural areas, from one village to the other. Their reactions were not, on the whole, a radical break with the values and beliefs of their social milieus. If Zionist and conservative-religious Jews adapted much more easily psychologically to the prospect of emigration, "assimilationists" and converts to Christianity strove to outlast Hitler's regime, reassuring themselves that the majority of Germans rejected the race-based antisemitism of the Nazis.

A commonality in Jewish writings is that by late 1935 the solidarity demonstrated by the German public, expressed openly and sometimes defiantly in the first months after 30 January 1933, had become increasingly passive. For many Aryan Germans, enthusiasm for the new regime eventually outweighed the indignities inflicted on "decent" Jews. They adapted quickly to the demands of the new government, either by rigorously pursuing their own personal and economic interests or by simply staying clear of any potential problems caused by having Jewish friends.[86] At the same time, however, Jewish experiences between 1933 and 1938 were also defined by a noticeable generational split. In 1940 Harvard University collected more than 230 testimonies on "life in Germany before and after January 30th 1933" as part of a project to analyze "the social and psychological effects of National Socialism on German society and on the German people."[87] Most of the authors had fled the Third Reich in the immediate aftermath of Kristallnacht, and so they were not far removed from the events they described, nor did they have any knowledge of the deportations and organized mass murder that were yet to happen. The texts describe, sometimes in harrowing detail, the gradual unraveling of German-Jewish relations up to Kristallnacht and after. Crucially, however, the diversity of the submissions—at least forty were written by former frontline combatants of World War I, and at least eleven by noncombat veterans—makes it possible to analyze how veterans experienced this period, and how these experiences differed from those of the general Jewish population.

A close reading of these texts reveals that Jewish war veterans continued to encounter contradictory messages from both the government and the German people. First there was a discernible tendency on the part of the Nazis to avoid molesting Jewish ex-servicemen in public. Nazi propaganda tirelessly glorified the Frontkämpfer of the First World War. Nazi officials were bound to this discourse, at least under the discerning gaze of the public, and were left without an acceptable way to justify their mistreatment of former military men. So while veterans suffered the loss of social status and the financial hardship that other Jews in Germany did, evidence suggests that Nazi efforts to undermine the public's recognition of Jewish sacrifices during World War I—to make them "invisible" to the general population—were largely unsuccessful. In routine, day-to-day interactions, Jewish Frontkämpfer continued to record positive encounters in public spaces, and it was not unusual, for instance, for Walter Tausk, despite the ratcheting up of antisemitic laws in his home city of Breslau, to take comfort in the fact that customers and business associates had not turned their backs on him, a situation that persisted until 1938.[88] And although an atmosphere of "insurmountable distance" persisted between Jews and other Germans after 1935, Karl Löwith described the ambiguous and often conflicting experience of being "a non-Aryan who was tolerated only because of his war service." Ordinary Germans, he wrote, including certain members of the NSDAP, "behaved with decency and restraint," for they "regretted the personal injustice that had been done to me as an ex-serviceman." Löwith immigrated to Japan in 1938. There, later that year, he encountered a German missionary, a man who was "completely indifferent" to the explosion of public violence against Jews on 9 November 1938: "[Yet] he was sensitive on one point: he protested loudly against the injustice (which he bombastically called 'metaphysical guilt') of these measures in a case like mine, that of an 'ex-serviceman.' The fact that thousands of Jews, whether they had taken part in the war or not, were deprived of any means of income, were robbed of their savings, had their homes demolished and their reputation destroyed, that most of them were in concentration camps to defend their bare existence—all this did not move this Christian missionary in the slightest."[89]

A second distinguishing feature of the Harvard manuscripts is that veterans were far more likely to retain a small circle of Aryan friends than nonmilitary German Jews, especially the generation born after 1900, who were too young to have served in the war. To be sure, comradeship was not immune to social pressures that called for Germans to distance themselves from Jews. In late 1933, Erich Leyens was informed by a longtime friend that their friendship would have to end. "He came to tell me personally that he had decided to join the National Socialist Party," Leyens wrote, "otherwise he would not be able to prevent his own store from being boycotted and ruined as well." Both men had served in the same regiment in World War I, and just a few months earlier, the man had stood at Leyens's side as stormtroopers attempted to boycott his store. Now, "fighting back tears," he informed Leyens they could no longer talk or meet again, nor could they exchange greetings in public.[90] This was the hardest for veterans to bear: not the regime's brutal antisemitic policies, but the collapse of comradeship—the willful and deliberate ending of long-standing relations that had resulted from shared military service. This "betrayal," as Albert Schwerin put it, constituted "among the most shameful things that I experienced during the entire Hitler period."[91]

Yet cases of outright betrayal or "bad" comradeship were the exception, not the rule. Even though Jews had been expelled from most veterans' associations by 1935, many private networks remained intact, especially longstanding friendships that resulted from the war or membership in a local ex-servicemen's association. Personal contacts became increasingly clandestine as time went on, and the files of the Würzburg Gestapo make it clear that meeting old comrades in public was increasingly fraught with risks. In October 1934, the housemaid working at the home of Ernst Schloss, a Jewish former officer, notified the police that uniformed members of the Reichswehr often showed up at the house. The maid surmised that the guests were "wartime comrades" of Schloss and found it "remarkable, from the National

Socialist standpoint, that this Jewish comradeship still exists."[92] One of the officers was identified as Lieutenant Colonel Max Siry, who had served in the same company as Schloss during the war. Both men had been taken prisoner in October 1918 after their position was overrun by the French.[93] When Siry petitioned to reenter the army after the war, he called on Schloss to testify as a character witness before a military evaluation board, which he did.[94] Under questioning by the Gestapo, Siry admitted having had a glass of wine with Schloss because, "as opposed to the other Jews in the regiment, he had earned the respect of his troops" and "is certainly not engaged in espionage." The Gestapo reported the incident to Siry's commanding officer, who ordered him to immediately break off further contact with Jews.[95]

By 1938, almost without exception, relations between Jewish veterans and their Aryan comrades remained "hidden,"[96] were sustained "in secret,"[97] typically "under the cover of night."[98] Hugo Moses received frequent visits from "old wartime comrades and school friends," but "mostly after nightfall."[99] And in Hermann Klugmann's case, the wartime bonds forged between him and several fellow soldiers evolved into a "deep, inner, sincere and lasting friendship . . . that even the upheavals of 1933 could not touch."[100] Two of Klugmann's comrades lived in his hometown, suggesting that an underlying factor in sustaining such informal networks was the German Army's practice of local recruitment.[101] The *Stammtisch* gatherings, private get-togethers, and other informal networks of affiliation that emerged from these encounters had often been merely a consequence of wanting to share stories and reminisce about common wartime experiences, but they also functioned to help comrades in times of hardship.[102] These connections proved to be crucial for Jewish ex-servicemen after 1935. They did more than offer psychological sustenance; they also saved Jews from imprisonment or the violent excesses of Nazi authorities. Otto Lewin's surviving personal papers reveal that his superiors protected him from the Aryan Paragraph until March 1936, when he was finally discharged from the German military. As a result of their efforts, Lewin was not only given a full pension but also awarded the Wehrmacht Long Service Award (Dienstauszeichung der Wehrmacht) in the name of the "Führer and Reichs Chancellor" for his "18 years of loyal service in the Armed Forces."[103] Lewin's expulsion from the army did not abruptly cast him into the social wilderness, however. Minden during the mid-1930s was a garrison town with a sizeable military presence, and Lewin received frequent visits from former comrades and attended regimental reunions and informal get-togethers at the local pub. For the time being, his connections to the military saved him from "social death," and ensured that he and his family were spared the violence that descended on Minden in November 1938.[104]

After the Gestapo arrested Hugo Gutmann in July 1937 for allegedly making "contemptuous, derogatory and untrue comments about the Führer," he spent three months in a Nuremberg jail. In a letter to a former comrade in 1946, he attributed his survival to the prison guards, who, unlike the Gestapo, had treated him well:

> I had the good fortune that a few of the men stationed in the Deutschhaus Barracks had been in my regiment. Particularly decent was a policeman who served as a guard in the prison. He visited me often and told me that as a good Catholic he despised the Nazis. Only under pressure was he here. I received all the food I wanted; he was even courageous enough to go into the Gestapo room at night where my files were kept. Through him I learned that they had nothing tangible against me, I mean no evidence. Furthermore, through him I was able to maintain contact with my wife.[105]

Gutmann was released after being held only for a few days, a development he credited to his former comrades of the List Regiment, several of whom had intervened on his behalf. They included Fritz Wiedemann, Hitler's adjutant at the time, and an unnamed active-duty general.[106] Like many former officers, Gutmann was able to make use of connections to higher-ups in the German government and the military. Comrades and former commanders often saw it as their duty to continue caring for their men by submitting character statements or letters of recommendation that testified to their comrade's "national reliability." A second group who could make use of such connections were Jews who were affiliated with the veterans' movement, especially their local association. As we have seen, regimental associations had been among the most visible areas in German society where Jews were successful in integrating themselves. Before Hitler, they had stood at the center of veterans' social and community life. They were places where comrades met and celebrated, where friendships were formed and rekindled, sometimes for life. Plans were underway in 1933 to "coordinate" these independent, unit-based associations and bring them under the institutional control of the Kyffhäuser League,[107] yet there was vehement resistance to this move, as protests to Hindenburg and the War Ministry were enough to preserve their special status as autonomous leagues until, in some cases, 1938.[108]

As independent organizations, many regimental associations openly resisted calls to expel their Jewish members. A preponderance of anecdotal evidence suggests that Jews' connections to the associations of their old regiments remained surprisingly strong until Kristallnacht. In fall 1935, for example, Klemperer described the predicament of his friend, Julius Sebba, who remained "bitter and bitterly German. . . . As an officer, he had just been to his annual regimental day. He had asked the commander beforehand whether he should *really* come. Reply: *Yes*, unreservedly, welcome from comrades, rank and file and active Reichswehr officers very warm."[109] Adolf Asch was not only reassured by the chairman of his regimental association that it would "stand by its Jewish comrades," but was given a signed letter to keep on his person in the event he got into trouble with Nazi authorities. The document, Asch wrote, was "complete with official insignia, attesting to my military accomplishments and bravery during the war. When I told the chairman that this letter was an exaggeration, he answered that this was merely the nature of things."[110] In Dresden, Friedrich Salzburg remained a member of the officer's association of Foot Artillery Regiment No. 19 until his immigration to Switzerland in 1937. The association defied the order to expel its two Jewish members, arguing that "if the two Jewish gentlemen were good enough to be our comrades at the Somme, Ypres, and Arras, then they are surely good enough to be our comrades now."[111] Such claims are supported by correspondence between General Ludwig Beck, the army chief of staff, and the chairman of a local association in Breslau in October 1937, in which the association chairman asked for clarification on whether or not Jews were still permitted to belong to these organizations. In a vaguely worded reply, Beck expressed reluctance to personally involve himself in the Jewish Question or to issue a formal policy statement. Yet in his "strictly personal opinion," he asserted that "whether or not it is necessary for a Jew to be denied membership in a regimental association can only be determined, I think, by the specific nature of the local and personal relations."[112]

This was indeed the "nature of things," for comradeship's ethical code demanded nothing less. Although the oft-used catchphrases "comradeship" and "Frontgemeinschaft" were frequently mere symbolic attempts to restore the dignity of the victims or preserve the reputation of the associations, there can be no doubt that the Great War constituted a powerful collective experience, one that often transcended racial and political contexts. When veterans invoked "comradeship," they were not merely indulging in rhetoric but referring to a lived reality. In some cases, it proved to be a lifelong asset that saved Jews from being thrust into a parallel existence. A case in point is Arthur Samuel, who received an invitation to attend the reunion of his old unit.[113] When he didn't respond to the letter, two members of the association showed up at his home, unannounced, having "traveled from Düsseldorf to Bonn to invite me to take part in the festivities that all comrades, those who were still alive, had pledged to attend." The incident is remarkable only because it was 1938. "Given the present climate," Samuel turned down the invitation. "I knew that if I gave in to the urgings of these gentlemen," he wrote, "something like this could lead to unpleasant consequences for the active-duty officers." A few weeks later, Samuel received a personal letter from the association chairman. "The entire medical company," he recalled, "led by the former commander, who had been promoted to an active-duty general, sent me a letter, expressing their condolences that I could not attend. Only those who know what such a document in the hands of a denunciant could lead to, are able to assess the courage it took in 1938 to send something like this to a Jew. This document is a testament of honor to everyone who signed it, from the general to the lowest enlisted man, who carried the severely wounded out of the trenches and onto my operating table."[114]

Samuel's case, however remarkable, was hardly unique. When Herbert Sulzbach returned to Berlin in 1938 to gather his family for the move to England, he met an old wartime comrade, a fellow named Ott, who had since become a sergeant in the Berlin Police. Ott invited Sulzbach out for drinks in a Berlin pub, an act that in Sulzbach's eyes "could have cost this brave man not only his profession, but also his life."[115] Such symbolic acts often remained the only bond between Jewish and gentile veterans. Yet they cultivated a sense of belonging under oppressive conditions, alleviating at least to a degree the traumatic effects of persecution and isolation, and strengthening Jewish veterans' identity as Germans, comrades, and honorable men. Proclamations of friendship, greetings, or encouragement "were not just words," as Klemperer later wrote. It "always made me happy when I met Germans who made it possible for me to preserve my feeling for Germany."[116] While the preservation of these relations alongside intensifying persecution by the Nazis added to the confusion that accompanied the rise of Hitler, this faint hope gave a decisive impetus to Jewish veterans' resolve to hold out.

A "Battle" for Germanness: The Diaries of Albert Herzfeld

The inconsistency in experience, the succession of contradictory and ambiguous messages from both the regime and the German public, generated an atmosphere of profound uncertainty for the Jewish Frontkämpfer. Nazi persecution on the one hand, yet limited legal protections and expressions of solidarity from the German public on the other, obscured the seriousness of the Nazi threat, oftentimes reinforcing Jewish determination to persevere. This ambivalence reveals itself in the writings of Albert Herzfeld, who, despite the increasingly dire situation in his home city of Düsseldorf, was certain that Germany would not betray him, as he struggled to preserve something of his former identity. His diary is a meticulous record of Germany under National Socialism from the perspective of both outsider and insider: a convert to Christianity and former officer who is persecuted by the Nazis for being a Jew. A successful businessman and philanthropist whose pride in his military service never wavered, Herzfeld saw himself as fully integrated into the German *Bildungsbürgertum* (educated middle-class society). Certain facets of Herzfeld's experience are unquestionably unique—he was a former member of the officers' corps, an upper-middle-class factory owner, and a baptized Protestant living in a liberal, predominantly Catholic region in Germany—but his writings exhibit remarkable similarities with other Jews who had been socialized by the front experience and imbued with a German "national" self-image, only to find themselves shunned by the Nazis after 1935. Most importantly, the diary throws light on how World War I not only governed Jewish veterans' thinking and behavior under National Socialism but also generated expectations of recognition and entitlement that did not abruptly end with the passage of the Nuremberg Laws.

Herzfeld had volunteered to fight in World War I at the age of forty-eight, ending the war as a senior lieutenant in command of a *Landsturm* (reserve) infantry company. He had been an active member of the *Garde Verein* veterans' league and his regimental association after the war, in addition to belonging to several philatelic and artists' clubs.[117] Yet when he began his diary in November 1935, Herzfeld had already been expelled from each of these organizations. He was a man consumed by inner turmoil, struggling to put his shattered sense of disbelief, disorientation, and bitterness into words as he was systematically driven to the margins of German society. The issue of identity is at the forefront of his early writing, as insults to honor seemed to weigh heavier than Nazi discrimination. His outrage over the Nazis' "dishonorable" treatment of former soldiers was especially pronounced when the government prohibited Jews from flying the old imperial flag, and when he was presented the Ehrenkreuz the very same week that the Nuremberg Laws were announced.[118] He was humiliated and profoundly disillusioned by the appearance of anti-Jewish signage throughout Düsseldorf, "suffering terribly under all the insults and degradations," especially so because "back then, we were constantly assured that the thanks of the Fatherland would be a certainty."[119] But the most disturbing aspect of life in Germany after 1935 was the aloofness of the German public—the "shocking" realization that "not a single high-ranking government official recognizes the egregiousness of the situation and lodges a complaint,"[120] and "not a single person steps forward and screams this injustice out to the world."[121] The years of humiliation and exposure to public indifference took a psychological toll, Herzfeld's diaries reveal, as he expressed increasing uncertainty and questioned his sense of belonging to Germany. It was no longer possible to disguise the scale of the calamity overtaking German Jewry, as he watched antisemitism spread rapidly and with little resistance from the populace. Everyday Germans often professed their loyalty and personal sympathy, yet more and more this support was accompanied by attempts to justify the "necessity" of the government's anti-Jewish policy. This—the increasing indifference of the public—was the hardest to bear. "It is all the same to me if I should die today or tomorrow," he wrote in January 1936, "for this treatment has taken all the joy from my life."[122] Herzfeld contemplated emigration several times and would have followed through "if I were 20 years younger, and if I were not so attached to Germany with every fiber of my being."[123]

In spite of the hardships and increasing estrangement from public life, Herzfeld retained a vital connection to Aryan society. Although he had been evicted in 1934 from both of the veterans' associations he had belonged to, he continued to receive regular visits from members of his old regiment. One of them was General Zedlitz-Lippe, whom Herzfeld had served with prior to the war, who showed up at his home after the passage of the Nuremberg Laws to express his solidarity.[124] Despite the humiliation of being banned from public spaces and daily exposure to antisemitic incitement, the preservation of these networks ensured that Herzfeld was not cast completely to the margins of German mainstream life. He interpreted visits by old comrades, the infrequent get-togethers at the local pub, and letters, postcards, and birthday greetings as a "sign of loyal comradeship," one that "brings me extraordinary joy, especially in these current times."[125] Against this backdrop, Herzfeld consoled himself that "none of my Aryan friends have pulled away, quite the opposite, each one of them, even those who aren't very close, continue to demonstrate sympathy."[126] These connections strengthened his belief that accommodation in the Third Reich was possible, even as late as 1936: "I will not give up hope that one day the situation of Jews and non-Aryans, who have proven their loyalty to the Fatherland, will be truthfully presented to high-ranking ministers of the government by a delegation of Aryans and non-Aryans. Did 12,000 Jews, and most likely an equal number of non-Aryans, in other words baptized Jews, really die for nothing? I tell myself that it cannot possibly continue on like this, a better situation must be forthcoming."[127]

Thus we see that Herzfeld's growing cynicism was juxtaposed with a seemingly unshakable belief that as a former officer, he would ultimately be spared the worst of the Nazi excesses. Although he contemplated emigration, in the end he never seriously considered leaving Germany, not even during a trip to Italy in 1937. He was frustrated and dismayed by Germans' indifference to Jewish suffering yet drew sharp distinctions between ordinary Germans and the Nazis, remaining convinced to the very end that the "broader public is absolutely not antisemitic."[128]

This inconsistency in experience resulted in a fundamental incongruence between expectations, perceptions, and reality, and defined life in Nazi Germany for the Jewish front generation. Like virtually all Jews in Germany by this time, Herzfeld remained irresolute, paralyzed by indecision, constantly vacillating between ideas and objectives. Time and again, he emerged shocked and demoralized as the Nazis pushed him to the margins of mainstream German life and made his daily existence increasingly unbearable. As he strove to find security in an increasingly perilous future, the torment inflicted by the Nazis was alleviated by his remaining friendships with comrades and sympathetic Germans, which strengthened and restored Herzfeld's German self-image. So while Herzfeld was "deeply shaken" after seeing signs forbidding entry to Jews at the public baths in the Kaiser Wilhelm Park in May 1936,[129] he was able to reassure himself a short time later "that despite all the official and systematic anti-Jewish agitation, not a single one of my 'Aryan' friends distanced themselves from me."[130] As late as 1937, he was certain that "a time will come when the German people will change their mind and denounce the antisemitic campaign as an egregious injustice against a segment of the population, from which thousands have died for their Fatherland."[131]

The leitmotif that emerges in the context of all the stories and tribulations Herzfeld recorded in his diary is the front experience of World War I. Again and again, Herzfeld harked back to the comradeship and sense of equality he felt during the war, when "there were no Jews or Christians, just soldiers" and "all combatants were to be rewarded with the thanks of the Fatherland." These memories were juxtaposed with the "egregious behavior" of the Nazis, which violated the most sacred principles of soldierly honor. These differences were stressed and repeated throughout his diary. As he attempted to reconcile antisemitism and societal indifference with his self-image as a German patriot, the Great War became a foil for his current predicament. The greater his sense of despair, the more this harking back to the war experience took the form of an idealized memory construct, a lens through which his self-identification as a German was interpreted and his decision to remain in Germany justified.

Herzfeld's case was not exceptional in this regard. A close reading of other Jewish writings from this period reveals that World War I held a profound significance for Jews during the Nazi years. It was a time when Jews were assessed by the yardstick of "performance of duty and achievement, and no distinctions were made on the basis of origin, regional identity, religion, or race," as Eugen Neter, a highly decorated medical officer, claimed.[132] "We—the older generation—still had not 'digested' the experience of 1914/1918," Herbert Sulzbach wrote after 1933. "One was still consumed by these tumultuous years, one thought about them, one dreamed about them, immersed oneself in diaries and photographs from this time; when war was still chivalrous, when one showed respect for the enemy and the enemy showed the same respect for us. To put in today's words: one had not yet reconciled this past."[133]

Even Willy Cohn, who by this time longed to start a new life in Palestine, had "tears streaming down [his] face" after reading newspaper accounts about the twentieth anniversary celebrations at Verdun. This memory brought him to the realization that "yes, even I had devoted myself with all my strength, and I don't regret that I did."[134] He continued to "quietly celebrate" the major milestones of his past life: Kaiser Wilhelm's birthday, the twenty-fifth anniversary of his mustering, and the 125th-year celebration of the establishment of the Iron Cross, each of which reminded him of "a nice bit of history I experienced."[135] Despite returning from the war disillusioned by the antisemitism he experienced in the army, Cohn admitted, "I enjoyed being a soldier . . . but wish I could have benefited Israel with all my experiences."[136]

What is remarkable about these invocations of the war is not only their frequency but also their timing. Twenty years onward, the First World War formed a central and functional part of the Jewish veterans' present identities. Their German sensibilities were thrown into disarray by the growing popularity of Hitler, but the remembered moments of comradeship from "back then" allowed them to detach from the environment of oppression and retreat to an idyllic past when they had been accepted as Germans. This was more than mere nostalgia: Jews searched for meaning in these memories, and were committed to making sense of the calamity unfolding around them. The war manifested itself as a self-affirming experience, a construction of myth driven by a longing for community with other Germans, and a sign that Germany would never abandon them, even when it already had.

At the heart of Herzfeld's diary is his struggle to remain German. No matter how much the indignities inflicted upon him by the Nazis disturbed him, he could never disown the German cause entirely. Identity became a coping mechanism: remaining German prevented him, psychologically, from falling victim to the Nazis. To be sure, identity became less of a pressing issue as matters of physical survival and his family's safety took precedence, but this inner crisis is an unbroken strand throughout Herzfeld's writings. A similar internal conflict arises in the diary of Victor Klemperer. As his circle of Aryan friends shrank, he grew disillusioned by the increasing alienation from the public and their indifference to his suffering. Yet even as his bitterness over his predicament grew, he vowed, "I am German forever, a German nationalist. The Nazis are un-German."[137] Several passages later, after seemingly reevaluating the indignity of being expelled from his professorship in 1935, Klemperer questioned his sense of belonging, admitting, "My principles over Germanness and the various nationalities are beginning to wobble like the teeth of an old man."[138] Seven years on, he again declared, "I am fighting the hardest battle for my Germanness now. I must hold on to this: I am German, the others are un-German. I must hold on to this. The spirit is decisive, not blood. I must hold on to this."[139] Like Herzfeld, Klemperer remained devoutly German by resisting the Nazis' attempts to define him as a Jew. By juxtaposing his Germanness with the un-Germanness of the Nazis, he convinced himself that the Third Reich was a mere distortion of the "real" Germany. As his world collapsed around him and he watched his neighbors being deported, preserving his identity provided the impetus to mentally endure the torment and uncertainty of the Nazi years.

Identity offered Herzfeld and Klemperer a means to psychologically survive Hitler's regime. For many "German" Jews and converts to Christianity, this vaguely defined sense of Germanness became a category that gave meaning to their personal struggles under Hitler, and it determined how and with which spiritual attitude they endured Nazi oppression. Similar assertions of identity emerge in the writings of other Jewish ex-servicemen, such as Martin Freudenheim, who refused to let the Nazis destroy his attachment to Germany. "Inwardly," he wrote, "I belonged [to Germany] more than many of these nationalistic screamers."[140] Walther Nord expressed the same sentiment as he left Germany for the United States in 1939: "I personally don't feel the least bit impacted or in any way moved by the Nazis' accusations against German or other Jews. They cannot change anything in my personal past. Neither their insults nor their behavior will impact it in any way. They cannot destroy or undermine my German past or uproot my Germanness, which they themselves cannot match, and which I have possessed for 60 years. I adhere to other German values and reject those preached by them."[141]

In their private writings, acculturated Jews like Nord tended to highlight the sympathy of ordinary Germans and their ability to cope under Nazi oppression. There was also a tendency to draw unambiguous distinctions between the "German people" and "the Nazis," while overlooking the nuances among Germans who eagerly accepted National Socialism or simply detached themselves from its reality. A different picture emerges in the writings of Zionists from the same period, where the issue of identity was far less of a problem. Willy Cohn, who admitted after Kristallnacht that, despite everything, his "great love for Germany still remains," was the exception in this regard.[142] Most Zionists, their letters and diaries suggest, felt vindicated by the Nazi rise to power and discriminated far less between the SA thugs who beat up Jews in the streets and everyday Germans who climbed without a party membership card because they learned to adapt. They contented themselves with the inevitable. "The love for Germany died in us," Max Kronenburg wrote in 1937. "Materially, we could have held out longer in Germany, but spiritually it had become impossible."[143]

The statements of defiance suggest that for many Jewish Frontkämpfer, identity became the sole means to endure Hitler's Reich; it represented the limits of their agency in defying the Nazis. Battered by life under National Socialism, alienated yet still fighting, in the end they refused to accept persecution and disavow their German sensibilities. The Nazis hoped to destroy this identity and Jews' connections to the fatherland through a series of repressive legal measures, harassment, and public humiliation. In this they were unsuccessful, for in the end many Jewish veterans chose to defy their oppressors.

CHAPTER 5

Under the "Absolute" Power of National Socialism, 1938–41

The year 1938 brought about a decisive transformation in the history of German Jewry. By the end of that year, virtually no Jewish businesses in Germany remained intact, a significant portion of Jewish wealth and property had been, or was about to be, confiscated by the government, and much of the male population aged eighteen to sixty-five years had been imprisoned in Nazi concentration camps. Jewish war veterans suffered the humiliation of arrest and physical abuse during Kristallnacht, and even those left unscathed by the events of 9 November were confronted with the powerlessness of being unable to defend their homes and families, and were racked by the uncertainty of what lay ahead. Germany's invasion of Poland on 1 September 1939 further altered the situation of Jews remaining in Germany. Travel routes over land and sea were immediately closed off, and the wartime situation allowed Hitler to dispense with political considerations in his search for a final "solution" to the Jewish Question. In October 1941, when the mass deportations of Jews from the Reich began, veterans were initially included in the transports, as Nazi authorities forged ahead with their plans to make the Reich *Judenfrei* (free of Jews). It marked the beginning of a prolonged struggle for existence that few would survive. Yet Jewish veterans made use of the limited resources at their disposal to preserve a sense of agency, whether in the Reich or in the extreme conditions of "the East." As members of the Jewish Order Police in the eastern ghettos of Lodz, Minsk, and Riga, they tried not only to survive physically, but also to retain their identity, their masculine honor, even as the last barriers to genocide were cast aside.

The Storm Breaks: Kristallnacht

Two landmark antisemitic measures foreshadowed the violence that erupted throughout the Reich on 9–10 November 1938, the first of which required all Jews to apply for a special ID card (*Kennkarte*) so they would henceforth be immediately recognizable as Jews when dealing with authorities.[1]

The second, announced on 17 August, was a new law that forced all Jews to adopt the "typically Jewish"-sounding names of "Sara" or "Israel" as their middle names.[2] As he had in the past, Friedrich Solmitz, a convert to Christianity whom the Nazis classified as a "full Jew" according to the Nuremberg Laws, immediately appealed to the Interior Ministry, seeking an exemption as a former officer and holder of the Iron Cross, only to be informed that his petition had been rejected. In addition to turning down his appeal, a letter from the Hamburg police reminded Solmitz that Jews were prohibited from using the greeting "Heil Hitler" in correspondence with government officials.[3] The ruling left Solmitz in a state of distress. "There is nothing worse than being homeless in one's own home," his wife, Luise Solmitz, wrote on 23 August 1938:

> One could hardly describe Fredy as a fearful man: despite all his comrades' warnings, he flew in Fokker's wooden planes held together with packing string. He spent four years of war fighting in the front lines . . . he could sleep right through when bombs were falling all around him. But on the morning after we got the first news about our Jewish first names from Strasbourg [radio station], he said, "I woke up bathed in sweat; it was nothing but a very ordinary, very nasty attack of fear." It's a kind of war, and we find ourselves in it without any defenses, without weapons, without the remotest possibility of defending ourselves.[4]

By this time any ambivalence on Hitler's part regarding the privileging of certain categories of Jews had disappeared. In a letter to Wilhelm Frick dated 4 November 1938, Hitler's secretary, Lammers, stressed that "the Führer is of the opinion that exemptions from special regulations for Jews have to be rejected without any exceptions."[5]

These developments should not obscure the impact of Kristallnacht, however, for it marked a decisive departure from the Nazis' strategy for "solving" the Jewish Question using legal and bureaucratic means. The assassination of Ernst vom Rath by Herschel Grynszpan in Paris provided the ideal pretext for the carefully orchestrated events that culminated in the pogrom of 9–10 November 1938, unleashing two days of terror that those who survived it would never forget.[6] The scenes that unfolded throughout Germany that night, as squads of SA and SS men descended on the unsuspecting Jewish population, were lucidly described by Samuel Honaker, the American consulate in Stuttgart, in his report to the U.S. ambassador: "The horror of midnight arrests, of hurried departures in a half dressed state from their homes in the company of police officers, the wailing of wives and children suddenly left behind, of imprisonment in crowded cells, and of the panic of fellow prisoners." What Honaker found particularly shocking was that "a number of Jews who had been arrested were forced to march in the streets of Kehl two-by-two, repeating in chorus: 'We are guilty of the murder in Paris and are traitors to Germany.' Among these were ex-servicemen, some of whom had been wounded during the Great War and some of whom had received war decorations."[7]

The events described by Honaker unfolded along the same lines in every city, village, and town throughout Germany. After the destruction of the local synagogue, the attacks shifted to Jewish businesses and homes, followed by the arrest and incarceration of the adult male population. In Pirmasens, on the morning of 10 November, Albert Schwerin encountered his friend Ernst Baer, a widely respected former officer and the chairman of the town's RjF chapter. Baer had been beaten so badly that Schwerin could hardly recognize him. "I mistook him for an old woman," Schwerin wrote, "for in haste someone had draped a woman's garment over him to protect him from the weather, as it must have been too painful for him to put on his own jacket. . . . The normally tall, erect, and confident man, although trying to hold his head up straight, was completely bent over, dragging his feet. Even as he turned to look at me, I didn't immediately recognize him." Baer had been woken up in the middle of the night and lured to the front door by three plainclothes stormtroopers, who pulled him outside, beat him into unconsciousness, and left him lying in an alleyway. He had somehow managed to crawl back to his home, where he then was arrested by the authorities.

In Berlin, Siegfried Neumann was assaulted by SA men outside the burning synagogue and dragged before an SS officer overseeing the *Aktion* (operation). "I opened my coat and pointed to the Iron Cross and War Service Cross which were affixed to my lapel. I told him: 'I was a war volunteer and Frontkämpfer and have the Iron Cross.' Him: 'Well, then you are in luck. Let's see if you can save yourself by climbing over that wall.' "[8] Before a jeering crowd of intoxicated stormtroopers, Neumann tried to jump the three-meter-high brick wall pointed out by the SS officer. After three failed attempts, Neumann decided to make his escape. He abruptly turned and sprinted headlong down a nearby alleyway, pursued by a "howling mob." By chance the commotion had drawn the attention of a sympathetic housemaid who beckoned Neumann into her home. The house belonged to a retired officer, "a nationalist who was anti-Nazi," who hid him as the drunken Nazi thugs combed the neighborhood in vain.[9]

That the perpetrators did not distinguish veterans from other Jews on Kristallnacht is all too evident in the after-action reports of the Gestapo. In Würzburg, Alfred Katzmann, the brother of the Julius Katzmann discussed in the introduction, committed suicide by throwing himself off his balcony after police and SA men broke through the front door his home.[10] Alfred Katzmann had volunteered for frontline military service in 1915 and spent three years on the Western Front, returning home in 1918 with the Iron Cross and a partially paralyzed shoulder. He had suffered immensely under Nazi repression, enduring harassment, ongoing pressure to aryanize his business, and several Gestapo interrogations related to false accusations of antiregime activities. Kristallnacht had been the final straw. In the case of Ernst Lebermann, a group of SA men stormed into his apartment and literally dragged him out of his bed and into the street, where he was then beaten so severely that he lost consciousness shortly after his arrival at the city jail. He died after being brought to the local hospital. The official police photograph in his Gestapo file, taken just before his death, shows a shocked and disheveled-looking Lebermann still wearing his bloodied nightshirt.[11]

The brutality described in the testimonies and police reports is striking in other ways. These sources make clear that the physical abuse and public shaming of war veterans was calculated: it was intended to show the victims, as well as the German public, that all Jews were the same in Hitler's Germany. The pogrom obliterated any remaining distinctions between different categories of Jews that had prevailed in public discourses; no preferences would be given to Frontkämpfer, baptized Jews, or any other type of "decent" Jew. In one fell swoop, the Nazis redefined what it meant to be Jewish in Nazi Germany. This was the message the regime sought to convey: every Jew belonged to a homogeneous group of enemies that had to be excluded from mainstream German life.

Yet older notions of status were not abruptly or completely swept aside. In some cases, Jewish veterans' status did save them from arrest. In a suburb of Würzburg, a former officer and holder of the Iron Cross managed to make his way to the town hall, where he pleaded with the mayor to spare his home from demolition. The mayor acquiesced and ordered the local SA leader to leave the man's house alone.[12] The troop of SA men who forced their way into Albert Dreyfuss's home were led by a Kripo (Criminal Police) officer who, after noticing Dreyfuss's old officer's saber, asked him to produce evidence of his frontline service. After looking over his military papers, the officer gathered his men and left. "With you we'll leave everything in order," he told him, also providing his name in case other stormtroopers showed up.[13] And "through a miracle," Joseph Levy and his son survived the pogrom unscathed because the latter presented his military ID to the SA men. "This made an impression on these ignorant chaps," Levy recalled, "and they left us and the apartment alone."[14] The decisive factor in these cases was that the perpetrators tasked with making the arrests were either overruled or restrained by regular policemen or public officials. Under certain conditions, invocations of military sacrifice offered some protection before regular law enforcement officials and "moderate" party members, for whom it was apparently preferable to move on and find easier victims.

In other situations, personal affiliations with old comrades who belonged to the NSDAP or sympathetic public officials proved crucial. Hugo Gutmann was tipped off by a local policeman just minutes before the SA stormed into his home and was able to escape with his family. They were hidden in a nearby Catholic hospital and later sheltered by relatives until the situation quieted down.[15] And in Düsseldorf, Albert Herzfeld woke up to the sound of screams and breaking glass; from his bedroom window he watched helplessly as a neighbor's house was demolished.[16] But when the perpetrators arrived at Herzfeld's doorstep, he heard a male voice from the street say, "This one we'll leave alone, he was my company commander," before they moved on.[17]

The behavior of the perpetrators often varied from town to town, neighborhood to neighborhood, even from one SA troop to the next. Albert Schwerin described how, in Pirmasens, the local *Kreisleiter* (district leader) tore the war medals from victims' jackets, "grinding them into the dirt," before putting them on the train to Dachau,[18] whereas in Frankfurt am Main, war invalids and Jews with "high medals for bravery and Wound Badges [Verwundetenabzeichen]" were "sent home."[19] In other cases, Jewish veterans were passed over entirely for reasons that remain unclear, either because of age or fortuitous circumstance, but most likely because the local jails and ad hoc detention facilities were already at full capacity.

The fact that under certain conditions, their status as veterans enabled some Jews to evade arrest on 9–10 November should not divert attention from the fate that awaited the Jewish veterans' community as a whole. Scholars are right to consider Kristallnacht a decisive watershed in Nazi Germany's anti-Jewish policies, and its implications for Jewish veterans were particularly egregious. By the evening of 10 November, most veterans shared the fate of other Jewish men, as they were rounded up and imprisoned in local jails and makeshift holding pens, awaiting transports that would take them to Himmler's concentration camps. A line had been crossed. Race was the sole and explicit reason for arrest. The distinctions separating Frontkämpfer from "ordinary" Jews had been rendered meaningless, as public space apparently no longer served as a brake on Nazi radicalism. The violence unfolded in the open, in hundreds of communities throughout Germany, in broad daylight, as thousands of Jewish former soldiers were physically assaulted, humiliated, and deported. There they would experience firsthand the "absolute" power of National Socialism.[20]

Inside the Nazi Camps

As the Jewish population in Germany struggled to come to terms with the magnitude of what had occurred, the roughly thirty thousand Jewish men arrested during the pogrom were delivered into the custody of the SS at Buchenwald, Sachsenhausen, or Dachau. Whatever restraint the Nazis still exercised in public up to this point was cast aside as Jews entered the barbed-wire enclosures and watchtowers of the Nazi camps, a development all too apparent to the victims from the moment of their arrival. Karl Rosenthal recalled what awaited him as his transport entered the gates of Sachsen-hausen: "We immediately heard deafening voices yelling at us: 'Out, you Jewish pigs, off the truck!' As we hurried to jump from the truck, several SS men armed with clubs and whips unleashed on us. Amid nasty epithets and screaming, their blows came down on us mercilessly: on our backs, our legs, our heads, and across our faces. . . . One of my less-fortunate comrades was thrown from the truck with such force that he remained lying on the ground, motionless, a large wound on his head and forehead . . . blood streaming over his face and jacket."[21]

Some veterans had brought their medals and military ID cards with them to the camps, in the desperate hope that this would make an impression on the SS. They quickly learned that evidence of past wartime bravery was not only meaningless but also dangerous, as the guards responded with particu-lar brutality against any Jews claiming German identity.[22] When he arrived at Sachsenhausen, Siegfried Neumann was told by another inmate to "ditch" his medals, the reasons for which soon became all too clear.[23] According to Fritz Schürmann, a sixty-year-old man arrived at the camp supported by a crutch, wearing the Iron Cross First Class and Silver Wound Badge he had earned during the war. When one of the guards spotted him, he relieved the

"old veteran" of his crutch and used it to beat him over the head. "The following day, this Jewish hero was forced to stand at attention for eleven hours
on the parade ground, in formation, despite his prosthetic leg," Schürmann
wrote. "Every time he lost his strength, several blows from an SS guard ensured that he came 'to his senses' again."[24] At Buchenwald, one of the new
arrivals went as far as reproaching the guards for their "dishonorable" treatment of a former officer and recipient of the Iron Cross. After receiving a
rain of blows by the SS guards, the man was dragged to the main parade
ground, tied face down on a wooden plank, his shirt removed, and, before
the assembled inmates, was lashed twenty-five times on his exposed back
with a thin wooden cane. The man's screams, Siegfried Oppenheimer wrote,
"stayed with me for days."[25]

Were Jewish veterans able to preserve their masculine honor under these
conditions? What did this experience mean for their identity as Frontkämpfer? On the surface, the writings of veterans who lived to describe these traumatic events did not differ much from those of other victims of Kristallnacht:
they offer vivid descriptions of the savagery of the SS guards and the appalling living conditions in the camp, from overcrowded, dirty barracks and
lack of drinking water to latrines overflowing with feces. Chronic hunger
and thirst, dysentery, infections, public floggings, suicides, and instances of
individuals completely losing their minds were a regular feature of daily life
in the camps, as the victims were subjected to unimaginable physical and
mental abuse.

Veterans' writings, however, reveal that their military background fulfilled
a vital psychological as well as a practical need. On a most basic level, the fact
that Jewish former soldiers were versed in the drill, commands, and codes of
discipline of the German military helped them endure the initial shock and
adapt to the "extreme" environment of the camp.[26] Many nonveteran prisoners suffered immensely in the first days after their arrival, finding it difficult
to adjust to the "military way of speaking" and "the senseless marching back
and forth."[27] To Hans Berger, however, the SS guards reminded him of "the
worst Prussian noncommissioned officer and sadist combined, many times
over." He remembered the military commands and the proper way to march
from his time in the army and knew what had to be done.[28] "Almost all of us
had been soldiers, many of us officers," wrote Hans Reichmann. "We pull
ourselves together and stand tall."[29] The war became a point of reference for
many Jewish prisoners, as former soldiers tapped into their wartime memories, contrasting the discipline, deprivations, and unpredictability of the
camp with the conditions they faced in the barracks yard or in the trenches
of the Western Front some twenty years earlier. They equated the hardships

they had experienced "back then"—shortages of food and clothing, close living space, lack of personal hygiene, and fear of death and mutilation—with the daily conditions in the camp, not only in terms of the military regimen but also in the existential threat the camp represented. "I know now that I am at war again," Julius Meyer wrote. "They have declared war against us, after they have already, for years, made us defenseless. . . . Now the nerves are strained as they can only be in combat."[30]

Physical survival, to be sure, was paramount in the camps, but Jewish veterans also strove to preserve their male self-worth through their ability to endure the brutality of the SS. When Albert Schwerin wrote that he had "never seen so many men cry as at Dachau" as he looked back on his arrival at the notorious Nazi concentration camp, he related these events as an observer, not a victim. Like all the other prisoners, Schwerin was subjected to unspeakable privations at Dachau: fear, uncertainty, hunger, and illness, as well as egregious mental and physical abuse. But he overcame these trials by maintaining his composure and not allowing himself to be cowed into submission. "From the very beginning, I was determined to rise to the occasion, to persevere and make it out in one piece," Schwerin wrote. "I did not allow anything to keep me down in Dachau: neither the frozen extremities, the despair of the other comrades, nor the sinister environment we found ourselves in. . . . I can think of no other time in my life where my self-reliance and self-confidence had been as strong."[31] He adapted to the camp: the tight living quarters, poor sanitation, and lack of privacy did not intimidate him, but merely reminded him of what he had endured years ago in the army.

Thus, despite attempts by the SS to strip away the last vestiges of a prisoner's soldierly identity, the Jewish Frontkämpfer were not relegated to impotence. To be sure, the sense of powerlessness and victimization that all inmates experienced had a damaging effect on male gender identity. The testimonies of veterans, however, suggest that this shame was mitigated by taking action, by not being reduced to passivity. Veterans also reappraised their masculine role by acting as protectors and father figures to the weaker prisoners, who seemed to lack the resolve to endure life in the camp. Schwerin juxtaposed his determination to overcome the hardships of Dachau against the "helplessness" and inaction of the other prisoners. He described "comforting" several "hysterical" or "deeply shaken" fellow inmates, his perseverance and composure serving as "a power of example to many."[32] Much of Heinrich Lichtenstein's description of Buchenwald relates how he consoled "countless fellow inmates who were in shock, who could no longer hold themselves together spiritually. We made sure that they cleaned their clothes and shoes . . . that they retrieved the rations allocated to them and that they ate and drank."[33] Invoking his experience as a soldier in the First World War and a POW in France, a "17-month battle with hopelessness that we as young men struggled through," Lichtenstein galvanized many of the weaker prisoners and motivated them to "pull through."[34] Implicit in this rhetoric was a certain moral superiority over nonmilitary Jews. As experienced men who had been tried and tested in battle, they saw themselves as proven leaders and masculine role models who could instill courage into the "weaker" prisoners. According to Hans Block, at Buchenwald several RjF members organized themselves into an internal "guard troop" that maintained discipline among the other inmates, in order to prevent unnecessary altercations with the SS. Those prisoners who did not comply were "made obedient by blows" if necessary.[35]

Even limited, seemingly self-destructive acts provided a means to alleviate the shame of powerlessness. Kurt Sabatzky recalled how another prisoner, a former officer, was struck repeatedly in the face by a sadistic guard yet refused to give in when "the SS man demanded he repeat the words: 'I am a traitor to the Fatherland.'"[36] It would have been easier and far less dangerous for the prisoner to simply concede to the guard's demands, but it was precisely this that made his defiance so remarkable. Examples like this remind us that although the SS considered all prisoners emasculated and powerless, in the end its power was not absolute. The pride expressed by the few men who acted in defense of honor also throws light on an important aspect of Jewish agency in the camps, and on the correlation between action and masculinity, something borne out in numerous testimonies. Not all veterans had the ability to act, of course. But those who did saw it as an important element in sustaining a strong male identity.

On 29 November 1938, an order issued by Hermann Göring released all frontline veterans arrested during Kristallnacht from the camps, bringing their four-week ordeal to an end.[37] As the other victims of the pogrom remained incarcerated for additional weeks or months, the Jewish Frontkämpfer were discharged in early December, an event depicted by Kurt Guggenheim as a moment of redemption: "Suddenly a command is issued from the middle of the crowd: 'March in formation!'—and a battle ready Jewish company of veterans marches in impeccable parade cadence through the gates of the concentration camp—leaving behind them the shocked and dumbfounded faces of the camp guards and the barely concealed smirks of the camp inmates. Even the noble knight Goetz von Berlichingen could not have bid a more suitable farewell."[38]

With Kristallnacht, a crucial transformation had taken place, for it changed how masculinity was performed. Self-assertion had been a core element of veterans' masculine identity, yet after November 1938, it was endurance that mattered. Their ability to withstand the wounds inflicted by the SS, all the while maintaining their composure—to not suffer or complain openly—was a reflection of their character. In their accounts of their ordeals, veterans invoked the dominant traits of masculinized soldierly identity: remaining calm and composed in the face of intense pressure, persevering in the face of overwhelming odds, rising above adversity, and refusing to succumb to momentary feelings of helplessness or defeat. This glorification of perseverance, a kind of sangfroid amid an atmosphere of powerlessness, defied the Nazis' efforts to strip Jews of their manhood, their honor. Crucially, by emphasizing the diminished coping capacity of the other prisoners, they simultaneously drew attention to their own resilience.[39] As veterans recorded the nervous breakdowns and scenes of "men crying," they did so as onlookers; they seemed unaffected by the suffering and indignities that had destroyed countless weaker men.[40]

To be sure, the survivor accounts under study here are not definitive; the writers had several months, even years, after November 1938 to merge these memories into a larger, coherent narrative. The themes of endurance, defiance, and defense of honor were a counterweight to the powerlessness that prevailed in the camps, and a means for the former prisoners to ensure that their ordeal would not be remembered as one of emasculation.[41] This leitmotif served a strategic purpose as well: to preserve the narrative of Jewish heroism. The accounts are meant to convey that the Jewish Frontkämpfer had not been broken, that despite the veterans' being subjected to the most inhuman conditions imaginable, the Nazis had been unable to sever their psychological connection to their former status. This was not a final, desperate act of self-delusion, of being lost or helpless while pretending to be in control, nor was it a peripheral development in the overall strategy of survival. Rather, it was a conscious effort to preserve an identity, a sense of agency, and it is reasonable to suspect that for many former soldiers, overcoming these ordeals while maintaining their dignity was synonymous with retaining their masculine honor. "The first three days were apparently the most horrendous of all," Walter Tausk wrote after speaking with several survivors of Buchenwald. "Only those who had the nerves necessary to endure them (and for the most part this was the case only with frontline soldiers) were able to persevere under everything else."[42]

After Kristallnacht

When Hugo Moses returned to his home after being discharged from Buchenwald in early December 1938, he recalled how his release from the notorious Nazi concentration camp coincided with his return from the war in 1918: "It was on this exact day twenty years ago that I returned from the Great War. Again I was coming home, yet this time from prison, innocent; again I was a tired, defeated man. . . . If back then I was inwardly broken over the fate of the German people and the defeat of the German Army, in my young heart there was still confidence and faith in the future, for I knew that I had endured the hardest trials and that this period of suffering would end."[43] But now, he wrote, "everything was lost. Today I went home, my heart filled with sadness and despair, racked with worry over my family and about our future. . . . After these latest events there was no staying in Germany any longer."[44] With Kristallnacht a watershed had been reached. Even those Jews who had not been directly targeted by the perpetrators could hardly sustain a sense of normalcy. Any lingering hope that a "tolerable situation" would persist, that medals for bravery or connections to old comrades could bring further reprieves, ended on 9 November 1938.

Testimonies collected by Harvard University in the immediate aftermath of the pogrom offer glimpses into individuals' emotions and psychological coping strategies as they contemplated the enormity of what had just occurred. Whatever uncertainties veterans had before Kristallnacht, the lesson they learned that day was clear: get out of Germany. Almost overnight, the confidence and self-assertion that characterized veterans' writings in the early years of the regime was replaced by the sobering realization that all along, the Nazis "had taken their battle cry—'Juda Verreck!' [Die Jews!]—quite literally," as Friedrich Solon phrased it.[45] "[We were] jolted from our illusion of our normal, bourgeois existence," wrote Alfred Schwerin. "With one violent blow, we were suddenly faced with the true reality of the lawlessness and brutality."[46] This feeling of powerlessness had been largely absent from Jewish veterans' writings before then, even in letters and diaries written between 1914 and 1918, during some of the bitterest fighting of World War I. "I have looked death straight in the eye repeatedly and found myself in horrifying situations, but I have never known fear," Alfred Oppler wrote in 1940. "It was not death that made one tremble, but the indignity; being tortured by beasts in human form; the physical and spiritual mutilation."[47] Many veterans contrasted the uncertainty and fear of death they had experienced in the trenches with their current circumstances, conceding that Kristallnacht had proven to be even more traumatic than the extreme experience of war. For Robert Lenneberg, danger had become routine at the front to the point where "feelings of fear rarely surfaced anymore." But what he experienced in November 1938 was "a kind of fear never known before, fear as a chronic condition. Anxiety, worry, grief, hate, rage, disgust, and revulsion, all converged to produce a feeling of utter hopelessness, of constant weariness and terror."[48] Incessant fear of arrest, denunciation, or simply the time when one's "luck would run out" left Walter Tausk "inwardly exhausted, spent, drained, and completely numb. . . . Only the war can be truly compared to the spiritual condition in which I find myself now."[49]

Many had lost all hope. Some saw suicide as the final act of defiance.[50] Before Kristallnacht, war veterans usually assessed their personal situation differently from that of the general Jewish population, not always perceiving what was happening to other Jews as having direct relevance for them. Given public attitudes throughout Germany, this is hardly surprising. But now Jewish veterans found themselves in the same situation as other Jews. They shared the danger of arrest and Nazi terror with the rest of the Jewish community—they were now "fair game," as Alfred Schwerin put it.[51] After their release from the camps, veterans, like the vast majority of the Jewish population, strained every resource to secure exit papers and visas and join the exodus of Jews fleeing the Reich.

Focusing exclusively on Jewish emigration after November 1938, however, obscures the private, inner struggles that many veterans waged. Amid all the chaos and uncertainty, they engaged in a process of reflection and self-justification as they strove to give meaning to the horrific events of the past months and make sense of their future. For many Jews, the pogrom was indeed a spiritual turning point that signaled a final and decisive break with Germany. Hugo Gutmann owed his life to former comrades; these connections saved him from arrest, prolonged imprisonment, or a far worse fate. In the end, however, he could no longer separate the nation he had sacrificed so much for during the Great War from Hitler's Reich. In January 1939, aboard the plane that took him out of Germany, Gutmann fought the urge to spit out the window, not literally but "in spirit," as it crossed the border into Belgium. For him, there was no "crisis" or inner struggle as he left Germany behind, for "these scumbags made my farewell easy."[52] Gutmann and his family fled to the United States via Portugal in August 1940 and eventually settled in Saint Louis. He would never talk or write or about his time as an officer in Hitler's wartime regiment. He changed his name to Henry Grant, telling a US immigration court that after the "harrowing experiences at the hands of the German government and its people," he wanted only to "disassociate himself from anything German."[53]

Gutmann's sweeping reevaluation of long-cherished values, memories, and beliefs hinged on the disappointment of a positive expectation: that the German public and conservative elites, especially the army, would keep the Nazis in check. This trust had been betrayed. It was the German public's inaction—their willingness to overlook, even tolerate, the excesses perpetrated against Jewish Germans—that led to a fundamental reassessment of his relationship to Germany.

Yet Jewish attitudes were also marked by continuity as well as radical change. When Albert Dreyfuss composed his memoirs shortly after immigrating to Palestine in 1940, he struggled to make sense of the horrific events he had experienced over the past seven years. As he recounted the incremental, step-by-step persecution of German Jews, from harassment and name-calling in the streets, estrangement from friends, and the "aryanization" of his business to the public violence that unfolded on 9 November, there was one thing that continued to give him hope. "Fortunately," Dreyfuss wrote, "the government and the Party are not the German people." Ordinary Germans did not share the antisemitism of the Nazi Party, he insisted, for if they had, "then not a single Jew or any other 'enemy of the state' would be alive in Germany today." Dreyfuss was convinced that the German people were Hitler's victims too. Had Germans tried to stand up to the regime's anti-Jewish policies, then "the thousands upon thousands of faithful, observant Protestants and Catholics, who were enemies of Nazism from the very beginning, would have shared the lot of the Jews."[54]

Historians have often dismissed such claims as naive or as a form of self-delusion. Yet they are crucial, for the fact that many acculturated Jews saw the regime and the German people as two distinct entities points to an ongoing identification with an abstract "German" self-consciousness. Even as they were deprived of their livelihood, property, and German citizenship, many Jewish veterans upheld the dichotomy between "Germans" and "Nazis" in their writings, claiming time and again that "the German population did not possess a mere fraction of the antisemitism of the government,"[55] "these scoundrels are not the German people,"[56] and "the crimes of the government were met with all-round condemnation [by everyday Germans]."[57] Such statements should not be seen as a testament to ordinary Germans' behavior during the Nazi years, for this was little more than a peripheral issue. Far more importantly, the veterans' writings tried to preserve the narrative of Jewish assimilation and national belonging underpinned by military wartime sacrifice, and with it, their sense of dignity. Anything less would have meant that the comradeship and sense of oneness with other Germans had been an illusion, that Jewish sacrifices in World War I had been in vain.

Most Jewish veterans dismissed the Nazi claim that Kristallnacht had been a spontaneous act carried out by an enraged populace, for even to contemporary observers, it was clear that the pogrom was a staged, tightly controlled undertaking that had been orchestrated from above.[58] Many veterans emphasized the help they received from former comrades, whether through extra handouts of food, help in securing exit visas, or nighttime get-togethers that provided much-needed psychological relief. After Heinrich Lichtenstein's release from Buchenwald, a comrade from his old regiment visited him, offering to help in any way he could, especially with food. "He brought us 1–2 dozen eggs every week until our departure from Germany. He collected them in his village and usually came by every Monday night, encouraging us to eat and to chat for a few hours," Lichtenstein wrote. "He was happy for us when we told him one day that we were able to go to England."[59]

There had also been individual acts of personal courage on the part of the German public on 9 November. In early 1939, the SD regional branch in Württemberg-Hohenzollern reported that certain officers' associations continued to "harbor" Jews and refused to comply with new racial laws requiring all members to prove their Aryan credentials. It further remarked that several local residents had assisted their Jewish comrades after the pogrom: "In individual cases there was evidence of a mild to pronounced Jew friendliness. For example, an 81-year-old Colonel (formerly Stahlhelm, now a party member) sent a flower arrangement to a Jew after the Aktion to show his solidarity. In Creglingen, an NSKK man and member of the NS-Reichskriegerbund [Kyffhäuser] helped a Jew go into hiding, so that he was able to evade arrest. Later on, the district leader of the Kyffhäuser also intervened on behalf of this Jew-friend."[60]

One of the only known collective interventions in the aftermath of Kristallnacht was the case involving Julius Katzmann, whose employees at H. A. Fränkel intervened after he was apprehended by the Gestapo and deported to Buchenwald. In addition to the petition they had sent to the Reichs Chancellery, the records of the Würzburg Gestapo reveal that a second letter had been sent to Franz Ritter von Epp, the *Reichsstatthalter* (governor) of Bavaria.[61] Based on the limited evidence, Epp may have been instrumental in securing Katzmann's early release from the camp.[62] As a committed National Socialist who was responsible for conceiving and implementing antisemitic policies in Bavaria throughout the early Nazi years, Epp was apparently willing to make exceptions for "comrades."[63] The Gestapo launched a follow-up investigation into the origins of the petition, yet its findings were inconclusive, due to either the exigencies of the situation or the desire to suppress any signs of public unrest. After three weeks, the Gestapo closed the case, commenting, "Surely a Jew was involved."[64]

Jewish veterans invested these events with great significance, even after they had fled the Third Reich. For Sulzbach and Leyens, both of whom would go on to fight in Allied armies, the memory of "brave Germans who risked their lives and careers" to help Jewish comrades, as Sulzbach put it, became an integral part of their memories of life under Hitler.[65] It enabled them to fight the Nazi enemy and "liberate" Germany from Adolf Hitler while never abdicating their sense of Germanness.

The fact that many Germans perceived the persecution of veterans and other "decent" Jews differently from measures targeting "Jewry" says something important about the prevalence of older, more traditional discourses in German society. Such reactions did not emerge out of a vacuum, but oriented themselves toward values and beliefs in Germany that already existed. Unlike Nazi Party hard-liners, most of whom never questioned the righteousness of Nazi Germany's anti-Jewish policies, everyday Germans had to decide repeatedly whether or not to participate, each time weighing their responses, the identity of the victim, and the likely costs of intervening. Although the German public's overall indifference to Jewish suffering undoubtedly emboldened Nazi leaders to forge ahead in their plans to unleash the pogrom on 9 November 1938, there was a perceptible sense of shame and discomfort when these measures were applied to ex-soldiers who bore the physical scars of four bloody years of fighting in the trenches.

Yet even the most optimistic of the victims could not deny the shift in the public's attitudes after November 1938. What had been lost during the pogrom was not just the feeling of entitlement that underpinned discourses on military sacrifice—in particular the expectation that the sacrifices of the Great War would be compensated by exemptions from antisemitic legislation—but also the hope that German public opinion would keep the "absolute power" of the Nazis at bay. Jewish veterans had drawn spiritual comfort from comradeship, the fleeting expressions of sympathy and encouragement, for as we have seen, this solidarity provided the impetus for individuals to endure the persecution of the Nazis and "wait out" the end of Hitler's Reich. After November 1938, everything became questionable. "People became used to the fact that Jews were persecuted and that they had to suffer," Alfred Oppler wrote. There was a perceptible "gradual numbing of the soul."[66] The relentless ratcheting forward of anti-Jewish measures made discrimination all too rapidly a "way of life," as it became clear to many Germans that sympathy with Jews had become a liability.[67] It was a development captured in a December 1938 diary entry by Victor Klemperer, who told of a policeman who in the past had been friendly to him and always greeted him in public. When he encountered him that month in the municipal office where the Klemperers lived, the same policeman passed by him, "staring ahead as he went past, as much a stranger as possible. In his behavior," Klemperer commented, "the man probably represents 79 million Germans."[68]

The First Deportations

The Second World War provided the context for Nazi Germany to intensify its anti-Jewish campaign, allowing Hitler to dispense with political considerations in his persecution of the Jews. After 1939, the regime's antisemitic policies were driven by two imperatives. First, the Nazis exploited the exigencies of the wartime situation to legitimize further measures against the Jewish population as a matter of national security. Second, the Nazis strove to dispel any remaining doubts among the Aryan public that Jews represented an existential threat to the Third Reich, one that had to be taken seriously, especially now that Germany was at war.

Between 1939 and 1941, Jews were evicted from their homes and moved into specially designated Jewish apartment buildings, so-called *Judenhäuser* (Jew houses), ordered to hand over their radios to the police, and prohibited from speaking to uniformed members of the armed forces (Wehrmacht). Curfews for Jews were established from 8:00 p.m. to 5:00 a.m. (during the summer, it was 9:00 p.m. to 5:00 a.m.), during which time they were not allowed to leave their homes. Unannounced "house searches" by the Gestapo, ostensibly to search for weapons, radios, or any signs of "enemy activity," became a routine part of daily life in Nazi Germany after 1939, and were occasions for brutal humiliation and physical abuse.

These measures were more than a mere reflection of a desire on the part of the authorities to monitor and control the Jewish population. They were a means to project the image of the Jewish enemy onto the "decent" German Jew. It was a process that culminated in the implementation of the *Judenstern* (Jewish badge) on 15 September 1941.[69] This decree, which required all Jews over the age of six to identify themselves by wearing a large yellow Star of David with the word *Jude* printed on it in bold black letters, was designed to close the gap between persisting notions of the unassimilated Eastern European Jew and the "German" Jew, to make clear to the German public that so-called "decent" Jews were no different from those depicted in Nazi newsreels. This had been the Nazis' goal from the beginning: to provoke public discourses on the domestic Jewish enemy, to alert everyday Germans that Jews were not merely un-German but composed a "fifth column" with the potential to sabotage the Reich's war effort.

The *Judenstern* decree simultaneously banned the wearing of "medals, decorations, and any other badges" by Jews. Thus the law would spare the German public the awkwardness of seeing Jews wearing an Iron Cross from the First World War, which was a source of ongoing embarrassment for the Nazis. The clause banning military decorations has been largely overlooked in the existing scholarship, yet its importance is difficult to overstate. As the previous chapters have argued, the public wearing of medals was part of a public identity; it signaled membership in an exclusive caste that enjoyed immense social prestige in Nazi Germany. More importantly, it was the only means available for Jews to identify themselves as former soldiers and challenge the derogatory classification "Jew." The law intended to obliterate this status, and there can be little doubt that it affected the external dynamics of German-Jewish relations. Nazi ideology refuted the Jewish claim to belonging by insinuating that Jewish military service had been self-interested, had been about acquiring power rather than serving the fatherland, but Jewish veterans had been able to speak out and display themselves against these accusations. The *Judenstern* decree took away Jewish veterans' ability to proclaim their status in public. It enabled the Nazis to achieve a goal that had eluded them until now: to make all Jews identical in the eyes of the German people.

Some Jewish veterans sarcastically referred to the yellow star as the "Orden Pour le Semite," a reference to Imperial Germany's highest wartime decoration, the Pour le Mérite, or quipped that they now had "one medal more," but any amount of humor failed to disguise the devastating psychological impact on the Jewish community.[70] "I myself feel shattered, cannot compose myself," Victor Klemperer wrote,[71] for now, as he later recalled, "every star-bearing Jew carried his own ghetto with him like a snail its house."[72] Although many Jewish ex-servicemen were already recognized as such by their Aryan neighbors, especially in smaller communities, the law forced old comrades and sympathetic Germans to publicly distance themselves from the so-called "star-bearers." A month after the decree went into effect, a follow-up directive declared that "people of German blood who show friendly contacts to Jews, will be temporarily placed in protective custody for educational reasons; in serious cases for a period of three months in a concentration camp." In each case the Jew was also to be sent to a concentration camp.[73]

After September 1939, the possibilities for Jewish veterans to exert influence on higher government offices or local officials in order to evade antisemitic measures were limited. In 1940, when the government "relocated" approximately 1,800 Jews from Stettin and Schneidemühl to Lublin in the Warthegau district between 10 and 15 March to make space for ethnic Germans, it deported veterans along with the rest of the Jewish population.[74] This was also the case on 22–23 October 1940, when 7,500 Jews from Baden and the Saar-Palatinate were deported to the former refugee camp Gurs in the Vichy zone of southern France.[75] It was Operation Barbarossa, however, Nazi Germany's invasion of the Soviet Union on 22 June 1941, that provided the impetus for the first mass deportations of Jews from Germany. By this time, some 165,000 Jews remained in Germany proper. That October, Nazi leaders decided that approximately 55,000 Jews from Germany (including Austria and the Protectorate) would be "resettled" to the occupied eastern territories over the next six months, a move that marked a dramatic departure from a policy of forced immigration to one of a "territorial solution to the Jewish Question." While the previous "resettlements" to Lublin and Gurs in 1940 had been local, extemporaneous measures, the deportations in fall 1941 were part of a larger plan involving massive resettlements of populations that coincided with the envisioned restructuring of Europe along racial lines.[76] The deportations were to be carried out in two "waves": The first, from 15 October to 3 November, would relocate 20,000 Jews (in addition to 5,000 Gypsies) from Vienna, Berlin, Prague, and Düsseldorf to the ghetto in Lodz. The second, scheduled to span 8 November 1941 through 15 February 1942, called for another 34,000 Jews in cities throughout Germany to be deported to Riga and Minsk.[77]

In order to determine which means were available for Jewish veterans to evade or delay these measures, it is necessary to establish who was responsible for drawing up the deportation lists and how victims were selected for transports. After the initial quotas were established by the Department of "Jewish Affairs and Evacuation" of the Reich Main Security Office (Reichssicherheitshauptamt, or RSHA), headed by Adolf Eichmann, the Gestapo issued guidelines to the local office of the Reich Association of Jews in Germany (Reichsvereinigung der Juden in Deutschland, or RV) for each transport, specifying which groups and which individuals were to be exempted from deportation in that particular transit. The RV selected names according to these criteria and submitted a preliminary list to the Gestapo, which then reviewed the names and decided who would be included on each transport.[78] The Gestapo, therefore, had the last word on who ended up on the lists, although the criterion they used to arrive at the final decision remains unclear.[79] Freed from the first two waves in 1941–42 were Jews in mixed marriages, foreign nationals, and forced laborers working in the armaments industry.[80] Beginning in November 1941, the sick, frail, and elderly over sixty-five years of age were also excluded.[81] Officially, the regime did not issue a collective exemption for Frontkämpfer at this early stage; war veterans were deported along with the other Jewish victims. Yet a close reading of the deportation lists from October 1941 reveals that the Gestapo rarely included former officers and recipients of high decorations (typically the Iron Cross First Class and higher) on transports to the East. The records of the Jewish Ghetto Administration at Lodz, for example, note that of the nine thousand German Jews deported to Lodz in October, only a single one had been a holder of the Iron Cross First Class.[82] A similar picture emerges in Würzburg, where the lists of deportees to Riga in November 1941 include no former officers or recipients of high decorations.[83]

Once the lists had been finalized by Nazi authorities, it was still possible for certain individuals to obtain exemptions. In fall 1941, according to an RV representative, "exemption requests were granted relatively generously," mainly because there was still a sufficiently large pool of replacements available to fill the void and so the Gestapo had no difficulty finding substitutes to meet the transport quota established by the RSHA.[84] Based on the high number of requests, it is not unreasonable to assume that former officers used connections to higher-ups to appeal their cases, as we have seen with Hugo Gutmann and Julius Katzmann.

Certain veterans, then, were able to evade deportation, most likely due to contacts in the government or the military. Thousands of other Jewish ex-servicemen, however—those without connections—were less fortunate. As the SS organized the deportations, noncombat veterans and those without serious war wounds or high medals for valor were ordered to report to local staging areas, along with the rest of the Jewish population, with fifty kilograms of baggage and five days of provisions for the trains headed to the East.

Life in the Extreme

On 15 October 1941, the first transports of Jews from the Reich arrived at Lodz (renamed Litzmannstadt by the Germans); they would be followed over the next four months by additional waves carrying Jews to the newly established Nazi ghettos in Minsk and Riga.[85] At first, the ghettos in Eastern Europe functioned as a kind of "dumping ground" for German Jews. The SS envisioned these deportations as a stopgap solution, a temporary means to relocate the Jewish population outside Germany's borders until their final fate had been decided.[86] Over time, however, they became a more permanent fixture in the Nazi system of annihilation and exploitation, using healthy Jewish prisoners for forced labor while murdering those "unfit" for work, and using the deportations as a pretext for confiscating the cash, valuables, and property of the victims.

Against this backdrop, having once belonged to a "privileged" group did not mean much once the victims arrived at Lodz. The sudden influx of Jews from Germany increased the population of the already overcrowded ghetto by nearly 20 percent; the new arrivals were placed in makeshift living quarters in evacuated school buildings, barracks, and assembly halls, where they were forced to sleep on the floor in buildings without heat, bathroom facilities, or running water. Exposed to disease and malnutrition and rendered defenseless against the arbitrary violence of the SS—and in some cases the indigenous Polish Jewish population—issues of status or identity were eclipsed by the need to survive physically.[87] Hans Biebow, the chief of the Nazi ghetto administration in Lodz, divided Jews into two groups: those capable and those incapable of work. Productivity was the sole guarantee for survival. It alone determined whether prisoners were allocated adequate rations and a place to live or placed in the dreaded category *nutzloser Fresser* (useless eater) and marked for further "resettlement" to a Nazi gassing facility. Veterans had to compete with other Jews for jobs that would spare them and their families from this fate. However, it was overwhelmingly younger men and skilled workers who received the highly coveted factory jobs, producing clothing and equipment for the Wehrmacht. Many of the new arrivals from Germany came from white-collar professions; they had been attorneys, architects, doctors, and small business owners, but only a few were craftsmen or farmers. The mostly middle-aged Great War veterans struggled under these conditions. Even the writers of the *Lodz Ghetto Chronicle*, a day-by-day community record of life in the ghetto, remarked that Jewish ex-servicemen from the Reich "have been doing manual labor in the ghetto, a great many of them working at garbage and excrement disposal," circumstances that produced "tremendous bitterness."[88]

Yet the records of the Jewish Ghetto Administration in Lodz reveal that war veterans, especially former officers and NCOs, were among those selected to serve in the Jewish Order Police (Ordnungsdienst).[89] At least a hundred former members of the German and Austro-Hungarian Armies were inducted into the Ordnungsdienst,[90] out of an overall veteran population of roughly four hundred.[91] A similar picture emerges in Minsk, where the Jewish police force in the "Hamburg" camp was composed of ex-soldiers.[92] In Riga, survivor testimonies and postwar trial records indicate that the chief of the Jewish police and several of his immediate subordinates were also ex-servicemen.[93]

Recent studies of Jewish masculinities during the Holocaust have proposed that ghettoization gave Jewish men a space to revitalize their masculine identity, for it created new power structures, laws, and hierarchies that afforded them opportunities to act.[94] Such was the case at Lodz, Riga, and Minsk, where service in the Jewish police made it possible for Jewish veterans to practice key elements of their normative gender roles, which would have been unthinkable in Nazi Germany during the years of persecution.

Established by German authorities to maintain public order inside the ghetto, the primary function of the police was to enforce the policies of both the Nazi ghetto administrators and the local Jewish Council (Judenrat). At Lodz, in addition to regular law enforcement duties, the Jewish police provided crucial logistical support to the SS when the "superfluous" ghetto population was periodically rounded up and deported to the makeshift gassing facilities at Chelmo.[95] In September 1942, when 15,681 prisoners, overwhelmingly children and the elderly, were violently separated from their parents and families and placed on trains that would take them to be gassed, it was the Jewish Order Police that cordoned off streets, apartment blocks, and sections of the ghetto, and guarded the victims as they boarded the trains to Chelmo.[96] Contemporary observers and historians writing after 1945 alike condemned the Jewish police as an agent of Nazi collaboration and, as Saul Friedländer put it, "morally and materially corrupt," a view that permeates the present literature on the Holocaust.[97] The 2014 publication of secret documents hidden by members of the Kovno Ghetto Police in 1942 and 1943 reveals that the boundary between collaboration and victimhood was often blurred.[98]

One of the reasons why there are no comprehensive studies on the Jewish police in general, or the German Jewish contingents at Lodz, Minsk, and Riga in particular, is that there were so few survivors.[99] Of the 5,000 German Jews deported to Minsk, only 5 are believed to have survived, while at the most a few hundred German and Austrian Jews sent to Lodz in October 1941 made it to the end of the war alive.[100] The highest survival rate among German Jews was in Riga, where it is believed that 1,100 lived to see the Allied liberation.[101] Karl Löwenstein, the Jewish police chief in Minsk (and later Theresienstadt) was the only Jewish former soldier to leave behind a detailed account of his experiences.[102] In the absence of substantial victims' testimony, the surviving files of the Lodz Ghetto administration (Ghettoverwaltung Litzmannstadt) yield some insights into the responsibilities and day-to-day inner workings of the Jewish Police.[103] Together with the Lodz Ghetto Chronicle and postwar trial records, these sources shed light on how membership in the police gave Jewish veterans a means to exert some agency in the confines of the "East," even as the Final Solution unfolded around them.[104]

In general it can be said that members of the Jewish Order Police were recruited from groups that could be relied on to obey and implement German orders. Their familiarity with the language and codes of discipline of the German military were traits that were deemed vital in order for the Jewish police to carry out their duties and simultaneously deal with German authorities. Membership in the police brought a number of tangible benefits, including greater freedom of movement, possibilities for obtaining extra rations, and protection of one's family from deportation. While Karl Löwenstein described the motivations of the Minsk Ghetto Police in highly altruistic terms, conceding only that his men occasionally received additional rations, "an extra warm soup . . . if there was any available,"[105] Ruth Alton's memoir of Lodz is far more frank in this regard. Among the rewards to be reaped by joining the Order Police was a highly coveted private apartment, a benefit the SS extended to Alton's husband, because he had accepted a job as a "transport assistant." Her memoir leaves little to the imagination as to what these privileges meant for people who had previously endured living in packed school classrooms where multiple families lived, in conditions so "wretched" that they "turned most humans into animals."[106] "The small room and the resulting privacy meant incredibly much for us," she wrote. "We were able to wash ourselves daily, rinse our work clothes, and spare our young boy from many things he had to hear and witness at the beginning."[107]

But survival was the overriding motive for Jews to join the Order Police. As a protected elite, they were provided immunity from further "resettlements" for both themselves and their families As a means to incentivize the Jewish police for the task of forcibly separating Jewish children from their mothers during the September 1942 deportations, Chaim Rumkowski, the head of the Lodz Jewish Council, personally guaranteed the safety of each policeman's family from future *Aktionen*.[108] A senior Gestapo official at Lodz, Günther Fuchs, went even further: he threatened the Jewish policemen that their own children would be deported if they did not deliver the exact quota of victims for the transports to Chelmo.[109]

Karl Löwenstein's memoir has been criticized by some scholars for its alleged self-serving retelling of events,[110] yet it provides key insights into how Jewish Frontkämpfer not only fought for their survival but also attempted to preserve their masculine honor in the extreme conditions of the East. Löwenstein served as a naval officer during World War I and went on to join the Freikorps after Germany's defeat, playing an active role in fighting Polish insurgents in Silesia in 1919–20.[111] A convert to Christianity, he was a founding member of the Confessing Church in Berlin, and his connections to conservative elites such as Helmuth James Graf von Moltke enabled him to elude the regime's anti-Jewish measures until late 1941. In November of that year, his situation abruptly changed. Without warning, the Gestapo arrested Löwenstein and placed him on a transport to Minsk the following day, so that his helpers would not have a chance to intervene. Upon his arrival at the ghetto, Löwenstein was selected by the Jewish Council to train a contingent of police to protect the female prisoners from "marauding" Russian POWs, who were being held in an adjoining camp. Löwenstein handpicked the Ghetto Police "from men who had served . . . from all ranks—up to captain—and from all branches of service from the old German, Austrian, and Czech armies, so that I was able to train and mold them into an effective troop."[112] Under Löwenstein's leadership, this "potent," "highly trained," and "first-class troop" acquired special insignia and even trained in Prussian-style military drill.[113] This carefully honed public image was not meant to impress the other Jewish prisoners, however. It was an attempt to distinguish the German prisoners from Eastern European Jews, to make clear to the SS that they were dealing with Jews who had fought in the German Army during World War I. Löwenstein's example shows how policemen went beyond the narrow confines of carrying out their duties to preserve their identity as military men, and defy the Nazi stereotype "Jew." Minsk was not an isolated case. In Riga, the roughly forty ghetto policemen led by Friedrich Frankenberg and his acting chief, Rudolf Haar, assumed a "purely German character," acquiring dark overcoats, riding breeches, army boots, and military-style peaked caps.[114] Surviving photographs from the Lodz Ghetto even show German Jewish policemen wearing the ribbon of the Iron Cross from the First World War on their uniforms.

Löwenstein's memoir suggests that one of the reasons he considered himself effective in his role as police chief was his ability to deal with the SS and Nazi bigwigs such as Wilhelm Kube. He credited his background as a German officer, which some of the camp officials shared or apparently respected, for his ability to adapt to the methods of the SS better than the other Jewish prisoners and interact with them on a completely different basis. At least, this is the recurring message in his writings; he presents himself as being more assertive, flexible, and confident than his nervous colleagues in the Jewish Council. A similar picture emerges in Zamość, a transit ghetto in the Lublin region, where the Order Police were led by Alwin Lippmann, a former fighter pilot and Freikorps officer. In Düsseldorf, the SS had exempted Lippmann from deportation, but in May 1942 he decided to join his wife, who, for reasons that are unclear, had not been exempted.[115] When he arrived at Zamość, he was appointed chief of the Jewish police, a capacity in which he served until the ghetto's liquidation in October 1942.[116] Thomas Blatt, another prisoner at Zamość, described Lippmann as a "typical" German—stoic and pedantic, thoroughly committed to his role, and also having a fondness for German military drill and discipline.[117] Taken together, these accounts embody a specific type of masculinity: not being incapacitated by fear, remaining composed in the face of intense pressure, and asserting one's identity in the face of Nazi intimidation. These were virtues extolled by German society, but even more so, they were associated with the image of the soldierly German male. This kind of self-assertion stood in contrast to the helplessness and inaction that prevailed in the ghetto, defying the Nazis' efforts to strip Jews of their manhood and German national identity.

Löwenstein claimed that the true purpose behind the military-style training of the Minsk Order Police was to one day fight back against the Nazis. "Already in late 1941," he wrote, "I took into account the possibility of Germany's defeat. In this case I wanted to ensure that the camp was not overrun without protection."[118] His success in molding the police into a well-disciplined, "first-class troop" did not go unnoticed by the SS. "Through informants," an SS after-action report stated, "it became known that the Order Service of the German Jews, comprising mainly former soldiers, was determined to wage armed resistance during a major clearing operation."[119] Out of fear that the Order Police could be dangerous, and "in order to prevent bloodshed on the German side," the SS lured them out of the ghetto on the pretense of fighting a fire that had erupted in the city. The Jewish policemen were loaded onto trucks and driven to a specially prepared location outside the perimeter, where they were gunned down by an SS firing squad.[120] This was also the fate of the Latvian Jewish police force in Riga. The SS discovered a secret weapons cache in the Latvian section of the ghetto in October 1942, and they responded by shooting all forty-one members of the police in a carefully prepared ambush. The importance of these seemingly unrelated developments is difficult to exaggerate. The fact that the SS viewed the Jewish policemen—overwhelmingly men with military training and experience—as a source of potential resistance would have far-reaching consequences for the Jewish Frontkämpfer, as Nazi Germany's military situation became increasingly precarious.

Interventions from Above

As the Nazis began deporting thousands of Jews to ghettos in Eastern Europe in October 1941, Ernst Hess had reason to remain optimistic. A former lieutenant in the List Regiment, Hess had served in the same unit as Hitler in World War I, a connection that led to the issuing of a so-called *Schutzbrief*—a protection letter—by the Reich Chancellery a year earlier. On 19 August 1940, Himmler's adjutant contacted the Düssseldorf chief of police to inform him that Hess had been granted immunity from deportation and was permitted to use his name without the mandatory "Israel" in official correspondence, a decision made "in accordance with the Führer's wishes."[121] The letter further stated that "H. is a full Jew with 4 Jewish grandparents. During the war 1914/18 he served in the same company as the

Führer and also temporarily served as the Führer's company commander. When Hess submitted a petition to obtain an exemption, the Führer, after declining the request, expressed his desire that H. be given an accommodation through other means. . . . I therefore request, in cooperation with all the relevant authorities and agencies, that H. remain unmolested for all intents and purposes."[122]

Hitler probably had little to do with the order protecting Hess. Most likely the letter was the result of an intervention by Fritz Wiedemann, Hitler's personal adjutant from 1934 to 1939, who had also served in the List Regiment during World War I. As we have seen, Wiedemann had helped engineer Hans Gutmann's release from prison several years before. His proximity to Hitler afforded him unfettered access to Heinrich Lammers, director of the Reich Chancellery, a connection that enabled him to secure special exemptions for old comrades. Wiedemann eventually fell out of favor with Hitler and was transferred to the United States in early 1939, where he assumed the post of consul general. This may explain why Hess was unexpectedly ordered to appear at the local Gestapo office in May 1941, only to be informed that his special status had been rescinded and that he was now "a Jew like any other."[123] Instead of being deported to a ghetto in eastern Europe, however, Hess was incarcerated at Milbertshofen, a labor camp outside Munich, where he worked as a forced laborer until his liberation on 20 April 1945.[124]

Hess was not the only Jewish former officer to take advantage of connections to higher-ups in order to evade deportation. In a postwar interview, Max Plaut, chairman of the Hamburg RV office, mentioned a baptized Jew who, as a comrade of Göring and Erhard Milch in World War I, received the "highest protection," allegedly without even having to submit any documents to the authorities. The man was allowed to change his name from Oppenheimer to a "less suspicious one," continued to live in his own home, and was even allowed to employ an Aryan housemaid. When the Bremen Gestapo got wind of the situation, they notified the chief of the Hamburg Gestapo, Claus Göttsche, who arrested Oppenheimer and threatened to have him shot. Only Göring's timely intervention by telephone saved Oppenheimer, and he was promptly released, apparently free to continue his life in the open, unmolested.[125] This highly unusual case cannot be confirmed by official records, yet other evidence indicates that Göring submitted a list—now lost—of two hundred individuals to the Berlin Gestapo in October 1941, with instructions to protect them from deportation.[126]

Some of the deferments emanating from Göring or the Reich Chancellery proved to be permanent, but most were not. After Heinrich Haake used his authority as *Landeshauptmann* (governor) to strike Stephan Prager's name from the deportation lists in October 1941, he contacted Wilhelm Frick, the interior minister, to arrange for a more permanent resolution, requesting that Prager be granted immunity from any future anti-Jewish measures. Because Prager, Haake argued, had "rendered invaluable services to the Fatherland in time of war and had joined the Stahlhelm early on, one can therefore make a strong case from the standpoint of the general public that Prager deserves an *exemption*, which I wholeheartedly endorse."[127] Haake's request was answered not by the Interior Ministry, but by Heydrich at the RSHA, who informed him that Hitler himself explicitly ordered that there would be no further exceptions, "regardless of the circumstances." What bothered Heydrich the most, however, was that Prager's case "would create a precedent, one that would lead to countless similar requests and create serious difficulties for the envisioned total solution of the Jewish Question in the Reich."[128]

If Heydrich was able to brush aside protests from midlevel party functionaries with relative impunity, a more serious challenge came from senior officers of the Wehrmacht. In February 1941, General Alfred Streccius, the commander of Wehrkreis (military district) 17 in Vienna, voiced his displeasure over the upcoming deportation of Austrian Jews to General Friedrich Fromm at the Army High Command (Oberkommando des Heeres, or OKH). Streccius had learned about the "resettlements" through Baldur von Schirach, the governor of Vienna, and what upset him was not that Viennese Jews were being "shoved off" to Poland, but that the names of "several former active officers and an even greater number of war-wounded" were included on the transport lists. In a letter to Fromm dated 24 February 1941, Streccius insisted that "former officers and war invalids with over 50% disability . . . be given the possibility to spend their remaining years on German soil. Aside from the fact that they have proven their worth in front of the enemy," he argued, "their expulsion is not compatible with the reputation of the Wehrmacht."[129] A follow-up letter to Schirach on 29 April indicates that Fromm endorsed Streccius's position, and that Hitler's adjutant at the Wehrmacht High Command (Oberkommando der Wehrmacht, or OKW), Colonel Rudolf Schmundt, also took up the issue. In the end, however, the intervention failed to provide sweeping protections to the groups Streccius mentioned. Schirach, the OKW, and the RSHA apparently reached a compromise, whereby "particularly serious cases" would be given consideration on a case-by-case basis.[130] Instead of categorically exempting the war wounded and former members of the officers' corps, a special commission at Wehrkreis 17 narrowed the original list of fifty names down to twelve individuals. The men on that list, all Jewish officers, would be "permitted to reside in the Reich" and entitled to "an easing of the measures pertaining to Jews currently in effect in Vienna."[131]

Several weeks later, in Berlin, Fritz Arnold and Julius Fliess, the Jewish war invalids who had petitioned Field Marshal Mackensen three years earlier, contacted Helmuth James von Moltke and Hans von Dohnanyi in German military intelligence (the Abwehr), after learning they were about to be deported to Minsk. Moltke and Dohnanyi were incensed that the Wehrmacht High Command countenanced the deportation of German Jews and did not intervene on behalf of war-wounded ex-servicemen. Writing to his wife on 11 November 1941, Moltke made no effort to hide his disgust: "Yesterday I said goodbye to a once famous Jewish lawyer who has the Iron Cross First and Second Class, the Order of the House of Hohenzollern, the Golden Wound Badge, who will kill himself with his wife today because he is to be picked up tonight."[132] After consulting Dohnanyi, Moltke brought the matter to the attention of his superiors, Admiral Wilhelm Canaris and General Georg Thomas, convincing them to sign a petition opposing the deportation of war-wounded Jews. "In fighting the latest decree against Jews," Moltke wrote on 11 November, "I have succeeded in getting the 3 most important generals of the Oberkommando der Wehrmacht to write to the 4th that he must immediately withdraw the approval he gave on behalf of the chief of the OKW."[133] Three days later, Moltke reported meeting with General Hermann Reinecke, the head of the Wehrmacht General Office (Allgemeines Wehrmachtsamt), and said that he had "secured a veto by the OKW."[134] Based on Fliess's and Arnold's postwar testimonies, Reinecke himself personally drove to Eichmann's office and demanded, in the name of the OKW, that their names be struck from the lists, which they were.[135] Moltke's letter from 17 November further implies that the "veto" extended beyond Fliess and Arnold, stating that an OKW "representative" was to meet with Field Marshal Wilhelm Keitel, chief of the OKW, the following day in order to register "an objection against the intended decree" that included war-wounded Jews in the deportations.[136] In the absence of documentary sources, it is not clear whether subsequent action was taken by Keitel, or how the RSHA responded. Reinecke's willingness to intervene on behalf of Jewish former soldiers, however, is corroborated by Leo Löwenstein, the former chairman of the RjF, who testified as a witness for the defense during Reinecke's war crimes trial in 1948, lauding him for his efforts to exempt Jewish veterans from having to wear the *Judenstern*.[137]

Complaints about the inclusion of veterans in the "evacuations" were not restricted to military circles. The year before, when seven thousand Jews from Baden were deported to Gurs in October 1940, a report by an official in the Foreign Office (Auswärtige Amt) dated 30 October noted with apparent surprise that "even men who had fought on the German side during the war as Frontkämpfer and former officers of the old army were sent away."[138] The Foreign Office also received several anonymous letters expressing anger that these measures were being applied to "men who had fought in the World War 1914–1918 on the German and Austrian side as front soldiers, some of them with officers' rank, including war cripples."[139] These protests were deemed serious enough to warrant a full Gestapo investigation.

Similar sentiments were recorded by the German diplomat Ulrich von Hassell. When he learned of the deportations that had taken place in Baden, he was shocked to discover that "reserve officers with the Iron Cross, First Class . . . were chased head over heels across the border toward Alsace."[140] Hassell visited Berlin the following year as the deportations to Lodz were in full swing, actions he described as "shameless measures . . . against harmless and often distinguished Jews in Berlin and other large cities."[141] His diary entry for 1 November 1941 suggests that many conservatives condemned such "shameless measures," in particular because they included former soldiers of the Great War: "Gritzbach, an intimate friend of Goering, called on Popitz. He was shocked by the expulsion of Jews from Berlin, including a holder of the Pour-le-Mérite, several Hohenzollern knights and numerous Iron Cross holders. Terrible scenes took place in their houses during the early hours. The populace in part was so disgusted that the Nazis found it necessary to distribute leaflets explaining that the Jews were to blame for everything, and anybody who sympathized with them was a traitor to the Volk."[142]

Such reactions reached the highest levels of the German government. If we believe Hassell, "Göring definitely shared the same sentiments" but was unwilling to do anything because the order to also deport Jewish veterans had been given by the Führer himself. "Hitler had been asked to exempt Jews who were war veterans, or at least those who had been awarded the Iron Cross, from expulsion or the wearing of the Star of David on their clothing," Hassell wrote. "The answer was: 'No, these swine got their decorations fraudulently.'"[143]

The objections raised by Streccius and Hassel in 1941 bear a striking similarity to Hindenburg and Manstein's protests seven years earlier. These rationales were also articulated in Carl Goerdeler's political manifesto, Das Ziel ("The Goal"), which called for the creation of a Jewish state where European Jews would be "resettled" after Hitler's demise, while making exceptions for Jewish veterans of World War I, who would be "entitled" to German citizenship.[144] Together, these cases throw light on the diverging positions on the Jewish Question between hard-liners in the NSDAP and traditional conservative elites. The latter shared many of the antisemitic principles of the Nazis, yet regarded military sacrifice as a qualifying factor for exemption from anti-Jewish legislation.[145] According to Hans Mommsen, these views were "largely consistent with the culturally inspired, disassimilationist anti-semitism that had manifested itself in the political right since the Kaiserreich and especially in the officers' corps."[146]

Displeasure over the government's treatment of Jewish war veterans extended not only into the ranks of the Nazi Party, as we have seen, but even into those organizations tasked with carrying out the Final Solution. Wilhelm Kube, the *generalkommissar* of Belarus, was shocked to discover during a visit to the Minsk Ghetto in November 1941 that "among these Jews are frontline veterans with the Iron Cross First and Second class, the war wounded, half-Aryans, and even a three-quarter Aryan." Writing to his superior, Hinrich Lohse, Kube declared, "I am certainly tough and ready to help solve the Jewish Question, but human beings who come from our cultural sphere are something other than the native bestial hordes."[147] Kube's racist credentials and his commitment to National Socialism were never in doubt: an antisemitic activist since his student days, he joined the NSDAP in the late 1920s and climbed rapidly through the party ranks.[148] As the governor of occupied Belarus, Kube was deeply implicated in the murder of the indigenous Jewish population, boasting to a superior in July 1942 that under his watch fifty-five thousand local Jews had been "liquidated" over a ten-week period.[149] Yet as far as Kube was concerned, it was "dishonorable" to treat former soldiers of the German Army in the same manner as the "bestial" Eastern European Jews, and he vowed to report the matter of such "unjustly resettled Jews" to the Führer.[150]

Not surprisingly, there was little tolerance for such a stance in the RSHA. Many in the SS were incensed by Kube's behavior and complained to Heydrich that his actions "demonstrate an absolutely impossible attitude regarding the Jewish Question."[151] Among the accusations SS officials leveled against Kube was that he openly berated camp guards for their "brutal, egregious" treatment of Jewish prisoners. In one incident, a report from 25 July 1943 claimed, Kube went as far as publicly dressing down a policeman after he had struck a Jewish prisoner, "screaming at him, asking him whether he was in possession of an Iron Cross like the Jew."[152] In the end, however, Kube's actions failed to save the Jewish veterans imprisoned in Minsk. Although spared from the March 1942 massacres, some 3,500 German Jews were murdered with Kube's consent in July; a further 2,600 were killed in March and September the following year. During the same period, 20,000 new arrivals from Germany were not even taken into the ghetto, but shot upon arrival.[153]

Several conclusions can be drawn from these developments. First, in fall 1941, the RSHA was being inundated by petitions seeking exemptions for certain individuals, especially Jewish veterans of the First World War. It was an issue raised repeatedly in correspondence between Heydrich, Eichmann, and other party officials, and at this early stage the RSHA was still willing to make exceptions on a case-by-case basis.[154] Second, the petitions overwhelmingly came from high-ranking active and retired officers in an effort to protect "their" Jews—that is, personal friends or comrades from the war. To treat an old comrade like Hess in this way was an "obligation" for fellow officers, one anchored in the military caste's code of honor. The moral code of comradeship demanded nothing less: old soldiers protected each other, especially from the "civilian rabble," and for their entire lives, whatever the circumstances.

Yet such cases throw light on the limits of these interventions. Protests from high-ranking officers and government officials often succeeded in saving certain Jews from deportation, but, importantly, they did not put a brake on the regime's genocidal ambitions. Quite the contrary: by protesting the government's "dishonorable" treatment of Jewish Frontkämpfer and claiming that these individuals had been exceptional because they had "proven their worth," Streccius, Canaris, Moltke, and others simultaneously reinforced the Nazis' rationale for pursuing their campaign against "Jewry." From the regime's point of view, it merely needed to maintain the appearance that certain types of "decent" Jews would be spared the fate of the other victims. The SS could therefore push the boundaries of what was tolerated. Because conservative elites, and the German public in general, were unwilling to respond to attacks against "Jews" but were hesitant to see these same measures applied to war veterans, the SS concluded—and rightly so—that they could exempt certain Jews while pursuing the rest without eliciting too much public disapproval.[155]

These developments raise critical questions: Did interventions from the Wehrmacht have any real impact? Did they succeed in effecting changes to anti-Jewish policy, either in the short or long term? How did Himmler, Heydrich, and the Nazi leadership respond? Despite the sparse and fragmented nature of the surviving sources, we can discern from Streccius's correspondence with Fromm and Schirach that a "meeting between the OKW and the Reichs Chancellery concerning the Zionist Star (*Judenstern*)" was set for September or October, and that Streccius urged the OKW to broach the issue of the "treatment of privileged Jewish officers."[156] Whether a formal meeting actually took place and what transpired there can no longer be established.

What is clear, however, based on Eichmann's notes from a gathering of RSHA leaders in Prague on 10 October 1941, is that a settlement had been negotiated. According to the internal meeting minutes, Heydrich remained adamant that "there shall be *no considerations for Jews with war decorations*. If a Jew in the Altreich possesses a war medal, the regulations will apply to him that have been agreed to by the OKW. These Jews should not remain in the Reich under any circumstances; quite the contrary, they will be evacuated in the appropriate percentages."[157]

War-decorated Jews, therefore, were to be deported along with the rest of the Jewish population. Most likely, the regulations that had been "agreed to by the OKW" stipulated that "serious cases" would be exempted on a case-by-case basis "in order to prevent a flood of letters on behalf of such Jews."[158] In practice, this loophole applied to ex-officers with high-level connections, which may explain why there were almost no former officers or recipients of "high wartime decorations" on the transports to Lodz during the first wave of deportations in October 1941.[159]

Yet six weeks after the Prague meeting, on 20 November, Eichmann circulated a memo outlining deportation guidelines, in which he complained about the increasing number of "interventions from certain Wehrmacht offices or individual officers."[160] Two days later, the Gestapo Main Office Nuremberg notified its Würzburg field office that Jewish war invalids and holders of the Iron Cross First Class or Bavarian Bravery Medal should be exempted from the upcoming "evacuations" to Riga. The order, dated 22 November, further stipulated that "if such persons have already been assigned to a transport, then they are, if protests opposing their deportation are forthcoming, to be removed (from the list)."[161] This was exactly five days after Helmuth James von Moltke wrote to his wife that he "managed to get all departments of the OKW behind me on this question. Tonight a colonel is travelling to see Keitel in order to propose to him tomorrow that an objection against the intended decree would be registered."[162] A few days later, on 28 November, Victor Klemperer noted in his diary, "Today an urgent communication from the Reich Association (RV). Who has war decorations? Will that be of any use against deportation?"[163] And a similar development was unfolding in Berlin, where in early December the Jewish Religious Union (Kultusvereinigung), the organization tasked by the Gestapo with assembling the deportation lists and informing individuals about upcoming "evacuations," began compiling the names of medal recipients and registering them in a separate list.[164]

The chronological sequence of events suggests that the objections raised by the OKW were a decisive factor in halting the deportations. On the basis of the sources cited, it is reasonable to assume that the decision to provisionally exempt certain Jewish wartime combatants had been reached sometime in mid-November. The decision was the consequence of a process stretching back over a period of at least nine months, from February to October 1941, during which multiple interventions from the OKW reached Heydrich's desk. The RSHA feared that deporting veterans might anger the military if news spread that Frontkämpfer and members of the old officers' corps were being killed along with other Jews, so Heydrich agreed to a series of exemptions for veterans of World War I. Unwilling to exempt too many, however, the RSHA imposed restrictions: only "serious cases"—that is, frontline veterans who had received high medals for bravery or had been wounded—were to be excluded, at least for the time being. Thus over the past eight years of Nazi rule, there had been a consistent and discernable pattern in the correlation between interventions from the military and the reining in of Nazi anti-Jewish policies by the RSHA, indicating that the regime's actions were heavily influenced and shaped by Heydrich's attempt to obviate potential zones of discontent. These developments culminated with the government's announcement on 24 November 1941 that a "privileged old persons' ghetto" for certain German Jews would be established at Theresienstadt.[165]

The aforementioned developments suggest some tentative conclusions in regard to the evolving structure of persecution of Jewish World War I veterans. Foremost, they show that interventions by senior officers of the Wehrmacht could be successful. The army was still able to persuasively articulate its moral indignation against Nazi policy in terms of honor and shame. Even at this late stage, as the war against the Soviet Union was entering its decisive phase, the Wehrmacht retained some of its political clout vis-à-vis Himmler and the RSHA. To their credit, Moltke and Streccius protested forcefully and also successfully, and their example demonstrates that a handful of mid-level, relatively inconsequential officers were able to wring concessions, albeit limited ones, from the regime. The fact that they pushed their proposals with apparently considerable support from other officers in the OKW and OKH further suggests these views were not individual. The traditional moral norms of the military caste, however antisemitic, still involved notions of comradeship and honor that demanded certain obligations toward former soldiers, especially members of the old officers' corps, ideas that were still alive in 1941.

These examples challenge recent scholarship on the behavior of ordinary Germans during the Holocaust, which emphasizes—rightly so—the widespread indifference of the population to the suffering of the Jews. Yet it is worth repeating here that the interventions by the German military did not challenge the regime's anti-Jewish policy on principle. Streccius, like other

German officers, was tormented by the damage to the German Army's reputation caused by its forfeiture of honor and submission to Nazi ideology. Even though the deportations exposed the murderous intentions of Hitler's regime, the generals were largely unreceptive to the suffering of Germany's Jewish population as a whole. They raised no objections on principle, perhaps because they feared the SS challenge to army authority or the potential damage to their professional careers, but also in large part because they shared the belief that Jews were an un-German ethnic minority, naturally predisposed to undermine Nazi Germany's war effort, and therefore had to disappear. Although the inclusion of former officers in measures targeting "Jewry" was seen as a stain on the army's honor, at no point were the deportations contested for what they were—a blatant assault on the most basic human rights of German citizens and incontrovertible evidence of the criminal nature of the Hitler regime.

"Proclamation No. 380"

On 29 April 1942, the ghetto administrators at Lodz distributed an announcement throughout the ghetto, alerting the population to an impending *Aktion*. Proclamation No. 380, as it was called, ordered all "Westjuden" (Western European Jews) to assemble on the main square with their luggage and personal belongings in preparation for "resettlement," ostensibly to a different labor camp. In what followed, between 4 and 14 May 1942, the SS sent away some 10,914 of the remaining German, Austrian, and Czech Jews, those too sick, old, or frail to work, to be gassed at Chelmo.[166] The move was part of a broader effort to reduce Jewish populations to a productive core that would be exploited for labor; only those capable of factory work were supposed to remain in the ghetto, which continued to serve as a center of production for the Wehrmacht until early 1944.[167] Yet the announcement contained a crucial passage, one that signaled a significant development in the Nazis' *Judenpolitik*. Excluded from the deportation to Chelmo were "1.) Holders of the Iron Cross, 2.) Holders of the Wound Badge, and 3.) Employed persons."[168] Thus even in the killing fields of the East, Jewish veterans were granted a reprieve, ostensibly on higher orders from Berlin. Who was responsible for the decision? And what did this latest development mean for the Jewish veterans interred at Lodz and the other ghettos in Eastern Europe?

Among the German Jewish population at Lodz, there was a frantic rush to submit medal certificates and military ID documents to the ghetto administration before the deadline passed. The less fortunate among them, those who no longer possessed their paperwork or awards, made impassioned pleas to the Judenrat, listing dates of service, battles, and names of commanding officers, in an all-out effort to substantiate their military service.[169] According to the *Lodz Ghetto Chronicle*,

> Holders of the Iron Cross were summoned yesterday to report to Balut Market today at 8 a.m. Around 100 of these summonses went out both to those who had been decorated with iron crosses and to those with medals for wounds suffered while in the German or Austrian army during WWI. . . . A few hundred old men marching down the streets of the ghetto by fours, military style, drew everyone's attention. Representatives of the secret police (Gestapo) examined their documents at Balut Market, and quite courteously, too. . . . The chief of secret police has spoken to the Chairman [Rumkowski] about assuring work to those with decorations. The next group of 100 has been summoned for tomorrow.[170]

This remarkable scene unfolded at a time when Nazi officials were working feverishly to coordinate a Europe-wide genocidal campaign, and as ten thousand German Jews from Lodz were gassed. In the end, approximately four hundred veterans and their families were spared from the deportations.[171] To be sure, this exemption was merely a stay of execution. But for those who escaped immediate gassing, the process of killing was in some cases protracted over a number of months, even years.

Proclamation No. 380 turned Nazi racial policy on its head. From the perspective of the RSHA and the Nazi ghetto managers at Riga, Minsk, and Lodz, the sole rationale for keeping Jews alive was for labor. Whatever concession was reached between the ideologically committed leadership of the SS, local *Gauleiter* (district governors), and members of the German military, the decree exempting Jewish war veterans from this policy contradicted this rationale. It went against the policy of murder, and the practice of destruction through labor (*Vernichtung durch Arbeit*), policies that had been endorsed and carried forward on the initiative and authority of the SS, above all the RSHA, with backing from Himmler and Hitler at the very top. Thus it appears that a concession was extracted from the SS, either by a handful of German military officers or due to anxieties over public opinion, but most likely a combination of both.

After 1941, even as the Nazis decreed the same fate for all Jews, ideological imperatives were subject to compromise as circumstances demanded, especially when it came to public opinion and to pacifying groups whose cooperation was deemed vital for the implementation of the Final Solution. Time and again, the Nazis did not go further than what they perceived everyday Germans and conservative elites would tolerate. This discrepancy in thinking between the military bureaucracy and the representatives of the RSHA, who were determined to classify Frontkämpfer the same as all other Jews, both legally and socially, and to include them in the measures aimed at genocide, exacerbated tensions that would not be resolved until the Wannsee Conference the following year.

FIGURE 1. Herbert Sulzbach, top, with fellow officers from the Sixty-Third Field Artillery Regiment on the Western Front.

Imperial War Museum, Q 94003.

FIGURE 2.   Erich, Heinrich, and Walter Leyens as war volunteers in 1914.

Courtesy of the Stadtarchiv Wesel.

FIGURE 3. Members of the Freikorps Würzburg, 1919. Three Jewish soldiers are present: Benno Schwabacher (third from left), Alfred Haas (middle, with army overcoat), and Siegfried Birn (behind Haas). Schwabacher and Haas emigrated from Germany and survived the Holocaust; Birn was murdered at Auschwitz in 1942.

FIGURE 4. "To German Mothers! 12,000 Jews fell in battle!" Illustrated leaflet of the Reichsbund jüdischer Frontsoldaten (RjF) from 1924, calling on Germans to remember Jewish sacrifices during the First World War.

Deutsches Historisches Museum.

FIGURE 5. Franz Seldte, the chairman of the Far Right veterans' association Stahlhelm, at the annual "front soldiers' day" in Magdeburg, 1929. Over Seldte's objections, the organization introduced an "Aryan Paragraph" in 1924, banning Jewish membership. Seldte would go on to become the Reich Minister of Labor under Hitler.

FIGURE 6. Richard Stern, who was awarded the Iron Cross during World War I, in front of his shop in Cologne during the Nazi boycott of Jewish businesses on 1 April 1933.

Courtesy of the NS Documentation Center of the City of Cologne.

An alle Frontkameraden und Deutsche!

Unser Herr Reichskanzler **Hitler** und die Herren Reichsminister **Frick und Göring** haben mehrfach folgende Erklärungen abgegeben:

> **Wer im III. Reich einen Frontsoldaten beleidigt, wird mit Zuchthaus bestraft!**

 Mein Bruder meldete sich mit 25 Jahren am 4. August 1914 als Kriegsfreiwilliger und war bis Ende 1918 an der Front. Ich selbst wurde als junger Bursche von kaum 18 Jahren zur Fahne berufen und stand dauernd **an der Front in vorderster Linie** bei der 2. Masch.-Gewehr-Komp. d. Landw.-Inf.-Regt. 31. Erhielt **für Tapferkeit vor dem Feinde das Eiserne Kreuz** und kehrte erst 1919 nach Hause zurück.

Unser verstorbener kranker Vater verrichtete mit 58 Jahren noch den Kriegshilfsdienst, während seine beiden Söhne im Felde standen. Müssen wir uns nach dieser Vergangenheit im Nationalen Dienst als guter Deutscher, jetzt öffentlich beschimpfen lassen? Soll das heute der Dank des Vaterlandes sein, daß durch Presse und Rundfunk über

65 Millionen Deutsche aufgefordert werden

nicht bei Deutschen Juden zu kaufen, ja jeder Deutsche Jude, selbst der kleinste Geschäftsmann oder Handwerker zu boykottieren sei?

Ist der Deutsche Jude nunmehr ein **Mensch II. Klasse** geworden, den man nur noch als Gast in seinem Vaterland duldet?

Wir fassen diese Aktion gegen das gesamte Deutsche Judentum auf als eine Schändung des Andenkens von

12 000 gefallenen Deutschen Frontsoldaten jüdischen Glaubens.

Wir sehen darüber hinaus in dieser Aufforderung eine Beleidigung für jeden anständigen Bürger. Es ist uns nicht bange darum, daß es in Köln auch heute noch die Zivilcourage gibt, die Bismarck einst forderte, und Deutsche Treue, die gerade jetzt zu uns Juden steht.

Bettwaren-Haus
Marsilstein 20

Der ehemalige Frontkämpfer
Richard Stern

FIGURE 7. "To all Frontline comrades and Germans!" Flier distributed by Richard Stern on 1 April 1933, calling on ordinary Germans to protest the Nazis' "dishonorable" treatment of Jewish veterans of the Great War.

FIGURE 8. Otto Lewin, one of the last German soldiers of Jewish descent to serve in the Wehrmacht, in a family portrait from 1934. The Nazis classified Lewin as a "full Jew" and discharged him from the army in 1936.

Ulrich Lewin, private collection.

FIGURE 9. Victor Klemperer, in a portrait taken in 1952.

BArch, Bild 183-16552-0001.

Figure 10. Julius Fliess in 1941. Note the miniatures of the Iron Crosses First and Second Class and Wound Badge affixed to his right lapel.

Jewish Museum Berlin, donated by Dorothee Fliess.

Figure 11. Jewish war commemoration organized by the Reichsbund jüdischer Frontsoldaten (RjF) in Berlin, 1936. Leading the procession is the association's chairman, Leo Löwenstein.

Bildarchiv Pisarek/akg-images.

Figure 12. Julius Katzmann, in a mug shot taken by the Gestapo after his arrest during Kristallnacht on 10 November 1938.

StAW, Gestapoakt Julius Katzmann, No. 3270.

FIGURE 13. Ernst Lebermann, shortly after his arrest on 10 November 1938. He is still wearing his bloodstained nightshirt, a result of the severe physical abuse he suffered at the hands of Nazi stormtroopers. Lebermann died shortly after the photo was taken.

StAW, Gestapoakt Ernst Lebermann, No. 5753.

FIGURE 14. Wiesbaden, Germany. Jews with war wounds or high decorations, along with those over sixty-five years old, board a transport to Theresienstadt, 1 September 1942.

Yad Vashem Photo Archive.

FIGURE 15. Another view of the 1 September 1942 transport from Wiesbaden to Theresienstadt. In order for the SS to maintain the appearance of Theresienstadt as a "privileged" destination, deportees were usually transported to the camp in third-class railway cars of regular passenger trains.

Yad Vashem Photo Archive.

FIGURE 16. Jewish Ghetto in Lodz, German-occupied Poland. A member of the Jewish Order Police wearing the ribbon of the Iron Cross Second Class on his lapel.

bpk Bildagentur/Wilhelm Holtfreter (photographer)/Art Resource, NY.

FIGURE 17. This contemporary sketch, part of an annual report prepared by the Theresienstadt Jewish self-administration, attests to the self-image and martial values cultivated by the camp's Jewish Order Police.

Yad Vashem Archives.

FIGURE 18. A satirical depiction of the Jewish Order Police at Theresienstadt and Karl Löwenstein's penchant for Prussian-style drill and discipline. The caption reads, "On the Bastion: The Ghetto Watch's morning salute (for Dr. Löwenstein): 'Good morning, Herr Doktor!'" Drawing by Erich Lichtblau, an inmate of Theresienstadt.

Erich Lichtblau-Leskly Collection, Los Angeles Museum of the Holocaust, Los Angeles.

FIGURE 19. General Alfred Streccius, second from left, at a conference in Vienna, 27 May 1941. Streccius objected to the deportation of Jewish World War I veterans from Vienna in February 1941.

bpk Bildagentur/Bayerische Staatsbibliothek, Munich, Germany/Heinrich Hoffmann (photographer)/Art Resource, NY.

FIGURE 20. Field Marshal August von Mackensen, left, and Prince August Wilhelm at the opening of the Prussian Council of State, September 1933.

bpk Bildagentur/Art Resource, NY.

FIGURE 21.   Former field marshal Erich von Manstein as a witness at the Nuremberg Trials, 1946. Manstein had protested the expulsion of Jewish soldiers from the army in 1934, yet as commander of the Eleventh Army in the Crimea during the Second World War, he countenanced the murder of thousands of Soviet Jews by the SS.

bpk Bildagentur/Art Resource, NY.

FIGURE 22.   Herbert Sulzbach at a British veterans' reunion in Ispwich, England, 1984. In addition to his British medals from World War II, Sulzbach wears the Iron Crosses First and Second Class that he earned during the Great War.

CHAPTER 6

Defiant Germanness

At the Wannsee Conference on 20 January 1942, the SS decreed that war-wounded and war-decorated Jews would not be deported to the East along with the rest of the Jewish population; rather, they were to be "relocated" to the privileged camp at Theresienstadt. To be sure, Theresienstadt was a theoretical construction, a way station on the road to Auschwitz. Yet the decision reveals that indecisiveness, expediency, and contradictory decision-making characterized Nazi policy against Jewish war veterans, which stood in sharp contrast to the deliberate, step-by-step process of annihilation of the Jewish population at large. When the Jewish Frontkämpfer arrived at Theresienstadt, their connection to their former status did not abruptly end. Whether as prisoners in Nazi camps and ghettos or confined to "Jew Houses" in the Reich, they remained invested in such masculine virtues as their physical capacity to endure hardship, protect their families, and preserve their sense of dignity. They continued to seek validation as brave soldiers and "real" men, endeavoring to project images of manliness in order to discredit the Nazi stereotype "Jew." At Theresienstadt, Auschwitz, and other Nazi ghettos and camps, status remained a key component of veterans' self-image. It is central to understanding how they thought, behaved, and reacted to new developments, even as they became victims of the Final Solution.

The Wannsee Conference

On 15 November 1941, local authorities informed Willy Cohn that he and his wife, Trudi, together with their two daughters, Tamara and Susanne, would be "evacuated" to a labor camp in the East.[1] His diary entry for that day gives the impression that he had little inkling of what was in store for them at the destination. The Breslau police took the Cohns into custody in the early morning hours of 21 November, and drove them by truck, together with the other Jewish victims, to a beer garden outside the city that served as a makeshift holding facility. The Cohns slept on bare floors for four days, their transport departing Breslau on 25 November, bound for Riga, where it was supposed to have arrived a few days later.[2] Just as it approached its destination, however, the train was diverted: due to poor coordination between the RSHA and the SS ghetto managers, the Breslau Jews had been dispatched to Riga before space for the new arrivals was made available. Instead of going to Riga, the Cohns' train was redirected to Kaunas (Kovno), Lithuania, and when it arrived there on the twenty-eighth, members of Einsatzkommando 3 and local militiamen were waiting. The Breslau Jews were herded off the trains and taken not to the local ghetto, but to Fort IX, a fortification dating back to tsarist times, where deep pits and firing positions had been readied by the SS. In small groups, the new arrivals were forced to undress and climb into the pits, whereupon the shooters opened fire, all the while revving the engines of nearby trucks in an attempt to drown out the gunfire and the screams of the victims. After the shooters threw hand grenades into the piles of bodies to finish off any survivors, the pits were filled in with earth. The SS officer supervising the executions noted in his after-action report, "693 male Jews, 1155 female Jews, 152 Jewish children. 2000 (total) (Resettled from Vienna and Breslau)."[3] In addition to Willy Cohn, the 4,943 victims murdered at Fort IX between 24 and 29 November 1941 included Walter Tausk. They were among the first German Jews murdered as part of the Final Solution.[4]

In Riga, a parallel development was taking place as 27,500 Latvian Jews were forced out of the city's ghetto and led into the nearby Rumbula Forest, where they were shot in a two-day killing operation aimed at freeing up space for the anticipated arrivals from Germany. The shootings were still underway on 30 November when a transport carrying 1,053 Jews from Berlin pulled into the Riga train station. But instead of being taken to the ghetto that had just been cleared for them, the Berlin Jews onboard were mistakenly marched into the forest and shot by members of Einsatzgruppe A and Latvian auxiliary police.[5] It is unclear why the SS ordered the killings. Friedrich

Jeckeln, the SS officer overseeing the Riga *Aktion*, had received instructions from Himmler several weeks before that "all Jews in the Ostland (German-occupied Baltic states) had to be destroyed to the last man."[6] Like many in the SS, Jeckeln did not make distinctions between German Jews and the Orthodox Eastern European Jews he was murdering in Latvia, and he ordered his men to proceed in the same fashion against the Jews from Berlin.

The massacres at Kaunas and Riga would have far-reaching repercussions for the course of Nazi Germany's anti-Jewish campaign. At 1:30 p.m. on 30 November 1941, the same day the Berlin Jews were murdered, after a telephone conversation with Heydrich, Himmler had noted in his appointment book, "Jewish transport from Berlin. No liquidation."[7] The order to prevent the execution of the Berlin Jews had arrived too late, however, for by the time Jeckeln received Himmler's message, the victims were already dead. When Himmler learned that the Berlin transport had been "liquidated" contrary to his explicit instructions, he reprimanded Jeckeln, warning him that "(German) Jews resettled to the territory Ostland are to be treated only according to the guidelines issued by me or by the Reich Security Main Office (RSHA) on my behalf. I will punish unauthorized actions or violations."[8] This order effectively gave the Einsatzgruppen authority to proceed with the systematic murder of Soviet and Eastern European Jews, while making the RSHA responsible for all German Jews, who were to be integrated into the forced labor system, not murdered outright. The incident sheds light on the unresolved tensions at the highest echelons of the Nazi leadership, which, although committed to eliminating the entire Jewish population, recognized the need for tactical restraint in order to prevent panic from arising among the Jews remaining in Germany, but also to avoid upsetting those Germans deemed too "soft."[9] Murdering Jews in the open in Russia and Lithuania hundreds of miles from the Reich borders was one matter, but subjecting German Jews, including decorated and war-disabled veterans, to the same fate as the Eastern European Jews was something altogether different.

The persecution of the Jews never provoked enough unrest among the German population to threaten Hitler's hold on power, but public opinion mattered, even if only in the minds of the Nazi leadership in Berlin.[10] They were well aware that the persecution of veterans antagonized traditional military elites and generated disquiet among the more conservative elements of the German population, leading to conflicts that ultimately forced the SS to modify its policies in the face of pressure, real or potential. Ever since the Nazi takeover in 1933, Hitler's *Judenpolitik* had followed a similar pattern: after each major piece of antisemitic legislation was introduced, the regime was forced to rescind or lessen the restrictions for Jewish war veterans. Eichmann and Heydrich expended a considerable amount of time during 1941–42 responding to interventions on behalf of "sensitive" categories, such as veterans and mixed marriages, as Nazi leaders, with Hitler and Himmler at the very top, were at pains to avoid causing discontent on the home front or antagonizing conservative elites, especially as the war entered its decisive phase.

The impetus behind Himmler's "no liquidation" order from 30 November 1941 remains a matter of contention. The only surviving documentary evidence is the internal meeting report from a gathering of Gestapo and SS officials in Berlin from March 1942, where Eichmann vaguely alluded to the forty to fifty-five cases of "unjustified evacuations" without specifically referencing whether or not the victims' veterans' status was a key issue.[11] Yet the chronology of events—Himmler's order came barely a week after the RSHA instructed local Gestapo officials to take Jews with medals off the lists—suggests that the presence of war-decorated Jews on the Berlin transport was a major factor in his decision to prevent its "liquidation." When Himmler and Jeckeln met with Hitler on 1 or 2 December, just after the massacre at Riga, the conversation revolved around the topic of mixed marriages, partial Jews, and most likely Jewish veterans, although the dialogue recorded by Hitler's stenographer is extremely vague.[12] Siegfried Seidl, the first commandant of Theresienstadt, further testified after the war that "Himmler was well aware that in the first transports of German Jews to Riga and Minsk there were medal recipients from the First World War and people over 65 years of age."[13] On the basis of the sources cited, therefore, it is reasonable to assume that the shootings unleashed a wave of protests, and that Himmler was anticipating more to follow.

The killings at Kaunas and Riga were a decisive factor leading to the meeting of representatives from the SS and various German government ministries at the Grosser Wannsee in Berlin on 20 January 1942 in order to discuss the "Final Solution of the Jewish Question."[14] The plan that emerged from the so-called Wannsee Conference was not radically new, for the systematic extermination of Soviet Jews had already been well underway since the start of Operation Barbarossa six months earlier. Rather, the topic of discussion was how to organize the murder of the eleven million Jews still living in Europe, for the logistics required to identify, apprehend, and transport victims from across Nazi-occupied Europe to the killing sites in the eastern territories were simply beyond the ability of the SS to carry out on its own. It was here that exemptions for certain groups of Jews, which up to this point had been administered on an ad hoc basis, were codified into official policy. The relevant passage of the Wannsee protocol states: "It is intended not to evacuate Jews over 65 years old, but to transfer them to an old-age ghetto—Theresienstadt is foreseen for this purpose. In addition to these age groups—of the approximately 280,000 Jews in Germany proper and Austria on 31 October 1941, approximately 30% are over 65 years old—severely wounded veterans and Jews with war decorations (Iron Cross First Class) will also be accepted in the old-age ghettos. With this expedient solution, the numerous interventions will be shut down in one fell swoop."[15]

The new camp at Theresienstadt would be used to intern German Jews considered controversial or "sensitive" cases, in order to "avoid these kinds of complaints under any circumstances."[16] To be sure, this arrangement was a temporary measure, a stay of execution, a means to postpone the "liquidation" of the privileged groups until it could be carried out either in greater secrecy or at a time when it would arouse less controversy among the German public.

Under the pretext of a "change of residence" to a "privileged camp" (*Vorzugslager*), the RSHA was able to secure the cooperation of the officers' corps and other members of this important stratum of German society, who did not share the virulent antisemitic convictions of the SS, and whose active support was necessary for the Holocaust to take place. Hitler's role in approving these exemptions is disputed. It is simply not true, however, as Bryan Mark Rigg has suggested with regard to Hitler's antisemitic views, that the Führer felt a grudging respect for the Jewish Frontkämpfer "because of his contact with Jews during World War I, through which he learned how brave many of them had been."[17] This claim is based on the writings of Major Gerhard Engel, Hitler's adjutant from 1938 to 1943, who, in his published diary, asserted that "much brought him [Hitler] sorrow, for one could say whatever one wants, but there were also brave Jewish soldiers in the World War, yes, even Jewish officers."[18] However, Engel edited his diary several times before it was published, and his entry is contradicted by numerous other sources and official documents.[19] In his earliest speeches, Hitler insisted that "the presence of Jews in frontline combat units was zero,"[20] and he considered it "shocking and a great shame" that Jewish comrades such as Hugo Gutmann, "a coward like no other," were awarded the Iron Cross.[21] Ulrich von Hassel also noted that Hitler referred to war-decorated Jews as "swine (who) got their decorations fraudulently.' "[22] It is true that on one occasion Hitler had admitted during a confidential talk that "there were Jews among us who were decent in the sense that they refrained from every measure directed against Germandom," and that "great suffering will undoubtedly fall upon the individual as a result of our racial policy." Yet he was adamant in his belief that such Jews were not conscious of the "destructive character of their being."[23] For this reason, he asserted, one should "not assess [Nazi racial policy] in respect to individual fates: in the future, an untold number of conflicts will be avoided!"[24]

Heydrich's concessions to war veterans, then, should be understood as a stroke of *realpolitik*, a compromise between ideologies. The veterans' provision was included on the assumption that the German public would not approve of such sweeping measures, and that at least sections of the military would oppose them. The creation of a racially pure German "people's community" could be achieved only with the cooperation of the Wehrmacht, which at that time was perceived by Hitler and the SS as reactionary and "not possessing sufficient understanding about the necessity of such measures."[25] By early 1942, after it had become clear that Operation Barbarossa had failed and that Germany would be engaged in a prolonged military struggle, sustaining public morale momentarily overrode other preoccupations of Hitler's regime. The result was a segmentation of policy, in which the SS was permitted to pursue its goal of exterminating the Jewish population, while Heydrich was making this important, albeit symbolic, concession to military elites.

Deportations to Theresienstadt, 1942–44

When the SS convened the conference at Wannsee on 20 January 1942, deportations from the Reich were already in high gear. Between 21 January and 8 February 1942, five transports from Austria and Germany departed for Riga, carrying approximately twenty thousand Jews to the East.[26] It was in this context that Victor Klemperer recorded in his diary on 17 January 1942, "Evacuation of all the Jews here on the coming Wednesday, excepting anyone who is over sixty-five; who holds the Iron Cross, First Class; who is in a mixed marriage, including one without children. Point 3 protects me—for how long?"[27]

For reasons that cannot be determined, however, the first deportation guidelines issued by the RSHA after the meeting at Wannsee did not specify the protections for decorated and war-wounded Frontkämpfer set down by Heydrich.[28] The orders issued on 31 January 1942 listed mixed-marriage partners, foreign citizens, Jews employed in the armaments industry, and those sixty-five years of age and older as the only categories exempted from deportation.[29] The omission is perplexing: there is neither anecdotal evidence nor any explanation in the official records as to why the veterans' clause was disregarded, and it is impossible to determine with any degree of certainty whether it was a bureaucratic oversight or a calculated move on Eichmann's part. There is the possibility that Eichmann did not deem it necessary to remind local authorities of a policy that was unwritten yet widely understood. Another possibility is that the passive attitude of the German populace encouraged the RSHA to forge ahead in its plans to deport all Jews, or that the inclusion of the veterans was a litmus test to gauge the reactions of the populace and conservative elites. But the tone of his follow-up meeting on 6 March, in which he reprimanded local officials for going beyond what had been ordered, does not support this explanation.[30] In light of the fact that both Eichmann and Heydrich were at pains to avoid further interference in their plans to implement the Final Solution, time and again admonishing local authorities to follow the established guidelines from Berlin, the lapse is confounding.[31]

Yet a closer examination of the deportation lists from Würzburg and Düsseldorf issued between February and June 1942, as over seventy thousand Jews were "evacuated" from Germany to Lublin, presents a mixed picture. On the one hand, the lists confirm that there were no "recipients of high decorations" or war-disabled Jews on the transports.[32] A comparison of the Gestapo personnel files in both cities to the deportation lists for 24 and 25 March (Würzburg and Düsseldorf, respectively) suggests that Eichmann's decree from 22 November 1941 was being followed: holders of the Iron Cross First Class and the seriously disabled were not being deported. On the other hand, the protections were not evenly applied to all war-wounded veterans as Heydrich had mandated at Wannsee. In Würzburg, Sally Mayer, who had received the Iron Cross First Class in World War I, was excluded from the "evacuations,"[33] but at least four other Jewish frontline veterans, three of them recipients of the Wound Badge, were deported to Izbica (Lublin) on 25 April 1942 along with the other Jews.[34] On 20 March, the Waldt company, a local plumbing firm based in Aschaffenburg, requested a deferment from the Gestapo for one of its Jewish employees, Siegfried Lewald, "who was nearly deaf as a result of a war wound." This was precisely the type of individual the Wannsee accord was supposed to exempt. But because the RSHA failed to issue the proper guidelines, Lewald was deported to Lublin, not to Theresienstadt, and murdered there.[35] Around the same time, Else Behrend-Rosenfeld, who worked as a nurse at the Jewish community center in Munich, wrote on 12 April 1942, "What really shocked and depressed me was that the married couple Altschüler was included on the deportation list. How is this man, who is handicapped because of a serious war wound, able to withstand the strains of the collection depot and the transport, not to mention what will come afterwards!"[36]

On 17 April 1942, Eichmann issued a new order to the Gestapo: "Jews who are recipients of the Wound Badge are *also* not to be evacuated to the East.

It is anticipated that these Jews will be transferred to a special Old People's Ghetto located on Reich territory at a later time."[37] This meant the Gestapo was supposed to spare all war-wounded Jews—not just the "serious cases"—from deportation, *in addition to* the categories already exempted. Eichmann made specific reference to a directive he issued on 20 November 1941, which had complained about the number of "interventions from certain Wehrmacht offices or individual officers."[38] However, the instructions failed to reach Würzburg or Düsseldorf in time to save any of the victims, and it does not appear that local authorities undertook any efforts to replace the war-wounded Jews already assigned to transports. In Düsseldorf, the Gestapo acknowledged Eichmann's order with the curt remark, "Because the telex directive was received after the deportation preparations had already been carried out, and cases in which Jews were recipients of the Wound Badge were not known, the dissemination of these guidelines to the subordinate offices is redundant."[39]

Such reactions highlight the tensions between center and periphery, whereby the regime's antisemitic policies were radicalized, exceeded, and pushed to their limits, not by the decision-makers in Berlin, but on the initiative of individual Gauleiter, mayors, and local party activists determined to make their towns and districts "Jew free." But the timing of Eichmann's order raises important questions. What were the circumstances driving this decision? What compelled him to abruptly alter course? That Eichmann was motivated by tactical imperatives is beyond question, for the regime was committed to obviating any criticism of the Final Solution. In light of the precarious military situation on the Eastern Front, especially after the debacle before Moscow in December 1941, those in power were increasingly sensitive to any disturbances or potential upheavals on the home front, which were to be avoided at all costs. It was precisely for this reason that Hitler temporarily suspended the murder of the handicapped under the so-called T4 program in August 1941.[40] If the inclusion of the war wounded was indeed seen as a litmus test, a means to gauge the reactions of the army or the German public, then they apparently had not acted as Eichmann had hoped.

The opinions of everyday Germans were crucial in this regard, for the Wound Badge (Verwundetenabzeichen) was a symbol of immense social prestige in Nazi Germany, awarded only to those soldiers "who had bled for the Fatherland."[41] If Jews generally were suspected of having shirked frontline combat in World War I, then war invalids refuted these allegations in the most powerful terms, offering physical evidence that they had risked death and injury for the fatherland, while creating moments of awkwardness and embarrassment for the Nazis. In his memoirs, Edmund Hadra recounted a scene that unfolded on a Berlin streetcar in mid-1942, as a train attendant stopped to help a wheelchair-bound Jewish man safely board the tram. The man was recognizable as a Jew by the yellow Star of David sewn onto his jacket, but also as a crippled former soldier, for not only was he missing both legs, but he was also blind, a result of having both eyes shot out during the war. When the attendant steered the man's wheelchair into the seating section reserved especially for war victims, an undercover Gestapo officer angrily confronted her. He berated the attendant for her "unseemly" behavior, accusing the woman of demonstrating a lack of "healthy racial awareness" because she, an Aryan, had "put her hands on a dirty Jew." The streetcar attendant stood her ground, however, declaring that in a case such as this she did not distinguish between Aryans and Jews. The altercation drew the attention of the other passengers, who came to the attendant's defense. "This can't be for real," "This is truly inhumane," "Unheard of," and "Leave the poor, blind, war cripple alone" could be heard among the chorus of protests. "When the Gestapo officer realized that the overall mood was directed against him," Hadra wrote, "he got off at the next stop without writing down the name of the attendant or the number of the streetcar. Nothing happened, no report."[42]

For most Germans, the ritual solidarity with former soldiers, even Jews, who had suffered wounds and disfigurement fighting the enemy was beyond question, and as late as 1942, these attitudes often transcended commitments to race and party ideology. In Estenfeld (Würzburg), the mayor, in a report to the local Gestapo office, demanded the immediate deportation of Leo Löwenthal, a war-disabled Jew, because he engendered sympathy from the otherwise "loyal" population. There had been no public opposition as other Jews in Estenfeld were rounded up and "evacuated," so the mayor could not understand why "there are still some who declare that it is not right that this decent Jew, who has done so much good, is in such misery."[43] Such cases remind us that the persecution of certain Jews provoked tensions between the public and the Nazi regime. They also serve as a reminder that public protests against the regime's anti-Jewish measures could be effective, that government officials tended to back down when faced with strong public opposition. Cases like this were not lost on those in power. From the RSHA's point of view, it was important to maintain the appearance that veterans and other types of "decent" or "harmless" Jews would be spared the fate of the other victims.[44]

The bureaucratic confusion over which types of Jewish veterans to exclude from deportations was eventually resolved by Gestapo chief Heinrich Müller on 21 May 1942. In an order disseminated to Gestapo station chiefs across Germany, he was explicit that "war invalids, recipients of the Wound

Badge, and recipients of high decorations for bravery (EK1 [Iron Cross First Class] Gold Bravery Medal, etc.) are *not* to be evacuated." Instead, the order read, "they will be accommodated in the old people's ghetto Theresienstadt in due course."[45] The tone and language of Müller's directive suggests that overzealous Nazi officials had not been following the original regulations, often going far beyond what had been called for. With the Gestapo now in line, two weeks later Eichmann reissued the official deportation guidelines, which included decorated and war-wounded veterans as a specific category to be "relocated to Theresienstadt."[46]

With the bureaucratic tensions resolved, deportations to the "privileged camp" began the next month. In what followed, 42,921 Jews from Germany and 17,000 from Austria would be sent to Theresienstadt over the next two years, including 2,000 war invalids and 1,000 Jews with high decorations.[47] This figure does not take into account those Jews deported to Theresienstadt under the category "over the age of 65." Although many elderly Jews had served in World War I, some were not classified as such because they had not received high decorations. Such was the case with Albert Herzfeld of Düsseldorf, who was deported to Theresienstadt on 21 July 1942 due to his age, not his military service record. The new regulations also meant that those Jewish Frontkämpfer without the prerequisite wounds or decorations would not receive special consideration. In Würzburg, Albert Heinemann's status as a frontline veteran had earned him reprieves from persecution until this point. Heinemann had fought as an infantryman at the Somme and was awarded the Iron Cross Second Class—but not the Wound Badge or the First Class of the Iron Cross—so in 1942, this status became meaningless. On 25 April, Heinemann was deported along with other Würzburg Jews to an unspecified location in the "East."[48]

We are afforded further insights into how these regulations were applied through the records of the central SS and police office in Amsterdam. It was here that the German occupiers meticulously compiled the names of the victims slated for Theresienstadt in four separate lists, each tallying the exact number of individuals "with Iron Cross First Class and above," "with Iron Cross Second Class and Wounded Badge," "with [only] a Wound Badge."[49] The fourth list for "wartime participant, no decorations" tallied the names of individuals who did not meet the minimum criteria, to whom no consideration was given.[50] In all, 186 German Jewish veterans who had fled to the Netherlands were sent to Theresienstadt between 1943 and 1944, while 330 others with "no decorations" were deported with the rest of the population to Auschwitz and Sobibor, where the SS murdered them through forced labor, starvation, and gassing.[51]

Thus the group of veterans protected from deportation was relatively small. It should be remembered that nine hundred Jewish soldiers received the Iron Cross First Class in World War I, many of whom were killed in the process, a figure slightly higher when adjusted for the undetermined number of converts to Christianity who were now designated "full Jews" by the regime.[52] All eight of the Jewish Iron Cross First Class recipients living in Würzburg had already emigrated from Germany when the Wannsee Conference took place,[53] and according to Victor Klemperer, by this time "there are [only] three or four holders of the Iron Cross, First Class in Dresden."[54] In Berlin, the city with the largest Jewish population, a census compiled by the RV in May 1942 listed 125 Iron Cross First Class holders and 220 Jews with serious war wounds,[55] while in Düsseldorf and its environs there were a total of 51 deferments for war service (out of 2,739 Jews).[56] The handful of exemptions were mostly former officers, men whose connections to higher-ups could, the RSHA believed, provoke interventions from the army or other government agencies. But not even this exclusive group of former officers was entirely safe from Nazi measures. In order to initiate the deportation of a prominent Jew, the Gestapo resorted to deporting his family members, as was the case with Alwin Lippmann, who voluntarily joined his wife after she was placed on the transport to Lublin in April 1942.[57]

Another tactic was to use past "offenses," which included even the most minor legal infractions, as a pretext for declaring an individual a "danger to state security." This was the fate of Ernst Bloch, who was working as a notary in Munich. In his capacity as the official Jewish legal "consultant," Bloch sent a letter to the Swiss consulate seeking better conditions for Jews to immigrate there. This was in violation of the Reich's ban on emigration, and it was probably for this reason that the Gestapo arrested Bloch on 10 February 1942 and charged him with committing "sabotage against the policies of the Reich Government." Bloch's wife pleaded with Gestapo officials, assuring them that despite "the government's negative attitude toward Jewry," her husband's patriotism was undiminished. "He often reminded me that he had been a German soldier and could no longer change his skin," she wrote, "and that true loyalty to the fatherland must prove itself even if it was no longer recognized." The appeal fell on deaf ears. Now a charged criminal, Bloch was deported not to Theresienstadt, but to Mauthausen, where he died less than one month later.[58] As Klemperer reported in April 1943, even a trivial misstep or infraction, real or perceived, was enough for a Jew to be arrested:

Yesterday evening news of Conradi's arrest. With that falls the last remaining barrier in my imagination between myself and death. Conradi is also a professor, pensioned-off civil servant, war veteran (surgeon-major), politically more right than left, in a mixed marriage, respected as a scholar, cautious and calm. . . . On Thursday he reported that he had been shouted at as he left a shop: "Watch that you don't cover your star; you know where you'll end up otherwise!" He had protested immediately; he was not covering it; it had probably been only a warning and intimidation; the man, whom he already knew as a Gestapo officer, had not taken his name . . . but telephoned the Community to identify the man.[59]

The Gestapo promptly arrested Conradi; the following morning, they announced that he'd died in custody. "It could strike me at any moment," Klemperer wrote. "I cannot get rid of the feeling of dread anymore."[60] The sense of dread, which Klemperer and others described so vividly, could also be fatal. In Minden, Otto Lewin's situation had taken a turn for the worse. Since Kristallnacht, he had been living in virtual isolation at his home. The visits by former comrades, which had sustained him following his dismissal from the army, had all but ceased after war broke out in 1939, when it became a serious offense for Aryan Germans to carry on friendships with Jews, especially for members of the armed forces. Lewin's psychological health rapidly deteriorated. He died in November 1942 at his home, most likely due to severe depression. According to his son, Ulrich, by that time "he was broken, mentally and spiritually, and simply unable to go on."[61]

Even after Wannsee, the majority of Jewish veterans found themselves in the same predicament as other Jews: increasingly isolated, they had to contend with arrest and deportation at any time, as the protections once afforded by their status as veterans was being reduced to an ever-greater state of irrelevance.

A Place for Jews to "Live and Die in Peace"

In order to reinforce the image of Theresienstadt as a privileged destination for Jewish ex-servicemen and obfuscate the fate that awaited the deportees after their arrival, the Nazis devised an elaborate deception to conceal the reality from both the victims and the German public. First, the deportations to Theresienstadt were presented not as "evacuations," as had been the case with transports heading to the East, but as "changes of residence" (Wohnsitzverlegung). Second, building on the image of Theresienstadt as a "privileged" destination, the RSHA coerced the victims into using their remaining savings to buy private apartments in the new ghetto, as if they were purchasing property in a kind of retirement community. These so-called "home purchase agreements" (*Heimeinkaufsverträge*) guaranteed the buyers lifelong room and board, including subsidized medical and elderly care. The contracts specified that the remaining assets of the undersigned would be transferred to the RV, and used to refurbish living quarters in the ghetto.[62] In reality, the money ended up in a special bank account of the RSHA.[63] This clever scheme went beyond mere extortion; it allowed the SS to reinforce the illusion of a "privileged" ghetto while concealing the genocidal ambitions of the perpetrators from public view.

The deception was successful: Theresienstadt had a calming effect. An internal memorandum from the RSHA Office Amsterdam from October 1943 reported that "the impression the camp leaves on outsiders is favorable. . . . Generally speaking, the Jews feel good in respect to their circumstances, and have reconciled themselves with their fate."[64] This assessment is supported by a multitude of private sources, which describe Theresienstadt as a positive corollary to the East, an "elite ghetto" where German Jews would enjoy healthier living conditions and better treatment.[65] Writing on 3 July 1942, Klemperer remarked that it was widely believed among the remaining Jews in Dresden that "things [there] are supposed to not be so bad at all. The general mood among Jews is that they do not fear evacuation quite as much as before and now even regard Theresienstadt as a relatively humane place."[66] There was no panic among the deportees when they learned of their upcoming "resettlement" to Theresienstadt, for they could reassure themselves that "Poland was far more dreadful."[67] Max Mannheimer (no relation to the Czech Holocaust survivor and activist of the same name), who was deported to Theresienstadt in early 1944, recalled after the war, "Neither myself nor the 1800 people who were detailed for transfer to Theresienstadt on the 25th of February 1944 were frightened when we heard about the deportation order. The name Theresienstadt, the model camp of the Nazis, did not imply horror. It was considered a special favor to be permitted to live in Theresienstadt. Ex-Servicemen of the First World War, with the Iron Cross, First Class, or the badge for wounded, descendants of mix marriages . . . etc. . . . people who had made some outstanding contribution to German life—these were the favored classes who were allowed to go to Theresienstadt."[68]

Theresienstadt's reputation as a "privileged ghetto" discouraged some Jews from going into hiding and allowed deportations to be well organized and orchestrated without the brutal roundups and street violence that many Germans found so upsetting. Yet the desire to prevent panic among the victims was merely a peripheral issue. According to the Wannsee minutes, Theresienstadt's primary aim was to silence the "numerous interventions" that interfered in the regime's genocidal intentions—to prevent the likes of Streccius, Donyahi, and Reinecke from meddling in Nazi plans for the Final Solution. With Theresienstadt, Eichmann could now dismiss objections to deporting veterans and former officers, claiming that they were being placed in a suitable residence for those who were "privileged" by virtue of their war record. From there they could eventually be sent to Auschwitz without anyone noticing or protesting.[69]

The pretexts "privileged camp" and "change of residence" served to hide the Final Solution from public view and enabled the SS to secure the further complicity—or indifference—of the German people. Theresienstadt sustained the premise that the rest of the Jewish population was actually being sent to Eastern Europe to perform hard labor, for suspicions had been aroused when the old and the war crippled were initially included in these transports. This semantic illusion enabled everyday Germans to sufficiently distance themselves from a frank appreciation of what awaited the Jewish victims at their destination. They could console themselves that Jews were merely being relocated, without evoking images of disease, starvation, shooting pits, or murder on an industrial scale. Theresienstadt allowed the Nazis to gain exceptional leverage over ordinary Germans by enabling them to accept distasteful elements of National Socialism and to take part in genocide, for it let the undecided or ambivalent fellow travelers disavow their involvement in Nazi crimes and liberate themselves from a moral dilemma.

Numerous sources suggest that Germans believed the claims of Nazi propaganda that portrayed Jewish Frontkämpfer as a protected minority in Nazi Germany and at least partially exempt from measures aimed at the general Jewish population. Take, for example, Klemperer's exchange with a public official at the Pensions Office in fall 1940:

A friendly, obliging senior official at the Pensions Office, where I had to make some complicated inquiries about church and Jewish taxes. We got into conversation, I unburdened myself a little cautiously, afterward asked for my remarks to be treated as a matter of confidence. That my house had been taken away from me, that I cannot leave Dresden, that I had been arrested, etc., etc.—He did not know any of it. "I thought, you as a frontline veteran . . . Can you not live in another town, where you can forget more easily? . . . Can you not receive your pension abroad?" He was genuinely shocked. At the same time stamped by National Socialism. "That it hits you like this! But you must admit that *the* Jew did us tremendous harm . . ."[70]

Not only is it remarkable that the official mentioned by Klemperer assumed that veterans were being treated differently from "the Jews," but his comments also reveal that he understood what was happening to Jews who were not veterans. Around the same time, Friedrich Solon described an encounter with a customs officer at Tempelhof Airport as he was boarding a plane to the United Kingdom. After checking Solon's emigration paperwork, which included his passport and military ID, the official exclaimed, "Surely *you* don't have to go, nobody would harm you."[71]

Such reactions are hardly surprising, for the general public had grown accustomed to the idea that veterans were exempted from antisemitic legislation, not only legally but also socially and informally. In part, Germans' denial of the actions being taken was a psychological coping mechanism: imagination and disbelief are crucial in freeing people from moral dilemmas, and here they created a reasonable doubt, a means to deny the Germans' knowledge of mass murder. But this explanation does not account for the fact that this belief was also expressed by some perpetrators of the Holocaust, from local Gestapo officials to senior-ranking members of the NSDAP. Otto Frank, the father of Anne Frank, described the reaction of the German police officer who arrested him in Amsterdam on 4 August 1944:

> Suddenly the man from the *Grüne Polizei* was standing fixated by my wife's bed, staring at a locker that was between the bed and the window and he said loudly, "Where did you get this?" He was referring to a grey foot locker with metal strips, like all of us had during WWI, and on the lid was written: Reserve Lieutenant Otto Frank. I answered: "It belongs to me." "What do you mean?" "I was an officer." That really confused him. He stared at me and asked, "Why didn't you come forward?" I bit my lip. "They certainly would have taken that into consideration, man. You would have been sent to Theresienstadt." I was silent. I just looked at him. Then he said, "Take your time."[72]

Wilhelm Kube, who had pulled strings to get Karl Löwenstein transferred out of the Minsk Ghetto to Theresienstadt in May 1942, also spoke about the camp as a "privileged ghetto." After securing Löwenstein's release from Minsk, Kube reassured him that he would be "taken back to the Reich" and "placed in a newly erected labor camp where there was no SS."[73] There is little reason to doubt the sincerity of Kube's statement, for he had already put his reputation on the line by extricating Löwenstein from the Minsk ghetto, a place he deemed "unbefitting of World War I veterans."[74] On the basis of this evidence, it is also reasonable to believe that members of the officers' corps as well as the German public were satisfied with the regime's assurances that Theresienstadt was a place where Jews would be able to "live and die in peace."[75]

Himmler and Heydrich, for their part, never intended for Theresienstadt to be a permanent Jewish settlement. Already in 1941, Heydrich had been clear about its role as a transit camp: "After the evacuation of the provisional collection camp (at which time the Jews will be strongly decimated) to the eastern territories, the entire region can be turned into a model German settlement."[76] Of course, the Nazi leadership would never utter these words in public. Amid reports and mounting rumors about mass shootings and gassings in the East, the utmost care was taken to maintain the illusion of the "privileged ghetto." When thousands of elderly and "unfit" Jews were deported from Theresienstadt to Auschwitz in December 1942, Gestapo chief Heinrich Müller went out of his way to reassure Himmler that "only Jews without special connections or relations and without high military decorations" would be selected.[77] Several months later, in February 1943, Himmler turned down a request by Ernst Kaltenbrunner, Heydrich's replacement at the RSHA, to deport five thousand Jews from Theresienstadt to Auschwitz. Kaltenbrunner also assured Himmler that "only those Jews will be selected without special connections or relations and those who do not possess any high wartime decorations,"[78] but the SS chief apparently worried that "such a transport would disrupt the perception that in the old age ghetto Theresienstadt, Jews are permitted to live and die in peace."[79] Himmler's reaction highlights the regime's concern over public opinion, which became all the more pressing in the wake of Stalingrad. If Nazi propaganda convinced many Germans that Jews constituted a genuine threat, it had failed to convince most Germans to see veterans in the same light as the Jewish enemy portrayed in *Der Stürmer* or Nazi newsreels. Himmler and other Nazi leaders feared that the murder of former soldiers could become a liability, a potential zone of discontent within the population, something the regime was not willing to risk as the war hung in the balance.

"The Paradise of Theresienstadt"

Based on appearances alone, Theresienstadt was an unlikely site for one of Nazi Germany's most infamous camps. The nineteenth-century fortress, named Theresienstadt in honor of the Hapsburg empress Maria Theresa, was situated about forty miles northwest of Prague in the idyllic countryside of northern Bohemia.[80] After Nazi Germany occupied Czechoslovakia in 1939 and created the Protektorat Böhmen und Mähren (Protectorate of Bohemia and Moravia), the SS transformed the fortress into a concentration camp for Czech Jews in November 1941. It was only after the Wannsee Conference that the site was selected as the destination for "privileged" German Jews, who began arriving there in June 1942.[81]

The camp comprised two fortresses, billets for troops, storage depots, magazines, and residential quarters designed to accommodate a garrison of about 10,000 soldiers and civilians. By September 1942, however, there were more than 53,000 prisoners, all living in an area encompassing no more than one square kilometer.[82] The hopelessly overcrowded living space, combined with inadequate sanitation, food, and medical care, led to repeated outbreaks of diseases that decimated the prisoner population, exacting an especially heavy toll on the new arrivals from Germany, most of whom were over sixty-five years old. Of the 42,000 German Jews deported to Theresienstadt by war's end, 20,848 (48.5 percent of the total population) succumbed to disease, infections, or organ failure resulting from malnourishment, overexertion, and lack of proper medical care.[83] An additional 16,098 inmates—some 37.5 percent—were deported to Auschwitz between June 1942 and October 1944; the majority were gassed on arrival. When the Red Army liberated the camp on 8 May 1945, barely 5,000 German Jews were still alive. Thus the mortality rate of the German Jews at Theresienstadt stood at approximately 85.85 percent, one of the highest of any prisoner group in the "privileged ghetto."[84]

Like the other Jewish inmates in their own writings, veterans described in horrific detail the brutality of the SS, tensions between the Czech and German prisoners, and the appalling living conditions in the camp. Their accounts convey the agony of living in overcrowded barracks where hundreds of people slept on the floors of dust-filled, unventilated attics; the lack of accessible latrines and washroom facilities; and insufficient rations of food and medical care. Chronic hunger; fatigue; lice; infections; outbreaks of tuberculosis, typhus, and other diseases; suicides; and the sight of the corpses of those who had died the night before being carried out from the barracks each morning and stacked onto handcarts for disposal in mass graves or the crematorium were features of everyday life at Theresienstadt. Prisoners endured them together, regardless of age, nationality, or past sacrifices for the fatherland.

Most of the victims bound for Theresienstadt had departed Germany in normal passenger trains, believing that "better conditions" would await them at their destination, clinging to the vague hope that the life promised to them by German authorities would at least be tolerable.[85] The reality came as a bitter surprise. From the moment of their arrival, any lingering expectations of privilege were shattered, as it became clear that the "model ghetto" touted by the Nazis had been a ruse. A year-end report prepared by the ghetto's Health and Welfare Department (Gesundheitswesen) in October 1943 described the arrival of the Jewish war invalids from Germany, giving an impression of their despair and sense of disbelief:

> With Transport III/1 from Cologne in mid-June 1942, the first large number of the severely war wounded from the Altreich arrived. Compared to their coreligionists, they had undoubtedly enjoyed a special status until their arrival here. Almost all of them were in possession of clothing- and tobacco cards, which entitled them to an allotment of soap, clothes, shoes, discounted transportation, and much more. Restrictions on provisions, which had hit everyone else hard, had not been applied to them; the majority even had permits to use the second-class cars in the train. They were treated in a markedly privileged manner. In addition, they were told that their resettlement meant moving into privileged accommodations inside the Reich's borders. The psychological shock of these patients was naturally far greater than that of the others.[86]

The German and Austrian deportees were placed in the hastily vacated attics of former troop barracks, where they were forced to sleep on bare floors in the dusty, unventilated upper stories of overcrowded buildings, where latrines and washrooms with running water were often located on a lower floor, or outside. This meant that each use of a lavatory or water spigot required having to descend—and then climb again—countless flights of stairs. For the disabled and blinded veterans, this was an excruciating, if not impossible, task. "University professors, the war wounded, recipients of war medals, wealthy industrialists . . . all lay on the bare floors of attics, in the sweltering heat, amid the unbearable stench, tortured by lice, dust, and their own feces," wrote Benjamin Murmelstein, who served as Theresienstadt's last Judenältester (Jewish Elder). "Their luggage had disappeared, their medal certificates were useless, and their company was constantly changing."[87] These conditions exacted a devastating toll on the veteran population. In the space of eight months, from July 1943 to March 1944, the Ghetto Health Department recorded that 17 percent of the overall veteran population perished, mainly from illnesses and infections resulting from insufficient rations and lack of medical attention, as well as from stress and overexertion.[88]

In theory, war-disabled Jews were freed from having to perform the mandatory labor required of other prisoners, and were allotted the same rations as regular workers (Normalarbeiter).[89] They were also issued a special ID card that entitled them to preferential medical treatment and entry into a new ghetto café reserved for prominent prisoners.[90] There, inmates could enjoy a serving of low-quality barley malt coffee, "seated at a table with white cloth, real chairs, and served by a prettily clad waitress," a place where "one could dream of earlier visits to a coffee house."[91] In practice, things looked quite different. In a diary entry from 16 August 1944, Ralph Oppenheim, a Danish Jew interred at Theresienstadt, described the daily struggle for survival facing the war wounded:

> Frederikke and I fetched our ration in the house next door, where the war invalids reside. This is possibly the greatest mark of shame for the Nazis, that these people, who sacrificed their limbs for Germany in the previous war, were dragged here into this misery. A number of them do not have arms, and others only one, one-and-a-half, or three-quarters of a leg. The completely legless ones do not collect their rations on their own—one only sees them hobble about on their stumps in the dirty, ground-floor rooms, using only the strength in their arms, like small kangaroos, not like humans. The ones who have it worst are those who had lost their eyes; they have to collect their rations by themselves and, in their blindness, are almost always tricked by the cooks.[92]

Many Jewish veterans shared the fate of Albert Herzfeld. As a recipient of the Iron Cross Second Class who had never suffered a wound in combat, the seventy-seven-year-old former officer was not considered a "Frontkämpfer with high decorations," but fell into the category, "Jews 65 years and older" when he was deported to Theresienstadt.[93] He was therefore required to perform forced labor like the other inmates, but because his failing health prevented him from working, Herzfeld was designated a "nonworker" and received a reduced rations allotment, consisting of a mere thirty-three and a half grams of bread per day.[94] The resulting malnutrition, together with the other stresses of the camp, led to a gradual weakening of his immune system, which had fatal consequences: Herzfeld became progressively weaker and vulnerable to even the most minor illnesses and infections. He died on 13 February 1943,[95] one of 2,210 Jews who perished in Theresienstadt that month.[96] His wife, Elsa, survived until the following year, having been deported to Auschwitz on 15 May 1944.[97]

Evidence of past wartime heroism carried little weight at Theresienstadt, where the native Czech Jews occupied the important positions in the camp bureaucracy.[98] Nor did it impress the SS. "One of those imprisoned was a cripple," Egon Redlich, a Czech prisoner, wrote in his diary, describing how several prisoners had been detained in the ghetto jail for minor infractions. "The Jewish police did not want to beat him. 'He was wounded in the war,' they said. 'He lost his arm for Germany.' 'Indeed,' replied the German commandant, 'he must get twenty-five lashes.' Such is the reward of the Fatherland, Germany's reward."[99] Veterans' status was not totally irrelevant, however: it is conceivable that the mortality rate among war invalids would have been even higher if it had not been for the additional ration allotments. Most importantly, until fall 1944, the war-decorated and war-wounded Jews were officially exempt from the deportations—euphemistically dubbed "work transports"—that took thousands of Jewish prisoners to Auschwitz and Treblinka.[100] Yet this status became increasingly uncertain during the final stages of the Second World War, as Nazi Germany faced destruction.

Life in the "Privileged Camp"

How did Jewish veterans perceive and react to events as they unfolded? What did they write about, how did they behave, and which developments did they endow with special meaning? The diary of Philipp Manes is one of the only surviving contemporary accounts by a German Jewish veteran at Theresienstadt. Manes kept a precise record of his experiences in the "privileged camp," and his writings offer a different perspective on veterans' attitudes, hopes, expectations, and personal agendas than that typically rendered by commentators and survivors writing after 1945. He recorded his experiences in minute detail, describing the events and routines of everyday life and his role as a member of the Orientation Service (Orientierungsdienst) and as an organizer of lectures.[101] Manes was sent to Theresienstadt because of his age, not on the basis of his military service. He had not seen frontline action in World War I, but was a draftee who served in a variety of support roles behind the lines, far removed from the actual fighting. But the war left a deep impression, one that held special significance for him, and he looked back on it as "the most interesting period in my life." Manes had been an enthusiastic soldier: he was promoted to the rank of sergeant, was awarded the Iron Cross Second Class, and referred to himself time and again in his diary as an "old soldier of the Great War," revealing that his time in the army was central to his sense of self.[102] Manes did not survive the Holocaust: he was deported to Auschwitz on 28 October 1944, and murdered upon arrival.[103] His diary and essays were entrusted to the care of a fellow inmate, who concealed them in a mattress until the camp's liberation.

Another crucial source is the memoir of Edmond Hadra. Written shortly after Soviet troops liberated the camp in 8 May 1945, the detailed manuscript offers a compelling glimpse into the experience of a Jewish former officer who was deported to Theresienstadt on the basis of his military service record.[104] Hadra had been a medical officer and served with the Second Prussian Foot Guards Regiment from 1914 to 1918. He was wounded three times and, in addition to receiving both classes of the Iron Cross, was awarded the Knight's Cross of the Royal Order of the Hohenzollerns (Ritterkreuz des königlichen Hausordens von Hohenzollern), an honor rarely bestowed on an officer of such junior rank (he was a captain). Hadra would survive the Holocaust. He briefly returned to Berlin in 1945 before immigrating to the United Sates in 1947.[105] To be sure, as an upper-middle-class convert to Christianity and a highly decorated member of the old Prussian officers' corps, Hadra's background and personal experience are atypical. Yet like Manes, his fate exemplifies the plight of the Jewish Frontkämpfer, whose habitus was shaped by the "front experience" and a pronounced "German" self-image, yet who struggled to reconcile the loss of status and betrayal by his country. Together with other postwar autobiographical sources, Manes's and Hadra's writings bring to light crucial similarities regarding veterans' behaviors, coping strategies, and spiritual attitudes as they became victims of the Final Solution.

By the time Manes and Hadra arrived at Theresienstadt, they had already endured nine years under National Socialism and witnessed how one exemption after another had been stripped away by the Nazis. And yet, by mid-1942, they still believed that as German former soldiers, they would receive better treatment than the rest of the Jewish population. Hadra had been genuinely shocked that as a decorated former officer, the Nazis "relocated" him to Theresienstadt along with the other Berlin Jews. "It was unheard of that I, a holder of the Knights' Cross, would be placed on this transport," he wrote. "Even then, I clung to the faint hope that, as a highly decorated war veteran, I would be left alone, or at least be among the last ones deported."[106] As late as 1943, nearly a year after his arrival at Theresienstadt, Hadra still expected to receive living quarters suited for "a Prussian officer and Knight's Cross holder." If Hadra had once imagined himself as belonging to a social elite, he soon discovered that acts of bravery performed during the war meant very little in the camp. It didn't matter if one was a former officer who had served in an elite Prussian regiment or a young Orthodox Jew from Berlin; each was forced to sleep on the same wooden bunks, wear the same clothes, eat the same rations, and wait in the same line to use a latrine. "This is not how we envisioned Theresienstadt," Hadra wrote. "No possibilities for weeks on end to get undressed. One was unable to change clothes. One had neither soap, nor a toothbrush, no spoon, no fork, no knife, no comb, no clothes brush. I did not have a pillow, no blanket to cover myself, and, of course, no bedsheets."[107]

Like all the prisoners, Hadra was subjected to significant physical and psychological torment: fear, anxiety, anger, uncertainty, hunger, illness, and separation from home and loved ones. Yet he endured these trials by not allowing himself to be cowed into helplessness and inaction. Several passages later, Hadra's writing abruptly strikes a defiant tone, as he admonishes himself for "complaining" and having become "soft" since leaving the army. "During the war, I had become used to all manner of things," he wrote. "But the long period of peace had undoubtedly softened me up. Back then, during the World War, I could sleep on the bare ground; yes, I had even been able to fall asleep on the stone floor of a church on one occasion."[108] Hadra remained resolute in the face of the squalor and adapted to the conditions in the camp, a resilience the self-described "old warrior" attributed to his experiences during the war, where he had made it through far worse. Theresienstadt was simply another challenge for the battle-tested former officer to overcome.

Hadra was not alone. As Philipp Manes watched other prisoners overcome by despair after they saw the cramped attics and primitive bathroom facilities in the camp, he reassured himself that "we men are familiar with this from our time in the military, and it doesn't put us out to constantly be in public. . . . The esthete, however, finds it difficult to stomach and endure, and wanders around despairingly."[109] It was a sentiment shared by Jacob Jacobsen, a war volunteer who had suffered a debilitating head wound in 1917, who remarked, "My experiences during the World War allowed me to easily endure many of the same hardships that caused others great physical and emotional torment."[110] As "old soldiers," they understood the ordeal ahead. Harking back to the dangers they had faced during the war strengthened their resolve to survive their current predicament, overcome self-pity and inaction, and never "lay down our arms," as Philipp Manes put it: "We do not want to be resigned to despair. Did we, as we stood at the front and stared so often into the pallid face of death? We stayed upright. Our sacred love of the fatherland kept us from losing courage. So it should be now. Have our German men not boldly and bravely faced the danger of being taken captive in the World War, the barbed wire, the distance from home? Here we are also prisoners of war, albeit under better conditions. We should always think about this!"[111]

Theresienstadt did not sever their psychological connection to their former status as Frontkämpfer and heroes of the Great War. They behaved as if this status still belonged to them. It is worth remembering that at Buchenwald, Sachsenhausen, and Lodz, as Jewish veterans were humiliated and stripped of their status, "honor" was redeemed through masculine toughness, by the preservation of one's composure and self-esteem. As long as they preserved their honor, the SS could not defeat them. Veterans like Manes and Hadra reassured themselves—and each other—that they had survived four years at the front, under hostile fire, surrounded by death, wounds, and mutilation. They had endured unspeakable privations in the trenches, amid the mud and the vermin, where they had no opportunities to wash or bathe, change their clothes, or properly relieve themselves. Theresienstadt did not intimidate them.

Based on the limited anecdotal evidence available, the Jewish Frontkämpfer interned at Auschwitz remained vested in these values as well. In his account of life in the infamous Nazi death camp, Primo Levi described a conversation with the "good soldier" Steinlauf, a recipient of the Iron Cross from World War I. Nothing is known about Steinlauf's background and his life before the Holocaust beyond what Levi related in his memoir. He encountered the "ex-sergeant" in a washroom, scrubbing himself vigorously with dirty water and drying himself on his jacket. Why wash? demanded Levi, to whom such an energy-consuming act of obeisance to bourgeoise respectability seemed to defy common sense. "We will all die," Levi pointed out, "we are all about to die." In the short time available between reveille and work, better to gaze at the sky and indulge in idleness than to get wet and dirtier. Yet Steinlauf responded that it was precisely because the camp was "a great machine to reduce us to beasts" that one must maintain at all costs the habits and principles of civilized life by keeping oneself clean, holding oneself upright, and going about one's business with "dignity and propriety."[112]

These invocations of honor during the darkest hours of the Final Solution point to a search for masculine identity in a community threatened with destruction. In March 1942, Klemperer, who was confined to a "Jew House" in Dresden during this time, remarked that the First World War remained "Jews' favorite topic," and this was also the case for many of the Jewish veterans incarcerated at Theresienstadt.[113] The "front experience" not only took center stage in veterans' writings; it was also a topic for the public lectures organized by the prisoner community, which stood at the center of the camp's cultural and intellectual life.[114] Some of the presentations included "The Last Battle of the Marne and Ludendorff's Error," "10 Days at the Somme, 3–13 July 1916," and "Two Days in Lemberg after Its Fall."[115] Hadra gave several talks about his experiences as a German officer, including a critique of Ludendorff's strategy during the spring 1918 offensive, while Leo Löwenstein, the former chairman of the RjF, delivered a presentation titled "The Jewish Soldier over the Millennia."[116] These lectures emphasized Jews' comradeship with other Germans, their unbroken loyalty to the fatherland, and their selfless devotion to a higher cause. They were an attempt to preserve some semblance of earlier status, for the Great War was the only connection to their past lives before Hitler, when their sacrifices for Germany had been crucial markers of identity.[117] Most importantly, these assertions of identity were intended to show the Nazis that although they tried to deprive them of their honor, the Jewish Frontkämpfer still possessed the same values and strong inner character as they did "back then," when they were soldiers fighting for Germany.

At Lodz, Minsk, and Riga, service in the Order Police provided a means for Jewish veterans to revitalize their masculine identity. The same was true at Theresienstadt, where the *Ghetto-Wache* (ghetto police) was headed by Karl Löwenstein. Löwenstein took over the camp's security services in September 1942; it was an umbrella organization that included the police, Orientation Service, and fire department, after the Jewish Council charged the old Czech police chief with corruption. As he had done at Minsk, Löwenstein appointed veterans to key positions of authority, equipped the policemen with special uniforms and truncheons, and trained his "troop" in Prussian drill and discipline. In May 1943, he presented the newly trained police to the senior delegates of the Jewish Council by organizing a military-style parade through the camp. Under the watchful gaze of the SS, the policemen marched in military formation past a makeshift reviewing stand with Jewish Council members. This remarkable scene was followed by a wreath-laying ceremony in honor of "fallen" policemen, to the accompaniment of the traditional German military hymn "Der gute Kamerad."[118] Many of the Czech inmates greeted this blatant display of German militarism with revulsion. "The police chief," Egon Redlich noted in his diary, "is very militant. Prussian to the hilt. He acts against thieves with a vengeance and great energy. But he is a dangerous fellow, a typical assimilationist and German to the core."[119] But for Philipp Manes, one of Löwenstein's subordinates, the veneration of soldierly tradition struck a positive chord, as "a reminder of our time in the military [that] delighted us old soldiers of the Great War."[120] Walter Unger, a former officer, expressed his admiration to Löwenstein in a personal letter, declaring, "Not only I, but all my comrades who were decorated during the war, are filled with deep gratitude and reassurance knowing that a person such as you is at the top of the Administration, someone who, according to the very best soldierly traditions, combines performance of duty [*Pflichterfüllung*] with a total commitment to his subordinates."[121]

The organizational culture of the *Ghetto-Wache* encouraged policemen to see themselves as protectors of the Jewish prisoner community, a role that reinforced the link between action, self-sacrifice, and a strong male identity.

As a member of the Orientation Service, Manes saw his confinement at Theresienstadt as a contest for the defense of personal and group honor and a means to redeem his self-worth.[122] "On the battlefield and in Theresienstadt," he wrote, "Jews put their lives on the line, sacrificed themselves for their people, to make life squashed together in these attics bearable. They did not talk about it; they did not ask questions. They carried out their mission, and many who might otherwise have lived died in the process."[123] Honor was defined by fearlessly rising to any challenge, to place the well-being of comrades and the greater community before self. These were the qualities that defined honorable men. The way they talked and wrote about their service at Theresienstadt, and their veneration for Germany's soldierly traditions, is striking. It was a means not only to regain lost status and preserve a sense of continuity from the trenches to the present day, but also to legitimate a sense of superiority and set themselves apart from the other Jewish prisoners.

"Our Homeland Is and Remains Ours."

Despite his enduring two years at Theresienstadt, Philipp Manes's inner sense of belonging to Germany never wavered. He was dismayed after learning that the Zeughaus (arsenal), Prussia's grand military museum on the Unter den Linden, had been reduced to rubble in an Allied air raid, and with it the great monuments to Germany's military past: "the atrium with the flags, the guns, the Schlüter masks of the 'dying warriors,' the beautifully curved stairs leading to the Hall of Fame."[124] They had left a far greater impression on him "than the boring history teacher who taught us only dates." Even more devastating to Manes was news of the destruction being wrought on German cities by British and American bombers: "That goes right to our hearts—this is our home, our city; our house in which our parents had died, where for half a century we had experienced joy and sorrow as citizens, and with the citizens. . . . Our homeland is and remains ours, and whatever evil befalls it also wounds us. We love our parents, honor and respect them even when they chastise us. Should our attitude toward the fatherland be different?"[125]

Manes wrote these passages in summer 1944, just three months before he was gassed at Auschwitz. Even in the midst of the Final Solution, after he witnessed how thousands of his coreligionists were murdered and countless more deported to an unknown fate, a discernible thread emerges throughout Manes's writing: the struggle to remain German—to preserve an identity that was under threat, or perhaps already lost. Identity offered him a diversion, a coping mechanism to psychologically survive Theresienstadt and make sense of his world.

Manes's revelations are a testament to the resilience of older values and expectations, suggesting that prewar beliefs played an important role in Jewish veterans' attempts to transcend the daily reality of the Holocaust. They also raise important questions about the extent to which the experience of persecution and loss shared by Jews during the Final Solution engendered a break with their German identity and strengthened—or created—a communal bond to Judaism. The majority of the Jewish veterans at Theresienstadt were acculturated Jews or converts to Christianity. Like Manes, they had not practiced Orthodox Judaism, in terms of either religion or culture, for several generations. They were German nationals with a long history in the country, and they identified themselves first and foremost as Germans rather than as Jews. They had willingly fought for Germany, believed in her cause, and—despite antisemitism—continued to look back on 1914–18 as "a decent business,"[126] and "a badge of honor."[127] This identification with Germany was, in part, a product of anticipated recognition and high status after the war—the expectation that their suffering would be compensated by social prestige. Veterans demanded reciprocation of their sacrifices, both from the state and from their communities, and it was this reciprocity that created a moral bond between them and the fatherland. This dilemma remained a source of chronic and unresolved tension throughout the Hitler years, as Jewish Frontkämpfer reassured themselves that the German people were not synonymous with the Nazis. But during the Holocaust everything became questionable. Had their sacrifices borne any positive results?

By 1942, even the most stalwart "German" Jews were deeply shaken. Despite ongoing affirmations of German identity, their diaries fail to conceal a simultaneous and increasing attachment to the Jewish community, at least in a cultural and historic sense. As they struggled to find a way to cope, practically and emotionally, assimilationists like Klemperer, Manes, and Hadra drew spiritual strength from a newfound sense of Jewishness, in order to overcome the "betrayal" inflicted on them by their government and cope with the uncertainty of what lay ahead. Nothing contributed as massively and violently to this process as the measures taken by Germany, especially after the Germans moved from persecution to genocide as a "solution" to the Jewish Question, and Omer Bartov is right in asserting that "numerous assimilated and converted Jews were forced by the Nazis to regain the Jewish identity they had relinquished, often just before being murdered for what they believed they no longer were."[128]

This tragedy was epitomized by the case of Paul Bauchwitz, a baptized Jew from Stettin who had been deported to the labor camp Majdanek. Not much is known about Bauchwitz's background and life in Germany before he was deported, but sometime in 1943, the camp commandant accused him of helping several Jewish prisoners escape and sentenced him to be hanged. As he was led to the gallows, Bauchwitz requested to be shot by firing squad, not hanged, in recognition of his service as an officer at Verdun, where he had received the Iron Cross First Class for bravery. To this the SS officer replied, "Whether you have the Iron Cross or not, whether you were an officer or not, in my eyes you are a stinking Jew, and you will be hanged." Before the sentence was carried out, Bauchwitz called on the gathered Jews to say Kaddish (the Jewish prayer for the dead) for him, proclaiming that since he could not die as a German, he would now die as a Jew.[129]

The acknowledgment of Jewishness should not be equated with a refutation of German identity or an embrace of Zionism, however. The Jewish veterans' writings contain little in the way of reflections on God or religion. But as they pondered their future prospects after the war, Jewish identity, one centered on fate and shared experiences, often promised a more secure and just postwar world than the thought of resuming their lives as Germans. This gradual transformation is especially poignant in Hadra's memoir: his initial idealism progressively gave way to cynicism, anger, and the realization that life in Germany after Theresienstadt would be unthinkable. He found emotional sustenance by cultivating friendships with Zionists, Czech Jews, and fellow German "assimilationists" who shared his disillusionment and could reassure each other that despite the broken promise of the "fatherland's thanks," they would emerge from their ordeal. A transformation had taken place in Manes's writings too. "It was only in Theresienstadt, through contact with men from the Zionist movement, with rabbis, and with the head of the Jewish section of the library," Manes revealed in summer 1944, "that I got to know the past and great intellectual and spiritual development of Judaism."[130]

Based on the diaries of Manes and Klemperer, and other contemporary writings, a different and far more complicated picture emerges, however. We have seen in previous chapters how allegiances to Germany were maintained by local acts of sympathy and solidarity by everyday Germans, however symbolic. Symbolic action often remained the only bond between Germans and Jews, yet these gestures cultivated a sense of belonging under horrific conditions and strengthened Jewish determination to hold out. At Theresienstadt, this illusion could no longer be sustained. Yet in the face of the perpetrators' attempts to deprive him of his Germanness, Manes defied his tormentors, refusing to submit to the Nazi stereotype "Jew" by stubbornly clinging to his German identity. Remaining German was more than a simple diversion or a coping mechanism to psychologically survive Theresienstadt. It became an act of defiance, for it is precisely this that the Nazis had sought to deprive Jews of from the beginning: the act of Jewish autonomy and self-assertion— that is, the assertion of German identity.

Manes's attitude bears a striking resemblance to that of Klemperer, who, at the time, was "fighting the hardest battle for [his] Germanness."[131] Despite his deferment due to his marriage to an Aryan German, Klemperer lived in an atmosphere saturated with fear and a sense of heightened anxiety. "I cannot rid myself of the fear of death anymore," he wrote in July 1942. "It is worse than in 1915. One can be hauled off at any moment."[132] As Klemperer struggled to reconcile his identities as a German and a persecuted Jew, expressions of German culture and nationalism transformed an environment of shame and repression into an act of resistance. He found redemption in defying the Nazis: "I must hold on to this: I am German, the others are un-German. I must hold on to this. The spirit is decisive, not blood. I must hold on to this."[133] As his world collapsed around him, as he suffered unspeakable abuse from the Gestapo and witnessed his neighbors being deported, "holding on" to his Germanness became the impetus to psychologically endure the Holocaust. It enabled him to construct an imagined landscape where the real Germans had gone underground, and he waited for them to reemerge when Hitler was gone.[134]

As his situation deteriorated, his ruptured German self-image was preserved by reinforcing the notion that it was Hitler's regime—not he—that was un-German. He abnormalized the Nazis as aberrations of "true Germanness," and in doing so distanced himself from the terror and the degradations psychologically, repeating over and over throughout his diary that "the National Socialists are not the German nation, the German nation of today is not all of Germany."[135] It was an attitude shared by the small circle of Jewish men confined with Klemperer, who continued to reassert German nationalism right up to the moment of defeat. For them, Klemperer wrote, "the war and the uniform were the tie to the wider German world," and "the biggest and best experience, one they always hark back to—as an adventure and as a time of completely shared interests with the Germans."[136] These men included Klemperer's friend Willy Katz, a former officer and "defiant nationalist . . . whose love for the German army is ineradicable,"[137] and the former Freikorps fighter Stefan Müller, who remained "ardently German even today."[138]

It is impossible to know how Albert Herzfeld or Philipp Manes reconciled this dilemma in the moments before they were murdered. But amid an atmosphere of profound uncertainty, "before we knew of gas chambers," as Hadra put it, Jewish veterans waged a personal struggle to remain German.[139] It was the final act of resistance against their oppressors.

The Fatherland's Thanks

On 22 July 1944, word spread throughout Theresienstadt that all Jewish former officers were required to register with the ghetto self-administration by the following day.[140] The announcement did not elicit panic among the veteran population at Theresienstadt; as a protected minority, they had thus far been excluded from deportations to the East, having been bystanders over the past two years as twenty-six thousand other Jews had been sent to their deaths. No official explanation was given for the order. At first, rumors abounded that the order was somehow linked to the failed 20 July plot against the Führer, an assumption grounded in the belief that the army had, until now, provided a kind of protective function for its old soldiers, and had kept the regime's genocidal ambitions in check. One contemporary observer expressed what was on the minds of many, predicting that "after the abortive assassination attempt on Hitler . . . all men between the ages of 15 to 55 would be deported."[141] This was a widespread belief among former officers such as Hugo Heumann, who remembered "the 24th of July [as] a day of great commotion. All of a sudden it was reported that all former officers, regardless of in which army they had served, had to come forward and would be registered. One attributed this to various assassination rumors and believed, of course, that deportations would follow."[142] In fact, the order signaled a radical change in Nazi policy: for the first time, Jews with high decorations and serious war wounds, in addition to all former officers, would be deported to the East along with the rest of the Jewish population.

Up to that point, the SS camp commandant had been responsible for initiating deportations from Theresienstadt to Auschwitz. He determined the exact number of people to be included in the transports, and then issued instructions as to which groups were to be excluded—which age categories, nationalities, racial categories (e.g., *Mischlinge*), types of veterans (e.g., seriously war wounded), mixed-marriage partners, and so on. These stipulations were then passed along to the office of the Judenälteste (Jewish Elders), who selected and compiled the individual names into the official deportation list. Yet in summer 1944, Eichmann personally intervened in this process. He dispatched SS-Hauptsturmführer Ernst Möhs from the RSHA Main Office Berlin to Theresienstadt to oversee the deportations that had been planned for that fall. At the gathering of the Jewish Elders, where the transport instructions were normally issued to the relevant departments of the ghetto administration, Möhs explicitly ordered that all former military officers, the same ones whose registration had been mandated weeks earlier, were to be included on the transports.[143]

A turning point had been reached, for until now, Theresienstadt had been part of an elaborate deception to show the outside world that there was no genocide targeting Jews. Under pressure to dispel rumors and foreign news reports about mass shootings and gassings in the East, the SS used Theresienstadt to contradict such claims by pointing out that Jews were actually living out their lives in relatively tolerable conditions. Nazi leaders in Berlin had expended considerable time and energy to preserve this illusion, famously inviting a delegation of the International Red Cross to tour the camp in June 1944.[144] Historians see the Red Cross visit as a turning point, for it was then that Theresienstadt, the "privileged ghetto" concocted by Himmler, Eichmann, and Heydrich as a means to "save face before the outside world," had lost its purpose.[145] These developments actually had little, if anything, to do with the attempted assassination of Hitler on 20 July, for the Wehrmacht had long since lost any interest in its Jewish comrades. Only a handful of astute observers such as Ralph Oppenheim correctly identified the true reason behind this dramatic shift in Nazi policy. "The Nazis removed former officers," he wrote, "so as to ensure that nobody would be left behind who could lead a revolt."[146]

The crucial development was not the failed attempt on Hitler's life, but the Warsaw Ghetto Uprising in April 1943. As we have seen at Minsk and Riga, the presence of armed, military-trained Jews in ghettos and camps behind the German lines unsettled the SS, provoking deep-seated anxieties about Jewish saboteurs conspiring to disrupt Nazi Germany's war effort. The SS had resisted the formation of paramilitary-style Jewish police units from the beginning, expressing fears that they would be not only capable of someday fighting back but also quite willing. "The Order Service of the German Jews, comprising mainly former soldiers, was determined to wage armed resistance," an SS-after-action report had claimed, as it justified the killing of the Jewish policemen in Minsk.[147] Yet the decisive moment came at Warsaw, when Jews opened fire on SS troops sent in to deport them: it was this event that alerted Himmler to the possibility of mass Jewish resistance, and the uprising became the catalyst for the further radicalization of Nazi policy.[148] In June 1943, the SS, on Himmler's orders, dissolved all Jewish ghettos in the Nazi-occupied East; from this point forward, Jews were permitted to work only within the secure barbed-wire perimeter of a concentration camp, while all "superfluous" nonworkers would be deported to Auschwitz.[149] The uprising also led Eichmann to disband the Theresienstadt *Ghetto-Wache*, for Löwenstein's "first-rate troop" had now become a liability, at least in the eyes of the SS.[150] To heighten such suspicions even further, that summer, Karl Rahm, the camp commandant, alerted higher-ups that Jewish former officers were holding regular, secret meetings inside the ghetto.[151] After the Jewish resistance in Warsaw had been crushed, Eichmann dispatched Möhs to Theresienstadt, where he personally supervised the dissolution of the *Ghetto-Wache*, reducing it to 150 men, all aged forty-five and older.[152] Möhs relieved Löwenstein from his position and placed most of the former policemen on a transport to Auschwitz to be gassed.[153]

Nazi Germany's deteriorating military situation in September 1944 further compounded fears that Theresienstadt could become a potential source of Jewish resistance. In the West, British and U.S. forces had reached the German border. On the Eastern Front the Red Army had crossed the Vistula, forcing the Wehrmacht to retreat into occupied Poland and Czechoslovakia.[154] As German units fell back into Bohemia in disarray, the SS received "alarming" reports that a coordinated mass uprising by Czech resistance groups was imminent.[155] Until now, enemy partisans had restricted their efforts to disrupting the flow of German supplies and reinforcements to the front. They also had, on occasion, freed Jewish prisoners from Nazi jails and labor camps.[156] With Germany losing its grip on the situation, the fact that Theresienstadt housed not only thousands of young Czech men of military age but also several hundred men with combat experience from World War I—all of them negatively predisposed toward the Nazi regime—posed a grave security risk, evoking images of a bloody partisan war behind German lines of the kind the Wehrmacht and the SS had suppressed with infamous brutality throughout the Second World War.

Amid increasing reports of sabotage, the dissemination of anti-German propaganda, and rising incidents of civil disobedience throughout the protectorate, in tandem with the worsening military situation, tensions mounted over the prospect of a coordinated, armed insurrection in Bohemia and Slovakia.[157] On 26 September 1944, Himmler instructed his police chief in Bohemia, Karl Hermann Frank, to hold his troops ready and prepare for the worst, as, he said, "I am convinced that any day now, over the next several weeks at the latest, we should count on an uprising of the Czechs."[158] The underlying fears expressed in these communiqués was that the Slovak resistance would link up with Theresienstadt and free the Jewish inmates, who would then join the ranks of the partisans, as had already happened before.

It was in this context that the decision was undertaken, most likely by Himmler, but perhaps by Eichmann and Kaltenbrunner as well, to neutralize any potential resistance in Theresienstadt and obviate the threat before it could materialize. Benjamin Murmelstein was present during the fateful meeting with Möhs in September 1944. "The SS demanded a list of all officers of the Czech Army," he wrote. "A week later, without comment, this demand was expanded to include all Austrian and German officers. The reason for the order was easy to surmise: the Germans feared an uprising of the Jews under the leadership of former military officers."[159] Once the former officers had been identified and registered, they were deported "root and branch" to the gas chambers at Auschwitz.[160] The first of eleven transports departed Theresienstadt on 28 September 1944, carrying 18,402 victims to their deaths, including the "privileged" former officers and Jewish war wounded.[161] Most of the victims had little inkling of what awaited them as they boarded the trains; only in hindsight did Hadra realize that it was Jewish resistance that the Nazis feared. "The Nazis had learned from past experience," he declared. "The uprising in the Warsaw Ghetto had cost the SS much blood. In all certainty, if our Jews had known that transport [to Auschwitz] meant death, they would have defended themselves and taken a number of their tormentors with them to their deaths. No matter how few weapons were available, the courage of despair would have made them dangerous."[162]

Over the past eleven years, evidence of military heroism and membership in the old officers' corps had enabled Frontkämpfer to evade the fate of the general Jewish population, forcing the Nazis time and again to rein in their genocidal intentions. They had obliterated the stereotype of the effeminate, cowardly Jew by presenting themselves as competent soldiers, reliable comrades, and tough men. Yet now, it was precisely these qualities that the Nazis feared. The Fall Transports (Herbstransporte) proved to be the final phase in the Nazi regime's policy toward Jewish veterans, marking its genocidal endgame.

The End

On 5 May 1945, the SS fled Theresienstadt. Manes, Herzfeld, and many others were dead. Some, like Edmund Hadra and Karl Löwenstein, were spared the final transports, and were still in the camp when it was liberated by the Red Army. Only a handful of those who had been rounded up and sent to Auschwitz in fall 1944 survived the ordeal that awaited them. The surviving records of the RSHA, Department IV B4-Amsterdam, afford some insights into the strikingly high mortality rate suffered by the "privileged" veterans who had been sent to Theresienstadt. On 18 January 1944, a transport carrying 870 Jews departed Westerbork, which included 49 war veterans and their family members.[163] All 49 were alive until May 1944, when, for unexplained reasons, 5 were deported to Auschwitz.[164] It is possible that they joined the transports voluntarily, believing the ruse of the "work transports," or were selected due to offenses or minor infractions. In September and October 1944, 35 of the veterans were deported to Auschwitz. Of these, 12 were gassed upon arrival, while the others perished over the following months. By war's end, each of the 40 veterans sent to Auschwitz in May and fall 1944 was dead. Of the original 49 who arrived at Theresienstadt in January 1944, only 8 were still alive when Nazi Germany capitulated on 8 May 1945.

Philipp Manes was deported to Auschwitz on 28 October 1944 as part of Transport "Ev." He did not make it past the initial "selection," and of the 2,038 victims on the transport, he was one of the 1,689 selected for immediate gassing.[165] The prospects for survival were even worse for Jewish war invalids. Helmut Lohn recalled his arrival at Auschwitz: "All of a sudden we come before an SS man. Age? 26. Healthy? Yes. A cursory, examining glance, a hand motion toward the right.—Age? 52. Healthy? 'War wound in the arm.' The SS man's thumb points to the left. And on it went."[166] The SS deported 600 war invalids to Auschwitz in fall 1944; only 175 would see the end of the war alive.[167]

Those who made it past the initial selection were subjected to inhumane working conditions, where the climate and the woefully inadequate supplies of water, food, and medicine, not to mention the brutality of the SS, exacted a devastating toll. Peter Gerzon's father, a former infantryman in World War I, had survived Theresienstadt and Auschwitz only to be deported a third time to Dachau in October 1944, where he was put to work building an underground armaments factory at Kaufering, Sub-Camp III. Lacking winter clothing and even the most basic construction tools, he perished along with most of the older men in the wretched conditions.[168] Others endured months of forced labor at Auschwitz only to succumb during the death marches. This was the case with the former Austrian field marshal Johann Friedländer, who was evacuated along with thousands of other prisoners on 18 January 1945 and marched back toward the Reich in temperatures approaching twenty degrees below Celsius. The sixty-three-year-old Friedländer collapsed from exhaustion on 20 January, after a forced march of over fifty kilometers, and was shot in the vicinity of Wodzislaw. An SS officer simply noted in the after-action report that "the Field Marshal got two bullets."[169]

Some veterans, however, did survive against all odds. One of them was Max Rosenstein, a former lieutenant, who had fled to Holland before 1940 only to be arrested by the Nazis and later "resettled" to Theresienstadt. He was deported to Auschwitz in October 1944 and transferred to Gleiwitz III, a satellite labor camp, together with his son, Gerald. Seemingly out of nowhere, one of the German guards approached Rosenstein and greeted him as he disembarked the trucks at Gleiwitz. The man recognized him from

World War I, when they had served together in the same unit. According to Gerald Rosenstein,

> In Gleiwitz, the second day we were there, my father was marched out on detail and there was an elderly guard, not SS but a German Wehrmacht guard, who looked at him and he said, "Aren't you Lieutenant Rosenstein? I served under you in World War I!" And he did recognize my father, it was just totally miraculous, and took the chance to speak to him. A very decent guy. My father told me that in the lining of his boot there is a 10 RM bill, and he managed to give that to the guard, and the guard occasionally dropped a newspaper and occasionally dropped a loaf of bread. A very decent man, who had certainly not volunteered to be a prison guard in a concentration camp at his age.[170]

The incident reveals the myriad of ways that Jewish veterans experienced the Holocaust and suggests that even at this late stage, wartime bonds between Jews and other Germans were still very much relevant. Rosenstein's case was by no means exceptional. Else Behrend-Rosenfeld, who was confined to a "Jew House" in Munich, reported that the only successful escape attempt was carried out by a former member of the Freikorps Epp, who was allegedly picked up and spirited away by several of his comrades just days before he was going to be deported.[171] And after Jacob "Köbes" Müller was arrested in Amsterdam in June 1940, it was his good fortune to be brought to a military prison, not a Gestapo jail, where he struck up a close friendship with the commandant. "It turned out that he also fought in 1914–18," Müller wrote, "and as soon as I explained to him that I, too, had the 'luck' to fight for the German fatherland, the friendship was more or less sealed." The commandant moved Müller to a better cell, provided him with extra rations, and even invited him for an occasional drink. The man was a "100% German," convinced of the righteousness of Germany's cause, and Müller's example demonstrates that personal allegiances based on shared war experiences often superseded ideological convictions, including antisemitism.[172] After his release from prison, Müller went into hiding and successfully eluded the Gestapo until the Allied liberation.

Even more remarkable was the case of Max Schohl. After several failed attempts to flee Nazi Germany and immigrate to the United States, Schohl found refuge in a small village about fifty miles outside Belgrade in April 1940.[173] The Wehrmacht invaded Yugoslavia the following year, and a squad of German soldiers arrived at Schohl's home, informing him that his property would be requisitioned to quarter German troops. When Schohl identified himself as a former officer and a German Jew, the young lieutenant assured him, "Don't worry, you are one of us."[174] Schohl's daughter, Kaethe, testified that the German soldiers were "decent" and "respectful" and "behaved correctly in every way" during their month-long encampment. They ate dinner every night with the family, where Schohl indulged them with his stories from the First World War. The behavior of the German soldiers reinforced his belief that his family would be safe, and as other Jews tried to flee Yugoslavia, Schohl had made up his mind: "I will not run anymore. I'm a German officer, they won't hurt me."[175]

In July 1941, after Belgrade and the surrounding areas were occupied by the Ustaše militia and a Croatian SS unit, Schohl was arrested during a raid carried out against local Jews. Schohl's wife immediately contacted the local German commander, who pressured SS officials to have him released.[176] The Ustaše arrested Schohl again in September 1942, and a third time in early 1943, for allegedly aiding partisans. Each time, the German commander used his authority to free Schohl from custody. Yet Schohl's luck ran out on 15 August 1943: this time he was arrested not by Croatian authorities, but by the Gestapo. The Wehrmacht officer informed Schohl's wife that he had been ordered not to interfere in Gestapo matters. Schohl was deported to Auschwitz, where he was declared dead on 1 December 1943, allegedly due to "heart failure as a consequence of Bronchopneumonia."[177]

Max Schohl's case reveals that the traditional moral norms of the officers' caste, however antisemitic, still involved notions of comradeship and honor that demanded certain obligations toward former comrades, values that were still alive during the Holocaust. As we have seen, interventions from former comrades helped some Jews go into hiding or escape from Nazi Germany. Sometimes they saved victims' lives, or delayed their murder for several months, even years. Yet a different picture emerges when examining the attitudes of the officers' corps in general as the murderous intentions of the Nazis became clear. To their credit, the likes of Blomberg, Manstein, and Mackensen protested on behalf of Jewish comrades, but in the end these same officers balked when confronted with the moral decision between comradeship and accommodation with the regime. Manstein, who courageously opposed the dismissal of Jews from the armed forces in 1934, was far more supportive of Nazi racial policy when he was given command of the Eleventh Army on the Eastern Front in September 1941. On 20 November of that year, he issued orders to his troops, reminding them that "the Jewish Bolshevik system must be wiped out once and for all and should never again be allowed to invade our European living space. . . . It is the same Jewish class of beings who have done so much damage to our own Fatherland by virtue of their activities against the nation and civilization, and who promote anti-German tendencies throughout the world, and who will be the harbingers of revenge."[178]

To be sure, the Wannsee Conference effectively negated the ability of German officers or government officials to intervene on behalf of old comrades. Before January 1942, officers could still pressure the SS to exempt comrades from deportation. After Wannsee, however, despite efforts by individuals like Donyahi and Moltke, the only concession granted was that the victims would be sent to Theresienstadt instead of the East, but not exempted from deportation outright.[179] Theresienstadt silenced the critics and removed a major obstacle to the radicalization of Nazi racial policy. It enabled the ambivalent fellow travelers to remain "good comrades"—that is, loyal to their Jewish comrades and true to the moral code of their caste and profession—by shielding their consciences from an awareness of the inevitable. Faced with the knowledge of the Final Solution, they deliberately adopted a policy of denial. In doing so, the officers' corps forfeited its responsibility to its former comrades. In failing to take a stand, the army was acting no differently from other institutions in Nazi Germany. The tragedy was, as Christopher Browning points out, that had the Wehrmacht acted differently, as "the one organization capable of removing Hitler from within, or at least setting limits on Nazi depravity abroad," it could have made a difference.[180]

Epilogue

In 1947, a German former prisoner of the British POW camp at Featherstone Park asked Herbert Sulzbach how he, as a Jewish victim of Nazi persecution and British officer, had been able to interact on a daily basis with captured officers of the Wehrmacht and Waffen-SS. Sulzbach's life had taken a dramatic turn since he immigrated to England in 1937. He had enlisted in the Voluntary Corps of the British Army and eventually accepted a position in a camp for German POWs, first as an interpreter and later as a reeducation officer tasked with schooling Hitler's military elites in democratic principles. It was a role that Sulzbach cherished, and he quickly acquired a reputation among the German prisoners for being not only a fair overseer but also a "good comrade." This is what perplexed the former POW: "You fought for Germany in the World War and were decorated for it. From 1933 on, members of the same people for whom you had risked your life maligned you, persecuted you, and cast you out, or murdered your family members and friends. How is it possible," he asked, "for someone to demonstrate a positive attitude and such great humanity toward the people who were partially responsible for your fate and those of your family?"[1]

To this Sulzbach replied, "After January 1945, since I have been working in this capacity, I came into contact with Germans again after many years, and I have come to the conclusion that 90% of Germans are not only decent, but had also been misled; their guilt lies in that they had been too passive. Passive in their conviction against something which they despised from the bottom of their hearts. . . . [Yet] I am of the opinion that it is just as easy to cultivate goodness in people, in this case the Germans, as Hitler and his criminals understood it, to cultivate evil."[2]

Sulzbach had dedicated himself to rehabilitating, not punishing, the German POWs under his watch, for Nazism had merely "covered up or concealed the good, even if, fortunately, temporarily."[3] In particular, he threw his energy into prisoners on so-called "black" lists—that is, those former officers and NCOs categorized by British military intelligence as "unrepentant Nazis." He was determined to work with these men in the hopes of "reawakening the old German qualities that had been buried for 12 years: honesty, ambition, diligence, dependability, benevolence, efficiency, zest for life," so that "Germany will once again become what it had been before the 30th of January 1933."[4] The fact that Sulzbach had been an officer in the German Army allowed him to build an extraordinary rapport with the POWs and develop bonds that persisted beyond the end of the Second World War and the prisoners' repatriation to Germany. "Despite everything he had to go through," a former Wehrmacht major wrote, "Captain Sulzbach's attitude was extremely positive and idealistic toward Germany and the German people. He did not shy away from hours-long conversations with unapologetic Nazis, in the hopes of convincing them that National Socialist ideology was wrong."[5] Sulzbach received hundreds of letters from the prisoners at Featherstone thanking him for his "humanity," "exemplary support," and "comradeship." Among them was a card signed by several members of the Waffen-SS, who pledged to "remember you with a feeling of gratitude and deep respect toward your personality . . . for you showed us the right way to contemplation, conversion, and to a fresh start."[6]

Featherstone Park had been a "fresh start" for Sulzbach as well. "My contact with some 8,000 German prisoners, I believe, is where I found my way back to Germany," he later wrote.[7] In another letter he said, "It was one of the most gratifying experiences in my life . . . and it restored my faith in the other Germany."[8] This was the moment of Sulzbach's redemption. Comradeship with the German POWs offered him a means to reclaim his former status, his honor, and with it his sense of belonging to Germany. It enabled Sulzbach to preserve something of his Germanness during the Nazi years, for to have given up on this would have meant abandoning his own identity. After his discharge from the British Army in 1948, the German government reinstated Sulzbach's citizenship. Three years later, he joined the staff of the German embassy in London as a cultural affairs officer, where he worked until his retirement. When several former German POWs established the Arbeitskreis Featherstone Park (Featherstone Park Working Group), an association dedicated to improving German-British relations, they chose Sulzbach as its president. He regularly attended the annual reunions in Düsseldorf, often wearing his British medals from World War II beside the Iron Cross the Kaiser had awarded him in 1918.[9]

National Socialism threatened to erase everything that Jewish veterans of World War I had achieved and sacrificed. It sought to destroy the identity they had constructed as soldiers in the service of the nation, as well as bonds with gentile Germans that had been forged under fire during the war. It also threatened to sever their connections to the status they had earned as soldiers of the Great War and defenders of the fatherland, on which their sense of masculinity and German identity rested. Yet despite feelings of disillusionment, anger, and bitter hatred toward their oppressors, the Nazi years had been a struggle for redemption, a battle to reclaim lost honor. Although they had been separated from their fatherland, to their minds, their values and their character remained intact. This is the message their writings were meant to convey. Jewish veterans preserved their sense of German identity based on a specific reading of their masculinity and their sacrifices during the Great War. Remaining German was not just a social and emotional resource when they faced persecution, however: it was the ultimate act of defiance against the Nazis. It meant choosing action over passive acceptance of their fate and it was intended to show that despite their being subjected to the most horrific conditions imaginable, their persecutors had failed to deprive them of their honor. These responses were grounded in thinking, perceptions, and behaviors that had been cultivated since their induction into the military and their participation in the First World War.[10] They influenced Jewish veterans' lives before Hitler and they are central to understanding their behavior in 1933, in 1938, and during the Holocaust.

Veterans' writings further reveal that Jews were hardened by the war experience just as their gentile comrades were, and that masculinity forged in war was central to their identity. As soldiers in the Kaiser's military, they came to idealize honor, perseverance, comradeship, and other concepts of military masculinity, obliterating stereotypes of effeminacy and lack of patriotism by demonstrating bravery in the front lines. When antisemitic activists questioned Jews' war record after 1918, the same social pressures that compelled Jewish soldiers to fight courageously in the trenches of the First World War also made it impossible for them to passively accept these degradations. They actively confronted radical nationalists during the Weimar years and stood up to Nazi thugs publicly after Hitler's seizure of power, exhibiting courage, assertiveness, and a refusal to let the perpetrators define who they were. These were the values that had kept them alive during the war, and they identified with these concepts for the rest of their lives, claiming and negotiating a special status for themselves throughout the early years of persecution and holding on to them even as they faced deportation to the Nazi death camps. The ways they confronted repression and carried themselves during the darkest hours of the Holocaust remind us that honor is not solely a feudal category; it was also an important cultural and emotional resource for Jewish veterans of World War I, most of whom had a middle-class background.

It would be a mistake to imagine that the survivors of the Holocaust were not profoundly shaken by their experiences. "Ten years have passed since I have described my life. In the meantime, the world—my world—has fundamentally changed," Friedrich Solon wrote in October 1950, in an addendum to the manuscript he had submitted to Harvard University a decade earlier.[11] "What seemed impossible became possible." Like all survivors, Solon began to think about his experiences under National Socialism in a fundamentally different way. As the magnitude of the Final Solution came to light, victims engaged in a process of reflection and reappraisal, as they struggled to attach meaning to the past twelve years under Hitler and to their survival, and contemplated what it meant for their future as German Jews. Experiences were rethought, reevaluated, and reshaped, and past events given new meaning, as the survivors transfigured the horrors of the Nazi years into memory. Solon had planned to return to Germany once Hitler was gone. "I never considered that we would be expelled from the Fatherland forever," he wrote. "Only after the collapse of the Nazis, the demise of the Reich, and the discovery of the until then incomprehensible mass murder of millions of innocents, did the true picture emerge." Yet for the self-described "old artilleryman," the perpetrators of these crimes were not the German people, but the SS and the Gestapo, who had "their hands splattered with blood." Ordinary Germans, he was certain, had been "duped by the press, speeches, and sloganeering, seeing only a glimpse of the secret nighttime deportations, and had thought, just like the Jews themselves, only about labor camps." As evidence of German inculpability, Solon pointed to his old friendships in Germany, which had survived the Nazi years intact: "I received many letters from old acquaintances. . . . Among them were those who anticipated my return and even offered to put their limited living space at my disposal. Others asked me to submit witness statements for their denazification cases. With these, I did not hold back if I knew or was relatively certain that their joining the Party occurred under considerable pressure."[12]

Such assertions of German identity by individuals who had suffered immensely under the Nazi regime demonstrate that Jewish attachment to German culture, customs, and nationalism did not abruptly end with the Holocaust. Solon had been spared the worst of the Nazis' excesses, and the support he received from friends and comrades profoundly affected how he remembered the Nazi years and his attachment to Germany. If we believe Solon, other Germans had never questioned his identity as a German citizen and former officer, and, in his eyes, this represented a victory over Hitler. From his home in London, Solon held considerably more positive views about the chances for a renewed life in Germany than most Jews, especially the survivors of the Nazi death camps. He was deeply grateful to those Aryans who had helped him during the Third Reich, and he never stopped identifying as a German and an "old soldier." The same was true for Siegmund Weltlinger, a former frontline soldier, who was hidden by members of the Confessing Church in Berlin during the war. When he reemerged after Hitler's downfall, he lauded the one thing that the inhumanity of Nazi crimes could never taint: his Germanness. Undergirding this conviction were "pronounced acts of sympathy" from ordinary Germans, especially the times where he was treated as a "comrade." These bonds remained unbroken during the darkest moments of Hitler's Reich, and were the one "decent" thing that came out of the Nazi years.[13]

Jewish veterans' outlook after 1945 inevitably reflected their experiences under Hitler. Those who had escaped in time or had survived underground tended both to have the most positive perspectives and to remain hopeful about eventual reconciliation. During the worst of the Nazi years, individuals like Solon, Sulzbach, and Weltlinger had encountered the best of the Germans. Like many Jews who left Germany in the 1930s, before the onset of the mass deportations, their writings speak about positive encounters with Germans during the Nazi years, emphasizing what united rather than what divided them. The Manichaean division of German society into "Germans" and "Nazis" served a functional purpose, for it led to the seamless renewal of an ideal that had survived Hitler's twelve-year Reich intact: Germany. This narrative offered Jews the possibility to reintegrate themselves into German society, or at the very least to preserve something of their former identity, and Sulzbach, Weltlinger, and Solon never stopped believing that National Socialists represented but a small minority of the German people.

Things looked very different, however, for the survivors of Auschwitz, Riga, and Theresienstadt. If the Jewish cohorts who fought in 1914–18 "emerged from the war more acculturated than any previous generation of German Jews," as Greg Caplan argues, there can be little doubt that 1945 was a watershed, one that signaled a distinct break with the past.[14] Those who had experienced the deportations and the unspeakable horrors of the Nazi camps demanded more than mere reintegration; they expected acknowledgment of their suffering and atonement for the injustice inflicted on them during Hitler's twelve-year Reich. For them, there would be no redemption. Atonement could be expected only from a society that acknowledged its crimes, where the perpetrators bore responsibility for their actions. This belief was absent in Germany after 1945, especially in the early phases of Allied occupation, where Germans overwhelmingly presented themselves as victims of the war, not only of the Allied bombings and Soviet brutality but of Hitler as well.[15]

As refugees like Fritz Beckhardt returned from exile abroad, they hoped to find old friends and neighbors, settle back into their old homes and ways of life, and participate in the rebuilding of their communities. Beckhardt had suffered immensely during the Nazi years. Despite his record as a distinguished fighter pilot, he was arrested in 1937 for having sexual relations with an Aryan woman—a serious offense in Nazi Germany—and spent nearly two years in jail. Once Beckhardt's sentence was up, the Nazis transferred him to Buchenwald, where he remained until March 1940. He owed his survival to Hermann Göring, who had briefly served in Beckhardt's squadron during World War I. Göring secured Beckhardt's release from Buchenwald and arranged for his safe passage to England via Portugal, where Beckhardt spent the next five years eagerly awaiting the Nazis' demise. But when he returned to his hometown of Wiesbaden in 1950, he found that more Germans were preoccupied with the misery caused by the lost war than with the fate of their Jewish neighbors. Beckhardt was distraught by the fact that no one, it seemed, admitted knowing anything about the atrocities committed against Jews, and by Germans' repeated pronouncements of innocence. Nobody confessed to having been a supporter of Hitler's or the regime's antisemitic policies, giving some truth to the cynical joke at the time, that there were no longer any Nazis in Germany after 8 May 1945. An even greater shock for Beckhardt was that many of his former acquaintances and neighbors who had profited during the Nazi years now resented him. They expected Beckhardt to demand restitution and feared that businesses and property acquired from Jews years earlier would now be taken away. Far from being welcomed back or compensated for his losses, Beckhardt was forced to endure a prolonged court battle in order to reclaim his old business. He remained in Wiesbaden but lived out his life in disillusionment, never finding what he had hoped would be the "Germany as it was before 30 January 1933."[16]

German indifference to Jewish suffering, as much as the Holocaust itself, was an experience that produced a sweeping reevaluation of traditional values and old allegiances, especially among those who had spent the past three years incarcerated at Auschwitz or Theresienstadt. Hugo Heumann, who had remained defiantly German in Theresienstadt under the most degrading conditions conceivable, found the prospect of resuming his life in Germany after 1945 "unthinkable."[17] This drastic shift of identity is captured in Max Mautner's writings. In 1942, Mautner had still believed that as a veteran of World War I, he would be spared deportation. When he learned that he was going to be "relocated" to Theresienstadt, Mautner reassured himself that conditions for veterans would at least be tolerable. But three years in the "privileged camp" and an unrepentant German populace had radically changed Mautner's outlook: "And here I leave the terror camp, brought here by the people for whom I had fought and for whom I suffered serious wounds. And this was the 'thanks of the Fatherland': instead of the decorations which had been pinned to my chest amid great fanfare in 1914–1918, I had to wear the yellow star on the very same spot, which they had devised as a mark of shame—the sign of Judas; but it is our sign now, the proud symbol of Israel!"[18]

What had been lost during the Holocaust was not just comradeship or the sense of entitlement associated with wartime military service, but also the self-identity of the Jewish Frontkämpfer, in particular the expectation that their sacrifices would be rewarded with the "thanks of the Fatherland." The Holocaust changed all that. Before 1945, Jewish veterans tried to convince themselves that Hitler and the SS were the sole perpetrators of the Holocaust, while transforming ordinary Germans into victims and reluctant bystanders. Yet this coping strategy was now stretched beyond its limits; it failed to transcend the annihilation of European Jewry and the unprecedented violence of a criminal war, nor was it able to overcome the indifferent attitudes of their fellow Germans. The Holocaust precipitated a decisive spiritual break, one that rendered the survivors of Auschwitz and Theresienstadt "homeless" after 1945.

For Victor Klemperer, too, a return to normalcy after 1945 was out of the question. Klemperer waged a courageous, yearslong battle to preserve his sense of German identity, despite having to bear witness to the regime's crimes. He narrowly escaped being deported to Theresienstadt only by the Allied bombing of Dresden on 13 February. The resulting firestorm that engulfed the city enabled him and his wife to flee into the countryside, where they managed to survive the rest of the war. Once the enormity of what had happened under twelve years of Hitler became clear, Klemperer's sense of belonging to Germany was shaken to its foundations. He doubted the sincerity of Germans as they repeatedly proclaimed their innocence. When Paul Hirche, the son of his longtime friend and a career army officer, asked Klemperer to write a character statement clearing him of any association with the Nazi Party, Klemperer refused. "The answer is certainly harsh," Klemperer wrote. "But . . . if the young Hirche made it all the way up to major in the General Staff, then he *must* have been a poster-child, politically, and *must* have also known to whom he was selling his soul."[19] Klemperer had endorsed Hirche as an officer candidate in 1932, and watched as Hirche rose through the ranks under the Nazis, becoming a General Staff officer before he was taken prisoner by the British in 1945. For Klemperer, who had experienced decent Germans throughout the worst of the Nazi years, individual acts of kindness and sympathy could not overcome the betrayal committed by the vast majority. Klemperer, who as late as 1938 had written that his "healthy Prussian militarism" and "love for the army" had endured well beyond 1933, went on to join the Communist Party in November 1945, believing that the East German Communist state was the "lesser evil" and offered the best— perhaps the only—bulwark against the resurgence of National Socialism in Germany.[20]

One of the survivors who chose to leave Germany and seek a fresh start abroad was Edmund Hadra. He began writing his memoirs in 1945, after his liberation from Theresienstadt, and finished writing in 1947, shortly after arriving in the United States. Hadra had remained German under the most trying conditions and was a bystander as thousands of his coreligionists in Berlin were being rounded up and deported to the East. Yet the long-awaited repatriation in 1945 came as a blow. He returned to Berlin expecting that the injustices of the Nazi years would be acknowledged, at the very least on a symbolic level. Instead he discovered that, despite the hopeful excitement of returning home, there would always be the realization that "if Germany had won the war, the same Germans who proclaimed their 'innocence' would now be standing with the Nazis cheering on their victory." Only in 1947, over two years after his liberation, as Hadra ended his memoirs, did he fully articulate the irrevocable loss of his fatherland. He had remained resolute through the worst of the Nazi years and had never disowned his German identity. In 1942, he had confined his condemnation of the perpetrators to the SS "henchmen" and "Gestapo thugs," yet now, back home in Berlin, he realized that it was the German people who bore responsibility for the Nazis' crimes. As Hadra traveled through the devastated ruins of Dresden, he was saddened at the scale of the destruction, lamenting that "beautiful Dresden, the city of baroque, the city of the *Rosenkavalier*, the Zwinger . . . was razed to the ground." After he reflected on the past twelve years, however, any feelings of sympathy for "the Germans" vanished. "And yet, it had to be," Hadra wrote. "Guilt comes crashing down on the heads of all barbarians!"[21]

Notes

Introduction

1. StAW, Gestapoakt Julius Katzmann, No. 3270. All translations from German language sources are my own, unless otherwise noted.

2. Ibid. Emphasis in the original.

3. Ibid.

4. Ibid.

5. See, for example, Dwork and Pelt, *Holocaust*, 86; and Kaplan, *Between Dignity and Despair*, 45–46.

6. Mosse, *Image of Man*, 44.

7. Although initially a term favored by both the nationalist Right and the Communists, *Frontkämpfer* quickly entered public parlance after World War I. See Ziemann, *Contested Commemorations*, 22–23; and Winkle, *Dank des Vaterlandes*, 243–46.

8. On the concept of military masculinity, see Goldstein, *War and Gender*; Horne, "Masculinity in Politics and War"; Morgan, "Theater of War"; and the collection of essays in Higate, *Military Masculinities*.

9. Krebs, *Fighting for Rights*, 3–29, 179–92.

10. On Jewish gender identities in nineteenth- and twentieth-century Germany, see Stefanie Schüler-Springorum, *Geschlecht und Differenz*; Penslar, *Jews and the Military*, 188–90; Caplan, "Germanising the Jewish Male"; and the essays in Baader, Gillerman, and Lerner, *Jewish Masculinities*.

11. Kühne, *Rise and Fall of Comradeship*, 17–44; Nelson, *German Soldier Newspapers*, 89–92; Reimann, *Große Krieg der Sprachen*, 120–24; and Bourke, *Dismembering the Male*, 136–56.

12. Zimmermann, *Deutschen Juden*, 58.

13. Ibid., 84–89.

14. Matthäus and Roseman, *Jewish Responses to Persecution*, xxix.

15. Regarding theories of identity construction, my analysis is grounded in Burke and Stets, *Identity Theory*; and Goffmann, *Stigma*.

16. Julius Meyer, "Buchenwald," YVA O 2/407.

17. Zechlin, *Deutsche Politik*; Brenner, "German Army"; Mendes-Flohr, "Kriegserlebnis"; Hoffmann, "Between Integration and Rejection"; and Rahden, *Jews and Other Germans*.

18. Rosenthal, *"Ehre des jüdischen Soldaten,"* 193.

19. Mosse, *Jews and the German War Experience*.

20. See, for example, Hank and Simon, *Feldpostbriefe*.

21. Caplan, "Wicked Sons, German Heroes"; Sieg, *Jüdische Intellektuelle im Ersten Weltkrieg*.

22. Grady, *German-Jewish Soldiers*, 1–21.

23. Penslar, *Jews and the Military*, 166–69; Panter, *Jüdische Erfahrungen und Loyalitätskonflikte*, 179–89.

24. Grady, *Deadly Legacy*.

25. See, for example, Cesarani, *Final Solution*; Hilberg, *Destruction*; Friedländer, *Years of Persecution*; Zimmermann, *Deutsche gegen Deutsche*; and Confino, *World without Jews*.

26. Exceptions in this regard are Matthäus and Roseman, *Jewish Responses to Persecution*; Wünschmann, *Before Auschwitz*; Carey, *Jewish Masculinity*; and Hájková, "Ältere deutsche Jüdinnen und Juden."

27. Kaplan, *Between Dignity and Despair*; Wildt, *Volksgemeinschaft als Selbstermächtigung*; Wünschmann, *Before Auschwitz*; Hájková, "Ältere deutsche Jüdinnen und Juden"; Fischer, *Ökonomisches Vertrauen*; and Carey, *Jewish Masculinity*.

28. See, further, Fischer, *Ökonomisches Vertrauen*, 9–30.

1. Reappraising Jewish War Experiences, 1914–18

1. Mosse, *German War Experience*; Brenner, "German Army"; Mendes-Flohr, "Kriegserlebnis"; Hoffmann, "Between Integration and Rejection."

2. See, further, Kaplan, *Jewish Daily Life*; Kauders, *German Politics*; and Rahden, *Jews and Other Germans*.

3. Anderson, *Practicing Democracy*, 188–90, 429–37.

4. Frevert, *Nation in Barracks*, 65–69. A newspaper editorial from 1908 countenanced the exclusion of Jews from the officers' corps, declaring, "What makes it impossible for Jews to belong to the officers' corps in Germany to this day is not their religion, but their un-German spirit and inherently unsuitable racial qualities." "Zur Frage der Juden im Heere," *Neues Tageblatt*, 6 October 1908, HStAS Kriegsministerium: Zentral-Abteilung, M 1/3 Bü 792.

5. Jochmann, "Ausbreitung des Antisemitismus," 421–23, 434.

6. Clemente, *For King and Kaiser!*, 57–59; Angress, "Jüdische Offizier," 72–73.

7. Schmidt, "Juden," 78–79.

8. Frevert, *Nation in Barracks*, 160–62.

9. Penslar, *Jews and the Military*, 36, 121; Lindner, *Patriotismus deutscher Juden*, 171–228; and Frevert, "Deutsche Juden."

10. Klemperer, *Curriculum Vitae*, 1:348–49.

11. Ibid.

12. Ibid., 1:352–53.

13. Krebs, *Fighting for Rights*, 3–29, 179–92.

14. Frevert, *Nation in Barracks*, 65–69, 90; also see Funck, "Meaning of Dying."

15. Verhey, *Spirit of 1914*; Ziemann, *War Experiences*.

16. "An die deutschen Juden," *Im deutschen Reich*, 9 September 1914, 339; "Aufruf!," *Israelitisches Gemeindeblatt*, 7 August 1914, 879.

17. "Kriegsaufruf," *Der jüdische Student*, 1 November 1914, 92.

18. Quoted in Heinrich Loewe, "Feinde Ringsum," *Jüdische Rundschau*, August 1914. Also see Penslar, *Jews and the Military*, 169–170; and Grady, *Deadly Legacy*, 26–34.

19. Herbert Sulzbach, diary entry for August 1914, "Tagebuchaufzeichnungen," BA-MA N 634/1.

20. Flade, *Juden in Würzburg*, 87.

21. Ernst Marcus, "Mein Leben in Deutschland vor und nach dem 30. Januar 1933," HHL bMS 91 (151).

22. Klemperer, *Curriculum Vitae*, 1:115.

23. Karl Löwith, HHL bMS 91 (147).

24. Fritz Goldberg's memoirs were written under the pseudonym "John Hay" in 1940, for fear of repercussions for family members still living in Germany: HHL bMS 91 (89). A later, revised introduction to his memoirs is located in Goldberg, "Mein Leben in Deutschland vor und nach dem 30. Januar 1933," LBINY ME 190.

25. Marcus, "Mein Leben in Deutschland."

26. Zuckmayer, *Als wär's ein Stück von mir*, 198–99.

27. David Kollander, HHL bMS 91 (117).

28. Max Kronenburg, HHL bMS 91 (123).

29. The exact number of Jewish war volunteers from the period 1914–18 is difficult to determine. Although a statistical study from 1922 documents the number of Jewish servicemen according to city and geographic region, by the author's own admission these figure are imprecise. See Segall, *Deutschen Juden*, 18–22.

30. Ibid., 22; Freudenthal, *Kriegsgedenkbuch*, 7–11. Also see Jochem, "Jüdische Soldaten aus Nürnberg."

31. Eckstein, *Haben die Juden in Bayern ein Heimatrecht?*, 62–77.

32. Mehler, "Entstehung eines Bürgertums."

33. Ziemann, *War Experiences*, 15–27; Fischer, *Ökonomisches Vertrauen*.

34. Liebmann, "Notes on My Life," LBINY ME 1183.

35. Langewiesche, "Nation, Imperium und Kriegserfahrungen"; and Ziemann, "'Fronterlebnis' des Ersten Weltkrieges."

36. On the conditions of trench warfare, see Watson, *Enduring the Great War*, 11–43.

37. On the dynamics of community building through military violence, see Kühne, *Rise and Fall*, 17–44; and Geyer, "How the Germans Learned to Wage War."

38. Edwin Halle, diary entry for 24 August 1915, "Kriegserinnerungen mit Auszügen aus meinem Tagebuch, 1914–1916," LBINY MM 31.

39. The "primary group," a term conceived by the American sociologist Charles Horton Cooley, is defined as a group of people with whom an individual comes into regular contact in intimate, face-to-face association and cooperation. In the form of family, school, and personal acquaintances, the group is an individual's major source of social influence through adulthood. Cooley, *Social Organization*, 25–31. For the importance of the primary group in contemporary military sociology, see Stachelbeck, *Militärische Effektivität*, 340–44; and Maleševićm, *Sociology of War and Violence*, 221–31.

40. US sociologists wrote extensively about the primary group after the Second World War, identifying small-group cohesion as the backbone of modern military organizations. See Shils and Janowitz, "Cohesion and Disintegration."

41. Kellet, "Soldier in Battle," 226; Simmel quoted in Langewiesche, "Nation, Imperium und Kriegserfahrungen," 214.

42. Alfred Koch, letter to mother, 23 June 1917, "Alfred Koch Briefe: Briefe und Gedichte unseres Alfred an Eltern, Geschwister und seine Kindheitsgefaehrtin und einzelne andere, 1910–1920," LBINY ME 1568.

43. Sulzbach, diary entry for November 1915, BA-MA N 634/5.

44. Joachim Friedrich Beutler, letters, 21 September 1916 and 8 January 1917, quoted in Reichsbund jüdischer Frontsoldaten, *Kriegsbriefe gefallener Deutscher Juden*, 12, 16.

45. On average, infantry regiments were withdrawn from the lines for a period of nine days for each eighteen-day deployment to the front. See Stachelbeck, *Militärische Effektivität*, 263–79; and Ziemann, "'Fronterlebnis,'" 51–52.

46. Kühne, *Rise and Fall*, esp. chap. 1.

47. Julius Fürst, "Literarischer Nachlass, 1914–1918," LBINY ME 163.

48. Halle, diary entry for 5 May 1915, LBINY MM 31.

49. Halle, diary entry for 7 May 1915, LBINY MM 31.

50. Halle, diary entry for 20 May 1915, LBINY MM 31.

51. Otto Meyer, letter, 2 April 1915, in *Als deutscher Jude*, 66.

52. Meyer, letter, 28 April 1915, in *Als deutscher Jude*, 71–72.

53. Meyer, undated letter to wife (probably August or September 1915), in *Als deutscher Jude*, 78–80.

54. Kühne, *Rise and Fall*, 17–44; Ziemann, *Gewalt im Ersten Weltkrieg*, 102.

55. Fritz Frank, diary entry for 29 January 1915, "Das Stahlbad," LBINY ME 133.

56. Koch, letter to mother, 10 October 1914, "Alfred Koch Briefe."

57. Koch, letter to parents, 9 October 1914, "Alfred Koch Briefe."

58. Koch, letter to brother, 23 November 1917, "Alfred Koch Briefe."

59. Koch, letter to brother, 13 March 1917, "Alfred Koch Briefe."

60. Kühne, *Rise and Fall*, 45–69, 290–96; Nelson, *German Soldier Newspapers*, 89–92; Reimann, *Große Krieg*, 120–24.

61. Walther Heymann, letter to wife, 12 September 1914, in *Kriegsgedichte und Feldpostbriefe*, 50–51.

62. Ibid.

63. Albrecht Mugdan, letter to mother, 5 April 1916, "Kriegstagebuecher, 1914–1916," LBINY ME 455.

64. For the quotation, see "Der Krieg," *Im deutschen Reich* 1–2, January 1915, 6.

65. Mugdan, letter to mother, 10 April 1915, "Kriegstagebuecher, 1914–1916."

66. Mugdan, letter to mother, 3 March 1915, "Kriegstagebuecher, 1914–1916."

67. Nelson, *German Soldier Newspapers*, 90.

68. Nathan Wolf, diary entry for 9 April 1915, "Kriegs-Tagebuch, 1914–1917," LBINY ME 1569.

69. This is also the case in Herbert Sulzbach's published diary, *Zwei lebende Mauern*.

70. Rosenzweig, letter to parents, 9 March 1918, in *Feldpostbriefe*, 594.

71. Koch, letter to mother, 18 June 1917, "Alfred Koch Briefe."

72. Koch, letter to parents, 9 April 1915, "Alfred Koch Briefe."

73. Koch, letter to brother, 27 March 1917, "Alfred Koch Briefe."

74. Marx, "Vorwort," in *Kriegstagebuch eines Juden*, 6.

75. In his memoirs, published in 1970, Marx states that his diary was based on notes he had taken during the war. Marx, *Georg Kaiser*, 37.

76. Ibid., 12–14. Also see Walther Huder, "Kriegs-Tagebuch eines Juden."

77. Marx, diary entry for 5 October 1914, in *Kriegstagebuch eines Juden*, 32. Emphasis added.

78. Marx, diary entry for 8 September 1916, 118. Emphasis added.

79. Marx, diary entry for 24 September 1916, 128–31.

80. Marx, diary entry for 5 October 1914, 32.

81. Beutler, letters, 21 September 1916 and 8 January 1917, quoted in Reichsbund jüdischer Frontsoldaten, *Kriegsbriefe gefallener Deutscher Juden*, 12, 16.

82. Ernst Löwenberg, letter to parents, 15 May 1917, HHL bMS 91 (145).

83. Koch, letter to parents, 25 November 1914, "Alfred Koch Briefe."

84. Ibid.

85. Koch, letter to brother, 18 April 1918, "Alfred Koch Briefe."

86. Crouthamel, " 'My Comrades.' "

87. Hermann Lehrer, letter, 24 April 1918, in Hank and Simon, *Feldpostbriefe*, 399–
402. Also see Spanier, *Leutnant Sender*, the edited letter collection of Gottfried Sender.

88. These incidents were lauded in the Jewish press. See, for example, "Wie
der Krieg Offiziere von ihrem Antisemitentum geheilt hat," *Im deutschen Reich*,
September 1917, 374; and "Unsere Gegner und Wir," *Im deutschen Reich*, July /
August 1917, 318.

89. Fritz Goldberg, HHL bMS 91 (89).

90. Barsqueaux, letter, 19 January 1918, in Hank and Simon, *Feldpostbriefe*, 105–6.

91. Bernhard Bing, diary entry for 4 December 1916, "Kriegstagebuch von Bernhard Hugo Bing," DTA 1920 / 1,2,3.

92. Bing, diary entry for 3 February 1917, "Kriegstagebuch."

93. Bing, diary entry for 14 March 1917, "Kriegstagebuch."

94. Bing was awarded the Iron Cross Second Class after the battles at the
Somme, a moment that brought him great "joy." See diary entry for 13 October 1916,
"Kriegstagebuch."

95. Koch, letter to parents, 2 March 1913, "Alfred Koch Briefe."

96. Ibid.

97. Koch, letter to brother, 30 September 1916, "Alfred Koch Briefe."

98. Ziemann, *War Experiences*, 328; Reimann, *Große Krieg*, 208–9. Also see
Crouthamel, " 'My Comrades.' "

99. See Jünger, *Kriegstagebuch*; Ludendorff, *Meine Kriegserinnerungen*; and Schauwecker, *Im Todesrachen*.

100. Statistics collected by Jacob Segall after the war document that thirty thousand Jewish soldiers were decorated and nineteen thousand were promoted. Segall,
Deutschen Juden, 35–37.

101. Offizierspersonalakten No. 6534, 6554, 1040, 28870, 28171, 27785, 25801,
28380, 31535, 39369, 40983, and 44544, BHStA / IV.

102. Klemperer, *Curriculum Vitae*, 2:316.

103. Zeise, letter to Fürst, undated, in Fürst, "Literarischer Nachlass."

104. Zeise, letter to Fürst's widow, 28 April 1918, in Fürst, "Literarischer
Nachlass."

105. Friedrich Solon, "Mein Leben in Deutschland vor und nach dem 30. Januar
1933," LBINY ME 607.

106. Order from Adolf Wild von Hohenborn on 11 October 1916, Kriegsministerium: Abteilung für allgemeine Armeeangelegenheiten, HStAS M 1/4, Bü
1271; "Nachweisung der beim Heere befindlichen (einschl. der noch vorhandenen

vertraglich angenommenen Ärzte) wehrpflichtigen Juden," 11 October 1916, Kriegsministerium: Abteilung für allgemeine Armeeangelegenheiten, HStAS M 1/4, Bü 1271. See, further, "Maßnahmen gegen angebliche 'Drückeberger' unter der wehrpflichtigen jüdischen Bevölkerung im 1. Weltkrieg," Sammlung zur Militärgeschichte, HStAS M 738, Bü 46.

107. Although decades old, the most comprehensive work on the Judenzählung remains Angress, "Deutsche Militär." For an excellent analysis of the census and its impact on German-Jewish soldier relations at the front, see Grünwald, "Antisemitismus im Deutschen Heer."

108. Less clear is how and to what extent the Jew Count was portrayed in the mainstream German press. More research is required in this area, but in several wartime newspapers examined, the census did not receive a great deal of attention. See, for example, "Die Konfessionsstatistik," *Frankfurter Zeitung*, 24 November 1916, 3 (HStAS M 1/4, Bü 1271).

109. These letters are reproduced in their entirety in Hank and Simon, *Feldpostbriefe*.

110. "Feldpostbriefe der Brüder Walther und Victor Strauss an ihre Eltern," Militärischer Nachlass Victor Strauss (1894–1966), HStAS M 660/325, Bü 1; and "Kriegstagebuch," HStAS M 660/325, Bü 3.

111. Friedrich Solon, a lieutenant serving in the Prussian Fifty-Sixth Field Artillery Regiment, reported learning "absolutely nothing" about the census during the war. Solon, "Mein Leben in Deutschland."

112. Grady, *Deadly Legacy*, 143–47. An example of such a reaction can be found in the diary of Paul Josephtal, an officer who had been transferred out of frontline service due to a wound suffered during the initial advance into France in October 1914. The census came as a particular shock to him because Josephtal was considered a rear-area soldier, despite having previously served in combat. The census is not mentioned again throughout the rest of the diary. Paul Josephtal, diary entry for 24 November 1916, "Kriegstagebuch," LBINY AR 4179.

113. Penslar, *Jews and the Military*, 172–73.

114. Sulzbach, diary entry for 28 October 1918, BA-MA N 634/13.

115. Sulzbach, entry for 8 December 1918, in *Zwischen zwei Mauern*, 287.

116. Beckhardt, *Jude mit dem Hakenkreuz*, 87.

117. Wilhelm Lustig, diary entry for 11 November 1918, "Kriegstagebuch," LBINY ME 6.

118. "Die Pflichten des Kompanieführers im Felde," undated, in Fürst, "Literarischer Nachlass."

2. The Politics of Comradeship

1. See, for example, Brenner, *Renaissance*; Mendes-Flohr, *German Jews*; Reichmann, "Bewußtseinswandel"; Rosenthal, *"Ehre des jüdischen Soldaten"*; and Rahden, *Jews and Other Germans*.

2. The most prominent examples of Jewish disillusionment from the war are Lewin, "Krieg"; and Simon, "Unser Kriegserlebnis (1919)." Also see Tucholsky, *Gesammelte Werke*.

3. Jacob Rosenthal, for example, claims that Jewish soldiers greeted the fall of the monarchy in 1918 enthusiastically: Rosenthal, *"Ehre des jüdischen Soldaten,"*

108–15. For socialist reactions to the November armistice, see Ziemann, *Contested Commemorations*, 49–51, 90–94.

4. Solon, "Mein Leben in Deutschland vor und nach dem 30. Januar 1933," LBINY ME 607.

5. On the individual and collective formation of war memories, see Koselleck, "Einfluß"; and Ziemann, "Konstruktion."

6. Ziemann, "Konstruktion." Also see Bessel, "Great War"; and Ulrich, *Augenzeugen*, 227–44.

7. Krebs, *Fighting for Rights*, 3–29, 179–92; Schilling, *"Kriegshelden,"* 289–315.

8. Sprenger, *Landsknechte*; Grady, *Deadly Legacy*, 196–200.

9. "Als Freikorpsführer in Oberschlesien," *Der Schild*, 15 August 1933, 125–27. Portions of Lippmann's military service record are located in his Gestapo file: HStADü RW 58, No. 18474.

10. Ernst Kantorowicz, "Curriculum Vitae," LBINY AR 7216; Gerhard Masur, IfZ ED 216/2. Also see Masur, *Das Ungewisse Herz*, 66–71.

11. "Rapport der Infanterie Battalion Scheuring Freikorps Würzburg," BHStA/IV Freikorps 745; "Verzeichnis der Offiziere des Freicorps Würzburg (1. Mai 1919)," BHStA/IV Freikorps 727. Further references to these officers' Freikorps service are found in their personnel files: Offizierspersonalakt Benno Schwabacher, BHStA/IV, No. 6554; and Offizierspersonalakt Eugen Stahl, BHStA/IV, No. 655.

12. See, further, Bergien, "Paramilitary Volunteers."

13. Kurt Sabatzky, "Meine Erinnerungen an den Nationalsozialismus," HHL bMS 91 (261).

14. "Verhalten gegenüber den Baltikumern," 21 January 1920, BA-MA RH 69/10. In November 1923, a battalion commander called for disciplinary measures against some thirty men who attacked and looted a Jewish business in Nuremberg. See Regt. Befehl vom 2.11.1923, Brigade Ehrhardt, BayHStA/II MInn 73725.

15. Joseph Kurt, "No Homesickness," LBINY MM 42.

16. Kauders, *German Politics*, 88.

17. Ibid., 56–57, 182–91; Berding, *Antisemitismus*, 163–89.

18. The Reichshammerbund was disbanded in 1919 and absorbed into the newly established Deutschvölkischer Schutz- und Trutzbund. See, further, Jackisch, *Pan-German League*, 25–29.

19. Bauer, *Große Krieg*; Ludendorff, *Kriegführung und Politik*, 108–55; Wrisberg, *Heer und Heimat*, esp. 93–95. Wrisberg was the deputy to Wild von Hohenborn, the initiator of the Jew Count in October 1916.

20. See, for example, Armin, *Juden im Heere*. This "analysis" was actually written by Alfred Roth, a one-time chairman of the Reichshammerbund, who wrote under the pseudonym Otto Armin. Also see Friedrich, *Juden im Heere*.

21. Samuel Jacobs, "Gedanken und Erinnerungen aus dem Weltkriege, 1914–1918," LBINY ME 328.

22. Quoted in Dunker, *Reichsbund jüdischer Frontsoldaten*, 62.

23. Many local communities published local statistics on Jewish wartime participation. See, for example, Freudenthal, *Kriegsgedenkbuch*; Reichsbund jüdischer Frontsoldaten, Ortsgruppe Dortmund, *Statistik*; Reichsbund jüdischer Frontsoldaten, Ortsgruppe Düsseldorf, *Gedenkbuch*; Reichsbund jüdischer Frontsoldaten, Ortsgruppe Essen, *Ehrentafel*; Reichsbund jüdischer Frontsoldaten, Ortsgruppe

München, *Unseren Gefallenen Kameraden*; and Württembergischer Landesverband des Centralvereins deutscher Staatsbürger jüdischen Glaubens, *Jüdische Frontsoldaten*.

24. Segall, *Die deutschen Juden*, 9–17. Also see Leiser, *Juden im Heer*; Oppenheimer, *Judenstatisktik*; and Eckstein, *Heimatrecht*.

25. Segall's results were not comprehensive. Certain regions in Germany, such as Alsace-Lorraine, Posen, and Hamburg, were omitted or incomplete. Segall, *Die deutschen Juden*, 30–31.

26. The prominence of Jews in these revolutionary movements was also a cause for concern among Jewish contemporaries. See, for example, Toller, *Eine Jugend in Deutschland*, 156–60.

27. See, further, Schröder, "'Jüdische Bolschewismus,'" 78–79, 88; Schumann, *Political Violence*, 200–206; and Bartov, "Defining Enemies."

28. See, further, Epkenhans, "'Wir als deutsches Volk.'"

29. On the effects of eastern Jewish immigration and the spread of antisemitism, see Sammartino, *Impossible Border*, 171–94.

30. Aschheim, *Brothers and Strangers*, 215–45; Walter, *Antisemitische Kriminalität und Gewalt*, 52–64.

31. Peukert, *Weimar Republic*, 61–66; Schumann, *Political Violence*, 113–41.

32. Stephan Kunreuther, "Memoiren, 1882–1942," LBINY ME 225.

33. Caplan, "Wicked Sons, German Heroes," 142–44.

34. Polizeibericht-Nürnberg, 11 November 1923, BayHStA MInn 73725.

35. Most studies reveal that ex-soldiers' organizations attracted only a small minority of veterans after the war. See, for example, Prost, *In the Wake of War*, 19–24, 42–46; Ziemann, *War Experiences*, 240–52; Bourke, *Dismembering the Male*, 152–55.

36. "Der Krieg," *Im deutschen Reich* 1–2, January 1915, 6. The so-called "contact hypothesis" holds that increased interaction between groups can dispel or weaken prejudicial stereotypes and misconceptions. See, further, Forsyth, *Group Dynamics*. For a counterargument, see Krebs, *Fighting for Rights*, 9–10.

37. Julius Fürst, "Literarischer Nachlass, 1914–1918," LBINY ME 163.

38. Nathan Wolf, diary entry for 1 April 1917, "Kriegs-Tagebuch, 1914–1917," LBINY ME 1569.

39. Volkov, "Antisemitism."

40. Willy Bornstein, HHL bMS 91 (34); Ernest Frank, HHL bMS 91 (66).

41. Richard Wolf, HHL bMS 91 (244).

42. "Hindenburg und die Juden: Eine Erinnerung an Leopold Rosenak," LBINY AR 1071.

43. Hindenburg to Rosenak, 23 February 1921, LBINY AR 1071.

44. On the attitudes of the postwar conservative-nationalist milieu, see Baranowski, *Sanctity of Rural Life*, 39–50; and Rohkrämer, *Single Communal Faith?*, 9–17, 52–54.

45. See, for example, Walter Bloem's remarks at the RjF's ten-year anniversary gathering in Hamburg in 1929. "Nachklänge zu Hamburgs Zehn-Jahr-Feier," *Der Schild*, 1 January 1930; and "Der deutschen Zwietracht mitten ins Herz!," *Der Schild*, 22 November 1929.

46. Remarque, *Weg Zurück*. This 1931 novel, the sequel to *All Quiet on the Western Front*, focuses on the immediate postwar period from 1918 to 1920 and describes how a tightly knit group of frontline soldiers is split up once they pursue different political

and professional endeavors after returning from the war. Max Weil, the lone Jewish protagonist, is chided by the other soldiers for shirking and later becomes the leader of a Marxist soldiers' council (*Soldatenrat*).

47. Hecht, *Deutsche Juden*, 400.

48. Rosenzweig, *Feldpostbriefe*, 594.

49. Cohn, *Verwehte Spuren*, 224–25.

50. Ibid., 224–25, 269–70.

51. Borut, "'Bin ich doch ein Isrealit,'" 120.

52. Poppel, *Zionism in Germany*, 176; Zimmermann, *Deutschen Juden*, 32–34.

53. Schindler, "Jüdische Studenten," 388.

54. Ibid.

55. Hermann Klugmann, HHL bMS 91 (113).

56. Quoted from the memoirs of Bernhard Kolb, whose personal experiences are documented in an unpublished manuscript: "Die Juden in Nürnberg, 1839–1945," LBINY AR 360. Also see Toury, "Krisenbewußtsein."

57. Wilhelm Lustig, "Erinnerungen aus der Volksabstimmung in Oberschlesien," LBINY ME 407a.

58. Edwin Landau, HHL bMS 91 (126).

59. On the radicalization of antisemitism at German universities after the war, see Barth, "Professoren"; and Levsen, "Constructing Elite Identities."

60. Erving Goffmann characterizes this behavior as indicative of "identity ambivalence," in which a stigmatized individual perceives with shame the acting out of negative stereotypes by another, more stigmatized member of his group. These individuals tend to view themselves in nonstigmatic terms, thus judging others in their group by the norms of "normal" society. See Goffman, *Stigma*, 304–9.

61. Joseph Levy, HHL bMS 91 (135).

62. Landau, HHL bMS 91 (126).

63. Cohn, *Verwehte Spuren*, 270–71.

64. These relations are explored by Remarque in *Der Weg Zurück*.

65. Prost, *In the Wake of War*, 27. This is an abridgement of Prost's seminal three-volume work on the French veterans' movement, *Anciens Combattants*.

66. Ibid.

67. On the regional recruitment practices of the German military, see Stachelbeck, *Militärische Effektivität*, 29–48.

68. Kühne, *Comradeship*, 17–44; Bessel, "'Front Generation'"; Cohen, *War Come Home*, 62–64.

69. Ziemann, "'Fronterlebnis' des Ersten Weltkrieges."

70. On the attitudes of pro-republican veterans, see Ziemann, *Contested Commemorations*, 24–59; and Kühne, *Comradeship*, 56–61.

71. For a concise overview of the Weimar-era German veterans' movement, particularly the organizations of the nationalist Right, see Elliot, "Kriegervereine."

72. See, further, Boris Barth, *Dolchstoßlegenden und politische Desintegration*.

73. "Ein Vaterländischer Bund jüdischer Frontsoldaten," *CV-Zeitung*, May 1919, 232.

74. There is a substantial body of literature on the RjF. The most comprehensive of these works are Dunker, *Reichsbund jüdischer Frontsoldaten*; Caplan, "Wicked Sons, German Heroes"; Pierson, "Embattled Veterans"; and Crim, *Antisemitism*, chap. 4.

75. Offizierspersonalakt Leo Löwenstein, BHStA/IV, No. 44544.

76. Paucker, "Der jüdische Abwehrkampf," 417.

77. Hermann Pineas, "Meine Erinnerungen an den Reichsbund jüdischer Front-soldaten," LBINY AR 94.

78. Caplan, "Wicked Sons, German Heroes," 128. In 1921, the RjF claimed fif-teen thousand members. By 1932, its membership officially approached fifty thou-sand, a number that included its affiliated youth association.

79. On the nationalist myth of the *Frontgemeinschaft*, see Kühne, *Comradeship*, 45–69.

80. "Entwicklung und Aufgaben unseres Bundes," *Der Schild*, November 1921, 1.

81. "Unzuverlässige Kritik am aktiven Offiziers- und Sanitätskorps," *Der Schild*, November 1921, 1–2.

82. Alfred Zweig, letter to parents, 31 December 1914, quoted in Reichsbund jüdischer Frontsoldaten, *Kriegsbriefe gefallener Deutscher Juden*, 133–34.

83. Toury, "Jewish Aspects," 245, 249.

84. On the Kyffhäuserbund's position on the Jewish Question, see Führer, "Deutsche Reichskriegerbund Kyffhäuser."

85. See Bloem, *Deutsche Zwietracht und Judentum*; Rudolf G. Binding, "Zwei jü-dische Offiziere im großen Kriege," *Der Jude* 9 (1925): 110–13; and "Der deutschen Zwietracht mitten ins Herz!," *Der Schild*, 22 November 1929.

86. These events were reported in *Der Schild* as well as in local Jewish community newspapers. For Berlin, see "Enthüllungsfeier des Gefallenen-Denkmals," *Der Schild*, 4 July 1927, 197; Nuremberg: *Nürnberg-Fürther Israelitisches Gemeindeblatt*, no. 6, 1 December 1922, 40; Konstanz: "Einweihung der Gedenktafel in der Synagoge," *Der Schild*, February 1924; Liegnitz: "Die Denkmalsweihe in Liegnitz," *Der Schild*, 8 February 1929.

87. Ziemann, *Contested Commemorations*, 198–200.

88. "Gedenkfeier der Ortsgruppe Düsseldorf," *Der Schild*, 13 November 1925; "Dem Geist der Treue und des Opfers: Zehn-Jahrfeier des Reichsbundes jüdischer Frontsoldaten," *Düsseldorfer Nachrichten*, 25 March 1929.

89. For commentary on and overviews of local press coverage during the RjF "front soldiers' day" in Düsseldorf in 1925, see "Rheinlandtagung und Presse," *Der Schild*, 13 November 1925.

90. Leo Löwenstein, IfZ ZS 2196/1.

91. Sabatzky, "Meine Erinnerungen an den Nationalsozialismus," HHL bMS 91 (261).

92. "Die antisemitische Hetze in der Reichswehr," *Im deutschen Reich*, June 1919, 373–76. For an analysis of antisemitism in the interwar German military, see Förster, "'Aber für die Juden'"; Schröder, "'Jüdischer Bolschewismus'"; and Crim, *Antisemi-tism*, 1–32. However, I disagree with Crim's characterization and analysis of antisemi-tism in the interwar German military.

93. "Verhalten gegenüber den Baltikumern," 21 January 1920, BA-MA RH 69/10.

94. "An meine Kameraden von der Lehrbrigade!," Militärischer Nachlass Walther Reinhardt, HStAS M 660/034, Bü 25.

95. Mulligan, *Creation*, 14, 206–8.

96. "Gedenktafel in der Synagoge," *Der Schild*, October 1922.

97. Fritsch, letter to Joachim von Stülpnagel, 16 November 1924, quoted in Carsten, *Reichswehr and Politics*, 203. Fritsch's statement refers to the social-demo-cratic president of the Weimar Republic, Friedrich Ebert, and the SPD paramilitary organization, Reichsbanner Schwarz-Rot-Gold.

98. Arthur Blum, "Mein Leben in Deutschland," HHL bMS 91 (29).

99. Although outdated, the standard work on the Stahlhelm remains Berghahn, *Stahlhelm*. Also see Fritzsche, *Rehearsals for Fascism*, 166–89; and Crim, *Antisemitism*, 33–64.

100. "Was ist der Stahlhem? Was will der Stahlhelm? Was wird der Stahlhelm?," undated flier, BArch R72/334.

101. Gestapoakt Stephan Prager, HStADü RW 58, No. 29013.

102. Quoted in Berghahn, *Stahlhelm*, 66.

103. Rundschreiben Nr. 87, 18 September 1928, BArch R72/273.

104. Stahlhelm to Ludwig Bernstein, 5 March 1933, BArch R72/273.

105. "Gedenkfeieren für unsere Gefallenen," *CV-Zeitung*, 19 June 1926; "Aus den Landesverbänden und Ortsgruppen," *Der Schild*, 26 July 1926.

106. "An den Stahlhelm, Bund der Frontsoldaten!," *Der Schild*, 1 February 1925, 1.

107. "Der 'Witz' im Stahlhelm," *Der Schild*, 15 February 1925.

108. "Stahlhelm-Glogau to RjF-Glogau," *Der Schild*, 29 November 1926.

109. Military journals and documents from the final months of the war and early postwar period suggest that most senior officers attributed defeat to Allied material superiority or the failure of combined military, political, and economic leadership. See, for example, Haller, *Militärzeitschriften*, 298–304.

110. Senator to 2. Bundesführer des Stahlhelm, 12 June 1929, BArch R72/273.

111. Vollmer (Stahlhelm Landesverband Mitteldeutschland) to Senator, 13 August 1929, BArch R72/273; and Stahlhelm to Senator, 27 December 1929, BArch R72/273.

112. Wedigo von Wedel (Stahlhelm Kreisführer Kolberg) to Gauführer, Stahlhelm Landesverband Pommern-Grenzmark, 1 October 1929, BArch R72/273.

113. Meteling, *Ehre, Einheit und Ordnung*, 410–12. Also see Scofield, "Veterans, War Widows."

114. Zimmermann, *"Der feste Wall,"* 303–12.

115. *Berliner Adreßbuch 1920*, 191–93 ("Krieger-Vereine").

116. The diversity in class and profession is reflected in the member lists of the 414th Infantry Regimental Association in Stuttgart: "Unterlagen zur Geschäftsführung der Regimentsvereinigung (Nr. 414) mit Korrespondenz," Militärischer Nachlass Paul Otto Hugo Flaischlen, Generalmajor (1868–1942), HStAS M 660/284 Bü 21, 22; and the Würzburg-based 9th Infantry Regiment: "Mitglieder- und Addressenverzeichniss," März 1928, StAW, Militär IV, Mappe 22 (Infanterie Regiment "Wrede"). Also see Weber, *Hitler's First War*, 275–82.

117. "Offizier und Kriegerverein," Nachrichten des Vereins der Offiziere usw. des ehemaligen 1. Unter-Elsässischen Infanterie-Rehiments Nr. 132, Nr. 25, Juni 1924, BA-MA MSG 3, 1175.

118. "Die Organisationen ehemaliger Heeresangehöriger und wir," *Der Schild*, 22 May 1926.

119. Tänzer, *"Kampfgenossenschaft."*

120. Kaethe Wells (Schohl), interview with the author, 10 July 2012. Also see Large, *World Closed Its Doors*, 1–12.

121. "Festprogramm 1928. 125 Jahre Neunertag in Würzburg vom 16.-18. Juni 1928," StAW, Militär IV, Mappe 22 (Infanterie Regiment "Wrede").

122. The resolution, passed in February 1925, was in response to the burial of Otto Rosenthal, father of the historian Jacob Rosenthal. The rabbi who orated the funeral

services apparently offended several right-leaning veterans in attendance when he mentioned attacks on the Jewish war record by a number of "high-ranking former military leaders." See "Judenfeindliche Bestrebungen in einem Kriegerverein," *Der Schild*, 1 May 1925; and Rosenthal, *"Ehre des jüdischen Soldaten,"* 9–11, 150–54.

123. Kühne, *Comradeship*, 19–21.

124. *Der Stürmer*, Nr. 6/1925, quoted in Zinke, *"An allem ist Alljuda Schuld,"* 102–3.

125. *Der Stürmer*, Nr. 21/1925, quoted in Zinke, *"An allem ist Alljuda Schuld,"* 102.

126. Adolf Asch, "Memoiren," LBINY ME 18.

127. Walter Gottheil, HHL bMS 91 (81).

128. Undated press clipping, Private Holdings of Dr. Roland Flade.

129. Grady, *German-Jewish Soldiers*, 97–98, 149–50.

130. On the incorporation of Jewish names into local war memorials in Bavaria, see Schwierz, *"Fur das Vaterland starben . . ."*

3. "These Scoundrels Are Not the German People"

1. Bauer, *Rethinking the Holocaust*, ix–xvi, 39–67.

2. Among the most important works in this area are Confino, *World without Jews*; Volkov, *Germans, Jews, and Antisemites*, 67–155; Friedländer, *Years of Persecution*, 87–112; and the essays in Bankier, *Probing the Depths*.

3. "Open Letter to Mr. Rabbi Dr. H. Fuchs, Chemnitz," *Oelsnizter Volksbote*, 23 July 1932, quoted in Szejnmann, *Nazism in Central Germany*, doc. 19, 273.

4. Matthäus, Kwiet, Förster, and Breitman, *Ausbildungsziel Judenmord?*, 179–83.

5. See, for example, Ernst Graf zu Reventlow, "Die Juden als Kriegsteilnehmer," in *Judas Kampf und Niederlage*, 113–18; and Hiemer, *Giftpilz*, 50–52.

6. "Gibt es 'nationale' Juden?," *Sensburger Zeitung*, 23 August 1934.

7. Kreisbefehl NSDAP Ortsgruppe Cochem, 20 July 1934, USHMMA RG-11.001M.31, reel 114 (SAM 721–1–2555, 186–87).

8. Krebs, *Fighting for Rights*, 3–29, 179–92.

9. Walter, *Antisemitische Kriminalität und Gewalt*, 222–31.

10. On Jewish reactions to 30 January 1933, see Matthäus and Roseman, *Jewish Responses to Persecution*, 1–18.

11. Ibid.

12. For a concise overview of the April Boycott, see Plum, "Wirtschaft und Erwerbsleben"; Friedländer, *Years of Persecution*, 19–26; and Matthäus and Roseman, *Jewish Responses to Persecution*, 16–24.

13. The RjF strongly encouraged veterans to wear their wartime decorations and distributed placards for business owners to display in their store windows. See "Plakat des Reichsbundes jüdischer Frontsoldaten," *Der Schild*, 13 April 1933.

14. Emphasis in the original. "Unser Herr Reichskanzler Hitler" (leaflet), USHMMA RG-11.001M.31, reel 101 (SAM 721–1–2321, 1200).

15. Erich Leyens, "Unter dem NS Regime, 1933–1938: Erlebnisse und Beobachtungen," LBINY ME 170. Leyens's memoir is published in Leyens and Andor, *Fremden Jahre*.

16. Leyens, "Unter dem NS Regime."

17. Erich Leyens, "Selbsthilfe eines jüdischen Frontkämpfers," unnamed newspaper, March 1933, LBINY ME 170. Based on internal CV correspondence, this clipping most likely came from the *Weseler Volksblatt*, a newspaper affiliated with the moderate-conservative Zentrum (Center Party).

18. CV regional office Rhinleland-Westphalia (Ernst Plaut) to CV head office Berlin, 20 March 1933, USHMMA RG-11.001M.31, reel 101 (SAM 721–1–2321, 1190–91).

19. Max Plaut, undated interview with Christian Riecke, LBINY ME 743.

20. Max Haller, "Briefe an die Redaktion: Seelische Klärung," *Jüdische Rundschau*, 30 May 1933.

21. Ibid.

22. "Würde bewahren!," *Der Schild*, 3 March 1933, 33.

23. Karl Löwith, HHL bMS 91 (147).

24. Edwin Landau, HHL bMS 91 (126).

25. Ibid.

26. Paul Rosenthal, "Bekenntnis eines jüdischen Frontsoldaten," *Deutsche Allgemeine Zeitung*, 26 March 1933.

27. Quoted in "Ein Schicksal: Brief eines kaufmännischen Angestellten," *Berliner Tageblatt*, 4 June 1933, HStADD 10702 Staatskanzlei, Nachrichtenstelle (Zeitungsausschnittsammlung), Nr. 582.

28. Willi Gans to Regierungspräsident Kassel, 6 June 1933, USHMMA RG-11.001M.31, reel 634 (SAM 721–1–2157, 235–37).

29. Hanns Silberschmidt to Hindenburg, handwritten letter, 21 March 1933, BArch R3001/4152.

30. Eugen Neter, "Der jüdische Frontsoldat: Erinnerungen aus dem 1. Weltkrieg," LBINY AR 1619. Neter was the chairman of the Mannheim chapter of the RjF until 1938 and a frequent contributor to *Der Schild*.

31. Gesetz zur Wiederherstellung des Berufsbeamtentum vom 7. April 1933, RGBl I, 175–77, Österreichische Nationalbibliothek, accessed 24 January 2020, http://alex.onb.ac.at/cgi-content/alex?aid=dra&datum=1933&size=45&page=300.

32. Büro des Reichspräsidenten to Reichskanzlei, 4 April 1933, BArch R43 II/600.

33. See correspondence between Hindenburg and Rabbi Leopold Rosenak quoted in chapter 2.

34. On Hindenburg's overall lack of intervention during the Nazis' persecution of Jews, see Pyta, *Hindenburg*, 832; and Goltz, *Hindenburg*, 174.

35. Kershaw, *Hitler: 1889–1936*, 500.

36. Reichskanzlei (Hitler) to Hindenburg, 5 April 1933, BArch R43 II/600.

37. The veterans' exemptions were unofficially referred to as the Frontkämpferprivileg (frontline veterans' exemption), the Frontkämpfergesetz (front soldiers' law), or quite simply as the "Hindenburg Law."

38. "Zur Begriffsbestimmung des 'Frontkämpfers,'" 20 June 1933, USHMMA RG-11.001M.31, reel 633 (SAM 721–1–2155, 1225).

39. "Fragebogen zur Durchführung des Gesetzes zur Wiederherstellung des Berufsbeamtentum vom 7. April 1933," copy dated 22 June 1933, Ernst Kantorowicz Collection, LBINY AR 7216.

40. On the role of Hitler's nationalist coalition partners in 1933, see Beck, *Fateful Alliance*. Beck's book overwhelmingly focuses on the shared goals and ideology of the Deutschnationale Volkspartei (German National People's Party) and Nazi Party, but largely overlooks the ambivalences and disagreements that persisted between the two camps.

41. "Aufruf an die deutschen Juden!," RjF pamphlet, May 1933, USHMMA RG-14.064M, A391.

42. RjF to Reichskanzlei, 4 April 1933, BArch R43 II/600.

43. On the RjF's discussions with Hindenburg and Mackensen, see the memoirs of Ernst Herzfeld, the CV chairman in the Rheinland: Herzfeld, "Meine letzten Jahre in Deutschland, 1933–1938," LBINY ME 287b. On Löwenstein's relationship to Blomberg, see Nachlass Leo Löwenstein, IfZ ZS 2196/1.

44. Quoted in "Selbsthilfe eines jüdischen Frontkämpfers," unnamed newspaper, April 1933, Erich Leyens Collection, LBINY ME 170. Also see Rohkrämer, *Single Communal Faith*, 91–93, 149.

45. This rationale was articulated in Hitler's April 5 letter to Hindenburg: Reichskanzlei (Hitler) to Hindenburg, 5 April 1933, BArch R43 II/600.

46. H. G. to Herbert Sulzbach, 15 August 1934, BA-MA N 634/89.

47. See, for example, Klemperer's entries for 19 August 1933, 13 May 1934, and 27 September 1936, in *I Will Bear Witness*, 1:29–31, 64–66, 190–93.

48. Karl Löwith, HHL bMS 91 (147).

49. Ibid.

50. Matthäus and Roseman, *Jewish Responses to Persecution*, 118.

51. The Centralverein argued that dismissal due to "national unreliability" pertained only to members of the Communist Party; however, it acknowledged that challenging the expulsion of Reichsbanner and SPD members from the civil service was "futile." CV main office Berlin (Goldschmidt) to P. Immerwahr, 12 September 1933, USHMMA RG-11.001M.31, reel 643 (SAM 721–1–2571, 1417–19).

52. Deutschkron, *Outcast*, 12–14.

53. Friedländer, *Years of Persecution*, 17; Johnson, *Nazi Terror*, 167–68.

54. Alfred Oppler, HHL bMS 91 (172).

55. Max Hirschberg, HHL bMS 91 (97). Also see Hirschberg, *Jude und Demokrat*.

56. Rosenthal was awarded both classes of the Iron Cross during World War I. See Karl Rosenthal, Offizierspersonalakt No. 27785, BHStA/IV.

57. Gestapo to Landgericht Würzburg, 19 November 1935, StAW, Gestapoakt Karl Rosenthal, No. 11141.

58. Ibid.

59. Status is defined as a group that is differentiated on the basis of noneconomic qualities such as honor, prestige, and religion. See Platt, "Social Psychology."

60. Gerstenberger, "Acquiescence?"; Bajohr, "Antijüdischen Konsens."

61. This sentiment is expressed in a multitude of contemporary internal government documents. See, for example, Document No. 33, "The Jewish Question—General," Situation Report from SD Main Office-Berlin, May/June 1934, reproduced in Kulka and Jäckel, *Secret Nazi Reports*, 538–68.

62. Quoted from the minutes of a meeting between CV lawyers and Nazi legal representatives regarding the rights of Jewish attorneys who were also war veterans: "Protokoll über die Unterredung zwischen dem Adjutanten des Preussischen Justizministers, dem Rechstanwalt Dr. Sting und den Referendaren Dr. Matzdorff und Dr. Swarenky," 29 May 1933, USHMMA RG-11.001M.31, reel 645 (SAM 721–1–2321, 1629–32).

63. RjF, press release, 19 March 1933, USHMMA RG-11.001M.31, reel 114 (SAM 721–1–2562, 587–91); "Stürmischer Ausspracheabend des Reichsbunds jüdischer Frontsoldaten," *Berliner Tageblatt*, 16 March 1933, BArch R72/1965.

64. "Aufklärung—trotz alldem: Kamerad Dr. Ludwig Freund spricht in Berlin," *Der Schild*, 23 March 1933.

65. Gerhard Lissa to Linder, 27 March 1933, DNVP, Politischer Schriftwechsel, BArch R8005/19. Other RjF members in attendance were Adolf Asch and Hermann Pineas, both of whom describe the event in their memoirs: Asch, "Memoiren," LBINY ME 18; and Pineas, "Erinnerungen," LBINY ME 502.

66. "Aufklärung—trotz alldem," *Der Schild*, 23 March 1933.

67. "Im Geist alter Frontkameradschaft," *Der Schild*, 14 September 1933. On the participation of non-Jewish organizations at RjF memorial services after 1933, see "Imposante Kundgebung in Hamburg," *Der Schild*, 14 September 1933.

68. "Aufklärung," *Der Schild*, 23 March 1933. Remarkably, the meeting also caught the attention of the international press: "German Veterans Hear Jewish Appeal," *New York Times*, 17 March 1933, 9.

69. "Ehre allen Gefallenen!," *C.V.-Zeitung*, 29 June 1933; "Im Geist alter Frontkameradschaft," *Der Schild*, 14 September 1933.

70. "Artikel aus der nationalsozialistischen Presse," undated press clipping, Dokumentationsstelle zur Erforschung der Schicksale der jüdischen Bürger Baden-Württembergs während der nationalsozialistischen Verfolgungszeit, 1933–1945, HStAS EA 99/001, Bü 251.

71. The continued presence of Jews in regimental associations drew Himmler's ire. In correspondence with Hitler in December 1934, he complained that these developments were "unacceptable" and "intended to devalue the movement and its program in the eyes of the public." Himmler to Reichskanzlei, December 1934, BArch R43 II/602.

72. Ziemann, *Contested Commemorations*, 261–65.

73. Ibid.

74. Elliott, "Kriegervereine"; Zimmermann, *"Der feste Wall,"* 144–53.

75. Führer, "Deutsche Reichskriegerbund Kyffhäuser"; Elliott, "Kriegervereine,"; "Kyffhäusererinnerungen," *Der Schild*, 13 October 1933.

76. Horn to Reichskanzler Hitler, 21 May 1933, BArch R43/824.

77. Per Führer, Horn's actions were intended to maintain the Kyffhäuser's autonomy, to prevent it from being absorbed into the SA. See Führer, "Deutsche Reichskriegerbund Kyffhäuser," 65–71.

78. "Parole-Buch des Kyffhäuser," No. 40, 1 October 1933, BA-MA RW 6/73a.

79. "Kyffhäuser-Bund schliesst Nichtarier aus," *CV-Zeitung*, 4 October 1933.

80. Max Schohl to General von Horn, 6 November 1933, USHMMA, Kaethe Wells Collection, 2010.242.1. Schohl's letter is reprinted in Large, *World Closed Its Doors*, 36–39.

81. Führer, "Deutsche Reichskriegerbund Kyffhäuser."

82. Verein "Garde" Düsseldorf to Vorstand des Reichskriegerbundes Kyffhäuser, 13 October 1933, USHMMA RG-11.001M.31, reel 116 (SAM 721-1-2598, 1225–28).

83. "Mitteilung Nr. 31 - Bericht über die 15. (ausßerordnetliche) Generalversammlung am 23. September 1933 im Artillerie-Klub in Stuttgart," November 1933, Offiziersverein des Feldartillerie-Regiments Nr. 29, HStAS M 740/10, Bü 1.

84. The Kameradschaftlicher Verein Deutscher Soldaten, founded in 1902 in Berlin, was a corporate member of the Kyffhäuserbund. Although statistics on the social and religious composition of its membership are unavailable, the few surviving association records suggest that it had a significant Jewish component. See "Leitsätze des Kameradschaftlichen Vereins Deutscher Soldaten," BA-MA MSG 2/7555.

85. "Protokoll zur Hauptversammlung des Kameradschaftlichen Vereins Deutscher Soldaten," 14 October 1933, BA-MA MSG 2/7555.

86. Ibid.

87. Ibid.

88. Kameradschaftlicher Verein Deutscher Soldaten, "Einladung-Mitglieder Versammlung am 4. April 1935," BArch R58/6405. In April 1935, the Gestapo launched an inquiry into Salomon and the association's activities, but it is not clear if follow-up actions were undertaken. See Bericht über Überwachung des Vereins und jüdische Mitglieder, 21 July 1935, BArch R58/6405.

89. See, for example, Wette, *Wehrmacht*, 74–94; and Rosenthal, *"Ehre des jüdischen Soldaten,"* 171–78.

90. Himmler to Reichskanzlei, "Betr. Verband der Bayerischen Offiziers-Regiments Vereine," December 1934, BArch R43 II/602.

91. Reichskanzlei (Lammers) to Himmler, 11 December 1934, BArch R43 II/602.

92. "Württ. Frontkämpferbund," press clipping from unnamed newspaper, 24 May 1933, Zeitungsausschnitts-Sammlung II, HStAS M 737, Bü 76.

93. Many Jewish members were notified of their expulsion by mail. However, some chapters apparently issued their expelled Jewish members a commemorative medal: see the records of Hans Sachs, JMB, No. 2010/24/2; and the experience of Arthur von Weinberg, in Groening, *Leo Gans und Arthur von Weinberg*, 142–62.

94. Bajohr, *Aryanization in Hamburg*, 16–42.

95. Messerschmidt, *Wehrmacht im NS-Staat*; Müller, *Heer und Hitler*; Streit, *Keine Kameraden*.

96. Hamburg Institut für Sozialforschung, *Verbrechen der Wehrmacht*.

97. Blomberg to Horn, 6 October 1933, BA-MA RW 6/73a. Horn responded by requesting a face-to-face meeting with Blomberg to discuss these and other "important and pressing questions" facing the military. It is unclear whether the meeting ever took place. See Horn to Blomberg, 19 October 1933, BA-MA RW 6/73a.

98. In late 1933, Blomberg issued statements to various newspapers such as *Fredericus*, claiming that no Jews served in the armed forces. Blomberg to *Fredericus—Die deutsche Wochenschrift*, 12 October 1933, BA-MA RW 6/73a. In January 1934, the press office of the Association of High-Ranking Civil Servants asked Blomberg to confirm whether it was true that over eight hundred non-Aryan officers served in the Reichswehr, and requested statistics to refute such allegations. Pressestelle des Reichsbundes der höheren Beamten an Reichswehrminsterium to Reichswehrministerium, 17 January 1934, BA-MA RW 6/73a.

99. Decree by Reichswehrminister v. Blomberg, 28 February 1934, BA-MA RW 6/73b.

100. The official Reichswehr documents report a total of fourteen officers and officer candidates, and thirty-six noncommissioned officers and enlisted men. "Durchfuhrung der Arierbescheinigung in der Wehrmacht," BA-MA RW 59 18/327. From this total, two officers, four officer candidates, and five noncommissioned officers and men were from the German Navy. Chef der Marineleitung to Reichswehrminister, "Zwischenmeldung über den Ariernachweis," 10 April 1934, BA-MA N 656/27.

101. Kershaw, *Hitler: 1889–1936*, 504. Also see Schäfer, *Werner von Blomberg*, 120–45; and Volkmann, "Von Blomberg zu Keitel."

102. This view is confirmed by the testimony of Hans Lebram, who was told by Blomberg's adjutant, Admiral Friedeburg, that the Aryan Paragraph was part of a strategy to exert pressure on the SA. Lebram to Vice Admiral Friedrich Ruge, 8 April 1976, BA-MA N 656/27.

103. Manstein to Beck, 21 April 1934, BA-MA RH 2/98. On Manstein's protest against the Aryan Paragraph, see Petter, "Wehrmacht und Judenverfolgung"; Wrochem, *Erich von Manstein*, 38–39; and Müller, *Generaloberst Ludwig Beck*, 142–44.

104. Manstein to Beck, 21 April 1934, BA-MA RH 2/98.

105. Ibid.

106. Quoted in Wrochem, *Erich von Manstein*, 58. Regarding Manstein's cooperation with Einsatzgruppe D during its anti-Jewish "actions" during the Crimean campaign, see 63–78; as well as Hürter, *Hitlers Heerführer*, 590–93.

107. Manstein to Beck, 21 April 1934, BA-MA RH 2/98. The officer was Klaus von Schmeling-Diringshofen, who later served under General Hans von Seekt as a military adviser to Chiang Kai-shek's Nationalist army. See Rigg, *Hitler's Jewish Soldiers*, 85–86.

108. "Gedanken zur nachträglichen Anwendung des Arier-Paragraphen auf die Wehrmacht," BA-MA RH 2/98.

109. Ibid. Emphasis in the original.

110. Manstein to Beck, 21 April 1934, BA-MA RH 2/98. Whether or not Manstein's memorandum ever reached Blomberg remains unclear. Sources confirm it was endorsed by his superior, Erwin von Witzleben, later a field marshal. It was also reviewed by Ludwig Beck, and subsequently the commander in chief of the army, General Werner von Fritsch (the original letter bears the handwritten initials of Beck [21 April 1934] and Fritsch [28 April 1934]). Manstein claimed in his memoirs that Blomberg and Reichenau sought to formally reprimand him, and that this was prevented only by an intervention from Fritsch and Beck, both of whom threatened to resign. However, there is no evidence to substantiate these claims. For Manstein's account, see *Aus einem Soldatenleben*, 209–10.

111. Hans Heinrich Lebram, letter to father, 7 May 1933, BA-MA N 656/2. Lebram enlisted in the German Navy in 1922, and was promoted into the officer ranks in 1926. By the time of his dismissal in May 1934, he had attained the rank of Kapitänleutnant.

112. Otto Lewin, "Mein Lebenslauf," Private Holdings of Ulrich Lewin; Ulrich Lewin, interviews and correspondence with the author, July 2012 and July 2019.

113. Militärpass Otto Lewin, issued October 1936, Private Holdings of Ulrich Lewin.

114. Memo by Böhme, "Entlassung wegen nichtarischer Abstammung," 19 February 1934, BA-MA N 656/27.

115. The Reichswehr's participation in, and reaction to, the so-called Röhm-Putsch on 30 June 1934 is described in detail in Müller, *Heer und Hitler*, 123–33.

116. Kühne, *Comradeship*, 70–103.

117. This sentiment was repeated in official documents as well as the personal writings of numerous German officers. According to one officer, "As embarrassing as these incidents were for me, I was unable to see the darkness ahead. As a captain in the Panzertruppe, I was completely immersed in new responsibilities and devoted myself with great passion into helping building this new arm." Quoted in Müller, *Heer und Hitler*, 125n.

118. These claims are corroborated by several local studies of Jewish life in Germany after 1933, including Abrams-Sprod, "Life under Siege," 283–97.

119. Richard Wolf, HHL bMS 91 (244). Also see Kaplan, *Between Dignity and Despair*, 36–40.

120. Karl Löwith, HHL bMS 91 (147).

121. Over the past decade, a number of works have claimed that Nazi violence came suddenly after 30 January. See, for example, Confino, *World without Jews*; and Beck, "Dictates of Conscience." However, the findings of this book support the contention that the intensity of persecution varied significantly from region to region, even village to village.

122. Ilse Strauss, "Lives in Crisis: Zwischen Krefeld and Frankfurt am Main," LBINY AR 3273. Also see Maurer, "Customers, Patients, Neighbors and Friends," 83.

123. Schwerin, *Von Dachau bis Basel*, 29, 147–48.

124. Ibid., 113.

125. "In Sachen Krebs gegen Deutsches Schuhwarenhaus," 28 October 1933, USHMMA RG-11.001M.31, reel 115 (SAM 721–1–2579, 1766–71).

126. Stephan Kunreuther, "Memoiren, 1882–1942," LBINY ME 225.

127. Ibid.

128. Klemperer, diary entry for 10 April 1933, in *I Will Bear Witness*, 1:12.

129. Alfred Oppler, HHL bMS 91 (172).

130. The verse is from "Ihr Sturmsoldaten jung und alt," a song highly popular with the Hitler Youth, the SA, and other auxiliary organizations of the NSDAP.

131. Annemarie Wolfram, HHL bMS 91 (247).

132. On antisemitic violence in small towns and rural communities, see Wildt, *Volksgemeinschaft als Selbstermächtigung*, 158–72, 205–13; Fischer, *Ökonomisches Vertrauen*, 212–34; and Stephenson, *Hitler's Home Front*, 135–52.

133. Julius Meyer, "Erinnerungen, 1914–1939," LBINY ME 439.

134. Leyens and Andor, *Fremden Jahre*, 33.

135. Fritz Goldberg (John Hay), HHL bMS 91 (89).

136. Ernst Marcus, HHL bMS 91 (151).

137. Klemperer, diary entry for 25 April 1933, in *I Will Bear Witness*, 1:15.

138. Bajohr, "Antijüdischen Konsens," 15–18.

139. Gellately, *Backing Hitler*, 132–44.

140. Rudi Hofmann to Max Strauss, 7 June 1933, StAW, Gestapoakt Max Strauss, No. 15622.

141. Wilhem Körngen, voluntary statement under oath, 8 April 1933, USHMMA RG-11.001M.31, reel 116 (SAM 721–1–2584, 49–50).

142. "Lagebericht der Staatspolizeistelle Potsdam für Juni 1935," undated report, in Ribbe, *Lageberichte der Geheimen Staatspolizei*, 287–88. Also see subsequent reports dated 31 July 1935 and August 1935, 310, 327–32.

143. "Lagebericht des Hildesheimer Regierungspräsidenten an den Reichsminister des Innern für die Monate April/Mai 1935," 1 June 1935, in Mylnek, *Gestapo Hannover meldet*, 375–83.

144. Karl Löwith, HHL bMS 91 (147).

145. Kaplan, *Between Dignity and Despair*, 15–16, 39.

146. Quoted in Strangmann, "Eduard und Hans Bloch," 256.

147. The Ehrenkreuz was awarded in three classes: frontline combatant, noncombat soldier, and next of kin of those killed in action. "Verordung des Reichspräsidenten über die Stiftung eines Ehrenkreuzes vom 13 Juli 1934," RGBl, 15 July 1934, 619–20, Österreichische Nationalbibliothek, accessed 24 January 2020, http://alex.onb.ac.at/cgi-content/alex?aid=dra&datum=1934&page=733&size=45.

148. "Zusammenstellung der vom Reichsministerium des Innern zur Durchführung des Verfahrens bei der Verleihung des Ehrenkreuzes des Weltkrieges herausgegebenen Richtlinien," 22 October 1934, BArch R1501/125280a/b.

149. Verleihung des Ehrenkreuzes an Nichtarier (para. 6), "Zweite Zusammenstellung der vom Reichsministerium des Innern zur Durchführung des Verfahrens bei der Verleihung des Ehrenkreuzes des Weltkrieges herausgegebenen Richtlinien," BArch R1501/125280a/b.

150. "Das Ehrenkreuz für Frontkämpfer," Der Schild, 20 July 1934; and "Das Ehrenkreuz," CV-Zeitung, 20 July 1934.

151. Cohn, diary entry for 5 February 1935, in Kein Recht, Nirgends, 1:208.

152. "Übersicht der Staatspolizeistelle Kassel über die politische Lage im April 1935," 4 May 1935, in Klein, Lageberichte der Geheimen Staatspolizei, 1:263.

153. "Lagebericht der Staatspolizeistelle Potsdam für Oktober 1934," 12 November 1934, in Ribbe, Lageberichte der Geheimen Staatspolizei, 210–11.

154. Albert Dreyfuss, HHL bMS 91 (54).

155. CV regional office Pomerania to Chief of Police, Stettin, 20 March 1935, USHMMA RG-11.001M.31, reel 145 (SAM 721–1–3019, 220–21).

156. Goltz, Hindenburg, 186–92.

157. Erna Albersheim, HHL bMS 91 (3).

158. "Reichspräsident von Hindenburg," Jüdische Rundschau, 3 August 1934. Also see the critical follow-up essay by Ernst Simon: "Kriegserlebnis des Jungen Juden," Jüdische Rundschau, 7 August 1934.

159. See, for example, "Übersicht der Staatspolizeistelle Kassel über die politische Lage im April 1935."

160. Klemperer, diary entry for 4 August 1934, in I Will Bear Witness, 1:80.

161. Fritz Goldberg (John Hay), HHL bMS 91 (89).

162. Cohn, diary entry for 2 August 1933, in Kein Recht, Nirgends, 1:143.

4. Jewish Frontkämpfer and the Nazi Volksgemeinschaft

1. Evans, Third Reich in Power, 42–50; Friedländer, Years of Persecution, 114–17.

2. Dwork and Pelt, Holocaust, 86; Kaplan, Between Dignity and Despair, 45–46.

3. Keene, "Long Journey Home"; Edele, Soviet Veterans.

4. See, further, Mosse, Image of Man; Goldstein, War and Gender; and Horne, "Masculinity in Politics and War."

5. Matthäus, "Evading Persecution."

6. Tausk, diary entry for 3 July 1933, in Breslauer Tagebuch, 87.

7. Kurt Rosenberg, diary entry for 1 May 1933, "Diaries, 1916–1939," LBINY AR 25279.

8. Johanna Neumann (daughter of Siegbert Gerechter), interview with the author, 29 November 2012. This interview took place at the United States Holocaust Memorial Museum, Washington, DC.

9. Statement by Curt Kochmann to Kriminalpolizei Beuthen, 24 July 1934, USHMMA, RG-11.001M.31, reel 116 (SAM 721–1–2604, 1898).

10. "Der Allensteiner Jude Levy überfällt den Standarten Adjudanten Nowack," 21 June 1933, *Nationalsozialistische Kreiszeitung Allenstein*, USHMMA, RG-11.001M.31, reel 101 (SAM 721–1–2316a, 520–21).

11. Ibid. Levy was deported to Theresienstadt on 17 March 1943, and to Auschwitz on 29 September 1944. He did not survive the Holocaust. See, further, "Levy, Max," *Gedenkbuch: Opfer der Verfolgung der Juden unter der nationalsozialistischen Gewaltherrschaft in Deutschland 1933–1945*, Bundesarchiv, accessed 2 July 2019, http://www.bundesarchiv.de/gedenkbuch/en1103753.

12. Edwin Landau, HHL bMS 91 (126).

13. Tosh, "Hegemonic Masculinity." Also see Wünschmann, "Konzentrationslagererfahrungen."

14. Carey, *Jewish Masculinity*, 53–58.

15. Gerhard Lissa to Linder, 27 March 1933, BArch R8005/19.

16. Landau, HHL bMS 91 (126).

17. Reichmann, *Deutscher Bürger*, 274.

18. Heinrich Lichtenstein, "Mein Leben in Deutschland vor und nach dem 30. Januar 1933," LBINY ME 1555.

19. Connell, *Masculinities*, 76. Also see Carey, *Jewish Masculinity*, 126–27.

20. "Tragt Ehrenzeichen!," *Der Schild*, 23 March 1933.

21. Marie-Luise Solmitz, diary entry for 20 May 1933, StAH 622–1/140, Bd. 31.

22. Siegfried Neumann, HHL bMS 91 (165).

23. Schwerin, *Von Dachau bis Basel*, 95.

24. Friedrich Solon, "Mein Leben in Deutschland vor und nach dem 30. Januar 1933," LBINY ME 607.

25. Winkle, *Dank des Vaterlandes*, 291–338; Weinrich, "Hitler-Jugend"; Löffelbein, *Ehrenbürger der Nation*, 65–71.

26. Ernst Fraenkel, "Brief an einen jungen Freund," *Der Schild*, 13 October 1933.

27. "Ein Beitrag zur Judenfrage in Briefen," *Euskirchener Beobachter*, March 1935, USHMMA, RG-11.001M.31, reel 114 (SAM 721–1–2555, 116–25).

28. Ibid.

29. See, for example, "Jüdische Frontsoldaten?," *Völkischer Beobachter*, 25 April 1933, quoted in Comité des Délégations Juives, *Schwarzbuch—Tatsachen und Dokumente*, 166–69.

30. Klemperer, *Curriculum Vitae*, 1:348–49.

31. Klemperer, diary entry for 27 September 1940, in *I Will Bear Witness*, 1:356–57.

32. Klemperer, diary entries for 12–19 March 1944, in *I Will Bear Witness*, 2:301–4.

33. Tausk, diary entry for 20 October 1933, in *Breslauer Tagebuch*, 87.

34. Tausk, diary entry for 3 July 1933, in *Breslauer Tagebuch*, 87.

35. Ibid.

36. Tausk, diary entry for 29 April 1933, in *Breslauer Tagebuch*, 68–70.

37. Tausk, diary entry for 16 May 1936, in *Breslauer Tagebuch*, 149.

38. Tausk, diary entry for 14 November 1938, in *Breslauer Tagebuch*, 191.

39. Tausk, diary entry for 8 February 1939, in *Breslauer Tagebuch*, 218.

40. Tausk, diary entry for 12 February 1939, in *Breslauer Tagebuch*, 219.

41. Wahlig, "Verdrängung Jüdischer Sportler."

42. Wehrgesetz vom 21 Mai 1935, RGBl I, 609–14, Österreichische Nationalbibliothek, accessed 24 January 2020, http://alex.onb.ac.at/cgi-content/alex?aid=dra&datum=1935&page=751&size=45.

43. CV Main Office-Berlin (Leo Baeck) to Reichswehrminister (Blomberg), 25 March 1935, USHMMA RG-11.001M.31, reel 616 (SAM 721–2–414, 258–61).

44. Max Vierfelder to Reichswehrminister Blomberg, 4 November 1933, BA-MA RW 6–73a; Herzfeld, diary entry for 17 January 1936, in *Nichtarischer Deutscher*, 37.

45. Kurt Sabatzky, HHL bMS 91 (261).

46. Kurt Rosenberg, diary entry for 30 April 1935, LBINY AR 25279.

47. "Versammlungstätigkeit der Juden," 21 June 1935, Bayerische Politische Polizei, IfZ Fa 119/1, 125–26.

48. "Allgemeine Übersicht der Staatspolizeistelle Frankfurt/Main über die innerpolitische Entwicklung im Berichtsmonat Juni 1935," 5 July 1935, in Klein, *Lageberichte der Geheimen Staatspolizei*, 254–65, 448–50.

49. "Lagebericht der Staatspolizeistelle Potsdam für Juni 1935," undated report, in Ribbe, *Lageberichte der Geheimen Staatspolizei*, 287–88.

50. For example, see Friedländer, *Years of Persecution*, 145–67; and Margaliot, "Reaction of the Jewish Public."

51. Erste Verordnung zum Reichsbürgergesetz, RGBl I, 14 November 1935, 1333, Österreichische Nationalbibliothek, accessed 24 January 2020, http://alex.onb.ac.at/cgi-content/alex?aid=dra&datum=1935&size=45&page=1479.

52. According to Victor Klemperer, this "shopwindow paragraph" entitled him, after deductions, to just 61 percent of his salary: diary entry for 31 December 1935, in *I Will Bear Witness* 1:141. Pension payments were substantially reduced in December 1938 by the Seventh Amendment to the Reich Citizenship Law.

53. Medical licenses for Jews were rescinded under Vierte Verordnung zum Reichsbürgergesetz, 25 July 1938, RGBl I, 969–70 (effective 30 September 1938), Österreichische Nationalbibliothek, accessed 24 January 2020, http://alex.onb.ac.at/cgi-content/alex?aid=dra&datum=1938&page=1147&size=45; for lawyers, see "Ausscheiden der Juden aus der Rechtsanwaltschaft," Fünfte Verordnung zum Reichsbürgergesetz, 27 September 1938, RGBl I, 1403–6 (effective 30 November 1938), Österreichische Nationalbibliothek, accessed 24 January 2020, http://alex.onb.ac.at/cgi-content/alex?aid=dra&datum=1938&size=45&page=1581.

54. Hermann Pineas, "Erinnerungen," LBINY ME 502.

55. Löffelbein, *Ehrenbürger der Nation*, 312–26.

56. Gesetz über die Versorgung der Militärpersonen und ihrer Hinterbliebenen bei Dienstbeschädigung (Reichsversorgungsgesetz), 12 May 1920, RGBl I, 989–1019, Österreichische Nationalbibliothek, accessed 24 January 2020, http://alex.onb.ac.at/cgi-content/alex?aid=dra&datum=1920&page=1223&size=45; also see Cohen, *War Come Home*, 157–62.

57. Löffelbein, *Ehrenbürger der Nation*, 75–91.

58. Gesetz über die Änderungen auf dem Gebiete der Reichsversorgung, 3 July 1934, RGBl I, 541–44, Österreichische Nationalbibliothek, accessed 24 January 2020, http://alex.onb.ac.at/cgi-content/alex?aid=dra&datum=1934&page=655&size=45. Also see "Kriegsopferrecht," *Der Schild*, 8 June 1934; Löffelbein, *Ehrenbürger der Nation*, 253–64; Cohen, *War Come Home*, 170–87; and Whalen, *Bitter Wounds*, 175–79.

59. Verordnung über die öffentliche Fürsorge für Juden, 19 November 1938, RGBl I, 1649, Österreichische Nationalbibliothek, accessed 24 January 2020, http://alex.onb.ac.at/cgi-content/alex?aid=dra&datum=1938&page=1827&size=45.

60. Erlaß des Reichsarbeitsministers an die Landesregierungen (Sozialverwaltung), "Betr. Fahrpreisvergünstigungen und Ausweise zur bevorzugten Abfertigung vor Amtsstellen für schwerkriegsbeschädigte Juden," 30 December 1939, HStAS EA 99/001, Bü 238.

61. RV, War Victims Welfare Office, to Hauptwirtschaftsamt Berlin, 4 February 1942, "Btr. Kontrollkarten für Tabakwaren," BArch R8150/752.

62. Erlaß des Reichsverkehrsministers to Württemberg Interior Ministry, "Btr. Einbeziehung der Führerscheine und Kraftfahrzeugscheine von Juden," 22 February 1939, in Sauer, *Dokumente*, doc. 324b, 2:68.

63. Directive, Reichsminister for Food and Agriculture to all District Governors et al., "Btr. Lebensmittelversorgung der Juden," 18 September 1942, BArch R8150/752. The original ordinance was enacted on 24 October 1940; it was confirmed by a similar decree on 18 September 1942.

64. See, for example, RV to Landeswohlfahrts- und Jugendamt, Vermittlungsstelle für Schwerbeschädigte, "Btr. Vermittlung jüdsicher Schwerkriegsbeschädigter in Arbeitsplätze," 26 April 1939, BArch R8150/753.

65. Württ. Landesfürsorgebehörde Abt. Hauptfürsorgestelle für Kriegsbeschädigte und Kriegshinterbliebene to Abwehrstelle Stuttgart, "Betr. Arbeitsfürsorge für den Schwerkriegsbeschädigten Siegfried Israel Horn," 11 March 1940, in Sauer, *Dokumente*, doc. 391a, 2:152–55.

66. Report of Württ. Landesfürsorgebehörde Abt. Hauptfürsorgestelle für Kriegsbeschädigte und Kriegshinterbliebene to Reich Labor Minister, "Btr. Arbeitsfürsorge für schwerkriegsbeschädigte Juden," 19 July 1943, in Sauer, *Dokumente*, doc. 391d, 2:157–64.

67. Leo Löwenstein, IfZ ZS 2196/1.

68. Kurt Sabatzky, HHL bMS 91 (261); also see the memoirs of Ernst Herzfeld, chairman of the CV-Rheinland: "Meine letzten Jahre in Deutschland, 1933–1938," LBINY ME 287b.

69. On the activities of Fritz Arnold and Julius Fliess, see Meyer, *Unternehmen Sieben*, 45–53.

70. Fliess to Reichsjustizministerium, 2 October 1935, copy sent to War Ministry, BA-MA RW 6/73b.

71. Arnold to Frhr. Von Wolf, Reichskriegsministerium, 19 November 1935, BA-MA RW 6/73b.

72. Reichskriegsminister (Blomberg) to Reichs- und Preußischen Ministern des Innern, 19 December 1935, BA-MA RW 6/73b.

73. Der Oberbefehlshaber des Heeres, "Betr. Ariernachweis," 28 December 1935, BA-MA RW 6/73b.

74. Reichskriegsministerium to Reichs- und Preußischen Ministern des Innern, undated (January 1936), BA-MA RW 6/73b.

75. Reichskriegsministerium, "Vortrag btr. Jüdische Notare mit Frontkämpfereigenschaft," December 1935, BA-MA RW 6/73b; and "Vortrag btr. Jüdische Notare," 16 January 1936, BA-MA RW 6/73b.

76. In the same memo, however, Blomberg stated that he supported pension and welfare payments for dismissed lawyers and civil servants. Reichskriegsminister to Reichs- und Preußischen Minister des Innern, 3 January 1936, BA-MA RW 6/73b.

77. Mackensen to Hitler, 3 December 1935, BA-MA RW 6/73b. A copy of this letter was forwarded to Blomberg on 11 January 1936.

78. Emphases in the original. Reichs- und Preußische Arbeitsminister (Rettig) to Reichs- und Preußische Minister des Innern, "Btr. Befreiung kriegsbeschädigter Notare von den Vorschriften des Reichsbürger- und des Blutschutzgesetzes," 31 December 1935, BA-MA RW 6/73b. Also see Reichs- und Preußische Arbeitsminister (Rettig) to Reichskriegsminister, "Btr. Kriegsbschädigte nichtarische Notare (Frontkämpfer)," 4 March 1936, BA-MA RW 6/73b.

79. On the Labor Ministry's role in formulating and administering Nazi anti-Jewish policies, and its involvement in the crimes of the Nazi regime, see the essays in Nützenadel, *Reichsarbeitsministerium im Nationalsozialismus.*

80. Verordnung über die öffentliche Fürsorge für Juden, 19 November 1938, RGBl I, 1649, Österreichische Nationalbibliothek, accessed 24 January 2020, http://alex.onb.ac.at/cgi-content/alex?aid=dra&datum=1938&page=1827&size=45.

81. Quoted in Cohen, *War Come Home,* 170, 255n144.

82. Reichsarbeitsminister to Preußische Minister des Innern, "Betr. Schutz Schwerkriegsbeschädigter," 5 October 1933, BArch R4901/6918.

83. Fünfte Verordnung zum Reichsbürgergesetz, 27 September 1938, RGBl 1938 I, 1403-6 (effective 30 November 1938), Österreichische Nationalbibliothek, accessed 24 January 2020, http://alex.onb.ac.at/cgi-content/alex?aid=dra&datum=1938&size=45&page=1581. The Labor Ministry, citing Mackensen's support, unsuccessfully pushed to extend the law's implementation to 30 December in order to ensure that the "proper" exemptions for veterans, especially the war disabled, were in place. Reichsarbeitsministerium to Reichsminister der Justiz, 29 July 1938, BArch R3001/20253.

84. Reichsminister der Justiz (Gürtner) to Mackensen, [illegible date] August 1938, BArch R3001/20253.

85. Hess is mentioned in correspondence as one of the proponents of the bill: RV to Landeswohlfahrts- und Jugendamt, Vermittlungsstelle für Schwerbeschädigte, "Btr. Vermittlung jüdsicher Schwerkriegsbeschädigter in Arbeitsplätze," 26 April 1939, BArch R8150/753; and Württ. Landesfürsorgebehörde Abt. Hauptfürsorgestelle für Kriegsbeschädigte und Kriegshinterbliebene to StadtKasse Horb, "Btr. Wertzuwachssteuerschuld des Schwerkriegsbeschädigten Willy Israel Gideon," 22 January 1940, in Sauer, *Dokumente,* doc. 390, 2:150–51. Also see Pfundtner (Interior Ministry) to Lammers, 8 April 1941, reproduced in Adler, *Verwaltete Mensch,* 498–99.

86. See Frank Bajohr, "Vom antijüdischen Konsens zum schlechten Gewissen"; Gellately, *Backing Hitler,* 121–26, 132–44; and Longerich, *"Davon haben wir nichts gewusst!,"* 85–92.

87. Allport, Bruner, and Jandorf, "Personality under Social Catastrophe."

88. Tausk, diary entries for 12 September 1933, in *Breslauer Tagebuch,* 110; and 14 October 1938, in *Breslauer Tagebuch,* 164.

89. Karl Löwith, HHL bMS 91 (147).

90. Leyens and Andor, *Fremden Jahre,* 23.

91. Schwerin, *Von Dachau bis Basel*, 136.

92. A. S. to Reichskanzlei, 10 October 1934, StaW, Gestapoakt Ernst Schloß, No. 12540.

93. BHStA/IV, Offizierspersonalakten/Ernst Schloß (No. 28171) and Max Siry (No. 47994).

94. "Bericht über die Gefangennahme des Herrn Oblt. Max Siry bez. der 5/2. bay.F.A.R.—Gutachten des Lt.d.R Schloss," 4 March 1920, BHStA/IV, Offizierspersonalakte/Max Siry, No. 47994.

95. Bayerische Politische Polizei München to Polizei Direktion Würzburg, "Btr. Bericht der Frau A.S. in Würzburg über angebliche Zusammenkünfte von Reichswehroffizieren bei dem Juden Schloss in Würzburg," 11 April 1935, StaW, Gestapoakt Ernst Schloß, No. 12540. Siry ended the war as a *Generalleutnant* commanding an infantry division on the Eastern Front. See Neitzel, *Abgehört*, 310.

96. According to Ulrich Lewin, after the dismissal of his father from the Wehrmacht, he received frequent visits from former comrades in Minden, yet increasingly after dark. Ulrich Lewin, interviews and correspondence with the author, July 2012 and July 2019.

97. Joseph Levy, HHL bMS 91 (135); Hugo Gutmann (Henry G. Grant) to Joseph Drexel, 6 November 1936, StArN E 10/24 Nr. 8.

98. Lichtenstein, "Mein Leben in Deutschland."

99. Hugo Moses, HHL bMS 91 (159).

100. Hermann Klugmann, HHL bMS 91 (113).

101. Stachelbeck, *Militärische Effektivität*, 29–48.

102. Kühne, *Comradeship*, 215–38; Echternkamp, *Soldaten im Nachkrieg*, 189–95.

103. Dienstauszeichung, "18-jährige treue Dienste in der Wehrmacht," October 1936, Private Holdings of Ulrich Lewin.

104. Lewin, interviews and correspondence with the author.

105. Hugo Gutmann (Henry G. Grant) to Joseph Drexel, 6 November 1936, StArN E 10/24 Nr. 8.

106. Ibid. Also see Weber, *Hitler's First War*, 300–301.

107. "Der Württ: Kriegerbund," 29 May 1933, *Tageblatt*, Zeitungsausschnits-Sammlung II, HStAS M 737, Bü 77; and "Ausgleichen der Regiments-Vereinigungen," press clipping from unnamed newspaper, 5 August 1933, Zeitungsausschnits-Sammlung II, HStAS M 737, Bü 77.

108. Oberst a.D. Reinhard to Reichskanzlei, "Betrifft: Eingliederung der alten Soldatenverbände und Vereinigungen in den Reichskriegerbund Kyffhäuser," 5 August 1933; and response from Reichskanzlei (Lammers), 14 August 1933, BArch R43 II/824.

109. Emphases in the original. Klemperer, diary entry for 16 September 1935, in *I Will Bear Witness*, 1:132.

110. Adolf Asch, "Memoiren," LBINY (ME 18).

111. Salzburg, *Mein Leben in Dresden*, 74.

112. Ludwig Beck to Major a.D. Schröder, "Betr. Mitgliedschaft von Nichtariern in Regimentsvereinen," 27 October 1937, in Müller, *General Ludwig Beck*, 497–98.

113. Letter to Arthur Samuel, "Betr. An alle ehemaligen Angehörigen der Res.San. Komp. 57 später 539 77.Res.Division 39. Korps," 23 April 1938, HHL bMS 91 (196).

114. Original document located in Arthur Samuel, HHL bMS 91 (196).

115. Herbert Sulzbach, "Privataufzeichnungen," unfinished book manuscript, BA-MA N 634/130.

116. Klemperer, diary entry for 28 August 1942, in *I Will Bear Witness*, 2:132–33.

117. See chapter 3 regarding the *Garde Verein*'s protest against the Aryan Paragraph. The incident is not mentioned by Herzfeld in his diary.

118. The Gestapo office in Düsseldorf noted that the flag ban "caused great dismay in Jewish circles. These circles cannot understand that even Jewish veterans, officers, and so on should be forbidden from raising the black, white, and red flag." Stapostelle Düsseldorf, Bericht für Februar 1935, in Kulka and Jäckel, *Nazi Reports*, CD-ROM, doc. 621.

119. Herzfeld, diary entry for 17 November 1935, in *Nichtarischer Deutscher*, 21.

120. Herzfeld, diary entry for 25 August 1936, in *Nichtarischer Deutscher*, 73.

121. Herzfeld, diary entry for 19 August 1938, in *Nichtarischer Deutscher*, 107. Also see entry for 1 October 1938, 113.

122. Herzfeld, diary entry for 1 January 1936, in *Nichtarischer Deutscher*, 37.

123. Herzfeld, diary entry for 5 February 1936, in *Nichtarischer Deutscher*, 47.

124. Herzfeld, diary entry for 3 December 1935, in *Nichtarischer Deutscher*, 27.

125. Herzfeld, diary entry for 6 May 1936, in *Nichtarischer Deutscher*, 61–62.

126. Herzfeld, diary entry for 5 February 1936, in *Nichtarischer Deutscher*, 47.

127. Herzfeld, diary entry for 1 January 1936, in *Nichtarischer Deutscher*, 37.

128. Herzfeld, diary entry for 5 February 1936, in *Nichtarischer Deutscher*, 47.

129. Herzfeld, diary entry for 24 May 1936, in *Nichtarischer Deutscher*, 62–3.

130. Herzfeld, diary entry for 22 August 1936, in *Nichtarischer Deutscher*, 71.

131. Herzfeld, diary entry for 9 March 1937, in *Nichtarischer Deutscher*, 78.

132. Eugen Neter, "Der jüdische Frontsoldat: Erinnerungen aus dem 1. Weltkrieg," LBINY AR 1619.

133. Sulzbach, "Privataufzeichnungen."

134. Cohn, diary entry for 13 July 1936, in *Kein Recht, Nirgends*, 1:337.

135. Cohn, diary entry for 27 January 1937, in *Kein Recht, Nirgends*, 1:376.

136. Cohn, diary entry for 1 October 1937, in *Kein Recht, Nirgends*, 1:474.

137. Klemperer, diary entry for 21 July 1935, in *I Will Bear Witness*, 1:128–29.

138. Ibid.

139. Klemperer, diary entry for 8 May 1942, in *I Will Bear Witness*, 2:49–51.

140. Martin Freudenheim, HHL bMS 91 (68).

141. Walther Nord, HHL bMS 91 (168).

142. Cohn, diary entry for 23 November 1938, in *Kein Recht, Nirgends*, 2:553.

143. Max Kronenburg, HHL bMS 91 (123).

5. Under the "Absolute" Power of National Socialism, 1938–41

1. Verordnung über Kennkarten, 22 July 1938, RGBl I, 913, Österreichische Nationalbibliothek, accessed 24 January 2020, http://alex.onb.ac.at/cgi-content/alex?aid=dra&datum=1938&size=45&page=1091.

2. Zweite Verordnung zur Durchführung des Gesetztes über die Änderung von Familiennamen und Vornamen, 17 August 1938, RGBl I, 1044, Österreichische Nationalbibliothek, accessed 24 January 2020, http://alex.onb.ac.at/cgi-content/alex?aid=dra&datum=1938&size=45&page=1222.

3. Diary entry for 25 August 1938, StAH 622–1/140, Nachlass Marie-Luise Solmitz, Bd. 31.

4. Ibid.

5. Quoted in Friedländer, *Years of Persecution*, 270–71.

6. On the background and events of Kristallnacht, see Steinweis, *Kristallnacht 1938*; and Friedländer, *Years of Persecution*, 269–84.

7. "Bericht des amerikanischen Generalkonsuls in Stuttgart, Samuel W. Honaker, an den amerikanischen Botschafter in Berlin, Hugh R. Wilson, Nr. 307, 12 November 1938," in Sauer, *Dokumente*, doc. 304, 2:33–37.

8. Siegfried Neumann, HHL bMS 91 (165).

9. Ibid.

10. StAW, Gestapoakt Alfred Katzmann, No. 3258.

11. StAW, Gestapoakt Ernst Lebermann, No. 5753.

12. StAW, Staatsanwaltschaft Würzburg, KLs 98/48.

13. Albert Dreyfuss, HHL bMS 91 (68). Hermann Pineas, too, was saved from arrest on 9 November, after policemen noticed his disfigured arm. See Pineas, "Unsere Schicksale seit dem 30.1.1933," LBINY AR 94.

14. Joseph Levy, HHL bMS 91 (135).

15. Hugo Gutmann (Henry G. Grant) to Joseph Drexel, 6 November 1946, StArN E 10/24 Nr. 8.

16. Herzfeld, diary entry for 8 December 1938, *Ein nichtarischer Deutscher*, 114–16.

17. Herzfeld, *Nichtarischer Deutscher*, 10, 124n34.

18. Schwerin, *Von Dachau bis Basel*, 44.

19. "Erinnerungen des Heinrich Baab, ehem. SS-Untersturmführer u. Kriminal-Sekretär an die Zeit 1937–1945 in Frankfurt/Main," USHMMA RG-14.064M A 256.

20. Sofsky, *Order of Terror*, 16–27.

21. Karl Rosenthal, HHL bMS 91 (192).

22. Dillon, *Dachau and the SS*, 212–13.

23. Siegfried Neumann, HHL bMS 91 (165).

24. Fritz Schürmann, HHL bMS 91 (206).

25. Siegfried Oppenheimer, "Meine Erlebnisse am 10. November 1938 u. mein Aufenthalt in Buchenwald bis zu meiner Rückkehr am 14 Dez. 1938 nach Bad Nauheim," LBINY MM 61.

26. Georg Simmel, quoted in Langewiesche, "Nation, Imperium und Kriegserfahrungen," 214.

27. Kurt Jutro, "Erlebnisse eines 'Schutzhaeftlings' in einem Konzentrationslager des Dritten Reichs waehrend der Monate November-Dezember 1938," LBINY ME 1046. For the concentration camp experiences of nonveteran Jews, also see Harvey Newton, "Erinnerungen an das KZ Buchenwald," LBINY ME 986; and Fritz Schürmann, HHL bMS 91 (206).

28. Hans Berger, "Erinnerungen an die Kristallnacht und meine Erlebnisse im Konzentrationslager Buchenwald," LBINY ME 46.

29. Reichmann, *Deutscher Bürger*, 155.

30. Julius Meyer, "Buchenwald," YVA O 2/407.

31. Schwerin, *Von Dachau bis Basel*, 84.

32. Ibid., 79, 84.

33. Heinrich Lichtenstein, "Mein Leben in Deutschland vor und nach dem 30. Januar 1933," LBINY ME 1555.

34. Ibid.

35. Hans Block, "Buchenwald," YVA O 1/49.

36. Kurt Sabatzky, HHL bMS 91 (261).

37. Chef der Sicherheitspolizei (Heydrich) to alle Stapoleit- und Stapostellen- et al., "Betr. Entlassung von jüdischen Häftlingen, die Frontkämpfer waren," 28 November 1938, ITS Digital Archive, 1.1.0.2/82340054, accessed at USHMMA. The order was disseminated the following day to all local law enforcement agencies. See, further, Gestapo Würzburg to all Landräte, "Betr. Entlassung von jüdischen Schutzhäftlingen, die Frontkämpfer waren," 29 November 1938, StAW LRA Bad Kissingen 3101.

38. Karl Guggenheim, "Der jüdische Widerstand," LBINY AR 179C. The same incident is described by Julius Meyer in "Buchenwald."

39. Jeffords, *Remasculinization of America*, 51.

40. Wünschmann, "Konzentrationslagererfahrungen"; Hájková, "'Poor Devils.'"

41. On the construction and shaping of biographical narratives, see Dausien, "Erzähltes Leben—erzähltes Geschlecht?"

42. Tausk, diary entry for 11 December 1938, in *Breslauer Tagebuch*, 208.

43. Hugo Moses, HHL bMS 91 (159).

44. Ibid.

45. Friedrich Solon, "Mein Leben in Deutschland vor und nach dem 30. Januar 1933," LBINY ME 607.

46. Schwerin, *Von Dachau bis Basel*, 161.

47. Alfred Oppler, HHL bMS 91 (172).

48. Robert Lenneberg, HHL bMS 91 (258).

49. Tausk, diary entry for 14 November 1938, in *Breslauer Tagebuch*, 191.

50. On Jewish suicides during the Third Reich, see Goeschel, *Suicide in Nazi Germany*, 96–118.

51. Schwerin, *Von Dachau bis Basel*, 161.

52. Gutmann to Drexel, 6 November 1946, StArN E 10/24 Nr. 8.

53. Ibid. On Gutmann's experience after immigrating to the United States, see Weber, *Hitler's First War*, 348–53.

54. Albert Dreyfuss, HHL bMS 91 (68).

55. Hugo Moses, HHL bMS 91 (159).

56. Ernst Marcus, HHL bMS 91 (151).

57. Alfred Oppler, HHL bMS 91 (172).

58. On the backgrounds of the perpetrators and the mobilization of Nazi agencies on the evening of 9 November, see Obst, *"Reichskristallnacht,"* 102–52.

59. Lichtenstein, "Mein Leben in Deutschland."

60. "Auszug aus dem Geheimbreicht des Sicherheitsdienstes Reichsführer-SS Unterabschnitt Württemberg-Hohenzollern für das 4. Vierteljahr 1938," 1 February 1939, in Sauer, *Dokumente*, doc. 318, 2:53–58.

61. Käthe Sauermann to Franz Ritter von Epp, 14 November 1938, ITS Digital Archive, Julius Katzmann/12310237.0.1–12310237.0.2, accessed at USHMMA.

62. Würzburg to Staatsministerium des Innern, "Btr. Aktion gegen Juden am 9./10.11.38," 29 December 1938, ITS Digital Archive, Julius Katzmann/12310240.0.1–12310240.0.2, accessed at USHMMA.

63. Regarding Epp's antisemitic convictions, see Wächter, *Macht der Ohnmacht*, 128–30, 200–202.

64. StAW, Gestapoakt Julius Katzmann, No. 3270.

65. Herbert Sulzbach, "Privataufzeichnungen," BA-MA N 634/130, pp. 34–35.

66. Alfred Oppler, HHL bMS 91 (172).

67. Confino, World without Jews, 99.

68. Klemperer, diary entry for 15 December 1938, in I Will Bear Witness, 1:283.

69. Polizeiverordnung über die Kennzeichnung der Juden vom 1 September 1941, RGBl I, 547, Österreichische Nationalbibliothek, accessed 24 January 2020, http://alex.onb.ac.at/cgi-content/alex?aid=dra&datum=1941&page=575&size=45.

70. Cohn, diary entry for 13 September 1941, in Kein Recht, Nirgends, 2:979–80.

71. Klemperer, diary entry for 15 September 1941, in I Will Bear Witness, 1:429.

72. Klemperer, LTI, 259.

73. "Btr. Verhalten Deutschblütiger gegenüber Juden," directive by RSHA, 24 October 1941, quoted in Walk, Sonderrecht für die Juden, 353.

74. Garbarini et al., Jewish Responses to Persecution, 322–24; Friedländer, Years of Extermination, 34–36.

75. On the October 1940 deportations to Gurs, see Teschner, Deportation; and Garbarini et al., Jewish Responses to Persecution, 325–42.

76. German plans for the racial restructuring of Europe and the Nazi-occupied eastern territories are discussed in Browning, Origins, 240–41; and Wildt, Uncompromising Generation, 331–34.

77. For a comprehensive overview of the 1941 deportations to Lodz, Riga, and Minsk, see Zimmermann, Deutsche gegen Deutsche, 106–9, 113–14.

78. Martha Mosse was an RV representative in Berlin tasked with compiling the transport lists. See Martha Mosse, "Erinnerungen," LBINY ME 751; and Meyer, Fatal Balancing Act, 111, 126–31.

79. Mosse, "Erinnerungen."

80. Meyer, Fatal Balancing Act, 147–52.

81. Besprechung in Berlin am 23.10.41 bei IVB4 unter dem Vorstitz von SS-Sturmbannführer Eichmann, "Btr. Führerbefehl (Evakuierung von 50000 Juden aus dem Altreich einschliesslich Ostmark und Protektorat Böhmen-Mähren," 24 October 1941, YVA TR 19/110.

82. Älteste der Juden in Litzmannstadt, Abteilung für die Eingesiedelten to Zentral-Sekretariat, "Betr. Registrierung der Besizter v. EK I, II, und VA," 26 May 1942; and "Vollständige Liste der Traeger von EKI, EKII und VA, in alphabetischer Reihenfolge," 14 June 1942, USHMMA RG-15.083M, reel 4.

83. Gestapo Würzburg, "Liste der zu evakuierenden Juden aus Würzburg," 19 November 1941, ITS Digital Archive, 1.2.3.0/82165171–82165185, accessed at USHMMA.

84. Mosse, "Erinnerungen."

85. Löw, Juden im Getto Litzmannstadt, 228–29; Barkai, "German-Speaking Jews," 252–55.

86. Matthäus et al., Jewish Responses to Persecution, 6.

87. On the living conditions of German Jews at Lodz, see Löw, Juden im Getto Litzmannstadt, 241–51.

88. "Proclamation No. 380," entry for 9 April 1942, in Dobroszycki, Chronicle, 156–57.

89. The Jewish Order Police were known by various names, depending on time and location, including Lager-Wache, Ordner-Wache, and Sicherheitswesen.

90. Löw, Juden im Getto Litzmannstadt, 256; Trunk, Lodz Ghetto, 308.

91. This number is based on lists of Iron Cross and Wound Badge recipients compiled by the Jewish Council from May through June 1942. "Vollständige Liste der Traeger von EKI, EKII und VA, nach Ankunftstransporten geordnet," Der Älteste der Juden in Litzmannstadt, Abteilung für die Eingesiedelten, 14 June 1942, Przełozony Starszeństwa Zydow w Getcie Łódzkim, USHMMA RG-15.083M.

92. Karl Löwenstein (Loesten), "Aus der Hölle Minsk in das 'Paradies' Theresienstadt, 1941–1945," LBINY ME 398. On the so-called German "Hamburg" camp at Minsk, see Hecker, "Minsker Ghetto,"

93. See, for example, Testimony of Sigmund Harf, recorded 23 March 1963, YVA TR 19/59; Testimony of Julius Rosengarten, recorded 22 January 1969, YVA TR 19/65; Gertrude Schneider, "Manuscript: Mass Grave and Concerts; The Riga Ghetto," LBINY AR 3348; and Angrick and Klein, "Final Solution," 214–15, 357.

94. Carey, Jewish Masculinity, chap. 3.

95. On the cooperation between the SS, the Ordnungspolizei, and the Jewish police during the ghetto-clearing operation at Lodz in September 1942, see Curilla, Judenmord in Polen, 129–32.

96. Ruth Alton, "Deportiert von den Nazis, 1941–1945," LBINY ME 9. Also see Curilla, Judenmord in Polen, 129–32; and Löw, Juden im Getto Litzmannstadt, 292–321.

97. Trunk, Judenrat, 475–527; Friedländer, Years of Extermination, 156.

98. Anonymous members of the Kovno Jewish Ghetto Police, Clandestine History.

99. The most detailed work is Trunk, Judenrat, which devotes chapter 18 to the Jewish police. Also see Hilberg, Destruction, 1:233–34.

100. Gottwaldt and Schulte, "Judendeportationen," 52–83, 90.

101. Angrick and Klein, "Final Solution," 437.

102. Löwenstein, "Hölle Minsk"; Testimony of Sigmund Harf, recorded 23 March 1963, YVA TR 19/59, pp. 98–102.

103. Bezpieczeństwo (Sicherheitswesen), Przełozony Starszeństwa Zydow w Getcie Łódzkim, USHMMA RG-15.083M.

104. Dobroszycki, Chronicle.

105. Löwenstein, "Hölle Minsk."

106. Ruth Alton, "Deportiert von den Nazis," LBINY ME 9.

107. Ibid.

108. Entry for 14 September 1942, in Dobroszycki, Chronicle, 252. Also see entry for 16 September 1942, in Singer, "Im Eilschritt . . . ," 133–37; and Curilla, Judenmord in Polen, 129–32.

109. Löw, Juden im Getto Litzmannstadt, 301.

110. Karny, "Deutsche Juden in Theresienstadt."

111. Löwenstein, "Hölle Minsk."

112. Ibid.

113. Ibid.

114. Schneider, "Manuscript," 51; Angrick and Klein, "Final Solution," 357.

115. Gestapoakt Alwin Lippmann, HStADü RW 58, No. 18474.

116. Kopciowski, "Der Judenrat in Zamość"; Berger, "Fallbeispiel."

117. Blatt, Ashes of Sobibor, 73.

118. Löwenstein, "Hölle Minsk."

119. Memo, Reichsführer SS (Himmler) to Chef der Bandenbekämpfung (von dem Bach), 25 July 1943, BArch NS 19/1770.

120. Ibid.; Löwenstein, "Hölle Minsk."

121. Reichsführer SS to Polizeipräsident Düsseldorf, 19 August 1940, "Vorg. Amstgerichtsrat i.R. Hess, geb. 20.3.1890 in Gelsenkirchen," Gestapoakt Ernst Hess, HStADü RW 58, No. 24484.

122. Ibid.

123. Gestapoakt Ernst Hess, HStADü RW 58, No. 24484. On Wiedemann's career during the Third Reich, see Weber, *Hitler's First War*, 321–25.

124. For further background on Ernst Hess, see Susanne Mauss, "Hitler's Jewish Commander and Victim," Jewish Voice from Germany, 4 July 2012, http://jewish-voice-from-germany.de/cms/hitlers-jewish-commander-and-victim/.

125. Max Plaut, interview with Christian Riecke, LBINY ME 743; Meyer, *"Jüdische Mischlinge,"* 152.

126. Meyer, *Fatal Balancing Act*, 149.

127. Emphasis in the original. Haake to Reichsminister des Innern (Frick), 19 November 1941, Gestapoakt Stephan Prager, HStADü RW 58, Nr. 29013.

128. Reichsführer SS to Haake, 21 May 1942, "Betr. Den Juden Stephan Friederich Israel Prager...," Gestapoakt Stephan Prager, HStADü RW 58, Nr. 29013.

129. Befehlshaber Wehrkreis XVII (Streccius) to Chef der Heeresrüstung (Fromm), 24 February 1941, IfZ MA 261, Bl. 9340.

130. Befehlshaber Wehrkreis XVII (Streccius) to Reichsleiter Baldur von Schirach, 29 April 1941, BA-MA RH 14–46.

131. Ibid. Also see the subsequent correspondence between Streccius and Fromm, 13 September 1941, BA-MA RH 14–46.

132. Helmuth James von Moltke to Freya Moltke, 11 November 1941, in Moltke, *Letters to Freya*, 181.

133. Ibid., 181.

134. Helmuth James von Moltke to Freya Moltke, 14 November 1941, in Moltke, *Letters to Freya*, 184–85.

135. Meyer, *Unternehmen Sieben*, 62–64. This account is based on postwar interviews with Fliess and Arnold, in addition to courtroom testimony related to restitution claims submitted by the victims.

136. Helmuth James von Moltke to Freya Moltke, 17 November 1941, in Moltke, *Letters to Freya*, 186–87.

137. Leo Löwenstein, "Eidesstattliche Aussage," 9 June 1948, IfZ ZS 2196/1.

138. "Bericht über Verschickung von Juden deutscher Staatsangehörigkeit nach Südfrankreich," 30 October 1940, in Sauer, *Dokumente*, doc. 441, 2:242–43.

139. Auswärtiges Amt (Rademacher) to RSHA (Hartmann), 20 February 1941, ITS Digital Archive, 1.2.7.11/82191504–82191507, accessed at USHMMA.

140. Hassell, diary entry for 11 November 1940, in *Ulrich von Hassell Diaries*, 103.

141. Hassell, diary entry for 1 November 1941, in *Ulrich von Hassell Diaries*, 144–46.

142. Ibid. Hassell's entry is factually inaccurate as there were no Jewish deportees with the Pour le Mérite. The only known Jewish recipient of the award was Wilhelm Frankl, a convert to Christianity who did not survive the war.

143. Ibid. Leo Löwenstein claimed that the efforts of German officers to exempt Jewish veterans from the wearing of the star "failed due to the intransigent attitude of Hitler." See Leo Löwenstein, IfZ ZS 2196/1.

144. Ernst Kaltenbrunner, "Btr. Stellung der Verschwörer zur Rassenfrage," 28 October 1944, BA-MA N 756/417b. For a closer analysis of *Das Ziel* and Goerdeler's antisemitism, see Hoffmann, *Carl Goerdeler*, 206–7.

145. On the antisemitic attitudes of the 20 July conspirators, see Dipper, "Deutsche Widerstand."

146. Schmitthenner and Buchheim, *Widerstand gegen Hitler*, 47.

147. Wilhelm Kube to Hinrich Lohse, 16 December 1941, ITS Digital Archive, 1.2.7.6/82176598–82176599, accessed at USHMMA.

148. Kube's antisemitic views are articulated in a series of newspaper articles he wrote in 1934, including "Und immer wieder die Judenfrage," *Generalanzeiger*, 19/20 May 1934, USHMMA, RG-11.001M.31, reel 101 (SAM 721–1–2308, 100). Also see Heiber, "Gauleiter Kube," 68.

149. Kube to Lohse, "Btr. Partisanenbekämpfung und Judenaktion im General-bezirk Weißruthenien," 31 July 1942, YVA O 53/132.

150. Aktenvermerk, Kommandeur der Sicherheitspolizei Weißruthenien, 20 July 1943, BArch NS 19/1770.

151. Reichsführer SS to Chef der Bandenbekämpfung (von dem Bach), 25 July 1943, BArch NS 19/1770.

152. Ibid.

153. Hecker, "Minsker Ghetto"; Zimmerman, *Deutsche gegen Deutsche*, 112.

154. Mosse, "Erinnerungen."

155. On the limitations of personal interventions in Nazi Germany, see Stoltzfus, *Hitler's Compromises*, 261–73.

156. Streccius to Fromm, 13 September 1941, BA-MA RH 14–46.

157. Emphasis in the original. "Notizen aus der Besprechung am 10.10.41 über die Lösung von Judenfragen," YVA O 51/204.

158. Ibid.

159. Of the nine thousand German Jews who arrived in Lodz in October 1941, only one was a holder of the Iron Cross First Class. See Memo, Älteste der Juden in Litzmannstadt, Abteilung für die Eingesiedelten to Zentral-Sekretariat, "Betr. Registrierung der Besizter v. EK I, II, und VA," 26 May 1942; and "Vollständige Liste der Traeger von EKI, EKII und VA, in alphabetischer Reihenfolge," 14 June 1942, USHMMA RG-15.083M, reel 4.

160. Eichmann to Gestapo Düsseldorf, 2 December 1941, in Meyer, *Unternehmen Sieben*, 236–37. Also see Gerlach, "Wannsee Conference," 770–71.

161. Memo from Stapo-Außendienststelle Würzburg, 22 November 1941, ITS Digital Archive, 1.2.3.0/82165154, accessed at USHMMA.

162. Helmuth James von Moltke to Freya Moltke, 17 November 1941, in Moltke, *Letters to Freya*, 186–87.

163. Klemperer, diary entry for 28 November 1941, in *I Will Bear Witness*, 1:446.

164. Klepper, diary entry for 2 December 1941, in *Unter dem Schatten deiner Flügel*, 995.

165. Officially, the preparations for Theresienstadt began on 24 November 1941. The editors of Himmler's *Dienstkalendar* state that a transit camp had already been planned as early as 23 October for certain German Jews. See Witte et al., *Dienstkalendar Heinrich Himmlers 1941/42*, 244.

166. Löw, *Juden im Getto Litzmannstadt*, 273–82.

167. On the policy of "destruction through labor" (*Vernichtung durch Arbeit*), see Tooze, *Wages of Destruction*, 513–51.

168. Bekanntmachung No. 380, "Betr. Aussiedlung von aus dem Altreich, Luxemburg, Wien und Prag nach Litzmannstadt-Getto eingesiedlten Juden," 29 April 1942, YVA O 34–389.

169. Applications for exemption, which included military documents and medal certificates from the war, are preserved in Przełozony Starszeństwa Zydow w Getcie Łódzkim (The Elders of the Jews in the Łódź Ghetto, 1939–1944), USHMMA RG-15.083M, reel 299–301. Also see entry for 1–3 May 1942, in Dobroszycki, *Chronicle*, 159.

170. Entry for 16 May 1942, in Dobroszycki, *Chronicle*, 173–74.

171. Memo, Älteste der Juden in Litzmannstadt, Abteilung für die Eingesiedelten to Zentral-Sekretariat, "Betr. Registrierung der Besizter v. EK I, II, und VA," 26 May 1942, and "Vollständige Liste der Traeger von EKI, EKII und VA," 14 June 1942, USHMMA RG-15.083M, reel 4. The authors of the *Chronicle* also report that of the 1,100 original members of the Berlin III transport, 50 former soldiers with war decorations "unanimously decided not to attempt to remain here and to leave together in the same transport. They have had enough of this paradise!" However, this claim cannot be substantiated by official sources. Entry for 9 April 1942, in Dobroszycki, *Chronicle*, 157.

6. Defiant Germanness

1. Cohn, diary entry for 15 November 1941, in *Kein Recht, Nirgends*, 2:1007–8.

2. Transport "Da 30," comprising a total of 1,005 Jewish victims, departed Breslau on 25 November 1941 and arrived at Kaunas on the twenty-eighth. Gottwaldt and Schulte, *"Judendeportationen,"* 108–9.

3. Matthäus et al., *Jewish Responses to Persecution*, 153–54.

4. Browning, *Origins*, 394–95.

5. The victims belonged to transport "Da 31," which had departed Berlin on 27 November 1941. Gottwaldt and Schulte, *"Judendeportationen,"* 121.

6. Angrick and Klein, *"Final Solution,"* 146–52; Klein, "Erlaubnis zum grenzenlosen Massenmord."

7. Heinrich Himmler, entry for 30 November 1941, in Witte et al., *Dienstkalendar*, 278.

8. Quoted in Angrick and Klein, *"Final Solution,"* 151.

9. Longerich, *Heinrich Himmler*, 549–50.

10. Benz, *Theresienstadt*, 35–39; Cesarani, *Becoming Eichmann*, 96; Longerich, "Davon haben wir nichts gewusst," 201–10.

11. Minutes, "Btr. Bericht über die am 6.3.42 im Reichssicherheithauptamt—Amt IV B 4 stattgefundenen Besprechung," 6 March 1942, YVA O 2–1163.

12. Jochmann, *Adolf Hitler*, 147–49. Also see Gerlach, "Wannsee Conference," 766.

13. Testimony, Siegfried Seidl, 16 October 1945, Eichmann Prozess Beweis Dokumente, IfZ G 01/17, No. 109.

14. For an overview of the Wannsee Conference, see Gerlach, "Wannsee Conference"; Roseman, *Wannsee Conference*; and the essays in Kampe and Klein, *Wannsee-Konferenz*.

15. Wannsee-Protokoll, 20 January 1942, ITS Digital Archive, 1.1.0.4/82292863–82292878, accessed at USHMMA.

16. Minutes, "Btr. Bericht über die am 6.3.42."

17. Rigg, *Hitler's Jewish Soldiers*, 176, 189.

18. Gerhard Engel, diary entry for 13 August 1938, in *Heeresadjutant bei Hitler*, 31–32.

19. Hildegard von Kotze, introduction to *Heeresadjutant bei Hitler*, 12–13.

20. Speech from February 1928, quoted in Löffelbein, *Ehrenbürger der Nation*, 314.

21. Hitler, monologue on 10–11 November 1941, in Jochmann, *Adolf Hitler*, 131–33.

22. Hassell, diary entry for 1 November 1941, in *Ulrich von Hassell Diaries*, 145.

23. Hitler, monologue on 1–2 December 1941, in Jochmann, *Adolf Hitler*, 147–49.

24. Ibid.

25. "Gerüchte über die Lage der Juden im Osten," 9 October 1942, in Longerich and Pohl, *Ermordung der europäischen Juden*, 433–34.

26. Gottwaldt and Schulte, "*Judendeportationen*," 133–36.

27. Klemperer, diary entry for 17 January 1942, in *I Will Bear Witness*, 2:6–7.

28. RSHA to all Stapo Offices et al., "Btr. Evakuierung von Juden," 31 January 1942, ITS Digital Archive, 1.2.3.0/82164542.0.1–82164544.01, accessed at USHMMA.

29. RSHA to Gestapo Würzburg, "Richtlinien zur technischen Durchführung der Evakuierung von Juden in das Generalgouvernement (Trawniki bei Lublin)," 22 March 1942, StaW, Gestapoakt 18876.

30. Minutes, "Btr. Bericht über die am 6.3.42."

31. Ibid.

32. On numerous occasions after January 1942, representatives of the RV also mentioned the exclusion of wounded and decorated veterans from the transports. See Meyer, "'Altersghetto,' 'Vorzugslager' und Tätigkeitsfeld."

33. StAW, Gestapoakt Sally Mayer, No. 7197.

34. Gestapo Würzburg, "Btr. Liste der zu evakuierenden Jude aus Mainfranken," 3 April 1942, StaW, Gestapoakt 18876. The deportees were Albert Heinemann (Gestapoakt No. 832), Richard Oppenheimer (No. 8959), Otto Reis (No. 10244), and Julius Neumann (No. 8590), none of whom survived the Holocaust.

35. Fr. Waldt to Gestpo Office Würzburg, 20 March 1942, StAW, Gestapoakt Siegfried Lewald, No. 18870.

36. Behrend-Rosenfeld, diary entry for 12 April 1942, in *Ich stand nicht allein*, 133.

37. Emphasis added. Eichmann to all Gestapo offices, 17 April 1942, StaW, Gestapoakt 18876.

38. Meyer, *Unternehmen Sieben*, 236–37. See also Gerlach, "Wannsee Conference," 770–71.

39. The comments, attached to the original telex, are mistakenly dated 13 April 1942, four days after the directive was issued. RSHA Berlin to all Gestapo offices, 17 April 1942, ITS Digital Archive, 1.2.3.0/82164585.0.1–82164585.0.2, accessed at USHMMA.

40. Friedländer, *Years of Extermination*, 201–2.

41. This was the inscription on the accompanying award certificate. See Winkle, *Dank des Vaterlandes*, 192–94.

42. Edmund Hadra, "Theresienstadt," part 1, LBINY AR 1249.

43. Bürgermeister Estenfeld to Gestapo Würzburg, "Btr. Umsiedlung des Juden Leo Israel Löwenthal und Emma Sara Löwenthal: Estenfeld, Hs. Nr. 122," 3 February 1942, StAW, Gestapoakt Leo Löwenthal, No. 6442.

44. On the attitudes of the German populace during the 1942 deportations, see Zimmermann, *Deutsche gegen Deutsche*, 144–45.

45. RSHA (Heinrich Müller), "Btr. Evakuierung von Juden," 21 May 1942, ITS Digital Archive, 1.2.3.0/82164650.0.1–82164651.0.2, accessed at USHMMA.

46. "Richtlinien zur technischen Durchführung der Evakuierung von Juden nach dem Osten (Izbica bei Lublin)," 4 June 1942, ITS Digital Archive, 1.2.3.0/82164669.0.1–82164672.0.2, accessed at USHMMA.

47. "Geschichte des Ghettos Theresienstadt," 31 December 1943, USHMMA RG-68.103M, reel 7, pp. 64–65; Biermann, "'Dank' ihres Vaterlandes." A statistical survey published by the International Tracing Service on 23 June 1943 indicated that there were 1,005 war-decorated Jews in the ghetto. MS, "KZ Theresienstadt," undated, USHMMA RG-14.058M. These statistics are also cited in Adler, *Theresienstadt, 1941–1945,* 828n299.

48. StAW, Gestapoakt Albert Heinemann, No. 832.

49. See, for example, the deportation lists issued for the 21 April 1943 transport to Theresienstadt: "Judentransport aus den Niederlanden von Amsterdam nach Theresienstadt am 21 April 1943," 14 April 1943, NIOD HSSPF 077/1292.

50. Willy Zöpf (IV B 4) to SD/Central Office for Jewish Emigration, "Btr. Kriegsteilnehmer die für eine Sendung nach Theresienstadt nicht in Frage kommen," 22 March 1943, NIOD HSSPF 077/1291.

51. Ibid. Zöpf's report included two lists of German Jews, with 179 and 151 names, respectively, whose military service record did not meet the minimum requirements for Theresienstadt.

52. Reichsbund jüdischer Frontsoldaten, *Jüdischen Gefallenen.*

53. Eckstein, *Heimatrecht,* 54–57.

54. Klemperer, diary entry for 17 January 1942.

55. Memo, RV Main Office Berlin, 22 May 1942, BArch R8150/753. Also listed were 164 officers and 817 holders of the Wound Badge.

56. Stapoleitstelle Düsseldorf to all Police Chiefs and District Offices, "Btr. Evakuierung von Juden," 22 May 1942, ITS Digital Archive, 1.2.3.0/82164652–82164662, accessed at USHMMA.

57. Gestapoakt Alwin Lippmann, HStADü RW 58, No. 18474.

58. Strangmann, "Eduard und Hans Bloch," 258.

59. Klemperer, diary entry for 25 April 1943, in *I Will Bear Witness,* 2:215–18.

60. Klemperer, diary entry for 26 April 1943, in *I Will Bear Witness,* 2:219.

61. Private Holdings of Ulrich Lewin; interviews and correspondence with the author, July 2012 and July 2019. Also see "Placement of a Death Notice for a Jew in a National Socialist Paper," in Kulka and Jäckel, *Secret Nazi Reports,* CD-ROM, doc. 663.

62. Memo, Reichsfinanzministerium, "Btr. Finanzierung des 'Altersghettos' Theresienstadt," 14 December 1942, BArch R2/12222.

63. Adler, *Theresienstadt, 1941–1945,* 89.

64. Memorandum, B.d.S. IV B4, "Lager Theresienstadt," 25 October 1943, NIOD HSSPF 077/1290.

65. Behrend-Rosenfeld, entry for 5 July 1942, in *Ich stand nicht allein,* 163–66.

66. Klemperer, diary entry for 3 July 1942, in *I Will Bear Witness,* 2:91–92. Also see Meyer, "'Altersghetto,' 'Vorzugslager' und Tätigkeitsfeld," 129–30.

67. Hadra, "Theresienstadt," part 1.

68. Max Mannheimer, "Theresienstadt and From Theresienstadt to Auschwitz," YVA O 1/118.

69. Hilberg, *Destruction,* 2:433–39.

70. Klemperer, diary entry for 27 September 1940, in *I Will Bear Witness,* 1:356–57.

71. Emphasis added. Friedrich Solon, "Mein Leben in Deutschland vor und nach dem 30. Januar 1933," LBINY ME 607.

72. Quoted in Lee, *Hidden Life*, 131.

73. Karl Löwenstein (Loesten), "Aus der Hölle Minsk in das 'Paradies' Theresienstadt, 1941–1945," LBINY ME 398.

74. "Erinnerungen des Heinrich Baab, ehem. SS-Untersturmführer u. Kriminal-Sekretär an die Zeit 1937–1945 in Frankfurt / Main," USHMMA RG-14.064M, A 256.

75. Himmler to Kaltenbrunner, "Btr. Abbeförderung von Juden aus Theresienstadt," 16 February 1943, BArch NS 19 / 352.

76. Heydrich's views were recorded and summarized in Adolf Eichmann, "Notizen aus der Besprechung am 10.10.41 über die Lösung von Judenfragen," YVA O 51 / 204.

77. Müller to Himmler, telex, "Btr. Transporte aus Theresienstadt nach Auschwitz," 16 December 1942, in Longerich and Pohl, *Die Ermordung der europäischen Juden*, doc. 65, 176–77.

78. Chef der Sicherheitspolizei und des SD (Kaltenbrunner) to Reichsführer SS (Himmler), "Btr. Abbeförderung von Juden aus Theresienstadt," February 1943, BArch NS 19 / 352.

79. Himmer to Kaltenbrunner, "Btr. Abbeförderung von Juden aus Theresienstadt," 16 February 1943, BArch NS 19 / 352.

80. The standard work on Theresienstadt remains Adler, *Theresienstadt, 1941–1945*, originally published in 1960 (Cambridge University Press published an English-language translation in 2017). Also see Benz, *Theresienstadt*; and Troller, *Theresienstadt*.

81. Karny, "Deutsche Juden in Theresienstadt."

82. Benz, *Theresienstadt*, 38.

83. Karny, "Deutsche Juden in Theresienstadt," 47–48.

84. Ibid. Karny lists the total number of German Jewish dead as 36,848, which represented 85.85 percent of their overall population.

85. Peretz Peter Gerzon, testimony, YVA O 33 / 8728.

86. "Kriegsbeschädigtenfürsorge," in *Gesundheitswesen-Abteilung Fürsorge, Ein Jahresbericht: Oktober 1942 bis Oktober 1943*, USHMMA RG-68.103M, reel 10, pp. 24–28.

87. Murmelstein, *Theresienstadt*, 45.

88. Adler, *Theresienstadt, 1941–1945*, 543.

89. Arbeitszentrale, "Btr. Punkt 7 der Richtlinien zur Führung der Brotkartei," 18 January 1943, USHMMA RG-68.103M, reel 8.

90. Tagesbefehl Nr. 423, "Btr. Schwerkriegsbeschädigten-Ausweis," 16 March 1944, USHMMA RG-68.103M, reel 6.

91. Hadra, "Theresienstadt," part 1.

92. Oppenhejm, diary entry for 16 April 1944, in *An der Grenze des Lebens*, 157–58.

93. Herzfeld was deported on transport "Da 70 / VII / 1," which departed Düsseldorf on 21 July 1942. See Gottwaldt and Schulte, *"Judendeportationen,"* 300.

94. Ältestenrat, Tagesbefehl Nr. 127, 17 May 1942, USHMMA RG-68.103M, reel 14.

95. "Herzfeld, Albert," *Gedenkbuch*, Bundesarchiv, last updated 4 December 2019, http:/ / www.bundesarchiv.de / gedenkbuch / en8ʃ.

96. Manes, *As If It Were Life*, 67–68.

97. "Herzfeld, Elsa," *Gedenkbuch*, Bundesarchiv, accessed 30 January 2020, https:/ / www.bundesarchiv.de / gedenkbuch / en861703.

98. Karny, "Deutsche Juden in Theresienstadt," 39–41.

99. Redlich, diary entry for 4 November 1942, in *Terezin Diary*, 82.

100. Tagesbefehl Nr. 135, "Richtlinien für Ostentransporte," 27 May 1942; and Tagesbefehl Nr. 272, "Ostentransporte," 10 January 1943, USHMMA RG-68.103M, reel 6. For the May 1944 transports, see Arbeitszentrale, "Verzeichnis der eingereihten Mitarbeiter, bei denen objective Transport-Ausschliessungsgründe vorliegen," undated (May 1944), USHMMA RG-68.103M, reel 6.

101. Manes, *Als ob's ein Leben wär*. An abridged version of the German original has been translated into English: Manes, *As If It Were Life*. Unless otherwise noted, all direct quotations are taken from the English edition.

102. Manes, *As If It Were Life*, 103.

103. "Manes, Philipp," *Gedenkbuch*, Bundesarchiv, accessed 14 June 2015, http://www.bundesarchiv.de/gedenkbuch/en873869.

104. Hadra, "Theresienstadt," parts 1 and 2. Hadra composed his memoirs between 1945 and 1947.

105. Hadra, "Theresienstadt," part 1.

106. Ibid.

107. Ibid.

108. Hadra, "Theresienstadt," part 2.

109. Manes, *As If It Were Life*, 24–25.

110. Jacob Jacobson, "Bruchstücke, 1939–1945," LBINY ME 329.

111. Manes, *As If It Were Life*, 88.

112. Levi, *Survival in Auschwitz*, 40–41.

113. Klemperer, diary entry for 16 March 1942, in *I Will Bear Witness*, 2:27.

114. Over 2,300 lectures were held by prisoners at Theresienstadt. See Adler, *Theresienstadt, 1941–1945*, 594–604.

115. Ibid.

116. Hadra, "Theresienstadt," part 1; Manes, *As If It Were Life*, 131.

117. Hájková, "Ältere deutsche Jüdinnen und Juden"; Wünschmann, "Konzentrationslagererfahrungen."

118. Löwenstein, "Hölle Minsk."

119. Redlich, diary entry for 3 November 1942, in *Terezin Diary*, 82.

120. Manes, *As If It Were Life*, 103.

121. Walter Unger to Löwenstein, 11 August 1943, USHMMA RG-68.103M, reel 12. Unger was deported to Auschwitz on 16 October 1944 and most likely was murdered on arrival.

122. On the redemption of honor and masculine self-worth, also see Biess, *Homecomings*; and Feltman, *Stigma of Surrender*.

123. Manes, *As If It Were Life*, 219.

124. Ibid., 97–98.

125. Ibid.

126. Klemperer, diary entry for 8 May 1942, in *I Will Bear Witness*, 2:48–49.

127. Manes, *As If It Were Life*, 219.

128. Bartov, *Mirrors of Destruction*, 144.

129. Testimony of David Wdowinski, in State of Israel, *Trial of Adolf Eichmann*, 3:1233–34.

130. Manes, *As If It Were Life*, 178.

131. Klemperer, diary entry for 8 May 1942, 2:49–51.

132. Klemperer, diary entry for 1 July 1942, in *I Will Bear Witness*, 2:89.

133. Klemperer, diary entry for 8 May 1942, in *I Will Bear Witness*, 2:49–51.

134. Klemperer, diary entry for 30 May 1942, in *I Will Bear Witness*, 2:63–64.

135. Klemperer, diary entry for 28 June 1942, in *I Will Bear Witness*, 2:88.

136. Klemperer, diary entry for 27 January 1943, in *I Will Bear Witness*, 2:192–94.

137. Klemperer, diary entry for 26 July 1942, in *I Will Bear Witness*, 2:108.

138. Klemperer, diary entries for 30 September and 7 October 1943, in *I Will Bear Witness*, 2:265–67.

139. Hadra, "Theresienstadt," part 1.

140. "Mitteilungen der jüdischen Selbstverwaltung Nr. 30," 22 July 1944, USHMMA RG-68.103M, reel 6.

141. Testimony of William W. Wermuth, 7 May 1968, YVA TR 19/41.

142. Hugo Heumann, "Theresienstadt," LBINY ME 165.

143. Karny, "Theresienstädter Herbsttransporte 1944," 17–19.

144. Friedländer, *Years of Extermination*, 578–80; Kerenji, *Jewish Responses to Persecution*, 78–84.

145. Minutes, "Btr. Bericht über die am 6.3.42."

146. Oppenhejm, diary entry for 5 June 1944, in *An der Grenze des Lebens*, 207.

147. Reichsführer SS (Himmler) to Chef der Bandenbekämpfung (von dem Bach), 25 July 1943, BArch NS 19/1770.

148. On the Warsaw Ghetto Uprising and armed Jewish resistance in general, see Kerenji, *Jewish Responses to Persecution*, 161–95.

149. Himmler to HSSPF Ostland, Chef des SS-Wirtschafts-Verwaltungsamtes, and Chef der Sicherheitspolizi, "Btr. Restliche sowjetische Juden in Konzentrationslager oder 'zu evakuieren,'" 21 June 1943, BArch NS 19/1790.

150. Löwenstein, "Hölle Minsk"; Murmelstein, *Theresienstadt*, 83–85.

151. Adler, *Theresienstadt, 1941–1945*, 187.

152. Memo, Ältestenrat der Juden, 22 August 1943, USHMMA RG-68.103M, reel 9.

153. Adler, *Theresienstadt, 1941–1945*, 82, 141–42.

154. On the military situation on the Eastern Front in late 1944, see Schönherr, "Kämpfe um Galizien."

155. Karny, "Theresienstädter Herbsttransporte 1944," 24–25.

156. Vella, "Czech Lands," Schönherr, "Kämpfe um Galizien."

157. Vella, "Czech Lands"; Karny, "Theresienstädter Herbstransporte 1944," 24–26.

158. A facsimile of the order is in Karny, "Theresienstädter Herbsttransporte 1944," 26.

159. Murmelstein, *Theresienstadt*, 158.

160. Resi Weglein, "Erlebnisse von Frau Resi Weglein aus Ulm im KZ Theresienstadt 1942–1945," IfZ, Ms 408.

161. Karny, "Theresienstädter Herbsttransporte 1944"; Benz, *Theresienstadt*, 92.

162. Hadra, "Theresienstadt," part 2.

163. IV B4 to Kommandant Theresienstadt (Burger), "Btr. Judentransport vom 18.1.1944 aus dem Lager Westerbork," 24 January 1944, NIOD HSSPF 077/1294. The individual deportation lists record seven Iron Cross First Class holders, nineteen recipients of the Iron Cross Second Class and Wound Badge, and twenty-three recipients of the Wound Badge only. See Anlage, "Theresiensadt-Transport 18.1.44: Frontkaempfer mit EK I, EKII und Verwundetenabzeichen," 24 January 1944, NIOD HSSPF 077/1294.

164. *Gedenkbuch*, Bundesarchiv, accessed 14 June 2015, http://www.bundesar-chiv.de/gedenkbuch.

165. "Transport: 'Ev' am 28.10.1944 zum KL Auschwitz," ITS Digital Archive, 4959579–4959646, accessed at USHMMA; and "Manes, Philipp," *Gedenkbuch*.

166. Helmut Lohn, "Wir fahren aus Theresienstadt," BArch DO 1/32590.

167. Biermann, "'Dank' ihres Vaterlandes."

168. Peretz Peter Gerzon, testimony.

169. Arno Lustiger, "Der Feldmarschall hat zwei Kugeln bekommen," *Die Welt*, 23 January 2010, http://www.welt.de/5950928.

170. Gerald Rosenstein, interview 22198, Visual History Archive, USC Shoah Foundation, accessed at USHMMA.

171. Behrend-Rosenfeld, diary entry for 26 July 1942, in *Ich stand nicht allein*, 166–70.

172. Jacob Müller, diary entry for 26 June 1940, "Aufzeichnungen (diaries), 1940–1945," LBINY ME 1028.

173. Schohl's numerous attempts to immigrate to the United States, Brazil, and Chile are documented in his personal papers. See USHMMA, Kaethe Wells Collection, 2010.242.1.

174. Käthe Wells (Schohl), interview with the author, 7 October 2012.

175. Ibid.; also see Large, *World Closed Its Doors*, 211.

176. Large, *World Closed Its Doors*, 211–12.

177. Death certificate, 26 December 1943, ITS Digital Archive, Max Israel Schohl/615486, accessed at USHMMA.

178. Quoted in Wrochem, *Erich von Manstein*, 58.

179. Meyer, *Unternehmen Sieben*, 121–22.

180. Browning, *Origins*, 20–21, 80.

Epilogue

1. Otto Kuehl to Herbert Sulzbach, 27 April 1947, BA-MA N 634/74.

2. Sulzbach to Kuehl, 29 April 1947, BA-MA N 634/74.

3. Ibid.

4. Sulzbach to Walter Meyer, 9 October 1945, BA-MA N 634/80.

5. Wolf-Dietrich Heimann to Baron von Seebach, undated letter, BA-MA N 634/80.

6. Emil Reinhard Stürzbecher to Sulzbach, 30 March 1948, BA-MA N 634/80.

7. Sulzbach to Ludovic Kennedy, 26 July 1978, BA-MA N 634/192.

8. Sulzbach to unknown recipient, 11 February 1969, BA-MA N 634/120.

9. Hannsjoachim Koch, foreword to Sulzbach, *Zwischen zwei Mauern*, 9–25.

10. Frevert, *Men of Honour*.

11. Friedrich Solon, "Anhang," 4 October 1950, LBINY ME 607.

12. Ibid.

13. Weltlinger, *Hast Du es schon vergessen?*, 11–13, 20–22. For Weltlinger's role in rebuilding Berlin's Jewish community after 1945, see Nielsen, "'I've Never Regretted Being a German Jew.'"

14. Caplan, "Wicked Sons, German Heroes," 312.

15. Grossmann, *Jews, Germans, and Allies*, 34–36; and Brenner, *After the Holocaust*, 51–57.

16. Lorzenz Beckhardt, interview with the author, 26 October 2011. Also see Beckhardt, *Jude mit dem Hakenkreuz*, 348–86.

17. Hugo Heumann, "Theresienstadt," LBINY ME 165.

18. Max Munisch Mautner, "Memoirs, 1938–1948," LBINY ME 1481.

19. Emphases in the original. Klemperer, diary entry for 11 November 1945, in *So sitze ich denn zwischen allen Stühlen*, 1:139–40.

20. Klemperer, *Curriculum Vitae*, 1:348–49.

21. Edmund Hadra, "Theresienstadt," part 1, LBINY AR 1249.

BIBLIOGRAPHY

Archival Sources

Bayerisches Haupstaatsarchiv, Abt. IV, Kriegsarchiv, Munich (BHStA/IV)
  Freikorps
  Offiziersakte
  Stahlhelm
  Vereine
Bayerisches Haupstaatsarchiv, Munich (BayHStA/II)
  MInn 73725 (Polizei Berichte)
  MA 97668 (Der Krieg und die Juden)
Bundesarchiv, Berlin (BArch)
  DO 1/32590 Theresienstadt
  NS 19 Persönlicher Stab Reichsführer SS
  NS 23 Sturmabteilung der NSDAP (SA)
  NS 26 Hauptarchiv der NSDAP
  R2 Reichsfinanzministerium
  R43 II Neue Reichskanzlei
  R58 Reichssicherheitshauptamt
  R72 Stahlhelm, Bund der Frontsoldaten e.V.
  R90 Reichskommissar für den Ostland
  R1501 Reichsministerium des Innern
  R1506 Reichsarchiv
  R3001 Reichsjustizministerium
  R3901 Beamtengelegenheiten
  R4901 Fürsorge für die Kriegsinvaliden, Volksbund deutsche
    Kriegsgräberfürsorge
  R8005 DNVP
  R8150 Reichsvereinigung der Juden in Deutschland
Bundesarchiv-Militärarchiv, Freiburg i. Br. (BA-MA)
  BW 1 Bundesministerium der Verteidigung
  MSG 2 Militärgeschichtliche Sammlung
  MSG 3 Verbandsdrucksachen (VDS)
  N 241 Nachlass Hans Meier-Welcker
  N 634 Nachlass Herbert Sulzbach
  N 656 Nachlass Hans Heinrich Lebram
  N 756 Nachlass Wolfgang Vopersal
  RH 1 Oberbefehlshaber des Heeres
  RH 2 OKH/Generalstab des Heeres

RH 14 Chef der Heeresrüstung und Befehlshaber des Ersatzheeres

RH 15 OKH/Allgemeines Heeresamt

RH 37 Stäbe, Verbände und Einheiten der Infanterie

RH 69 Freikorps

RW 6 Allgemeines Wehrmachtsamt

RW 59 Personalverwaltende Stellen der Wehrmacht

Deutsches Tagebucharchiv, Emmendingen (DTA)

1920/1,2,3 Kriegstagebuch von Bernhard Hugo Bing

Haupstaatsarchiv Dresden (HStADD)

Bezirkstag/Rat des Bezirkes Dresden, VdN-Akten

Ministeriums der auswärtgen Angelegenheiten "Judentum."

Polizeipräsidium Dresden

10702 Staatskanzlei, Nachrichtenstelle (Zeitungsausschnittsammlungen)

Haupstaatsarchiv Düsseldorf (HStADü)

RW 58 Gestapo-Akten

Hauptstaatsarchiv Stuttgart (HStAS)

EA 99/001 Dokumentationsstelle zur Erforschung der Schicksale der jüdischen Bürger Baden-Württembergs während der nationalsozialistischen Verfolgungszeit, 1933–1945

M 1/3 Kriegsministerium

M 1/4 Kriegsministerium

M 33/2 Generalkommando XIII: Armeekorps

M 400/1 Heeresarchiv Stuttgart

M 430/3 Personalakten

M 660 Militärischer Nachlässe

M 737 Zeitungsausschnitt-Sammlung

M 738 Sammlung zur Militärgeschichte

M 740 Vereine

Houghton Library—Harvard University, Cambridge, MA (HHL)

bMS 91 My Life in Germany Contest

Institut für Zeitgeschichte, Munich (IfZ)

ED 216/2 Nachlass Gerhard Masur

Fa 119 Bayerische Politische Polizei

Fa 282/1 Aktenstücke zur Judenverfolgung

G 01/17 Eichmann Prozess Beweis-Dokumente Nr. 51–110

MA 261 Reichswehrministerium

Ms 408 Nachlass Resi Weglein

ZS 2196/1 Nachlass Leo Löwenstein

ZS 2359 Theresienstadt Testimonies

ZS 2399 Theresienstadt Briefe

Jüdisches Museum Berlin (JMB)

2410 Nachlass Hans Sachs

9691 Mein Deutschland: Bekennerworte, den nicht-arischen Frontsoldaten gewidmet

Leo Baeck Institute Archive, New York (LBINY)

Ruth Alton, "Deportiert von den Nazis, 1941–1945," ME 9

Rudolf Apt Collection, AR 71880

Adolf Asch, "Auszug aus den Memoiren," ME 18

Kurt Ball-Kaduri Collection, MF 52/4

Rudolf Bauer Collection, AR 6608

Hans Berger, "Erinnerungen an die Kristallnacht und meine Erlebnisse im Konzentrationslager Buchenwald," LBINY ME 46

George Bergmann Collection, ME 43

Willy Bernheim Collection, ME 1570

Rudolf Bing, "Mein Leben in Deutschland vor und nach dem 30. Januar 1933," ME 267

Eduard Blumberg Collection, AR 4818

Arthur Czellitzer Collection, ME 100

Moritz Dahlerbruch Collection, AR 2384

Richard A. Ehrlich Collection, AR 11

Phillip Flesch, "Mein Leben in Deutschland vor und nach dem 30. Januar 1933," AR 25197

Fritz Frank, "Das Stahlbad. Aufzeichnungen eines Arztes, 1914–1918." ME 133

Ludwig Frankenthal Collection, AR 6751

Walter Freudenthal, "Champagne Tagebuch," ME 152

Helmut Freund Collection, ME 264

David Friedmann Collection, MM 26

Julius Fürst Collection, ME 163

Fritz Goldberg, "Mein Leben in Deutschland vor und nach dem 30. Januar 1933," ME 190

Fritz Goldschmidt, "Mein Leben in Deutschland vor und nach dem 30. Januar 1933," ME 193

David Gruenspecht Collection, ME 218

Karl Guggenheim Collection, AR 1441, AR 179C

Edmund Hadra Collection, AR 1249

Edwin Halle, "Kriegserinnerungen mit Auszügen aus meinem Tagebuch, 1914–1916," MM 31

Ernst Herzfeld, "Eine Autobiographie," ME 287a

Ernst Herzfeld, "Meine letzten Jahre in Deutschland, 1933–1938," ME 287b

Richard Herzstein, "Meine Kriegszeit," ME 245

Hugo Heumann, "Erlebtes-Erlittenes," ME 165

Fritz Heymann Collection, AR 764

Hartwig Heymann Collection, MM 37

Paul von Hindenburg Collection, AR 6178

Adolf Hohenstein, "Lebenslauf," AR 1489

Samuel Jacobs, "Gedanken und Erinnerungen aus dem Weltkriege, 1914–1918," ME 328

Jacob Jacobson Collection, ME 329

Max Jacobson, "Mein Leben und Erinnerungen," ME 330

Jewish Veterans' Association, AR 7012

Fritz Joseph, "Erlebnisse in Theresienstadt," ME 1430

Kurt Joseph, "No Homesickness," MM 42

Paul Josephtal, "Kriegserinnerungen, 1914," ME 341

Paul Josephtal Collection, AR 4179

Kurt Jutro, "Erlebnisse eines 'Schutzhaeftlings' in einem Konzentrationslager des Dritten Reichs waehrend der Monate November-Dezember 1938," ME 1046

Ernst Kantorowicz Collection, AR 7216

Felix Kaufmann, "Erlebnisse in der Gefangenschaft," ME 233

Alfred Koch Collection, ME 1568

Bernhard Kolb Collection, AR 360

Siegfried Koppel, "Kristallnacht and Aftermath," MM 115

Hans Kronheim Collection, AR 3156

Stephan Kunreuther, "Memorien, 1882–1942," ME 225

Erich Leyens Collection, ME 170 / AR 4868

Heinrich Lichtenstein, "Mein Leben in Deutschland vor und nach dem 30. Januar 1933," ME 1555

Louis Liebmann, "Notes on My Life," ME 1183

Karl Löwenstein, "Aus der Hoelle Minsk in das 'Paradies' Theresienstadt, 1941–1945," ME 398

Karl Löwenthal Collection, AR 6503

Wilhelm Lustig Collection, ME 781 / ME 6 / ME 407a / 407b

Max Hermann Maier Collection, ME 415

Ernst Marcus Collection, AR 25006

Mayer Family Collection, AR 2007

Julius Meyer, "Erinnerungen, 1914–1939," ME 439

Oscar Meyer Collection, AR 25056

Martha Mosse, "Erinnerungen," ME 751

Albrecht Mugdan, "Kriegstagebücher, 1914–1916," ME 455

Jacob Müller, "Aufzeichnungen (diaries), 1940–1945," ME 1028

Max Munisch Mautner, "Memoirs, 1938–1948," ME 1481

National Socialism Collection, AR 119

Eugen Neter Collection, AR 1619

Harvey Newton, "Erinnerungen an das KZ Buchenwald," ME 986

Siegfried Oppenheimer, "Meine Erlebnisse am 10. November 1938 u. mein Aufenthalt in Buchenwald bis zu meiner Rückkehr am 14 Dez. 1938 nach Bad Nauheim," MM 61

Stephanie Perlstein Collection, AR 10056

Hermann Pineas Collection, AR 94

Hermann Pineas, "Erinnerungen," ME 502

Max Plaut Collection, ME 743 / AR 7094

Reichsbund jüdischer Frontsoldaten Collection, AR 3242

Leopold Rosenak Collection, AR 1071

Kurt Rosenberg, "Diaries, 1916–1939," AR 25279

Willy Rosenstein, "Autobiographical Note," ME 527

Hans Rothmann Collection, AR 2122

Kurt Sabatzky, "Meine Erinnerungen an den Nationalsozialismus," ME 541

Leopold Samolewitz, "Poldi's Memoris," ME 1293

Albert Samson Collection, AR 11623

Gertrude Schneider Collection, AR 3348

Emil Schorsch Collection, MM 67

Benno Schwabacher Collection, AR 6335

Carl Schwabe, "Mein Leben in Deutschland vor und nach dem 30. Januar 1933," ME 586

Alfred Schwerin, "Erinnerungen von Dachau bis Basel," ME 593

Kurt Silberstein Collection, AR 10407

Friedrich Solon, "Mein Leben in Deutschland vor und nach dem 30. Januar 1933," ME 607

Rudolf Stahl, "Memoirs," ME 1011

Alfred Stierstadt Collection, AR 164

Ilse Strauss, "Lives in Crisis: Zwischen Krefeld and Frankfurt am Main," AR 3273

Max Strauss Collection, AR 11009

Sussmann-Hirsch Family Collection, AR 25042

Arnold Taenzer Collection, AR 485

Heinrich Toczek Collection, AR 4763

Willi Wertheimer, "Erinnerungen," AR 798

Nathan Wolf, "Kriegs-Tagebuch, 1914–1917," ME 1569

Robert Wolfers Family Collection, AR 1312

NIOD Instituut voor Oorlogs-, Holocaust- en Genocidestudies, Amsterdam (NIOD)

    001 Wehrmachtsbefehlshaber in den Niederlanden (WbN)

    077 Generalkommissariat für das Sicherheitswesen / Höhere SS- und Polizeiführer (HSSPF) Nordwest, 1940–1945

Private Holdings of Dr. Roland Flade

    Juden in Würzburg collection

Private Holdings of Ulrich Lewin

    Personal Papers of Otto Lewin

Staatsarchiv Hamburg (StAH)

    614–1 / 29 Vereinigung ehemaliger Offiziere des Infanterie-Regiments 187

    622–1 / 140 Nachlass Marie-Luise Solmitz

Staatsarchiv Würzburg (StAW)

    Gestapo-Akten

    LRA Alzenau

    LRA Aschaffenburg

    LRA Bad Kissingen

    LRA Hammelburg

    Staatsanwaltschaften

Stadtarchiv Freiburg i. Br. (StArFr)

    Nachlass Max Mayer (K1 / 83)

Stadtarchiv Nürnberg (StArN)

    E 10 / 24 Nr. 8 Nachlass Hugo Gutmann

    Stürmerarchiv

Stadtarchiv Würzburg (StArW)

    Militär IV, Mappe 22 (Infanterie Regiment "Wrede")

United States Holocaust Memorial Museum Archives, Washington, DC
(USHMMA)
International Tracing Service (ITS)
RG-11.001M.01 Reichssicherheitshauptampt (RSHA)
RG-11.001M.04 Gestapo in Stettin
RG-11.001M.31 Centralverein
RG-14.002M Staatsarchiv Leipzig Records
RG-14.035M Leipzig Jewish Community, 1933–1945
RG-14.056M Jüdische Gemeinde Mannheim
RG-14.058M Institut für die Geschichte der deutschen Juden, Hamburg,
1935–1954
RG-14.064M Selected Records of the Jewish Museum Frankfurt
RG-15.083M The Elders of the Jews in the Łódź Ghetto, 1939–1944
RG-15.127M Records of the City of Łódź, Stadtverwaltung Litzmannstadt
RG-68.103M Theresienstadt Collection
USC Shoah Foundation, Visual History Archive
Alfred Grünwald (30700)
Erich Leyens (963)
Gerald Rosenstein (22198)
Yad Vashem Archives, Jerusalem (YVA)
O 1 K. J. Ball-Kaduri Testimonies and Reports of German Jewry Collection
O 2 Wiener Library Testimonies Collection, London
O 8 Germany Collection
O 29 Belgium Collection
O 33 Testimonies, Diaries and Memoirs Collection
O 34 Zonabend Collection: Documentation from the Lodz Ghetto
O 51 Nazi Documentation
O 52 Jewish German Community Collection (Pinkas Kehillot Germania)
O 53 Ludwigsburg, USSR Collection
TR 19 Documentation from the Trial of Bovensiepen and others, Germany

Published Primary Sources

Adler, H. G. *Die Verheimlichte Wahrheit: Theresienstädter Dokumente*. Tübingen: J. C. B.
Mohr, 1958.
Anonymous members of the Kovno Jewish Ghetto Police. *The Clandestine History of
the Kovno Jewish Ghetto Police*. Translated and edited by Samuel Schalkowsky.
Bloomington: Indiana University Press, 2014.
Armin, Otto. *Die Juden im Heere: Eine statistische Untersuchung nach amtlichen Quellen*.
Munich: Deutscher Volks-Verlag, 1919.
Bajohr, Frank, Beate Meyer, and Joachim Szodrzynski, eds. *Bedrohung, Hoffnung, Skep-
sis: Vier Tagebücher des Jahres, 1933*. Göttingen: Wallstein Verlag, 2013.
Bauer, Max. *Der große Krieg in Feld und Heimat: Erinnerungen und Betrachtungen*. Tübin-
gen, Osiander, 1921.
Behrend-Rosenfeld, Else R. *Ich stand nicht allein: Erlebnisse einer Jüdin in Deutschland,
1933–1944*. Frankfurt: Europäische Verlagsanstalt, 1949.

Berliner Adreßbuch 1920. Berlin: August Scherl Deutsche Adreßbuch Gesellschaft, 1920.

Blatt, Thomas Toivi. *From the Ashes of Sobibor: A Story of Survival.* Evanston, IL: Northwestern University Press, 1997.

Bloem, Walter. *Deutsche Zwietracht und Judentum: Festrede bei der Feier des zehnjährigen Bestehens der Ortsgruppe Hamburg des Vaterländischen Bundes jüdischer Frontsoldaten am 17. November 1929 gehalten.* Leipzig: Grethlein, 1929.

Cohn, Willy. *Kein Recht, Nirgends: Tagebuch vom Untergang des Breslauer Judentums, 1933–1941.* 2 vols. Cologne: Böhlau Verlag, 2007.

——. *Verwehte Spuren: Erinnerungen an das Breslauer Judentum vor seinem Untergang.* Cologne: Böhlau Verlag, 1995.

Comité des Délégations Juives, eds. *Das Schwarzbuch—Tatsachen und Dokumente: Die Lage der Juden in Deutschland, 1933.* Frankfurt: Ullstein, 1984.

Deutschkron, Inge. *Outcast: A Jewish Girl in Wartime Berlin.* New York: Fromm, 1989.

Dobroszycki, Lucjan, ed. *The Chronicle of the Lodz Ghetto, 1941–1944.* New Haven, CT: Yale University Press, 1984.

Eckhardt, Albrecht, and Katharina Hoffmann, eds. *Gestapo Oldenburg meldet . . . Berichte der Geheimen Staatspolizei und des Innenministers aus dem Freistaat und Land Oldenburg, 1933–1936.* Hannover: Verlag Hahnsche Buchhandlung, 2002.

Eckstein, Adolf. *Haben die Juden in Bayern ein Heimatrecht? Eine geschichtswissenschaftliche Untersuchung mit kriegsstatistischen Beilagen.* Berlin: Philo Verlag, 1928.

Ernst, Fritz, ed. *Aus dem Nachlass des Generals Walther Reinhardt.* Stuttgart: Kohlhammer, 1958.

Felsch, Volkmar. *Otto Blumenthals Tagebücher: Ein Aachener Mathematikprofessor erleidet die NS-Diktatur in Deutschland, den Niederlanden und Theresienstadt.* Konstanz: Hartung-Gorre Verlag, 2011.

Freudenthal, Max. *Kriegsgedenkbuch der israelitischen Kultusgemeinde Nürnberg: Herausgegeben von Rabbiner Dr. Max Freudenthal.* Nuremberg: J. Rosenfeld, 1921.

Friedrich, Hans. *Die Juden im Heere.* Munich: J. F. Lehmann's Verlag, 1922.

Geiger, Ludwig. *Die deutschen Juden und der Krieg.* Berlin: C. A. Schwetschket & Sohn, 1915.

Groscurth, Helmuth. *Tagebuch eines Abwehroffiziers, 1938–1940.* Edited by Helmut Krausnick and Harold C. Deutsch. Stuttgart: Deutsche Verlags-Anstalt, 1970.

Hank, Sabine, and Hermann Simon, eds. *Feldpostbriefe jüdischer Soldaten, 1914–1918.* Potsdam: Hentrich & Hentrich Verlag, 2002.

Hassell, Ulrich von. *The Ulrich von Hassell Diaries, 1938–1944: The Story of the Forces against Hitler inside Germany.* London: Frontline Books, 2011.

Heeresadjutant bei Hitler, 1938–1943: Aufzeichnungen des Majors Gerhard Engel. Edited and annotated by Hildegard von Kotze. Stuttgart: Deutsche Verlags-Anstalt, 1974.

Herzfeld, Albert. *Ein nichtarischer Deutscher: Die Tagebücher des Albert Herzfeld, 1935–1939.* Edited by Hugo Weidenhaupt. Düsseldorf: Triltsch Verlag, 1982.

Heymann, Walther. *Kriegsgedichte und Feldpostbriefe.* Munich: G. Müller, 1915.

Hiemer, Ernst. *Der Giftpilz.* Nuremberg: Der Stürmer Verlag, 1938.

Hirschberg, Max. *Jude und Demokrat: Erinnerungen eines Münchener Rechtsanwalts, 1883 bis 1939.* Edited by Reinhard Weber. Munich: R. Oldenbourg Verlag, 1998.

Huder, Walther. "Kriegs-Tagebuch eines Juden: Ein Beitrag zur Geschichte des deutschen Judentums." *Bulletin des Leo Baeck Instituts* 8, no. 29 (1965): 240–49.

Huser, Karin, ed. *"Haltet gut Jontef und seid herzlichst geküsst": Feldpostbriefe des Elsässer Juden Henri Levy von der Ostfront (1916–1918)*. Zurich: Chronos Verlag, 2014.

Jacobsen, Hans-Adolf, ed. *"Spiegelbild einer Verschwörung": Die Opposition gegen Hitler und der Staatsstreich vom 20. Juli in der SD-Berichterstattung; Geheime Dokumente aus dem ehemaligen Reichssicherheitshauptamt*. Stuttgart: Seewald Verlag, 1984.

Jochmann, Werner, ed. *Adolf Hitler: Monologue im Führerhauptquartier, 1941–1944*. Munich: Orbis Verlag, 2000.

Johnson, Eric A., and Karl-Heinz Reuband, eds. *What We Knew: Terror, Mass Murder, and Everyday Life in Nazi Germany; An Oral History*. Cambridge: Basic Books, 2005.

Jünger, Ernst. *Kriegstagebuch, 1914–1918*. Edited by Helmuth Kiesel. Stuttgart: Klett-Cotta, 2010.

Katz, David. "Frontjahre im Ersten Weltkrieg." *Bulletin des Leo Baeck Instituts* 26, no. 80 (1988): 13–17.

Katz, Josef. *One Who Came Back: The Diary of a Jewish Survivor*. New York: Herzl, 1973.

Klein, Thomas. *Die Lageberichte der Geheimen Staatspolizei über die Provinz Hessen-Nassau, 1933–1936*. 2 vols. Cologne: Böhlau Verlag, 1986.

Klemperer, Victor. *Curriculum Vitae: Erinnerungen, 1881–1918*. 2 vols. Berlin: Aufbau-Verlag, 1996.

——. *Ich will Zeugnis ablegen bis zum letzten: Tagebücher, 1933–1945*. 2 vols. Berlin: Aufbau-Verlag, 1996.

——. *I Will Bear Witness: A Diary of the Nazi Years, 1933–1945*. 2 vols. Translated by Martin Chalmers. New York: Random House, 1998.

——. *Leben sammeln, nicht fragen wozu und warum: Tagebücher, 1918–1932*. 2 vols. Berlin: Aufbau-Verlag, 1996.

——. *LTI: Notizbuch eines Philologen*. Berlin: Aufbau Verlag, 1947.

——. *So sitze ich denn zwischen allen Stühlen: Tagebücher, 1945–1959*. 2 vols. Berlin: Aufbau-Verlag, 1999.

Klepper, Jochen. *Unter dem Schatten deiner Flügel: Aus den Tagebüchern der Jahre, 1932–1942*. Stuttgart: Deutsche Verlags-Anstalt, 1956.

[Korodi, Walter] (published under Anonymous). *Ich kann nicht Schweigen: Ein Nationalsozialist enthüllt*. Zurich: Europa-Verlag, 1936.

Kriegsbriefe gefallener deutscher Juden: Mit einem Geleitwort von Franz Josef Strauß. Stuttgart: Seewald, 1961.

Kuropka, Joachim, ed. *Meldungen aus Münster, 1924–1944: Geheime und vertrauliche Berischte von Polzei, Gestapo, NSDAP und ihren Gliederungen, staatlicher Verwaltung, Gerichtsbarkeit und Wehrmacht über die politische und gesellschaftliche Situation in Münster*. Münster: Verlag Regensberg, 1992.

Leiser, Walter. *Die Juden im Heer: Eine Kriegsstatisktik*. Berlin: Philo Verlag, 1919.

Levi, Primo. *Survival in Auschwitz*. New York: Touchstone, 1996.

Lewin, Reinhold. "Der Krieg als jüdisches Erlebnis." *Monatsschrift für die Geschichte und Wissenschaft des Judentums* 63 (1917): 1–14.

Leyens, Erich, and Lotte Andor. *Die Fremden Jahre: Erinnerungen an Deutschland*. Frankfurt: Fischer Verlag, 1994.

Liebrecht, Heinrich F. *"Nicht mitzuhassen, mitzulieben bin ich da": Mein Weg durch die Hölle des Dritten Reiches*. Freiburg: Verlag Herder, 1990.

Loewenstein, Karl. *Minsk: Im Lager der deutschen Juden*. Bonn: Bundeszentrale für Heimatdienst, 1961.

Longerich, Peter, and Dieter Pohl, eds. *Die Ermordung der europäischen Juden: Eine umfassende Dokumentation des Holocaust, 1941–1945*. Munich: Piper Verlag, 1989.

Ludendorff, Erich. *Meine Kriegserinnerungen, 1914–1918*. Berlin: Mittler & Sohn, 1919.

——. *Kriegführung und Politik*. Berlin: E. S. Mittler & Sohn, 1922.

Manes, Philipp. *Als ob's ein Leben wär: Tatsachenbericht; Theresienstadt, 1942–1944*. Berlin: Ullstein, 2005.

——. *As If It Were Life: A WWII Diary from the Theresienstadt Ghetto*. New York: Palgrave Macmillan, 2009.

Manstein, Erich von. *Aus einem Soldatenleben, 1887–1939*. Bonn: Athenäum-Verlag, 1958.

Marx, Julius. *Georg Kaiser, ich und die anderen: Alles in einem Leben; Ein Bericht in Tagebuchform*. Gütersloh: C. Bertelsmann Verlag, 1970.

——. *Kriegstagebuch eines Juden*. Frankfurt: Ner-Tamid-Verlag, 1964.

Masur, Gerhard. *Das Ungewisse Herz: Berichte aus Berlin—über die Suche nach dem Freien*. Holyoke: Blenheim, 1978.

Meyer, Otto. *Als deutscher Jude im Ersten Weltkrieg: Der Fabrikant und Offizier Otto Meyer*. Edited by Andreas Meyer. Berlin: be.bra Wissenschaft Verlag, 2014.

Moltke, Helmuth James von. *Letters to Freya, 1939–1945*. New York: Alfred A. Knopf, 1990.

Moser, Julius. *KZ Theresienstadt: Erlebnisse eines "Nichtariers" in den letzten Monaten des Naziregimes*. Pforzheim: Stadt Pforzheim, 1995.

Müller, Klaus-Jürgen, ed. *General Ludwig Beck: Studien und Dokumente zur politischen-militärischen Vorstellungswelt und Tätigkeit des Generalstabschefs des deutsches Heeres, 1933–1938*. Boppard am Rhein: Harald Boldt Verlag, 1980.

Murmelstein, Benjamin. *Theresienstadt: Eichmann's Vorzeige-Ghetto*. Vienna: Czernin Verlag, 2014.

Mylnek, Klaus. *Gestapo Hannover meldet . . . Polizei- und Regierungsberichte für das mittlere und südliche Niedersachsen zwischen, 1933 und 1937*. Hildesheim: Verlag Augst Lax, 1986.

Oppenheimer, Franz. *Die Judenstatisktik des preußischen Kriegsministeriums*. Munich: Verlag für Kulturpolitik, 1922.

Oppenhejm, Ralph. *An der Grenze des Lebens: Theresienstädter Tagebuch*. Hamburg: Rütten & Loening Verlag, 1961.

Österreichische Nationalbibliothek. "Deutsches Reichsgesetzblatt Teil I 1867–1945." ALEX Historische Rechts- und Gesetzetexte Online. 2011. http://alex.onb.ac.at/tab_dra.htm.

Redlich, Gonda. *The Terezin Diary of Gonda Redlich*. Edited by Saul S. Friedman. Translated by Laurence Kutler. Lexington: University Press of Kentucky, 1992.

Reichmann, Hans. *Deutscher Bürger und verfolgter Jude: Novemberpogrom und KZ Sachsenhausen, 1937 bis 1939*. Munich: R. Oldenbourg Verlag, 1998.

Reichsbund jüdischer Frontsoldaten, ed. *Die jüdischen Gefallenen des deutschen Heeres, der deutschen Marine und der deutschen Schutztruppen, 1914–1918: Ein Gedenkbuch*. Berlin: Verlag der Schild, 1932.

——. *Kriegsbriefe gefallener Deutscher Juden.* Berlin: Vortrupp, 1935.

Reichsbund jüdischer Frontsoldaten, Ortsgruppe Dortmund, ed. *Statistik des Bundes jüdischer Frontsoldaten Dortmund-Hörde (Stadt und Land).* Dortmund: Gebrüder Wolff, 1921.

Reichsbund jüdischer Frontsoldaten, Ortsgruppe Düsseldorf, ed. *Gedenkbuch zur Ehren der im Weltkrieg 1914/1918 gefallenen jüdischen Krieger der Stadt Düsseldorf.* Düsseldorf: Lintz A. G., 1923.

Reichsbund jüdischer Frontsoldaten, Ortsgruppe Essen, ed. *Ehrentafel: Unseren gefallenen Kameraden zum Gedenken.* Essen: Fredebeul & Koennen, 1924.

Reichsbund jüdischer Frontsoldaten, Ortsgruppe München, ed. *Unseren Gefallenen Kameraden: Gedenkbuch für die im Weltkrieg Gefallenen Münchner Juden.* Munich: Verlag B. Heller, 1929.

Remarque, Erich Maria. *Der Weg Zurück.* Cologne: Kiepenheuer & Witsch, 2014.

Reventlow, Ernst Graf zu. *Judas Kampf und Niederlage in Deutschland: 150 Jahre Judenfrage.* Berlin: Zeitgeschichte Verlag, 1937.

Ribbe, Wolfgang. *Die Lageberichte der Geheimen Staatspolizei über die Provinz Brandenburg und die Reichshauptstadt Berlin, 1933 bis 1936.* Cologne: Böhlau Verlag, 1998.

Rosenfeld, Oskar. *In the Beginning Was the Ghetto: Notebooks from Lodz.* Evanston, IL: Northwestern University Press, 2002.

Rosenzweig, Franz. *Feldpostbriefe: Die Korrespondenz mit den Eltern (1914–1917).* Freiburg: Verlag Karl Alber, 2013.

Salzburg, Friedrich. *Mein Leben in Dresden vor und nach dem 30. Januar 1933.* Dresden: Stiftung Sächsische Gedenkstätte, 2001.

Sauer, Paul, ed. *Dokumente über die Verfolgung der jüdischen Bürger in Baden-Württemberg durch das Nationalsozialistische Regime, 1933–1945.* 2 vols. Stuttgart: W. Kohlhammer Verlag, 1966.

Schauwecker, Franz. *Im Todesrachen: Die deutsche Seele im Weltkrieg.* Halle: Heinrich Diekmann, 1919.

Schoenaich, Paul Freiherr von. *Mein Finale: Mit dem geheimen Tagebuch, 1933–1945.* Flensburg: Verlagshaus Christian Wolff, 1947.

Schwerin, Alfred. *Von Dachau bis Basel: Erinnerungen eines Pfälzer Juden an die Jahre, 1938 bis 1940.* Kaiserslautern: Institut für pfälzische Geschichte und Volkskunde, 2003.

Segall, Jacob. *Die deutschen Juden als Soldaten im Kriege 1914–1918.* Berlin: Philo-Verlag, 1922.

Simon, Ernst. "Unser Kriegserlebnis (1919)." In *Brücken: Gesammelte Aufsätze*, 17–23. Heidelberg: Verlag Lambert Schneider, 1965.

Singer, Oskar. *"Im Eilschritt durch den Gettotag . . .": Reportagen und Essays aus dem Getto Lodz.* Berlin: Philo Verlag, 2002.

Spanier, M., ed. *Leutnant Sender: Blätter der Erinnerung für seine Freunde.* Hamburg: Verlag von M. Glogau, 1916.

Spiegel, Marga. *Retter in der Nacht: Wie eine jüdische Familie in einem münsterländischen Versteck überlebte.* 5th ed. Berlin: LIT Verlag, 2009.

State of Israel, ed. *The Trial of Adolf Eichmann: Record of Proceedings in the District Court of Jerusalem.* 9 vols. Jerusalem: Trust for the Publication of the Proceedings of the Eichmann Trial, 1992.

Steinwascher, Gerd, ed. *Gestapo Osnabrück meldet . . . Polizei- und Regierungsberichte aus dem Regierungsbezirk Osnabrück aus den Jahren, 1933 bis 1936*. Osnabrück: Verein für Geschichte und Landeskunde von Osnabrück, 1995.

Stern, Fritz. *Five Germanies I Have Known*. New York: Farrar, Straus & Giroux, 2006.

Stern, Norbert. *Theresienstadt: Bericht aus einem Ghetto*. Edited by Gustav Zerres. Cologne: Nordwestdeutscher Rundfunk, 1955.

Sulzbach, Herbert. *Zwei lebende Mauern: 50 Monate Westfront*. Berlin: Bernhard & Graefe, 1935.

——. *Zwischen zwei Mauern: 50 Monate Westfront, 1914–1918*. Berg am See: Kurt Vowinckel Verlag, 1986.

Tänzer, Aaron. *Die Geschichte des Veteranen- und Militärvereins "Kampfgenossenschaft" in Göppingen, 1871–1921: Eine Festschrift zur Feier seines 50 jährigen Bestehens*. Göppingen: Buchdruckerei der Göppinger Zeitung, 1921.

Tausk, Walter. *Breslauer Tagebuch, 1933–1940*. Berlin: Siedler Verlag, 1988.

Theilhaber, Felix A. *Jüdische Flieger im Weltkrieg*. Berlin: Verlag der Schild, 1924.

Toller, Ernst. *Eine Jugend in Deutschland*. Stuttgart: Philipp Reclam, 2011.

Tucholsky, Kurt. *Gesammelte Werke in 10 Bänden*. Edited by Mary Gerold-Tucholsky and Fritz J. Raddatz. Reinbek: Rowohlt-Verlag, 1975.

Weltlinger, Siegmund. *Hast Du es schon vergessen? Erlebnisbericht aus der Zeit der Verfolgung*. Berlin: Gesellschaft für Christlich-Jüdische Zusammenarbeit, 1954.

Westmann, Stephan Kurt. *Surgeon with the Kaiser's Army*. Barnsley, UK: Pen and Sword Books, 2014.

Wrisberg, Ernst von. *Heer und Heimat, 1914–1918*. Leipzig: Koehler, 1921.

Württembergischer Landesverband des Centralvereins deutscher Staatsbürger jüdischen Glaubens, ed. *Jüdische Frontsoldaten aus Württemberg und Hohenzollern*. Stuttgart: J. Fink, 1926.

Zuckmayer, Carl. *Als wär's ein Stück von mir: Horen der Freundschaft*. Frankfurt: S. Fischer Verlag, 1966.

Secondary Sources

Abrams-Sprod, Michael E. "Life under Siege: The Jews of Magdeburg under Nazi Rule." PhD diss., University of Sydney, 2006.

Adam, Uwe Dietrich. *Judenpolitik im Dritten Reich*. Düsseldorf: Droste Verlag, 1972.

Adler, H. G. *Die Juden in Deutschland: Von der Aufklärung bis zum Nationalsozialismus*. Munich: Kösel-Verlag, 1960.

——. *Theresienstadt, 1941–1945: Das Anlitz einer Zwangsgemeinschaft*. Göttingen: Wallstein Verlag, 2012. Reprint of 1960 edition.

——. *Der Verwaltete Mensch. Studien zur Deportation der Juden aus Deutschland*. Tübingen: J.C.B. Mohr (Paul Siebeck), 1974.

Allport, G. W., J. S. Bruner, and E. M. Jandorf. "Personality under Social Catastrophe: Ninety Life-Histories of the Nazi Revolution," *Character and Personality* 10, no. 1 (1941): 1–22.

Anderson, Margaret Livinia. *Practicing Democracy: Elections and Political Culture in Imperial Germany*. Princeton, NJ: Princeton University Press, 2000.

Angress, Werner T. "Das deutsche Militär und die Juden im Ersten Weltkrieg." *Militärgeschichtliche Mitteilungen* 19 (1976): 77–146.

——. "The German Army's 'Judenzählung' of 1916: Genesis-Consequences-Signifi-cance." *Leo Baeck Institute Yearbook* 23 (1978): 117–37.

——. "Der jüdische Offizier in der neueren deutschen Geschichte, 1813–1918." In *Willensmenschen: Über deutsche Offiziere*, edited by Ursula Breymayer, Bernd Ul-rich, and Karin Wieland, 67–78. Frankfurt: Fischer Verlag, 1999.

Angrick, Andrej, and Peter Klein. *The "Final Solution" in Riga: Exploitation and An-nihilation, 1941–1944*. New York: Berghahn Books, 2009.

Appelbaum, Peter C. *Loyal Sons: Jews in the German Army in the Great War*. London: Valentine Mitchell, 2015.

Arndt, Ludwig. *Militärvereine in Norddeutschland: Vereinsleben, Abzeichen, Auszeichnun-gen, Denkmäler*. Norderstedt: Books on Demand GmbH, 2008.

Aschheim, Steven. *Brothers and Strangers: The East European Jew in German and German Jewish Consciousness, 1800–1923*. Madison: University of Wisconsin Press, 1982.

Baader, Benjamin Maria, Sharon Gillerman, and Paul Lerner, eds. *Jewish Masculini-ties: German Jews, Gender, and History*. Bloomington: Indiana University Press, 2012.

Bajohr, Frank. *Aryanization in Hamburg: The Economic Exclusion of Jews and the Con-fiscation of Their Property in Nazi Germany*. New York: Berghahn Books, 2001.

——. "Vom antijüdischen Konsens zum schlechten Gewissen: Die deutsche Ge-sellschaft und die Judenverfolgung, 1933–1945." In *Massenmord und schlechtes Gewissen: Die deutsche Bevölkerung, die NS-Führung und der Holocaust*, edited by Frank Bajohr and Dieter Pohl, 15–79. Munich: Fischer Verlag, 2006.

Bankier, David. *The Germans and the Final Solution: Public Opinion under Nazism*. Cam-bridge: Blackwell, 1995.

——, ed. *Probing the Depths of German Antisemitism: German Society and the Persecution of the Jews, 1933–1941*. New York: Berghahn Books, 2000.

Baranowski, Shelley. *The Sanctity of Rural Life: Nobility, Protestantism, and Nazism in Weimar Prussia*. New York: Oxford University Press, 1995.

Barkai, Avraham. "German-Speaking Jews in Eastern European Ghettos." *Leo Baeck Institute Yearbook*, 34 (1989): 247–66.

Barth, Boris. *Dolchstoßlegenden und politische Desintegration: Das Trauma der deutschen Niederlage im Ersten Weltkrieg, 1914–1933*. Dusseldorf: Droste, 2003.

——. "Professoren, Studenten und die Legende vom Dolchstoß." In *"Wir Siegen oder Fallen": Deutsche Studenten im Ersten Weltkrieg*, edited by Marc Zirlewagen, 377–96. Cologne: SH-Verlag, 2008.

Bartov, Omer. "Defining Enemies, Making Victims: Germans, Jews, and the Holo-caust." *American Historical Review* 103, no. 3 (1998): 771–816.

——. *Germany's War and the Holocaust: Disputed Histories*. Ithaca, NY: Cornell Univer-sity Press, 2003.

——. *Mirrors of Destruction: War, Genocide, and Modern Identity*. Oxford: Oxford Uni-versity Press, 2000.

Bauer, Yehuda. *Rethinking the Holocaust*. New Haven, CT: Yale University Press, 2001.

Beck, Hermann. "Between the Dictates of Conscience and Political Expediency: Hit-ler's Conservative Alliance Partner and Antisemitism during the Nazi Seizure of Power." *Journal of Contemporary History* 41, no. 4 (2006): 611–40.

——. *A Fateful Alliance: German Conservatives and Nazis in 1933: The Machterergreifung in a New Light*. New York: Berghahn Books, 2008.

Beckhardt, Lorenz. *Der Jude mit dem Hakenkreuz.* Berlin: Aufbau Verlag, 2014.

Beer, Ulrich. *Dr. Horst Berkowitz: Ein jüdisches Anwaltsleben (1898–1983).* Tübingen: Klöpfer & Meyer, 2004.

Benz, Wolfgang, ed. *Dimension des Völkermords: Die Zahl der Opfer des Nationalsozialismus.* Munich: R. Oldenbourg Verlag, 1991.

———. *Die Juden in Deutschland: Leben unter nationalsozialistischer Herrschaft.* Munich: Verlag C. H. Beck, 1989.

———. "Der Novemberpogrom 1938." In *Die Juden in Deutschland: Leben unter nationalsozialistischer Herrschaft,* edited by Wolfgang Benz, 499–544. Munich: Verlag C. H. Beck, 1989.

———. "Theresienstadt." In *Der Ort des Terrors: Geschichte der nationalsozialistischen Konzentrationslager,* edited by Wolfgang Benz and Barbara Distel, vol. 9, 476–78. Munich: Verlag C. H. Beck, 2009.

———. *Theresienstadt: Eine Geschichte von Täuschung und Vernichtung.* Munich: Verlag C. H. Beck, 2013.

Berding, Helmut. *Moderner Antisemitismus in Deutschland.* Frankfurt: Suhrkamp, 1988.

Berger, Michael. *Eisernes Kreuz und Davidstern: Die Geschichte Jüdischer Soldaten in Deutschen Armeen.* Berlin: Trafo Verlag, 2006.

———. "Fallbeispiel: Alwin Lippmann—Ein Frontsoldat in Auschwitz." In *Jüdische Soldaten-Jüdischer Widerstand in Deutschland und Frankreich,* edited by Michael Berger and Gideon Römer-Hillebrecht, 364–70. Paderborn: Ferdinand Schöningh, 2012.

Bergerson, Andrew Stuart. *Ordinary Germans in Extraordinary Times: The Nazi Revolution in Hildesheim.* Bloomington: Indiana University Press, 2004.

Berghahn, Volker R. *Der Stahlhelm: Bund der Frontsoldaten, 1918–1935.* Düsseldorf: Droste, 1966.

Bergien, Rüdiger. "Paramilitary Volunteers for Weimar Germany's 'Wehrhaftmachung': How Civilians Were Attracted to Serve with Irregular Military Units." In *War Volunteering in Modern Times: From the French Revolution to the Second World War,* edited by Christine G. Krüger and Sonja Levsen, 189–210. New York: Palgrave Macmillan, 2010.

Bergmann, Werner. "Das antisemitische Bild vom jüdischen Soldaten von der Emanzipation bis zum Ersten Weltkrieg—am deutschen Beispiel." In *Weltuntergang: Jüdisches Leben und Sterben im Ersten Weltkrieg,* edited by Marcus G. Patka, 52–60. Vienna: Jüdisches Museum Wien, 2014.

Bessel, Richard. "The 'Front Generation' and the Politics of Weimar Germany." In *Generations in Conflict: Youth Revolt and Generation Formation in Germany, 1770–1968,* edited by Mark Roseman, 121–36. Cambridge: Cambridge University Press, 1995.

———. *Germany after the First World War.* Oxford: Oxford University Press, 1993.

———. "The Great War in German Memory: The Soldiers of the First World War, Demobilization, and Weimar Political Culture." *German History* 6, no. 1 (1988): 20–34.

———. "Die Heimkehr der Soldaten: Das Bild der Frontsoldaten in der Öffentlichkeit der Weimarer Republik." In *Keiner fühlt sich hier mehr als Mensch . . .: Erlebnis und Wirkung des Ersten Weltkriegs,* edited by Gerhard Hirschfeld, Gerd Krumeich, and Irina Renz, 221–39. Essen: Klartext Verlag, 1993.

———. *Nazism and War.* New York: Modern Library, 2004.

Biermann, Hildegard. "Der 'Dank' ihres Vaterlandes: Kriegsbeschädigte in There-sienstadt." *Aufbau* 13 (22 August 1947): 17.

Biess, Frank. *Homecomings: Returning POWs and the Legacies of Defeat in Postwar Germany.* Princeton, NJ: Princeton University Press, 2009.

Birken, Lawrence. "Prussianism, Nazism, and Romanticism in the Thought of Victor Klemperer." *German Quarterly* 72, no. 4 (1999): 33–43.

Borut, Jacob. "'Bin ich doch ein Isrealit, ehre ich auch den Bischof mit': Village and Small-Town Jews within the Social Spheres of Western German Communities during the Weimar Period." In *Jüdisches Leben in der Weimarer Republic—Jews in the Weimar Republic*, edited by Wolfgang Benz, Arnold Paucker, and Peter Pulzer, 117–33. Tübingen: Mohr Siebeck, 1998.

Bösch, Frank. *Das konservative Milieu: Vereinskultur und locale Sammlungspolitik in ost- und westdeutschen Regionen (1900–1960).* Göttingen: Wallstein, 2002.

——. "Militante Geselligkeit: Formierungsformen der bürgerlichen Vereinswelt zwischen Revolution und Nationalsozialismus." Special issue, *Geschichte und Gesellschaft* 21 (2005): 151–82.

Bourke, Joanna. *Dismembering the Male: Men's Bodies, Britain and the Great War.* London: University of Chicago Press, 1996.

Brenner, Michael. *After the Holocaust: Rebuilding Jewish Lives in Postwar Germany.* Princeton, NJ: Princeton University Press, 1997.

——. "The German Army Orders a Census of Jewish Soldiers, and Jews Defend German Culture." In *Yale Companion to Jewish Writing and Thought in German Culture, 1096–1996*, edited by Sander L. Gilman and Jack Zipes, 348–54. New Haven, CT: Yale University Press, 1996.

——. *The Renaissance of Jewish Culture in Weimar Germany.* New Haven, CT: Yale University Press, 1996.

Browning, Christopher. *The Origins of the Final Solution: The Evolution of Nazi Jewish Policy, September 1939–March 1942.* With contributions by Jürgen Matthäus. Lincoln: University of Nebraska Press, 2004.

Burke, Peter, and Jan E. Stets. *Identity Theory.* Oxford: Oxford University Press, 2009.

Busche, Jürgen. *Heldenprüfung: Das verweigerte Erbe des Ersten Weltkriegs.* Munich: Deutsche Verlags-Anstalt, 2004.

Caplan, Gregory. "Germanising the Jewish Male: Military Masculinity as the Last Stage of Acculturation." In *Towards Normality? Acculturation and Modern German Jewry*, edited by Rainer Liedtke and David Rechts, 159–84. Tübingen: Mohr Siebeck, 2003.

——. "Wicked Sons, German Heroes: Jewish Soldiers, Veterans, and Memories of World War I in Germany." PhD diss., Georgetown University, 2001.

Caplan, Jane, and Nikolaus Wachsmann. *Concentration Camps in Nazi Germany: The New Histories.* New York: Routledge, 2010.

Carey, Maddy. *Jewish Masculinity in the Holocaust: Between Destruction and Construction.* London: Bloomsbury, 2017.

Carsten, F. L. *The Reichswehr and Politics, 1918–1933.* Berkeley: University of California Press, 1973.

Cesarani, David. *Becoming Eichmann: Rethinking the Life, Crimes, and Trial of a "Desk Murderer."* Cambridge, MA: Da Capo, 2006.

——. *The Final Solution: The Fate of the Jews, 1933–1949.* New York: St. Martin's, 2016.

Chickering, Roger. *Imperial Germany and the Great War, 1914–1918*. Cambridge: Cambridge University Press, 2014.

Clemente, Steven E. *For King and Kaiser! The Making of the Prussian Army Officer, 1860–1914*. New York: Greenwood, 1992.

Cohen, Deborah. *The War Come Home: Disabled Veterans in Britain and Germany, 1914–1939*. Berkeley: University of California Press, 2001.

Confino, Alon. *A World without Jews: The Nazi Imagination from Persecution to Genocide*. New Haven, CT: Yale University Press, 2015.

Connell, R. W. *Masculinities*. Berkeley: University of California Press, 2005.

Cooke, Phillip, and Ben H. Shepherd, eds. *Hitler's Europe Ablaze: Occupation, Resistance, and Rebellion during World War II*. New York: Skyhorse, 2014.

Cooley, Charles Horton. *Social Organization: A Study of the Larger Mind*. New York: Charles Scribner's Sons, 1909.

Corbach, Dieter. *"Ich kann nicht Schweigen!" Richard Stern, Köln, Marsilstein 20*. Cologne: Scriba, 1988.

Crim, Brian E. *Antisemitism in the German Military Community and the Jewish Response, 1914–1938*. Lanham, MD: Lexington Books, 2014.

——. "'Was It All Just a Dream?' German-Jewish Veterans and the Confrontation with Völkisch Nationalism in the Interwar Period." In *Sacrifice and National Belonging in Twentieth-Century Germany*, edited by Greg Eghigian and Matthew Paul Berg, 64–89. College Station: Texas A&M University Press, 2002.

Crouthamel, Jason. *The Great War and German Memory: Society, Politics, and Psychological Trauma, 1914–1945*. Liverpool: Liverpool University Press, 2010.

——. *An Intimate History of the Front: Masculinity, Sexuality, and German Soldiers in the First World War*. New York: Palgrave Macmillan, 2014.

——. "'My Comrades Are for the Most Part on My Side': Comradeship between Gentile and German-Jewish Front Soldiers in the First World War." In *Beyond Inclusion and Exclusion: Jewish Experiences of the First World War in Central Europe*, edited by Jason Crouthamel, Michael Geheran, Tim Grady, and Julia Köhne, 228–53. New York: Berghahn Books, 2018.

——. "Paul Lebrechts Kriegstagebuch." In *Krieg! Juden zwischen den Fronten 1914–1918*, edited by Ulrike Heikaus and Julia B. Köhne. Berlin: Hentrich & Hentrich Verlag, 2014.

Curilla, Wolfgang. *Der Judenmord in Polen und die deutsche Ordnungspolizei, 1939–1945*. Paderborn: Ferdinand Schöningh, 2011.

Dausien, Bettina. "Erzähltes Leben—erzähltes Geschlecht? Aspekte der narrativen Konstruktion von Geschlecht im Kontext der Biographieforschung." *Feministische Studien* 19, no. 2 (2001): 57–73.

Davis, Belinda. *Home Fires Burning: Food, Politics, and Everyday Life in World War I Berlin*. Chapel Hill: University of North Carolina Press, 2000.

Diehl, James M. *Paramilitary Politics in Weimar Germany*. Bloomington: Indiana University Press, 1977.

Dillon, Christopher. *Dachau and the SS: A Schooling in Violence*. Oxford: Oxford University Press, 2016.

Dipper, Christof. "Der Deutsche Widerstand und die Juden." *Geschichte und Gesellschaft* 9, no. 3 (1983): 349–80.

Dörner, Bernward. *Die Deutschen und der Holocaust: Was niemand wissen wollte, aber jeder wissen konnte*. Berlin: Ullstein Buchverlag, 2007.

Dunker, Ulrich. *Der Reichsbund jüdischer Frontsoldaten, 1919–1938: Geschichte eines jüdischen Abwehrvereins.* Düsseldorf: Droste Verlag, 1977.

Duppler, Jörg, and Gerhard Groß, eds. *Kriegsende 1918: Ereignis, Wirkung, Nachwirkung.* Munich: Oldenbourg Verlag, 1999.

Dwork, Debórah, and Robert Jan van Pelt. *Holocaust: A History.* New York: W. W. Norton, 2003.

Echternkamp, Jörg. *Soldaten im Nachkrieg: Historische Deutungskonflikte und westdeutsche Demokratisierung, 1945–1955.* Munich: De Gruyter Oldenbourg Verlag, 2014.

Edele, Mark. *Soviet Veterans of the Second World War: A Popular Movement in an Authoritarian Society.* Oxford: Oxford University Press, 2008.

Eichenberg, Julia, and John Paul Newman, eds. *The Great War and Veterans' Internationalism.* New York: Palgrave Macmillan, 2013.

Elliott, Christopher James. "The Kriegervereine and the Weimar Republic." *Journal of Contemporary History* 10, no. 1 (1975): 109–29.

Epkenhans, Michael. " 'Wir als deutsches Volk sind doch nicht klein zu kriegen . . .': Aus den Tagebüchern des Fregattenkapitäns Bogislav von Selchow 1918/19." *Militärgeschichtliche Mitteilungen* 55 (1996): 165–224.

Essner, Cornelia. *Die "Nürnberger Gesetze" oder Die Verwaltung des Rassenwahns, 1933–1945.* Paderborn: Ferdinand Schöningh, 2002.

Evans, Richard J. *The Third Reich in Power, 1933–1939.* New York: Penguin, 2005.

Farbstein, Esther. "Diaries and Memoirs as a Historical Source—The Diary and Memoir of a Rabbi at the 'Konin House of Bondage.' " *Yad Vashem Studies* 26, vol. 1 (1998): 87–129.

Feltman, Brian K. *The Stigma of Surrender: German Prisoners, British Captors, and Manhood in the Great War and Beyond.* Chapel Hill: University of North Carolina Press, 2015.

Fine, David J. *Jewish Integration in the German Army in the First World War.* Berlin: De Gruyter, 2012.

Fischer, Stefanie. *Ökonomisches Vertrauen und antisemitische Gewalt: Jüdische Viehhändler in Mittlefranken, 1919–1939.* Göttingen: Wallstein Verlag, 2014.

Flade, Roland. *Juden in Würzburg, 1918–1933.* Würzburg: Freunde Mainfränkischer Kunst und Geschichte, 1985.

——. *Die Würzburger Juden: Ihre Geschichte vom Mittelalter bis zur Gegenwart.* Würzburg: Königshausen & Neumann, 1996.

Förster, Jürgen. " 'Aber für die Juden wird auch noch die Stunde schlagen, und dann wehe ihnen!' Reichswehr und Antisemitismus." In *Deutsche, Juden, Völkermord: Der Holocaust als Geschichte und Gegenwart,* edited by Jürgen Matthäus and Klaus-Michael Mallmann, 21–37. Darmstadt: Wissenschaftliche Buchgesellschaft, 2006.

——. "Complicity or Entanglement? Wehrmacht, War, and Holocaust." In *The Holocaust and History: The Known, the Unknown, the Disputed, and the Reexamined,* edited by Michael Berenbaum and Abraham Peck, 266–84. Bloomington: Indiana University Press, 1998.

——. "Das Verhältnis von Wehrmacht und Nationalsozialismus im Entscheidungsjahr 1933." *German Studies Review* 18, no. 3 (1995): 471–80.

Forsyth, Donelson R. *Group Dynamics.* Belmont, CA: Cengage Learning, 2013.

Frevert, Ute. "Deutsche Juden und die Liebe zum Militär." In *Krieg! Juden zwischen den Fronten, 1914–1918*, edited by Ulrike Heikaus and Julia B. Köhne, 45–64. Berlin: Hentrich & Hentrich Verlag, 2014.

———. *Men of Honour: A Social and Cultural History of the Duel*. Cambridge: Polity, 1995.

———. *A Nation in Barracks: Modern Germany, Military Conscription, and Civil Society*. Oxford: Berg, 2004.

Friedländer, Saul. *Nazi Germany and the Jews: The Years of Persecution, 1933–1939*. New York: HarperCollins, 1997.

———. "Politische Veränderungen der Kriegszeit." In *Judentum in Krieg und Revolution, 1916–1923*, edited by Werner E. Mosse and Arnold Paucker, 27–66. Tübingen: Mohr Siebeck, 1971.

———. *The Years of Extermination: Nazi Germany and the Jews, 1939–1945*. New York: HarperCollins, 2007.

Frieser, Karl-Heinz. *Das Deutsche Reich und der Zweite Weltkrieg*. Vol. 8, *Die Ostfront 1944*. Munich: Deutsche Verlags Anstalt, 2007.

Fritzsche, Peter. *Life and Death in the Third Reich*. Cambridge, MA: Harvard University Press, 2008.

———. *Rehearsals for Fascism: Populism and Political Mobilization in Weimar Germany*. New York: Oxford University Press, 1990.

Führer, Karl. "Der Deutsche Reichskriegerbund Kyffhäuser, 1930–1934: Politik, Ideologie und Funktion eines 'unpolitischen' Verbandes." *Militärgeschichtliche Mitteilungen* 36, no. 2 (1984): 57–76.

Funck, Marcus. "The Meaning of Dying: East Elbian Noble Families as 'Warrior Tribes' in the Nineteenth and Twentieth Centuries." In *Sacrifice and National Belonging in Twentieth-Century Germany*, edited by Greg Eghigian and Matthew Paul Berg, 26–63. College Station: Texas A&M University Press, 2002.

———. "Ready for War? Conceptions of Military Manliness in the Prusso-German Officer Corps before the First World War." In *Home/Front: The Military, War and Gender in Twentieth-Century Germany*, edited by Karen Hagemann and Stefanie Schüler-Springorum, 43–67. Oxford: Berg, 2002.

Garbarini, Alexandra, Emil Kerenji, Jan Lambertz, and Avinoam Patt. *Jewish Responses to Persecution*. Vol. 2, *1938–1940*. Lanham, MD: AltaMira, 2011.

Geheran, Michael. "Remasculinizing the Shirker: The Jewish Frontkämpfer under Hitler." *Central European History* 51, no. 3 (2018): 440–65.

———. "Rethinking Jewish Front Experiences." In *Beyond Inclusion and Exclusion: Jewish Experiences of the First World War in Central Europe*, edited by Jason Crouthamel, Michael Geheran, Tim Grady, and Julia Köhne, 111–43. New York: Berghahn Books, 2018.

Gellately, Robert. *Backing Hitler: Consent and Coercion in Nazi Germany*. Oxford: Oxford University Press, 2001.

———. *The Gestapo and German Society: Enforcing Racial Policy, 1933–1945*. Oxford: Clarendon, 1991.

Gerber, David A. "Disabled Veterans, the State, and the Experience of Disability in Western Societies, 1914–1950." *Journal of Social History* 36, no. 4 (2003): 899–916.

Gerlach, Christian. "The Wannsee Conference, the Fate of German Jews, and Hitler's Decision in Principle to Exterminate All European Jews." *Journal of Modern History* 70, no. 4 (1998): 759–812.

Gerson, Judith. "Family Matters: German Jewish Masculinities among Nazi Era Refugees." In *Jewish Masculinities: German Jews, Gender, and History*, edited by Benjamin Maria Baader, Sharon Gillerman, and Paul Lerner, 210–31. Bloomington: Indiana University Press, 2012.

Gerstenberger, Heide. "Acquiescence?" In *Probing the Depths of German Antisemitism: German Society and the Persecution of the Jews, 1933–1941*, edited by David Bankier, 19–35. New York: Berghahn Books, 2000.

Geyer, Michael. "How the Germans Learned to Wage War: On the Question of Killing in the First and Second World Wars." In *Between Mass Death and Individual Loss: The Place of the Dead in Twentieth-Century Germany*, edited by Paul Betts, Alon Confino, and Dirk Schumann, 25–50. New York: Berghahn Books, 2008.

——. "War in the Context of General History in an Age of Total War: Comment on Peter Paret, 'Justifying the Obligation of Military Service,' and Michael Howard, 'World War One: The Crisis in European History.'" *Journal of Military History* 57, no. 5 (1993): 145–63.

Glad, Betty, ed. *Psychological Dimensions of War*. Newbury Park, CA: Sage, 1990.

Goeschel, Christian. *Suicide in Nazi Germany*. Oxford: Oxford University Press, 2009.

Goffman, Erving. *Stigma: Notes on the Management of Spoiled Identity*. New York: Touchstone, 2009.

Goldbaum, Silvia. "'Wir erfuhren was es heißt, hungrig zu sein': Aspekte des Alltagsleben dänischer Juden in Theresienstadt." In *Alltag im Holocaust: Jüdisches Leben im Großdeutschen Reich, 1941–1945*, edited by Andrea Löw, Doris Bergen, and Anna Hájková, 199–216. Munich: Oldenbourg Verlag, 2013.

Goldstein, Joshua. *War and Gender*. Cambridge: Cambridge University Press, 2001.

Goltz, Anna von der. *Hindenburg: Power, Myth, and the Rise of the Nazis*. Oxford: Oxford University Press, 2009.

Gottwaldt, Alfred, and Diana Schulte. *Die "Judendeportationen" aus dem Deutschen Reich, 1941–1945*. Wiesbaden: Marix Verlag, 2005.

Grady, Tim. *A Deadly Legacy: German Jews and the Great War*. New Haven, CT: Yale University Press, 2017.

——. "Fighting a Lost Battle: The Reichsbund Jüdischer Frontsoldaten and the Rise of National Socialism." *German History* 28, no. 1 (2010): 1–20.

——. *The German-Jewish Soldiers of the First World War in History and Memory*. Liverpool: Liverpool University Press, 2011.

Groening, Monika. *Leo Gans und Arthur von Weinberg: Mäzenatentum und jüdische Emanzipation*. Frankfurt: Societäts Verlag, 2012.

Grossmann, Atina. *Jews, Germans, and Allies: Close Encounters in Occupied Germany*. Princeton, NJ: Princeton University Press, 2007.

Gruner, Wolf. *Jewish Forced Labor under the Nazis: Economic Needs and Racial Aims*. Cambridge: Cambridge University Press, 2006.

Grünwald, Michal. "Antisemitismus im Deutschen Heer und Judenzählung." In *Jüdische Soldaten-Jüdischer Widerstand in Deutschland und Frankreich*, edited by Michael Berger and Gideon Römer-Hillebrecht, 129–44. Paderborn: Ferdinand Schöningh, 2012.

Hagemann, Karen, and Stefanie Schüler-Springorum. *Home/Front: The Military, War and Gender in Twentieth-Century Germany*. Oxford: Berg, 2002.

Hájková, Anna. "Ältere deutsche Jüdinnen und Juden im Ghetto Theresienstadt." In *Deutsche Jüdinnen und Juden in Ghettos und Lagern (1941–1945): Lodz. Chelmo. Minsk. Riga. Auschwitz. Theresienstadt*, edited by Beate Meyer, 201–20. Berlin: Metropol Verlag, 2017.

——. "'Poor Devils' of the Camps: Dutch Jews in Theresienstadt, 1943–1945." *Yad Vashem Studies 43*, no. 1 (2015): 77–111.

Haller, Christian. *Militärzeitschriften in der Weimarer Republik und ihr soziokultureller Hintergrund: Kriegsverarbeitung und Milieubildung im Offizierskorps der Reichswehr in publizistischer Dimension*. Trier: Kliomedia, 2012.

Hamburg Institut für Sozialforschung, ed. *Verbrechen der Wehrmacht: Dimensionen des Vernichtungskrieges, 1941–1944*. Hamburg: Hamburg Edition, 2002.

Hart, Peter. *The Great War: A Combat History of World War I*. Oxford: Oxford University Press, 2013.

Hayes, Joseph, Jeff Schimel, Jamie Arndt, and Erik H. Faucher. "A Theoretical and Empirical Review of the Death-Thought Accessibility Concept in Terror Management Research." *Psychological Bulletin 136*, no. 5 (2010): 699–739.

Hecht, Cornelia. *Deutsche Juden und Antisemitismus in der Weimarer Republik*. Bonn: Dietz Verlag, 2003.

Hecker, Clara. "Deutsche Juden im Minsker Ghetto." *Zeitschrift für Geschichtswissenschaft 56*, no. 8 (2008): 823–43.

Heer, Hannes, ed. *Im Herzen der Finsternis: Victor Klemperer als Chronist der NS Zeit*. Berlin: Aufbau-Verlag, 1997.

Heiber, Helmut. "Aus den Akten des Gauleiter Kube." *Vierteljahreshefte für Zeitgeschichte 4*, no. 1 (1956): 67–92.

Heidel, Caris-Petra, ed. *Ärzte und Zahnärzte in Sachsen, 1933–1945: Eine Dokumenation von Verfolgung, Vertreibung, Ermordung*. Frankfurt: Marbuse-Verlag, 2005.

Heim, Susanne, Beate Meyer, and Francis R. Nicosia, eds. *"Wer bleibt, opfert seine Jahre, vielleicht sein Leben": Deutsche Juden, 1938–1941*. Göttingen: Wallstein Verlag, 2010.

Herf, Jeffrey. *The Jewish Enemy: Nazi Propaganda during World War II and the Holocaust*. Cambridge, MA: Harvard University Press, 2006.

Higate, Paul, ed. *Military Masculinities: Identity and the State*. Westport, CT: Praeger, 2003.

Hilberg, Raul. *The Destruction of the European Jews*. 3rd ed. 3 vols. New Haven, CT: Yale University Press, 2003.

Hirschfeld, Gerhard, Gerd Krumreich, Dieter Langewiesche, and Hans-Peter Ullmann, eds. *Kriegserfahrungen: Studien zur Sozial- und Mentalitätsgeschichte des Ersten Weltkriegs*. Essen: Klartext Verlag, 1997.

Hoffmann, Christhard. "Between Integration and Rejection: The Jewish Community in Germany, 1914–1918." In *State, Society, and Mobilization in Europe during the First World War*, edited by John Horne, 89–104. Cambridge: Cambridge University Press, 1997.

Hoffmann, Peter. *Carl Goerdeler and the Jewish Question, 1933–1942*. Cambridge: Cambridge University Press, 2011.

——. *Carl Goerdeler gegen die Verfolgung der Juden*. Cologne: Böhlau Verlag, 2013.

Hoffstadt, Anke. "Frontgemeinschaft? Der 'Stahlhelm. Bund der Frontsoldaten' und der Nationalsozialismus." In *Nationalsozialismus und Erster Weltkrieg*, edited by Gerd Krumreich, 191–206. Essen: Klartext Verlag, 2010.

Horne, John. "Masculinity in Politics and War in the Age of Nation States and World War, 1850–1950." In *Masculinities in Politics and War: Gendering Modern History*, edited by Stefan Dudnik, Karen Hagemann, and John Tosh, 22–39. Manchester: Manchester University Press, 2004.

Huppauf, Bernd. "Schlachtenmythen und die Konstruktion des 'Neuen Menschen.'" In *Keiner fühlt sich hier mehr als Mensch . . .: Erlebnis und Wirkung des Ersten Weltkriegs*, edited by Gerhard Hirschfeld, Gerd Krumeich, and Irina Renz, 43–84. Essen: Klartext Verlag, 1993.

Hürter, Johannes. *Hitlers Heerführer: Die deutschen Oberbefehlshaber im Krieg gegen die Sowjetunion, 1941/42*. Munich: R. Oldenbourg Verlag, 2007.

Jackisch, Barry A. *The Pan-German League and Radical Nationalist Politics in Interwar Germany, 1918-39*. Farnham: Ashgate, 2012.

Jeffords, Susan. *The Remasculinization of America: Gender and the Vietnam War*. Bloomington: Indiana University Press, 1989.

Jochem, Gerhard. "Jüdische Soldaten aus Nürnberg im Ersten Weltkrieg und ihre Schicksale nach 1918." *Der Melder 3*, no. 1 (2007): 28–42.

Jochmann, Werner. "Ausbreitung des Antisemitismus." In *Judentum in Krieg und Revolution, 1916–1923*, edited by Werner E. Mosse and Arnold Paucker, 409–510. Tübingen: Mohr Siebeck, 1971.

Johnson, Eric A. *Nazi Terror: The Gestapo, Jews, and Ordinary Germans*. New York: Basic Books, 1999.

Jones, Larry Eugene. "Nationalists, Nazis, and the Assault against Weimar: Revisiting the Harzburg Rally of October 1931." *German Studies Review 29*, no. 3 (2006): 483–94.

Junginger, Horst. *The Scientification of the Jewish Question in Nazi Germany*. Leiden: Brill, 2017.

Kampe, Norbert, and Peter Klein, eds. *Die Wannsee-Konferenz am 20. Januar 1942: Dokumente, Forschungsstand, Kontroversen*. Cologne: Böhlau, 2013.

Kaplan, Marion. *Between Dignity and Despair: Jewish Life in Nazi Germany*. New York: Oxford University Press, 1998.

——. *Jewish Daily Life in Germany, 1618–1945*. New York: Oxford University Press, 2005.

Karny, Miroslav. "Deutsche Juden in Theresienstadt." *Theresienstädter Studien und Dokumente 1* (1994): 36–53.

——. "Die Theresienstädter Herbsttransporte 1944." *Theresienstädter Studien und Dokumente 2* (1995): 7–37.

Karny, Miroslav, and Terezinska Iniciativa, eds. Theresienstaedter Gedenkbuch: Die Opfer der Judentransporte aus Deutschland nach Theresienstadt, 1942–1945. Prague: Academia Verlag, 2000.

Karras, Steven. *The Enemy I Knew: German Jews in the Allied Military in World War II*. Minneapolis: Zenith, 2009.

Kauders, Anthony. *German Politics and the Jews: Düsseldorf and Nuremberg, 1910–1933*. New York: Oxford University Press, 1996.

Keene, Jennifer D. "The Long Journey Home: African American World War I Veterans and Veterans' Policies." In *Veterans' Policies, Veterans' Politics: New Perspectives on Veterans in the Modern United States*, edited by Stephen R. Ortiz, 146–70. Gainesville: University Press of Florida, 2012.

Kellet, Anthony. "The Soldier in Battle: Motivational and Behavioral Aspects of the Combat Experience." In *Psychological Dimensions of War*, edited by Betty Glad, 215–35. Newbury Park, CA: Sage, 1990.

Kerenji, Emil, ed. *Jewish Responses to Persecution*. Vol. 4, *1942–1943*. Lanham, MD: Rowman & Littlefield, 2015.

Kershaw, Ian. *Hitler: 1889–1936; Hubris*. New York: W. W. Norton, 1998.

——. *Hitler: 1936–1945; Nemesis*. New York: W. W. Norton, 2000.

——. *Popular Opinion and Political Dissent in the Third Reich: Bavaria, 1933–1945*. Oxford: Clarendon, 2002.

Kiesel, Doron, Cilly Kugelmann, Hanno Loewy, and Dietrich Neuhauß, eds. *"Wer zum Leben, wer zum Tod . . .": Strategien jüdischen Überlebens im Getto*. Frankfurt: Campus Verlag, 1992.

Klein, Peter. "Die Erlaubnis zum grenzenlosen Massenmord—das Schicksal der Berliner Juden und die Rolle der Einsatzgruppen bei dem Versuch, Juden als Partisanen 'auszurotten.'" In *Die Wehrmacht: Mythos und Realität*, edited by Rolf-Dieter Müller and Hans-Erich Volkmann, 923–47. Munich: Oldenbourg Verlag, 1999.

——. *Die "Gettoverwaltung Litzmannstadt," 1940 bis 1944: Eine Dienststelle im Spannungsfeld von Kommunalbürokratie und staatlicher Verfolgungspolitik*. Hamburg: Hamburger Edition, 2009.

Knipping, Franz, and Klaus-Jürgen Müller. *Machtbewußtsein in Deutschland am Vorabend des Zweiten Weltkrieges*. Paderborn: Schöningh, 1984.

Kopciowski, Adam. "Der Judenrat in Zamość." *Theresienstädter Studien und Dokumente 9* (2002): 221–45.

Korb, Alexander. *Reaktionen der deutschen Bevölkerung auf die Novemberpogrome im Spiegel amtlicher Berichte*. Saarbrücken: VDM Verlag, 2007.

Koselleck, Reinhart. "Der Einfluß der beiden Weltkriege auf das soziale Bewußtsein." In *Der Krieg des kleinen Mannes: Eine Militärgeschichte von unten*, edited by Wolfram Wette, 324–43. Munich: Piper Verlag, 1992.

Krausnick, Helmut. "Goerdeler und die Deportation der Leipziger Juden." *Vierteljahrshefte für Zeitgeschichte 13*, no. 3 (1965): 338–39.

Krebs, Ronald R. *Fighting for Rights: Military Service and the Politics of Citizenship*. Ithaca, NY: Cornell University Press, 2006.

Kreutzmüller, Christoph. "Die Erfassung der Juden im Reichskommissariat der besetzten niederländischen Gebiete." In *Besatzung, Kollaboration, Holocaust: Neue Studien zur Verfolgung und Ermordung der europäischen Juden*, edited by Johannes Hürter and Jürgen Zarusky, 21–44. Munich: Oldenbourg Verlag, 2008.

Krüger, Christine G. *"Sind wir nicht Brüder?" Deutsche Juden im nationalen Krieg, 1870/71*. Paderborn: Ferdinand Schöningh, 2006.

Krumeich, Gerd. "Aux origins de l'antisémitisme nazi: Compter les Juifs pendant la Grande Guerre." *Revue d'histoire de la Shoah 189*, no. 2 (2008): 359–72.

Kuhlman, Erika. *The International Migration of German Great War Veterans: Emotion, Transnational Identity, and Loyalty to the Nation, 1914–1942*. New York: Palgrave Macmillan, 2016.

Kühne, Thomas. *Belonging and Genocide: Hitler's Community, 1918–1945*. New Haven, CT: Yale University Press, 2010.

———. "Comradeship: Gender Confusion and Gender Order in the German Military, 1918–1945." In *Home/Front: The Military, War and Gender in Twentieth-Century Germany*, edited by Karen Hagemann and Stefanie Schüler-Springorum, 233–54. Oxford: Berg, 2002.

———. *Kameradschaft: Die Soldaten des nationalsozialistischen Krieges und das 20. Jahrhundert*. Göttingen: Vandenhoeck & Ruprecht, 2006.

———. *The Rise and Fall of Comradeship*. Cambridge: Cambridge University Press, 2017.

Kulka, Otto Dov, and Eberhard Jäckel, eds. *The Jews in the Secret Nazi Reports on Popular Opinion in Germany, 1933–1945*. New Haven, CT: Yale University Press, 2010.

Kwiet, Konrad. "Nach dem Pogrom: Stufen der Ausgrenzung." In *Die Juden in Deutschland: Leben unter nationalsozialistischer Herrschaft*, edited by Wolfgang Benz, 545–659. Munich: Verlag C. H. Beck, 1989.

Langewiesche, Dieter. "Nation, Imperium und Kriegserfahrungen." In *Kriegserfahrungen: Krieg und Gesellschaft in der Neuzeit; Neue Horizonte der Forschung*, edited by Georg Schild and Anton Schilling, 213–30. Paderborn: Ferdinand Schöningh, 2009.

Laqueur, Walter. "Three Witnesses: The Legacy of Victor Klemperer, Willy Cohn, and Richard Koch." *Holocaust and Genocide Studies* 10, no. 3 (1996): 252–66.

Large, David Clay. *And the World Closed Its Doors: The Story of One Family Abandoned to the Holocaust*. New York: Basic Books, 2004.

Lee, Carol Ann. *The Hidden Life of Otto Frank*. New York: HarperCollins, 2002.

Lerner, Robert E. *Ernst Kantorowicz: A Life*. Princeton, NJ: Princeton University Press, 2017.

Levsen, Sonja. "Constructing Elite Identities: University Students, Military Masculinity and the Consequences of the Great War in Britain and Germany." *Past and Present* 198, no. 1 (2008): 147–98.

Limberg, Margarete, and Hubert Rübsaat, eds. *Germans No More: Accounts of Jewish Everyday Life, 1933–1938*. New York: Berghahn Books, 2006.

Lindner, Erik. *Patriotismus deutscher Juden von der napoleonischen Ära bis zum Kaiserreich: Zwischen korporativen Loyalismus und individueller deutsch-jüdischer Identität*. Frankfurt: Peter Land, 1997.

Lockenour, Jay. *Soldiers as Citizens: Former Wehrmacht Officers in the Federal Republic of Germany, 1945–1955*. Lincoln: University of Nebraska Press, 2001.

Löffelbein, Nils. *Ehrenbürger der Nation: Die Kriegsbeschädigten des Ersten Weltkriegs in Politik und Propaganda des Nationalsozialismus*. Essen: Klartext Verlag, 2013.

Longerich, Peter. *"Davon haben wir nichts gewusst!" Die Deutschen und die Judenverfolgung, 1933–1945*. Munich: Siedler, 2006.

———. *Heinrich Himmler*. Oxford: Oxford University Press, 2012.

———. *Wannseekonferenz: Der Weg zur "Endlösung."* Munich: Pantheon Verlag, 2016.

Loose, Ingo, and Thomas Lutz, eds. *Berliner Juden im Getto Litzmannstadt, 1941–1944: Ein Gedenkbuch*. Berlin: Stiftung des Topographie des Terrors, 2009.

Löw, Andrea. *Juden im Getto Litzmannstadt: Lebensbedingungen, Selbstwahrnehmungen, Verhalten*. Göttingen: Wallstein Verlag, 2006.

Ludwig, Ulrike, Markus Pöhlmann, and John Zimmermann, eds. *Ehre und Pflichterfüllung als Codes militärischer Tugenden*. Paderborn: Ferdinand Schöningh, 2014.

Lustiger, Arnold, ed. *Zum Kampf auf Leben und Tod! Vom Widerstand der Juden, 1933–1945.* Munich: DTV, 1994.

Maleševićm, Siniša. *The Sociology of War and Violence.* Cambridge: Cambridge University Press, 2010.

Margaliot, Abraham. "The Reaction of the Jewish Public in Germany to the Nuremberg Laws." *Yad Vashem Studies* 12, no. 1 (1977): 75–107.

Matthäus, Jürgen. "Evading Persecution: German-Jewish Behavior Patterns after 1933." In *Jewish Life in Nazi Germany: Dilemmas and Responses*, edited by Francis R. Nicosia and David Scrase, 47–70. New York: Berghahn Books, 2010.

Matthäus, Jürgen, Emil Kerenji, Jan Lambertz, and Leah Wolfson. *Jewish Responses to Persecution.* Vol. 3, *1941–1942.* Lanham, MD: AltaMira, 2013.

Matthäus, Jürgen, Konrad Kwiet, Jürgen Förster, and Richard Breitman. *Ausbildungsziel Judenmord? "Weltanschauliche Erziehung" von SS, Polizei und Waffen-SS im Rahmen der "Endlösung."* Frankfurt: S. Fischer Verlag, 2003.

Matthäus, Jürgen, and Mark Roseman. *Jewish Responses to Persecution.* Vol. 1, *1933–1938.* Lanham, MD: AltaMira, 2010.

Maurer, Trude. "Customers, Patients, Neighbors and Friends: Relations between Jews and Non-Jews in Germany, 1933–1938." In *Nazi Europe and the Final Solution*, edited by David Bankier and Israel Gutman, 73–92. Jerusalem: Yad Vashem, 2003.

——. *Ostjuden in Deutschland, 1918–1933.* Hamburg: Christians, 1986.

Mayer, Michael. *Staaten als Täter: Ministerialbürokratie und "Judenpolitik" in NS-Deutschland und Vichy-Frankreich; Ein Vergleich.* Munich: R. Oldenbourg Verlag, 2010.

Megargee, Geoffrey P. *War of Annihilation: Combat and Genocide on the Eastern Front, 1941.* Lanham, MD: Rowman & Littlefield, 2007.

Mehler, Richard. "Der Entstehung eines Bürgertums unter den Landjuden der bayerischen Rhön vor dem Ersten Weltkrieg." In *Juden, Bürger, Deutsche: Zur Geschichte von Vielfalt und Differenz, 1800–1933*, edited by Andreas Gotzmann, Rainer Liedtke, and Till van Rahden, 193–216. Tübingen: Mohr Siebeck, 2001.

Meinen, Insa. *Die Shoah in Belgien.* Darmstadt: Wissenschaftliche Buchgesellschaft, 2009.

Meinen, Insa, and Ahlrich Meyer. *Verfolgt von Land zu Land: Jüdische Flüchtlinge in Westeuropa, 1938–1944.* Paderborn: Ferdinand Schöningh, 2013.

Mendes-Flohr, Paul. *German Jews: A Dual Identity.* New Haven, CT: Yale University Press, 1999.

——. "The *Kriegserlebnis* and Jewish Consciousness." In *Jüdisches Leben in der Weimarer Republik*, edited by Wolfgang Benz, 225–38. Tübingen: Mohr Siebeck, 1998.

Messerschmidt, Manfred. "Juden im preußisch-deutschen Heer." In *Deutsche Jüdische Soldaten: Von der Epoche der Emanzipation bis zum Zeitalter der Weltkriege*, edited by the Militärgeschichtliches Forschungsamt, 39–62. Hamburg: Mittler & Sohn, 1996.

——. *Die Wehrmacht im NS-Staat: Zeit der Indoktrination.* Hamburg: R. v. Decker's Verlag, 1969.

Meteling, Wencke. *Ehre, Einheit und Ordnung: Preußische und französcishe Städte und ihre Regimener im Krieg, 1870/71 und 1914/19.* Baden-Baden: Nomos, 2010.

Meyer, Beate. "'Altersghetto,' 'Vorzugslager' und Tätigkeitsfeld: Die Repräsentanten der Reichsvereingung der Juden in Deutschland und Theresienstadt." *Theresienstädter Studien und Dokumente* 12 (2006): 125–51.

——. *A Fatal Balancing Act: The Dilemma of the Reich Association of Jews in Germany, 1939–1945*. New York: Berghahn Books, 2013.

——. *"Jüdische Mischlinge": Rassenpolitik und Verfolgungserfahrung, 1933–1945*. Hamburg: Dölling & Galitz, 1999.

——. *Die Verfolgung und Ermordung der Hamburger Juden, 1933–1945: Geschichte. Zeugnis. Erinnerung*. Göttingen: Wallstein Verlag, 2006.

Meyer, Michael A., ed. *Deutsch-Jüdische Geschichte in der Neuzeit*. Band 4, *Aufbruch und Zerstörung, 1918–1945*. Munich: Verlag C. H. Beck, 1997.

Meyer, Winfried. *Unternehmen Sieben: Eine Rettungsaktion für vom Holocaust Bedrohte aus dem Amt Ausland/Abwehr im Oberkommando der Wehrmacht*. Frankfurt: Verlag Anton Hain, 1993.

Militärgeschichtliches Forschungsamt, ed. *Deutsche Jüdische Soldaten: Von der Epoche der Emanzipation bis zum Zeitalter der Weltkriege*. Hamburg: Mittler & Sohn, 1996.

Moeller, Robert G. "'The Last Soldiers of the Great War' and Tales of Family Reunions in the Federal Republic of Germany." *Signs: Journal of Women in Culture and Society* 24, no. 1 (1998): 129–45.

Mommsen, Hans. *Aufstieg und Untergang der Republik von Weimar, 1918–1933*. Berlin: Ullstein, 2009.

——, ed. *Der Erste Weltkrieg und die europäische Nachkriegsordnung: Sozialer Wandel und Formveränderung der Politik*. Cologne: Böhlau Verlag, 2000.

Morgan, David H. J. "Theater of War: Combat, the Military, and Masculinities." In *Theorizing Masculinities*, edited by Harry Brod and Michael Kaufman, 165–82. Thousand Oaks: Sage, 1994.

Morris, Douglas G. *Justice Imperiled: The Anti-Nazi Lawyer Max Hirschberg in Weimar Germany*. Ann Arbor: University of Michigan Press, 2005.

Mosse, George L. *The Image of Man: The Creation of Modern Masculinity*. Oxford: Oxford University Press, 1998.

——. *The Jews and the German War Experience, 1914–1918*. New York: Leo Baeck Institute, 1977.

Mosse, Werner E., and Arnold Paucker, eds. *Entscheidungsjahr 1932: Zur Judenfrage in der Endphase der Weimarar Republik*. Tübingen: J. C. B. Mohr (Paul Siebeck), 1966.

——. *Judentum in Krieg und Revolution, 1916–1923*. Tübingen: Mohr Siebeck, 1971.

Müller, Klaus-Jürgen. *Generaloberst Ludwig Beck: Eine Biographie*. Paderborn: Ferdinand Schöningh, 2009.

——. *Das Heer und Hitler: Armee und nationalsozialistisches Regime, 1933–1940*. Stuttgart: Deutsche Verlags-Anstalt, 1969.

Müller, Klaus-Jürgen, and Eckardt Opitz, eds. *Militär und Militarismus in der Weimarer Republik*. Düsseldorf: Drotse Verlag, 1978.

Müller, Rolf-Dieter, and Hans-Erich Volkmann, eds. *Die Wehrmacht: Mythos und Realität*. Munich: Oldenbourg Verlag, 1999.

Mulligan, William. *The Creation of the Modern German Army: General Walther Reinhardt and the Weimar Republic, 1914–1930*. New York: Berghahn Books, 2005.

Neitzel, Sonke. *Abgehört: Deutsche Generaäle in britischer Gefangenschaft, 1942–1945.* Berlin: List, 2007.

Nelson, Robert L. *German Soldier Newspapers of the First World War.* Cambridge: Cambridge University Press, 2011.

Nielsen, Philipp. *Between Heimat and Hatred: Jews and the Right in Germany, 1871–1935.* Oxford: Oxford University Press, 2019.

——. "'I've Never Regretted Being a German Jew': Siegmund Weltlinger and the Reestablishment of the Jewish Community in Berlin." *Leo Baeck Institute Yearbook* 54 (2009): 275–96.

Nützenadel, Alexander, ed. *Das Reichsarbeitsministerium im Nationalsozialismus: Verwaltung—Politik—Verbrechen.* Berlin: Wallstein Verlag, 2017.

Obst, Dieter. *"Reichskristallnacht": Ursachen und Verlauf des antisemitischen Pogrome vom November 1938.* Frankfurt: Peter Lang, 1991.

O'Byrne, Darren. "Political Civil Servants and the German Administration under Nazism." PhD diss., Cambridge University, 2016.

Ophir, Baruch Z., and Falk Wiesenmann, eds. *Die jüdischen Gemeinden in Bayern, 1918–1945.* Munich: R. Oldenbourg Verlag, 1979.

Panter, Sarah. *Jüdische Erfahrungen und Loyalitätskonflikte im Ersten Weltkrieg.* Göttingen: Vandenhoeck & Ruprecht, 2014.

Paucker, Arnold. "Der jüdische Abwehrkampf." In *Entscheidungsjahr 1932: Zur Judenfrage in der Endphase der Weimarar Republik,* edited by Werner E. Mosse and Arnold Paucker, 405–99. Tübingen: J. C. B. Mohr (Paul Siebeck), 1966.

Pegelow, Thomas. "'German Jews,' 'National Jews,' 'Jewish Volk,' or 'Racial Jews'? The Constitution and Contestation of 'Jewishness' in Newspapers of Nazi Germany, 1933–1938." *Central European History* 35, no. 2 (2002): 195–221.

Penslar, Derek. "The German-Jewish Soldier: From Participant to Victim." *German History* 29, no. 3 (2011): 445–69.

——. *Jews and the Military: A History.* Princeton, NJ: Princeton University Press, 2013.

Petter, Wolfgang. "Wehrmacht und Judenverfolgung." In *Die Deutschen und die Judenverfolgung im Dritten Reich,* edited by Ursula Büttner, 194–214. Frankfurt: Fischer Verlag, 2003.

Peukert, Detlev J. K. *The Weimar Republic.* New York: Hill & Wang, 1987.

Picht, Clemens. "Zwischen Vaterland und Volk: Das deutsche Judentum im Ersten Weltkrieg." In *Der Erste Weltkrieg: Wirkung, Wahrnehmung, Analyse,* edited by Wolfgang Michalka, 736–55. Munich: Piper Verlag, 1994.

Pierson, Ruth. "Embattled Veterans: The Reichsbund Jüdischer Frontsoldaten." *Leo Baeck Institute Yearbook* 19 (1974): 139–54.

Platt, G. M. "Social Psychology of Status and Role." In *International Encyclopedia of the Social & Behavioral Sciences,* edited by Neil J. Smelser and Peter Baltes, 15090–95. Amsterdam: Elsevier, 2001.

Plum, Günter. "Wirtschaft und Erwerbsleben." In *Die Juden in Deutschland, 1933–1945: Leben unter nationalsozialistischer Herrschaft,* edited by Wolfgang Benz, 272–80. Munich: Verlag C. H. Beck, 1996.

Poppel, Stephen. *Zionism in Germany, 1897–1933: The Shaping of Jewish Identity.* Philadelphia: Jewish Publication Society of America, 1976.

Prost, Antoine. *Les Anciens Combattants et la societé francaise, 1914–1939.* 3 vols. Paris: Presse de la Foundation Nationale des Sciences Politiques, 1977.

——. *In the Wake of War: "Les Anciens combattants" and French Society, 1914–1939.* Oxford: Berg, 1992.

Pulzer, Peter. *Jews and the German State: The Political History of a Minority, 1848–1933.* Oxford: Oxford University Press, 1992.

Pyta, Wolfram. *Hindenburg: Herrschaft zwischen Hohenzollern und Hitler.* Munich: Siedler Verlag, 2007.

Rahden, Till van. *Jews and Other Germans: Civil Society, Religious Diversity, and Urban Politics in Breslau, 1860–1925.* Madison: University of Wisconsin Press, 2008.

Reichardt, Sven. "Die SA im 'Nachkriegs-Krieg.'" In *Nationalsozialismus und Erster Weltkrieg,* edited by Gerd Krumreich, 243–59. Essen: Klartext Verlag, 2010.

Reichmann, Eva G. "Der Bewußtseinswandel der deutschen Juden." In *Judentum in Krieg und Revolution, 1916–1923,* edited by Werner E. Mosse and Arnold Paucker, 511–612. Tübingen: Mohr Siebeck, 1971.

Reimann, Aribert. *Der große Krieg der Sprachen: Untersuchungen zur historischen Semantik in Deutschland und England zur Zeit des Ersten Weltkriegs.* Essen: Klartext Verlag, 2000.

Richarz, Monika, ed. *Jüdisches Leben in Deutschland: Selbstzeugnisse zur Sozialgeschichte, 1918–1945.* Stuttgart: Deutsche Verlags Anstalt, 1982.

——. *Jüdisches Leben in Deutschland: Selbstzeugnisse zur Sozialgeschichte im Kaiserreich.* Stuttgart: Deutsche Verlags Anstalt, 1982.

Rigg, Bryan Mark. *Hitler's Jewish Soldiers: The Untold Story of Nazi Racial Laws and Men of Jewish Descent in the German Military.* Lawrence: University Press of Kansas, 2002.

Rohkrämer, Thomas. *Die fatale Attraktion des Nationalsozialsmus: Zur Popularität des Unrechtsregimes.* Paderborn: Ferdinand Schöningh, 2013.

——. *Der Militarismus der "kleinen Leute": Die Kriegervereine im Deutschen Kaiserriech, 1871–1914.* Munich: R. Oldenbourg Verlag, 1990.

——. *A Single Communal Faith? The German Right from Conservatism to National Socialism.* New York: Berghahn Books, 2007.

Röhm, Eberhard, and Jörg Thierfelder. *Juden, Christen, Deutsche.* Band 1, *1933–1935.* Stuttgart: Calwer Verlag, 1990.

Roseman, Mark. *The Wannsee Conference and the Final Solution: A Reconsideration.* New York: Metropolitan Books, 2002.

Rosenthal, Jacob. *"Die Ehre des jüdischen Soldaten": Die Judenzählung im Ersten Weltkrieg und ihre Folgen.* Frankfurt: Campus Verlag, 2007.

Sammartino, Annemarie H. *The Impossible Border: Germany and the East, 1914–1922.* Ithaca, NY: Cornell University Press, 2010.

Sauer, Bernhard. "Freikorps und Antisemitismus in der Frühzeit der Weimarer Republik." *Zeitschrift für Geschichtswissenschaft* 56, vol. 1 (2008): 5–29.

Sauer, Paul, ed. *Die Schicksale der jüdischen Bürger Baden-Württembergs während der nationalsozialistischen Verfolgungszeit, 1933–1945.* Stuttgart: W. Kohlhammer Verlag, 1968.

Schaar, Sebastian. *Wahrnehmungen des Weltkrieges: Selbstzeugnisse Königlich Sächsischer Offiziere, 1914 bis 1918.* Paderborn: Ferdinand Schöningh, 2014.

Schäfer, Kirstin A. *Werner von Blomberg: Hitler's erster Feldmarschall; Eine Biographie.* Paderborn: Ferdinand Schöningh, 2006.

Schilling, René. *"Kriegshelden": Deutungsmuster heroischer Männlichkeit in Deutschland, 1813–1945.* Paderborn: Ferdinand Schöningh, 2002.

Schindler, Thomas. "Jüdische Studenten im Ersten Weltkrieg: Versuch einer Charakterisierung-mit Schwerpunkt auf der Entwicklung im zionistischen 'Kartell Jüdischer Verbindungen.'" In *Jüdische Soldaten-Jüdischer Widerstand in Deutschland und Frankreich*, edited by Michael Berger and Gideon Römer-Hillebrecht, 373–89. Paderborn: Ferdinand Schöningh, 2012.

Schleunes, Karl A. *The Twisted Road to Auschwitz: Nazi Policy toward German Jews, 1933–1939.* Urbana: University of Illinois Press, 1970.

Schmidt, Herbert. *Der Elendsweg der Düsseldorfer Juden: Chronologie des Schreckens, 1933–1945.* Dusseldorf: Droste Verlag, 2005.

Schmidt, Wolfgang. "Die Juden in der Bayerischen Armee." In *Deutsche Jüdische Soldaten: Von der Epoche der Emanzipation bis zum Zeitalter der Weltkriege*, edited by Militärgeschichtliches Forschungsamt, 63–85. Hamburg: Mittler & Sohn, 1996.

Schmitthenner, Walter and Hans Buchheim, eds. *Der deutsche Widerstand gegen Hitler: Vier historisch-kritische Studien von Hermann Graml, Hans Mommsen, Hans Joachim Reichhardt und Ernst Wolf.* Cologne: Kiepenheuer & Witsch, 1966.

Schoeps, Julius H., and J. Schlör, eds. *Bilder der Judenfeindschaft: Antisemitismus, Vorurteile und Mythen.* Augsburg: Weltbild Verlag, 1999.

Schönherr, Klaus. "Die Kämpfe um Galizien und die Beskiden." In *Das Deutsche Reich und der Zweite Weltkrieg*, vol. 8, *Die Ostfront 1944*, edited by Karl-Heinz Frieser, 679–730. Munich: Deutsche Verlags Anstalt, 2007.

Schrafstetter, Susanna, and Alan E. Steinweis, eds. *The Germans and the Holocaust: Popular Responses to the Persecution and Murder of the Jews.* New York: Berghahn Books, 2016.

Schröder, Joachim. "Der Erste Weltkrieg und der 'jüdische Bolschewismus.'" In *Nationalsozialismus und Erster Weltkrieg*, edited by Gerd Krumreich, 77–96. Essen: Klartext Verlag, 2010.

Schüler-Springorum, Stefanie. *Geschlecht und Differenz.* Paderborn: Ferdinand Schöningh, 2014.

——. "A Soft Hero: Male Jewish Identity in Imperial Germany through the Autobiography of Aron Liebeck." In *Jewish Masculinities: German Jews, Gender, and History*, edited by Benjamin Maria Baader, Sharon Gillerman, and Paul Lerner, 90–113. Bloomington: Indiana University Press, 2012.

Schultheis, Herbert. *Juden in Mainfranken, 1933–1945: Unter besonderer Berücksichtigung der Deportationen Würzburger Juden.* Bad Neutstadt an der Saale: Rötter Druck & Verlag, 1980.

——. *Die Reichskristallnacht in Deutschland nach Augenzeugenberichten.* Bad Neutstadt an der Saale: Rötter Druck & Verlag, 1985.

Schumann, Dirk. *Political Violence in the Weimar Republic, 1918–1933: Fight for the Streets and Fear of Civil War.* New York: Berghahn Books, 2009.

Schwierz, Isreal. *"Fur das Vaterland starben . . .": Denkmäler und Gedenktafeln bayerisch-jüdischer Soldaten.* Aschaffenburg: Eduard Krem-Bardischewski Verlag, 1998.

Scofield, Devlin. "Veterans, War Widows, and National Belonging in Alsace, 1871–1953." PhD diss., Michigan State University, 2014.

Shils, Edward A., and Morris Janowitz. "Cohesion and Disintegration in the Wehrmacht in World War II." *Public Opinion Quarterly* 12, no. 2 (1948): 280–315.

Showalter, Dennis. *Little Man, What Now? Der Stürmer in the Weimar Republic.* Hamden, CT: Archon Books, 1982.

Sieg, Ulrich. *Jüdische Intellektuelle im Ersten Weltkrieg: Kriegserfahrungen, weltanschauliche Debatten und kulturelle Neuentwürfe.* Berlin: Akademie-Verlag, 2001.

——. "'Nothing More German Than the German Jews?' On the Integration of a Minority in a Society at War." In *Towards Normality? Acculturation and Modern German Jewry,* edited by Rainer Liedtke and David Rechts, 201–16. Tübingen: Mohr Siebeck, 2003.

Smelser, Neil J., and Peter Baltes, eds. *International Encyclopedia of the Social & Behavioral Sciences.* Amsterdam: Elsevier, 2001.

Sofsky, Wolfgang. *The Order of Terror: The Concentration Camp.* Princeton, NJ: Princeton University Press, 1997.

Sprenger, Matthias. *Landsknechte auf dem Weg ins Dritte Reich? Zu Genese und Wandel des Freikorpsmythos.* Paderborn: Ferdinand Schöningh, 2008.

Stachelbeck, Christian. *Deutschlands Heer und Marine im Ersten Weltkrieg.* Munich: Olbenbourg Verlag, 2013.

——. *Militärische Effektivität im Ersten Weltkrieg: Die 11. Bayerische Infanteriedivision, 1915 bis 1918.* Paderborn: Ferdinand Schöningh, 2010.

Stadt Pirmasens, ed. *Juden in Pirmasens: Spuren eine Geschichte.* Pirmasens: Stadtverwaltung, 2004.

Stadtarchiv Trier. *Juden in Trier: Katalog einer Ausstellung von Stadtarchiv und Stadtbibliothek Trier, März-November 1988.* Trier: Stadtbibliothek and Universitätsbibliothek Trier, 1988.

Stargardt, Nicholas. *The German War: A Nation under Arms, 1939–1945.* New York: Basic Books, 2015.

Steer, Martina. "Nation, Religion, Gender: The Triple Challenge of Middle-Class German-Jewish Women in World War I." *Central European History* 48, no. 2 (2015): 176–98.

Steinweis, Alan E. *Kristallnacht 1938.* Cambridge, MA: Belknap Press of Harvard University Press, 2009.

Stephenson, Jill. *Hitler's Home Front: Württemberg under the Nazis.* London: Hambledon, 2006.

Stoltzfus, Nathan. *Hitler's Compromises: Coercion and Consensus in Nazi Germany.* New Haven, CT: Yale University Press, 2016.

Strangmann, Sinja. "Eduard und Hans Bloch—Zwei Generationen jüdischer Soldaten im Ersten Weltkrieg." In *Krieg! Juden zwischen den Fronten, 1914–1918,* edited by Ulrike Heikaus and Julia B. Köhne, 239–62. Berlin: Hentrich & Hentrich Verlag, 2014.

Strätz, Rainer. *Biographisches Handbuch Würzburger Juden, 1900–1945.* Würzburg: Schöningh, 1989.

Streit, Christian. *Keine Kameraden: Die Wehrmacht und die sowjetischen Kriegsgefangenen, 1941–1945.* Stuttgart: Deutsche Verlags-Anstalt, 1978.

Strzelecki, Andrzej. *The Deportation of Jews from the Lodz Ghetto to KL Auschwitz and Their Extermination.* Oświęcim: Auschwitz-Birkenau State Museum, 2006.

Szejnmann, Claus-Christian W. *Nazism in Central Germany: The Brownshirts in "Red" Saxony*. New York: Berghahn Books, 1999.

Teschner, Gerhard J. *Die Deportation der badischen und saarpfälzischen Juden am 22 Oktober 1940: Vorgeschichte und Durchführung der Deporation und das weitere Schicksal der Deportierten bis zum Kriegsende im Kontext der deutschen und französischen Judenpolitik*. Frankfurt: Peter Lang, 2002.

Tooze, Adam. *The Wages of Destruction: The Making and Breaking of the Nazi Economy*. London: Allen Lane, 2006.

Tosh, John. "Hegemonic Masculinity and the History of Gender." In *Masculinities in Politics and War: Gendering Modern History*, edited by Stefan Dudnik, Karen Hagemann, and John Tosh, 41–57. Manchester: Manchester University Press, 2004.

Toury, Jacob. "Gab es ein Krisenbewußtsein unter den Juden während der 'Guten Jahre' der Weimarer Republik, 1924–1929?" *Tel Aviver Jahrbuch für deutsche Geschichte* 17 (1988): 145–68.

——. "Jewish Aspects as Contributing Factors to the Genesis of the Reichsbanner Schwarz-Rot-Gold." *Leo Baeck Institute Yearbook* 37 (1992): 237–57.

Troller, Norbert. *Theresienstadt: Hitler's Gift to the Jews*. Chapel Hill: University of North Carolina Press, 1991.

Trunk, Isaiah. *Judenrat: The Jewish Councils in Eastern Europe under Nazi Occupation*. New York: Stein & Day, 1972.

——. *Lodz Ghetto: A History*. Edited by Robert M. Shapiro. Bloomington: Indiana University Press, 2006.

Turner, Henry Ashby, Jr. "Victor Klemperer's Holocaust." *German Studies Review* 22, no. 3 (1999): 385–95.

Ullrich, Volker. "Fünfzehntes Bild: Drückeberger." In *Bilder der Judenfeindschaft: Antisemitismus, Vorurteile und Mythen*, edited by Julius H. Schoeps and J. Schlör, 210–17. Augsburg: Weltbild, 1999.

Ulmer, Martin. *Antisemitismus in Stuttgart, 1871–1933: Studien zum öffentlichen Diskurs und Alltag*. Berlin: Metropol Verlag, 2011.

Ulrich, Anna. " 'Nun sind wir geziechnet'—Jüdische Soldaten und die 'Judenzählung' im Ersten Weltkrieg." In *Krieg! Juden zwischen den Fronten, 1914–1918*, edited by Ulrike Heikaus and Julia B. Köhne, 215–38. Berlin: Hentrich & Hentrich Verlag, 2014.

Ulrich, Bernd. *Die Augenzeugen: Deutsche Feldpostbriefe in Kriegs- und Nachkriegszeit, 1914–1933*. Essen: Klartext Verlag, 1997.

——. "Die Desillusionierung der Kriegsfreiwilligen von 1914." In *Der Krieg des kleinen Mannes: Eine Militärgeschichte von unten*, edited by Wolfram Wette, 110–26. Munich: Piper Verlag, 1992.

Ulrich, Bernd, and Benjamin Ziemann, eds. *Frontalltag im Ersten Weltkrieg: Ein historisches Lesebuch*. Essen: Klartext Verlag, 2008.

——. *Krieg im Frieden: Die umkämpfte Erinnerung an den Ersten Weltkrieg*. Frankfurt: Fischer Verlag, 1997.

Vella, Christina. "The Czech Lands." In *Hitler's Europe Ablaze: Occupation, Resistance, and Rebellion during World War II*, edited by Phillip Cooke and Ben H. Shepherd, 52–76. Barnsley: Praetorian Press, 2013.

Verhey, Jeffrey. *The Spirit of 1914: Militarism, Myth, and Mobilization in Germany.* Cambridge: Cambridge University Press, 2000.

Vogel, Rolf. *Ein Stück von uns: Deutsche Juden in deutschen Armeen, 1813–1976; Eine Dokumentation.* Mainz: v. Hase & Koehler Verlag, 1977.

Volkmann, Hans-Erich. "Von Blomberg zu Keitel—Die Wehrmachtführung und die Demontage des Rechtstaats." In *Die Wehrmacht: Mythos und Realität*, edited by Rolf-Dieter Müller and Hans-Erich Volkmann, 47–65. Munich: Oldenbourg Verlag, 1999.

Volkov, Shulamit. "Antisemitism as a Cultural Code: Reflections on the History and Historiography of Antisemitism in Imperial Germany." *Leo Baeck Institute Yearbook* 23 (1978): 25–46.

———. *Germans, Jews, and Antisemites: Trial in Emancipation.* Cambridge: Cambridge University Press, 2006.

Wachsmann, Nikolaus. *KL: A History of the Nazi Concentration Camps.* New York: Farrar, Straus & Giroux, 2015.

Wächter, Katja-Maria. *Die Macht der Ohnmacht: Leben und Politik des Franz Xaver Ritter von Epp.* Frankfurt: Peter Lang, 1999.

Wahlig, Henry. "Die Verdrängung Jüdischer Sportler aus dem öffentlichen Raum in NS-Deutschland." In *"Volksgemeinschaft" als soziale Praxis: Neue Forschungen zur NS-Gesellschaft vor Ort*, edited by Dietmar von Reeken and Malte Thießen, 257–74. Paderborn: Ferdinand Schöningh, 2013.

Walk, Joseph, ed. *Das Sonderrecht für die Juden im NS-Staat: Eine Sammlung der gesetzlichen Maßnahmen und Richtlinien—Inhalt und Bedeutung.* Heidelberg: C. F. Müller Juristischer Verlag, 1981.

Walser, Martin. *Das Prinzip Genauigkeit: Laudatio auf Victor Klemperer.* Frankfurt: Suhrkamp, 1996.

Walter, Dirk. *Antisemitische Kriminalität und Gewalt: Judenfeindschaft in der Weimarer Republik.* Bonn: Dietz, 1999.

Watson, Alexander. *Enduring the Great War: Combat, Morale and Collapse in the German and British Armies, 1914–1918.* Cambridge: Cambridge University Press, 2008.

———. "'For Kaiser and Reich': The Identity and Fate of the German Volunteers, 1914–1918." *War in History* 12, no. 1 (2008): 44–74.

Weber, Reinhard. *Das Schicksal der jüdischen Rechtsanwälte in Bayern nach 1933.* Munich: R. Oldenbourg Verlag, 2006.

Weber, Thomas. *Hitler's First War: Adolf Hitler, the Men of the List Regiment, and the First World War.* Oxford: Oxford University Press, 2010.

Wehler, Hans-Ulrich. *Deutsche Gesellschaftsgeschichte.* Band 4, *Vom Beginn des Ersten Weltkriegs bis zur Gründung der beiden deutschen Staaten, 1914–1949.* Munich: Verlag C. H. Beck, 2003.

Weinrich, Arndt. "Die Hitler-Jugend und die Generation der 'Frontkämpfer.'" In *Nationalsozialismus und Erster Weltkrieg*, edited by Gerd Krumreich, 271–82. Essen: Klartext Verlag, 2010.

Wette, Wolfram, ed. *Der Krieg des kleinen Mannes: Eine Militärgeschichte von unten.* Munich: Piper Verlag, 1992.

———. *Die Wehrmacht: Feindbilder, Vernichtungskrieg, Legenden.* Frankfurt: Fischer Verlag, 2002.

Whalen, Robert. *Bitter Wounds: German Victims of the Great War, 1914–1939.* Ithaca, NY: Cornell University Press, 1984.

Wildt, Michael. *An Uncompromising Generation: The Nazi Leadership of the Reich Security Main Office.* Madison: University of Wisconsin Press, 2009.

———. *Volksgemeinschaft als Selbstermächtigung: Gewalt gegen Juden in der deutschen Provinz, 1919 bis 1939.* Hamburg: Hamburger Edition, 2007.

Winkle, Ralph. *Der Dank des Vaterlandes: Eine Symbolgeschichte des Eisernen Kreuzes.* Essen: Klartext Verlag, 2007.

Winkler, Heinrich August. "Hans Rothfels—Ein Lobredner Hitlers? Quellenkritische Bemerkungen zu Ingo Haars Buch, 'Historiker im Nationalsozialismus.'" *Vierteljahresheft für Zeitgeschichte* 49, no. 4 (2001): 643–52.

Winter, Jay. *Remembering War: The Great War between Memory and History in the Twentieth Century.* New Haven, CT: Yale University Press, 2006.

Witte, Peter, Michael Wildt, Martina Voigt, Dieter Pohl, Peter Klein, Christian Gerlach, Christoph Dieckmann, and Andrej Angrick, eds. *Der Dienstkalendar Heinrich Himmlers 1941/42.* Hamburg: Hans Christian Verlag, 1999.

Wollenberg, Jörg, ed. *"Niemand war dabei und keener hat's gewußt": Die deutsche Öffentlichkeit und die Judenverfolgung.* Munich: Piper Verlag, 1989.

Wrochem, Oliver von. *Erich von Manstein: Vernichtungskrieg und Geschichtspolitik.* Paderborn: Ferdinand Schöningh, 2006.

Wünschmann, Kim. *Before Auschwitz: Jewish Prisoners in the Prewar Concentration Camps.* Cambridge, MA: Harvard University Press, 2015.

———. "Cementing the Enemy Category: Arrest and Imprisonment of German Jews in Nazi Concentration Camps, 1933–8/9." *Journal of Contemporary History* 3, no. 3 (2010): 576–600.

———. "Die Konzentrationslagererfahrungen deutsch-jüdischer Männer nach dem Novemberpogrom 1938." In *"Wer bleibt, opfert seine Jahre, vielleicht sein Leben": Deutsche Juden, 1938–1941,* edited by Susanne Heim, Beate Meyer, and Francis R. Nicosia, 39–58. Göttingen: Wallstein, 2010.

Zechlin, Egmont. *Die deutsche Politik und die Juden im Ersten Weltkrieg.* Göttingen: Vandenhoeck & Ruprecht, 1969.

Ziemann, Benjamin. *Contested Commemorations: Republican War Veterans and Weimar Political Culture.* Cambridge: Cambridge University Press, 2013.

———. "Das 'Fronterlebnis' des Ersten Weltkrieges—eine sozial historische Zäsur? Deutungen und Wirkungen in Deutschland und Frankreich." In *Der Erste Weltkrieg und die europäische Nachkriegsordnung: Sozialer Wandel und Formveränderung der Politik,* edited by Hans Mommsen, 43–82. Cologne: Böhlau Verlag, 2000.

———. *Gewalt im Ersten Weltkrieg: Töten-Überleben-Verweigern.* Essen: Klartext Verlag, 2013.

———. "Die Konstruktion des Kriegsveteranen und die Symbolik seiner Erinnerung, 1918–1933." In *Der Verlorene Frieden: Politik und Kriegskultur nach 1918,* edited by Jost Düffler and Gerd Krumeich, 101–18. Essen: Klartext Verlag, 2002.

———. *War Experiences in Rural Germany, 1914–1923.* Oxford: Berg, 2007.

Zimmermann, Harm-Peer. *"Der feste Wall gegen die rote Flut": Kriegervereine in Schleswig-Holstein, 1864–1914.* Neumünster: Karl Wachholtz Verlag, 1989.

Zimmermann, Mosche. *Deutsche gegen Deutsche: Das Schicksal der Juden, 1938–1945.* Berlin: Aufbau Verlag, 2008.

——. *Die Deutschen Juden, 1914–1945.* Munich: R. Oldenbourg Verlag, 1997.

Zinke, Peter. *"An allem ist Alljuda Schuld": Antisemitismus während der Weimarar Republik in Franken.* Nuremberg: ANTOGO Verlag, 2009.

Zirlewagen, Marc, ed. *"Wir Siegen oder Fallen": Deutsche Studenten im Ersten Weltkrieg.* Cologne: SH-Verlag, 2008.

Index